PRAISE FOR ELIJAH C. NEALY

"Here's the book that caregivers and family members of transgender children have been waiting for. With equal measures sound scientific reasoning and genuine human compassion, Elijah Nealy provides a thoughtful roadmap for anyone trying to support our precious—and endangered—trans youth. An invaluable resource."

—**Jennifer Finney Boylan**, author of *She's Not There* and *Long Black Veil*

"Elijah Nealy's book is an incredibly complete and empathic guide to supporting gender expansive youth, their families, and their communities. While remaining accessible, it embraces the complexities of gender diversity, intersectionality, and the role of caregivers and professionals in their lives. You will finish this book feeling equipped to be a better ally, and probably a better person."

—**Jean Malpas, LMHC, LMFT,** Director, Gender and
Family Project, Ackerman Institute for the Family

"*Transgender Children and Youth* creates space for families to gain a deeper understanding of gender diversity and provides tools to best support and affirm living authentically with unconditional love. Although every family's journey is unique, this resource remains relevant at every stage of transition, lending honest, compassionate, and empowering insight into questions, challenges, and celebrations parents of transgender and gender-variant children experience."

—**Michelle Honda-Phillips**, Parent Advocate,
Transgender & Gender-Expansive Youth

"There could hardly be a better time for this insightful, thoughtful guide to supporting transgender children and youth. . . . Through vignettes illustrating common counseling sit...

experiences with parents and teens going through the coming-out process and provides an enormous amount of guidance for those facing gender questions for themselves or family and friends. In fact, this should be considered a critical volume for anyone involved with schools or working or volunteering with children and teens. . . . Nealy powerfully makes the case for what can be done to ease the pain of these children. A must-read for anyone who wants to help trans youth."

—*Booklist, starred review*

"Elijah Nealy has presented very complex issues in an incredibly clear and accessible manner. In order to really understand transgender adults coming into treatment it will help immensely if we understand the experiences of transgender youth. Many of the principles and guidelines presented are relevant to working with transgender-identified individuals of any age. . . . [I]ncredibly illuminating, even for the most experienced counselor."

—*NALGAP: The Association of Lesbian, Gay, Bisexual and Transgender Addiction Professionals and Their Allies* **Newsletter**

"In writing his book, Nealy has accomplished a huge and valuable feat that will serve to foster the healthy development of transgender and gender non-conforming youth, the acceptance and well-being of families, and the ability of therapists to improve their skills with youth and families."

—*International Journal of Transgenderism*

"[A]n accessible, meticulously explained and supported introduction to the particular issues trans children and teenagers face, and how best to address them. . . . Nealy illustrates repeatedly through *Transgender Children and Youth* that acceptance can be fostered, schools held accountable, and progress made."

—*Psych Central*

"*Transgender Children and Youth* fundamentally humanises a population that has been long been pathologised. It presents a stark image of the damage that can be done to young transgendered individuals. More importantly, it stands as a positive framework to nurture young people and celebrate diversity in all its forms."

—*British Journal of Psychiatry*

"In this age of ever-expanding gender creativity, every mental professional working with children and families will inevitably meet up with a transgender youth. Elijah Nealy has given us the gift of an extraordinary, comprehensive, insightful, and empathic book to guide us in their care and ensure gender health for the children, families, and surrounding social world. A must-read for anyone who will have a transgender child in their life."

—**Diane Ehrensaft, Ph.D.**, author of *Gender Born, Gender Made* and *The Gender Creative Child*, Director of Mental Health, Child and Adolescent Gender Center, UC San Francisco

"This book will serve as an essential reference to assist in better care of TGNC youth, and for families to learn more and come to accept and support their TGNC children. Dr. Nealy writes about this often confusing and controversial area in a clear, lucid style, discussing the meanings of gender variations and the uses and misuses of gender identity diagnoses, providing a helpful review of the diagnostic process and caveats involved. The very helpful vignettes he presents bring to life the various topics with insightful suggestions and practical examples—even a top 10 list! I will be recommending Dr. Nealy's contribution to my trainees, families, and colleagues."

—**Richard R. Pleak, M.D.**, Founding Member, Center for Transgender Health, Northwell Health

"Nealy's writing is both profound and personal, offering readers an enormous amount of solid information along with deep insights and suggestions that everyone in our society needs to challenge our traditional, oversimplified, bifurcated understanding of sex, sexual orientation, gender identity, and gender expression. Nealy draws you in with clear and honest personal exploration of the clinical dilemmas in working with children, their families, and the systems in which they are embedded."

—**Monica McGoldrick, MSW, Ph.D. (h.c.)**, Director, Multicultural Family Institute

TRANS KIDS AND TEENS

TRANS KIDS AND TEENS

PRIDE, JOY, AND FAMILIES IN TRANSITION

Elijah C. Nealy

W. W. NORTON & COMPANY

INDEPENDENT PUBLISHERS SINCE 1923

NEW YORK LONDON

For information about permission to reproduce selections from this book,
write to Permissions, W. W. Norton & Company, Inc.,
500 Fifth Avenue, New York, NY 10110

For information about special discounts for bulk purchases, please contact
W. W. Norton Special Sales at specialsales@wwnorton.com or 800-233-4830

Manufacturing by Sheridan Books
Production manager: Katelyn MacKenzie

Library of Congress Cataloging-in-Publication Data

Names: Nealy, Elijah C., author.
Title: Trans kids and teens : pride, joy, and families in transition / Elijah C. Nealy.
Other titles: Transgender children and youth
Description: New York : W.W. Norton & Company, [2019] | "Previous edition
published as TRANSGENDER CHILDREN AND YOUTH: Cultivating Pride and
Joy with Families in Transition." | Includes bibliographical references and index.
Identifiers: LCCN 2019019881 | ISBN 9780393713992 (pbk.)
Subjects: LCSH: Gender nonconformity. | Transgender children—Mental health. |
Transgender youth—Mental health. | Transgender people—Identity. | Transgender
people—Family relationships. | Transgender people—Services for.
Classification: LCC HQ77.9 .N43 2019 | DDC 306.76/80835—dc23
LC record available at https://lccn.loc.gov/2019019881

W. W. Norton & Company, Inc., 500 Fifth Avenue, New York, N.Y. 10110
www.wwnorton.com

W. W. Norton & Company Ltd., 15 Carlisle Street, London W1D 3BS

1 2 3 4 5 6 7 8 9 0

Dedicated to Dr. Barbara E. Warren, with gratitude for her pioneering and persistent advocacy on behalf of trans people in New York City and beyond, inviting me onboard at the LGBT Community Center in NYC and championing my own personal and professional journey, and so generously mentoring a generation of trans-identified advocates, leaders, and clinicians.

CONTENTS

INTRODUCTION TO THE

PAPERBACK, 2019

"MY ELEVEN-YEAR-OLD JUST CAME OUT TO ME AS A TRANS-gender girl," the mom said, with her voice cracking. "My heart has been breaking ever since." She paused to pull a tissue from her bag. "Why didn't she tell me sooner? Did she think I wouldn't accept her?"

We were in a room of 60 parents, all of them listening intently as this mother shared. I had just presented about the range of feelings and challenges families can encounter when a child comes out as transgender. The mom went on crying openly now. "I must have done something wrong that she didn't feel safe to tell me when she was younger. I feel so bad she carried this inside all this time."

"Wait a minute," I said, as I stepped away from the lectern. "You just told us that your eleven-year-old child came out to you as a transgender girl, yes?" The mother nodded. "That tells me that you haven't done anything wrong. In fact, it tells me you've actually done an incredible job as a parent," I said, aware I not only had the mom's attention now, but also the attention of every parent in the room.

"What you just shared tells me you've raised an eleven-year-old with a strong enough sense of self that she knows who she is, even when every adult in her world has told her differently since the day she was born." I walked down the side aisle to be close to the mom where she sat in the middle of the room. "Your child is confident enough to declare who she is and claim her place in the world as an eleven-year-old girl, in spite of the fact that the world around her does not always affirm her truth. That tells me you've done an incredible job as a parent."

I paused to take in the emotional intensity I could feel among parents around the room. "Yes, she told you at eleven years old and not at five or eight years old. But she felt sure enough of your love and support that she came out to you now, and not at fifteen, twenty, or thirty years old. From my perspective as a parent and a therapist, it's clear you have done a lot of things right as a mom."

I felt the other parents take a deep breath with this mom and begin to relax. I went on, "We all know there's no road map for being parents, and certainly not one for being the parents, grandparents, aunt, uncle, or sibling of a transgender child. As parents, we don't always get everything right. Sometimes we make mistakes. Sometimes even big mistakes. But when your child has a strong enough sense of self to know who they are, and then come out in their authentic gender, that's definitely effective parenting."

Since I wrote this book, I've talked with hundreds of parents. I am more convinced than ever that almost every parent wants the best for their child. That almost every parent loves their child deeply. That almost every parent wants to see their child be healthy and happy. That almost every parent wants their child to grow up to have a rich and meaningful life full of love and joy and purpose. Parents of transgender kids and teens are no exception.

That doesn't mean parents of transgender children don't face challenges; they do. Some parents of transgender children aren't sure whether they can support their transgender child moving forward and transitioning. But in my experience, a parent's inability to support or embrace their transgender child is never about not loving their child. Their perceived rejection is not about not wanting the best for their child. Instead, my work with families has convinced me that when parents or families appear rejecting or struggle to be supportive of their transgender children and teens, there is always an underlying conflict or emotional struggle. There is always more to the family's story when a child is rejected or lacks support for their identity.

The family may need education about sex, gender, gender identity, or gender expression. There may be misunderstandings, an absence of knowledge about, or a lack of connection with trans people, and thus the family needs more information. Parents may experience conflicts between their different roles and responsibilities as a parent—for example, when to protect versus when to allow children to take risks. Some families experience major tensions between their deeply-held religious beliefs and values and their love for their children. In other families, underlying feelings of fear, sadness, or loss can challenge their ability to fully support their trans child.

If you are a member of a family that's struggling with how to parent your trans kid or teen, my hope is that the material in this book will offer what you need to work through your questions and emotions, so your transgender child grows up to be the very healthiest and happiest adult they deserve to be.

If you are already fully committed to the trans kid or teen in your life, my hope is that this book will add to your knowledge of what it means to grow up trans, that the stories and reflection questions will help you better understand the challenges and emotional nuances that are often part of being a transgender child or teen.

This is a challenging time to parent and care for transgender children and youth. Since the hardback edition was published, there has been continued, and even greater, visibility of trans children and teens and their families. Through film, literature, and social media, we know more about their lives than ever before. At the same time, the legal environment has rapidly shifted, often in punitive ways. Issues such as the transgender bathroom debates, rescinding federal guidelines to protect transgender students, and the very real possibility that the Affordable Care Act will be dismantled—eliminating access to health insurance coverage for trans-related medical needs—are continuously evolving. (For the most current information about legal protections and changes, visit the National Center for Transgender Equality [https://transequality.org/] or Lambda Legal [https://www.lambdalegal.org/]).

Over the past two years a growing number of states have passed "restoration of religious freedom" laws that allow discrimination against LGBT people on the basis of a "moral objection." This includes healthcare providers and healthcare facilities, child welfare agencies, employers, schools, businesses, landlords, public accommodations, restaurants—essentially any organization, institution, or person in these jurisdictions can refuse to serve or provide care for trans kids and teens and their families (Moreau, 2017).

Just weeks before I finished this introduction, the U.S. Department of Health and Human Services proposed a definition of "sex" that eradicates any distinction between sex and gender/gender identity. This proposed legal definition of sex that specifies: *"Sex means a person's status as male or female based on immutable biological traits identifiable by or before birth. The sex listed on a person's birth certificate, as originally issued, shall constitute definitive proof of a person's sex unless rebutted by reliable genetic evidence"* (Green, Benner, & Pear, 2018). The potential impact is far reaching, with HHS calling for this definition to be adopted by the Departments of Education, Justice, Health and Human Services, and Labor. In essence, this definition would eradicate any recognition of the estimated 1.4 million U.S. transgender people, including trans kids and teens.

To be clear, this proposed definition would invalidate every piece of identification I hold as a man of transgender experience—my birth certificate, passport, social security card, potentially even my driver's license, despite currently living in a state that prohibits discrimination on the basis of gender identity/expression. Each of these documents would revert back to a female sex designation, placing me and every other transgender adult and young person at even higher risk of harassment, discrimination, and violence, simply while attempting to navigate our day-to-day lives as human beings.

Alongside these changes, we are witnessing increased violence directed toward transgender, gender diverse, and non-binary individuals, especially trans women, and more so, trans women of color and poor trans women. In the face of harsh and persistent ridicule, rejection, discrimination, and violence, 41% of transgender adults have attempted suicide compared to 1.6% in the general population (James et al, 2016). In the week following the publication of the proposed HHS ruling, calls to Trans Lifeline, a transgender suicide hotline, quadrupled (Sobel, 2018). A recent study found 50.8% of trans-masculine, 29.9 % of trans-feminine, 41.8% of non-binary adolescents have attempted suicide, compared to rates among cisgender female (17.6%) and cisgender male (9.8%) teens (Toomey, Syvertsen, & Shramko, 2018). As the adults in their lives, transgender children and teens need us, more than ever, to believe them when they tell us who they are and to have their back each and every day as they move through the world.

Since the hardback edition was published, the number of young people coming out and identifying as agender, bigender, non-binary, and gender fluid continues to grow, further challenging the binary understandings of sex and gender with which most adults grew up. Within the past two years California, Oregon, Washington State, and New York City began offering non-binary designations on birth certificates (Newman, 2018). Colorado, Maine, Minnesota, and New Jersey begin issuing drivers' licenses with a non-binary designation within the next year (Intersex & Genderqueer Recognition Project, 2018; Sevits, 2018). In addition, non-binary gender markers have been granted to at least one individual in the following jurisdictions: Arkansas, the District of Columbia, Maine, Ohio, and Utah (Intersex & Genderqueer Recognition Project, 2018). There is no question we are moving toward a world where gender will be "imagined less as an announcement made at birth and more as a future to hold in mind" (Farley & Kennedy, 2016).

In a recent pushback against affirmative therapy for transgender youth, the term "rapid onset gender dysphoria" has emerged. It is important for parents and providers to be aware this is not a DSM-5 diagnosis. Instead, it is a phrase coined by a group of providers who oppose social transition for transgender youth. These individuals suggest the increased visibility of transgender youth who want to transition and live in their authentic gender is the result of "social contagion," meaning that adolescents come out as transgender because they have peers who identify as transgender (Littman, 2018). Their opposition to transgender youth being allowed to socially transition is rooted in now debunked older studies that indicated high rates of gender non-conforming children not identifying as transgender once they moved into their adult lives. One of the major methodological flaws in older studies was their failure to differentiate between children whose gender expression was diverse (not conforming to societally expected norms) and children who asserted a gender other than the sex assigned at birth or a transgender identity (Olson, 2016; Steensma, McGuire, Kreukels, Beekman, & Cohen-Kettenis, 2013). (See Chapter 2 for further discussion of these older studies).

There is no substantial or reputable research to support a claim of social contagion as a precipitant for transgender identity. The single published study (Littman, 2018) has serious methodological problems, including a biased sample comprised solely of parents who disbelieve or oppose their adolescents' trans identity, data collection from these parents alone and not transgender youth themselves, blurring the distinctions between onset of gender dysphoria and the emergence of trans identity and coming out to others, and equating parental awareness of their teen's transgender identity (when the teen came out to their parents) with the young person's onset of gender dysphoria (Jones, 2018; Serrano, 2018; Tannehill, 2018).

As a result, the study cannot be assumed valid or reliable in supporting the claim that social contagion is responsible for the growing visibility of transgender youth. In fact, the journal itself, PLoS One, issued a follow up statement ten days after publishing Littman's article acknowledging they were aware of the concerns about the study's content and methodology and committed to "seek further expert assessment on the study's methodology and analyses... and provide a further update once we have completed our assessment and discussions" (PLoS One Staff, 2018). Similarly, Brown University—which initially published a press release about the study—released a statement five days later stating, "In light of questions raised about research design and data collection related to Lisa Littman's study on "rapid-onset gender dysphoria," Brown determined that removing the article from news distribution is the most responsible course of action" (News from Brown, 2018).

In reality, the increased number of children and adolescents coming out as transgender and seeking to live in their authentic gender (transition) reflects a greater awareness of gender identity and trans identities that enables gender diverse youth to name who they are earlier than previous generations of transgender people could, and an increased societal acceptance of transgender people, creating greater support and safety for transgender people to live rich, meaningful lives in their authentic gender (See Chapter 6 for further discussion of the increase in teens coming out as transgender).

A growing body of methodologically sound and well-substantiated research documents no difference between trans and cisgender preschool children in the development of gender constancy, the understanding that gender is a stable and consistent aspect of our identity (Fast & Olson, 2018; Olson & Gülöz, 2018). More recent research indicates that children and teens who come out as transgender and socially transition continue to identify as transgender as they mature (Steensma, et al, 2013). Numerous studies now indicate transgender children who socially transition with parental support are mentally, emotionally, and socially healthy and experience no greater degree of mental health challenges than do their cisgender counterparts (Becerra-Culqui, Liu, Nash, Cromwell et al, 2018; Durwood, McLaughlin,

& Olson, 2017; Olson, Durwood, DeMeules, & McLaughlin, 2016). For more information about affirmative therapy for trans children and teens and the critique of social contagion as a determinant of transgender identity among youth, see The Gender Dysphoria Affirmative Working Group, https://www.gdaworkinggroup.com/.

As I provide trainings in both health and mental healthcare settings, I consistently find counselors and therapists who are encountering increasing numbers of trans youth in their schools, medical centers, social service agencies, and clinical practices. While growing numbers of therapists and school counselors are aware of transgender children and youth, many still need basic education about the differences between sex, gender identity/expression, and sexual orientation, as well as the unique needs of transgender children and adolescents.

There is a profound need for therapists equipped to work with families—especially when parents or other family members are not on the same page, or are unsure about supporting a young person's authentic gender identity or expression. There is a critical need for family therapists who can validate the unique joys and challenges of parenting a transgender child, yet also frame these experiences within the context of "normative" parenting tasks. Equally crucial are therapists who can build alliances and work affirmatively with families from conservative faith traditions that have historically viewed trans identities as sinful. These clinicians may be within these religious communities, or therapists who have learned to work across religious differences without devaluing the families' beliefs.

For those of you who are faith leaders or members of religious communities, in my work with trans youth and their families over the past twelve years, I've come to believe that regardless of our specific religious tenets our essential task is to hold love to be most important. As faith leaders and members, we hold the power to bless or withhold blessing; our witness to God's love holds the possibility that a trans child, teen, or adult may experience themselves as lovable again—or perhaps for the very first time. Our compassionate presence can relieve the fear and stress resulting from past and present experiences of injustice and marginalization; our genuine prayers, without hint of condemnation or condescension, can bring healing of mind and spirit; our embrace of trans kids and teens for who they are, as they are, can heal mental, emotional, and physical trauma; our willingness to bear witness to love as most important can bring about reconciliation and wholeness within families.

If you are a medical or mental health provider and you've picked up this book, know that you have the ability to make an incredible difference in the lives of the transgender kids and teens with whom you work. I want you and the families you work with to have a road-map for supporting the transgender children and teens in your lives. I want you to understand the differences between gender diversity and transgender identities and be able to engage youth in these explorations. I want you to have a resource to turn to in the face of the feelings that sometimes emerge when a child comes out as transgender. I want you to have the information you need to make the best decisions about social and medical transitions if these are the next steps in their lives.

If you are the birth, foster/adoptive parent, grandparent, aunt, or uncle of a transgender kid or teen and you've picked up this book: remember, the very fact that your child has come out to you as trans or talks with you about their gender identity/expression says you've already done an incredible job. No matter how challenging or over-whelming it might be in the moment, my hope is that the stories and material in this book will provide what you need to always hold love to be the most important thing in your relationship with your child.

Holding love to be the most important can not only transform the lives of the transgender children and teens and families we encounter, but our very own lives, our communities, and even our world. As parents, counselors, youth workers, healthcare providers, clinicians, and faith leaders, I believe this is our calling, our unique task, and our sacred privilege.

INTRODUCTION TO THE

HARDCOVER, 2017

Late one summer afternoon when I was nine years old, my best friends, Charley and Nick, and I were out traipsing through the woods near our homes. We'd been there for hours playing our favorite game—police detectives hot on the trail of a murderer. The woods weren't much to speak of, but they were ours. We hiked there, played there, caught tadpoles and built tree forts there. It was mostly just a field with trees that stretched on along the railroad tracks, but it was overgrown enough to be our private place away from watchful parental eyes. Just off from the woods behind a row of houses was the open field where we played baseball when we weren't playing murder detectives.

That day we were deep into our roles, searching for clues to find the killer, when Nick raced off a few hundred feet ahead. A few minutes later, Charley and I rounded the path and caught up with Nick. On the left in the weeds was a dirty white 5-gallon bucket—the kind you buy paint in. It was nearly full of water. In an instant I could see the surface was bubbling. The air was thick with the smell of warm pee. Nick was zipping up his pants.

My crotch exploded—hot and tingly—with my own need to urinate. The urgency overwhelmed me. I wanted to unzip my pants and relieve myself like Nick. But what was even more overwhelming that afternoon was the crushing realization that I could not.

Charley and I were inseparable at that age, with Nick often in tow. We went everywhere together. We walked to school together. We played in each other's yards. We teased our little sisters together. We sold snow cones together at the neighborhood teenage boys' baseball games. Left to my own devices, inside my own head, I was one of them. I dressed like them, talked like them, felt like them. But in that moment by the paint bucket it was painfully clear that I was not just like them. My body was not like theirs.

By the age of 12, with the approach of puberty, I was depressed and suicidal. It was 1970. No one talked about gender identity or transgender people. There were no visible transgender role models, no transgender talk shows, and definitely no media stories about transgender teenagers. In the fundamentalist environment that surrounded me, no one even discussed lesbian or gay people. I was 16 years old before I knew what the words meant.

As a result, I spent my adolescence nearly drinking and drugging myself to death, trying to numb out all the ways it felt like my body was betraying me. I hated the way my chest was changing. I hated the monthly menstrual reminders that my body didn't match the way I felt inside. I was profoundly self-conscious about my body and about people seeing my body. I wore long-sleeved shirts and long pants all summer. I didn't go swimming unless forced to. Being in a bathing suit where my breasts were visible was unbearably dysphoric.

At that age and in that historical context, I did not have words to describe what was going on inside me. And I was afraid to begin to try telling anyone. Almost everyone I knew was a fundamentalist Christian, and I sensed they would not be OK with what I felt. I kept quiet and kept taking phenobarbital and drinking to keep my dysphoria and depression at bay.

I knew I was attracted to girls, and so, in late adolescence, when I discovered lesbians, I figured that must be what I was. A bit later I discovered there was such a thing as butch lesbians. That helped things fit a bit more—at least I could wear the clothes that felt like me, preferably a suit and tie.

Despite these struggles, I survived adolescence, graduated college with a bachelor's in social work, and moved into my adult life. In my early thirties, I obtained my graduate degrees in social work and divinity and got sober. I moved through my life visibly Queer, given my masculine gender expression. Being a butch dyke was in many ways an alternate gender identity for me during this time. It didn't fit quite right, but it seemed to be the best and only accommodation available.

After receiving my graduate degrees, I went to work at the Lesbian, Gay, Bisexual, and Transgender Community Center (then the

Lesbian and Gay Community Center) in New York City. It was here that I began to understand gender identity and meet transgender women (at that time, trans men were still largely invisible). I left the Center to work as the regional director for a network of Metropolitan Community Church congregations in Texas, Oklahoma, Arkansas, and Louisiana (a denomination founded in 1968 with primarily a ministry in the LGBT community). When I returned to the Center four years later, I was actively thinking about my own gender identity and becoming increasingly aware that being a lesbian did not match my internal understanding of myself.

It took me a number of years to find the courage to come out. By this point, I was a well-established and respected social worker with a part-time private clinical practice and a wide network of colleagues throughout and beyond New York City. When I imagined coming out as a transgender man and beginning to transition, it felt like this would be the equivalent of throwing the deck of cards that was my life up in the air, not knowing where any one of them would land. I grappled over and over with whether being a man in the world was "worth" upsetting the entire apple cart of my life and relationships. I also wasn't sure I had the courage it would take to come out and begin visibly and very publicly changing how I was viewed in the world.

Nevertheless, one morning I woke up and knew without a doubt that I must make this change. Despite having spent my adult life to date managing to live as a butch dyke, I knew I could not finish out the rest of my life that way. No matter what the consequences might turn out to be, it was no longer tolerable being perceived in a way that did not match my internal sense of myself, and so I began my own gender transition.

Since then, my clinical practice has become increasingly focused within the transgender community, and for the past nine years I have worked almost entirely with gender-diverse and transgender children, adolescents, and young adults and their families. The work is incredibly rich and meaningful to me. I am aware at the end of each day of the ways I make a difference in their immediate and emerging lives. I watch the ways they are able to become who they are in the world much, much earlier than those in my age cohort did. I am amazed at the incredible ways most of their parents show up for them and support them, even when the parents struggle to understand everything or perhaps aren't entirely sure it's truly OK to be transgender.

My own life narrative has been radically different on this front. There still is not much room within fundamentalist faith communities for LGBT people. When I came out initially as a lesbian, there was tremendous pushback. There were phone calls and letters about how being a lesbian was a sin. I was told being gay was an abomination to God and urged to repent and begin dating guys. As a result of coming out as a lesbian, I lost my family and my faith community.

My passion for working with transgender and gender-nonconforming youth and their families has evolved out of my own life narrative. It is rooted within my own loss and motivated by my desire to ensure that other trans youth and their families stay connected. Despite increased visibility, many transgender people continue to encounter hostility and discrimination in the world around them.

In a recent national study of over 27,000 transgender adults, nearly half (48%) of all respondents reported being denied equal treatment, verbally harassed, and/or physically attacked in the previous year because of being transgender. Nearly one-third (29%) of respondents were living in poverty, more than twice the rate in the U.S. adult population (14%) (James et al., 2016).

Unemployment rates for transgender people were three times higher than those of the general population, with trans people of color unemployed two – three times more often (James et al., 2016). Sixteen percent (16%) of respondents who had ever been employed reported losing at least one job because of their gender identity or expression. Twenty-seven percent of those who held or applied for a job the prior year reported being fired, denied a promotion, or not hired for a job they applied for because of their gender identity or expression; fifteen percent (15%) of respondents employed in the previous year were verbally harassed, physically attacked, and/or sexually assaulted at work because of their gender identity or expression (James et al., 2016).

HIV infection rates among transgender people were nearly five times the national average, with rates higher among transgender people of color. One-third (33%) of respondents reported having at least one negative experience with a healthcare provider in the prior year related to being transgender (James et al., 2016).

While there is increased media coverage about transgender

children and teens, our world is still not an easy place to grow up transgender. Most parents, daycare workers, and kindergarten and elementary school teachers do not know much about gender difference among children. Many people still believe that gender-nonconforming or diverse behavior among children is "wrong" and should not be tolerated, let alone accepted.

There are still medical doctors and mental health professionals who counsel parents to correct or "punish" young boys who like to play with girls' toys, like the colors pink and purple, or want to wear a princess nightgown to bed. They tell parents to take away the girls' toys, to not allow their gender-different boys to play with girls or play girls' games or activities, and instead to insist upon only stereotypical masculine clothes, toys, activities, and playmates.

Many people, even mental health professionals, believe that a child cannot know they are transgender. They insist it is impossible for a 4-year-old, 7-year-old, 11-year-old, or even a 14-year-old to know yet that they are transgender. So the first hurdle for any transgender child or adolescent is simply getting people to believe that they are who they say they are, that they are in fact who they know themselves to be in terms of their gender identity, that they are capable of knowing whether they are a boy or a girl (or both or neither).

If the young person manages to convince their parents that they are who they say they are despite the sex they were assigned at birth, the next hurdle often involves whether or not that child or adolescent should be allowed to begin living in their identify gender. Gender transition is still challenging for adults. It can be even more difficult to navigate for children and adolescents.

All of us as human beings, whether children or adults, want to be seen in the world. And all of us want to be seen for who we really are, for who we know ourselves to be. We also want our identity to be acknowledged and validated by those around us—particularly by the people who are important to us, the people we love and who love us, our family.

All of us long to be in relationships where we are free to be who we are, where we are loved for who we are—and not in spite of who we are. All of us long to be in relationships and communities where we can bring our whole selves. None of us want to have to hide parts of who we are. None of us want to compartmentalize parts of ourselves, to be forced to pick and choose which parts of us are "acceptable" or "safe" within a particular relationship or environment. Transgender children and adolescents want these things too.

During December 2014, the story of Leelah Alcorn, a 17-year-old transgender girl, went viral. Leelah was raised in a conservative religious home. When she came out as transgender at age 14, her parents did not accept her identity as a young woman. When she requested to begin medically transitioning at age 16, her parents sent her to a religious therapist whose goal was to convince Leelah to accept her birth-assigned sex as male. When Leelah began coming out to friends, her parents pulled her out of school and took away her Internet privileges.

Leelah's profound gender dysphoria, coupled with the refusal of those she loved to acknowledge her identity as a young woman and her increasing isolation, led, as it often does in transgender adolescents, to depression, despair, and hopelessness.

On December 28, 2014, Leelah posted a note to go live on Tumblr and then ended her life by walking out into traffic on an interstate near her home in Ohio. Excerpts from the note she left spoke directly to those left behind:

> If you are reading this, it means that I have committed suicide.
>
> Please don't be sad, it's for the better. The life I would've lived isn't worth living ... To put it simply, I feel like a girl trapped in a boy's body, and I've felt that way ever since I was 4. I never knew there was a word for that feeling ... so I never told anyone...
>
> When I was 14, I learned what transgender meant and cried of happiness. After 10 years of confusion I finally understood who I was. [My family told] me that it was a phase ... that God doesn't make mistakes, that I am wrong. If you are reading this, parents, please don't tell this to your kids... That won't do anything but make them hate them self. That's exactly what it did to me...
>
> The only way I will rest in peace is if one day transgender people aren't treated the way I was, they're treated like humans, with valid feelings and human rights. Gender needs to be taught about in schools, the earlier the better. My death

needs to mean something. My death needs to be counted in the number of transgender people who commit suicide this year. I want someone to look at that number and say "that's fucked up" and fix it. Fix society. Please.

Goodbye,

(Leelah) ~~Josh~~ Alcorn (Lowder, 2014)

For many transgender people, one aspect of gender dysphoria is the profound feeling or awareness that your body does not match your own sense of who you are. This can be particularly acute for adolescents as they enter puberty and begin developing secondary sex characteristics that do not match their internal gender identity as a young man or young woman. For nonbinary or transgender adolescents who have sensed from early childhood that their gender identity, or the ways their gender identity was perceived in the world, did not fit them, it can seem like their body is betraying them when puberty begins.

Some preteen transgender children harbor the belief that when they grow up, they will be the woman or man they know themselves to be—even if people around them can't see that now. The emergence of secondary sex characteristics shatters that belief. Instead of becoming the young woman or young man they know they are, it is suddenly apparent that their bodies are developing into an adult self that matches the sex they were assigned at birth rather than their internal sense of identity. For these transgender adolescents, the risk of depression, hopelessness, and suicide is acute, especially when coupled with lack of family acceptance (Ryan, Russell, Huebner, Diaz, & Sanchez, 2010).

National studies of transgender adults indicate that 40% have attempted suicide at some point in their lives, compared to only 4.6% in the general population (James et al., 2016). Rates are even higher among those who had lost a job due to bias (55%), have been harassed or bullied in school (51%), have experienced homelessness (59%), or have been the victim of physical assault (61%) or sexual assault (64%) (Grant et al., 2011; James et al., 2016).

These statistics indicate the profound risks of living with gender dysphoria and not being recognized and accepted for who we are in the world. Leelah Alcorn is only one of many transgender adolescents who have taken their own lives because they despaired of ever being able to be who they were in the world or ever being accepted for who they were. Two years ago, on the heels of several local and national trans people committing suicide, I spent an entire summer listening to my transgender clients talk about nothing else. Their grief was palpable. It also triggered all the moments they, too, had despaired about navigating their trans identities in a still often unaccepting world.

These realities compelled me to write this book. The more social workers, psychologists, school counselors, family therapists, and other mental health providers understand gender identity and expression, and the more we learn about the experiences and needs of transgender and gender-diverse youth and their families, the greater the possibility that we can not only prevent other transgender children and adolescents from taking their own lives but also enable them to live rich and fulfilling lives as adults. The more families, teachers, and youth workers know how to communicate acceptance and support for the trans and gender-diverse youth in their lives, the greater the possibility these young people will grow up to become healthy, happy, productive happy young adults. Sometimes even one person can make a difference.

I have woven vignettes throughout each chapter because I believe in the power of stories to illuminate the nuances of our varied lives. Stories touch our minds and emotions enabling us to connect across our differences. I have chosen to respect the stories young people and families have shared with me by creating composite characters and families that reflect the varied, yet common, experiences of transgender children and adolescents and the people who love and cherish them.

None of the vignettes reflect a single young person or one specific family. Instead, I have interlaced themes, questions, joys, and challenges in ways I hope will lead you to a greater understanding and appreciation for their incredible creativity, courage, resilience, and determination to hold love as the most important thing in our lives.

How This Book Is Organized

PART ONE: FOUNDATIONS FOR UNDERSTANDING TRANSGENDER YOUTH includes six chapters that provide basic information needed for understanding transgender and gender-diverse youth and their families.

CHAPTER 1 defines core concepts and ideas such as sex, gender expression, gender identity, and sexual orientation and covers basic vocabulary used within trans and gender-nonconforming communities by both young people and adults.

CHAPTER 2 explores gender variance and gender diversity among children and adolescents. It reviews historical responses to gender-nonconforming children as well as historical and current theoretical and clinical approaches for working with these children and their families. It offers an overview of the evolution of DSM criteria for gender identity disorder (DSM-III and DSM-IV) alongside commentary on the advantages and limitations of the current DSM-5 shift to a diagnosis of gender dysphoria.

CHAPTER 3 focuses on how to understand gender diversity and dysphoria among children and adolescents in today's culture. It outlines what is needed for a diagnosis of gender dysphoria and discusses the benefits and costs of the diagnosis. It also explores the process of supporting young children whose gender expression does not conform to what is stereotypically viewed as normal for either young boys or girls. These are children who have not declared a transgender identity in the sense of stating that their birth-assigned sex conflicts with their gender identity. Their understanding of themselves may or may not evolve over time to the point of wanting to gender transition.

CHAPTER 4 explores the scope and challenges of disclosing a transgender identity for youth and their families and outlines the basic steps involved with social (no medical interventions) transition.

CHAPTER 5 describes the various aspects of medical transition, including hormone therapy and different surgical interventions. Detailed information about the use, potential benefits, and possible concerns about the use of hormone blockers is presented. Feminizing and masculinizing hormone therapy is reviewed, including basic protocols, possible risks, and benefits. Information about various surgical interventions is presented in the latter section of the chapter.

CHAPTER 6 discusses the emergence of transgender identity in adolescence, including the role of the onset of puberty-specific dynamics unique to nonbinary youth. Risk factors for trans adolescents are highlighted as well as aspects of their resilience. The chapter discusses the range of challenges trans youth of color may encounter and presents guidelines for effective work with these young people.

PART TWO: TRANS YOUTH AND THE WORLD AROUND THEM moves beyond foundational concepts and processes to address the challenges transgender youth face in the world around them.

CHAPTER 7 describes dynamics affecting parents and caregivers of gender-diverse and transgender children and adolescents with the goal of preparing mental health professionals to support these young people and their families, as well as normalize family tasks and challenges. Almost all families, and parents in particular, experience a wide range of emotional responses as they navigate their child's journey with gender diversity and/or gender transition. The chapter concludes by outlining the knowledge and resources families of transgender and gender-nonconforming children need to effectively parent these young people as well as interact with a variety of medical and mental health providers.

CHAPTER 8 explores more complex work with families, including situations when families disagree about whether a child is transgender or what steps should be taken next in a child's transition. It addresses work with parents from more conservative faith traditions and strategies for moving parents toward greater acceptance.

CHAPTER 9 focuses on issues that often arise within schools, as well as needs and potential challenges that may emerge within other types of youth programs and settings. The role of parents and professionals as advocates in ensuring that these environments are inclusive and affirming is emphasized. The final section presents ways to create a welcoming environment for transgender children and teens.

CHAPTER 10 explores more advanced clinical interventions with trans adolescents, focusing on the kinds of challenges and themes that may emerge after the initial wave of coming out and transitioning to life in their affirmed gender. There is very little existing literature that addresses advanced clinical work with trans youth.

CHAPTER 11 discusses questions that can arise as transgender young people are launched and move into the world of work or attend college.

PART THREE: SUPPORTING TRANS YOUTH addresses the specific role and responsibilities of mental health providers and concludes with a review of life-affirming practices that can make a difference in the lives of transgender and gender-diverse children and adolescents.

CHAPTER 12 reviews the role and tasks of mental health professionals as outlined in the World Professional Association for Transgender

Health (WPATH) Standards of Care, including the challenges that can emerge as a result of the "gatekeeper role." The chapter explores our internalized attitudes and beliefs and how these may interfere with effective clinical practice with trans youth. Possible provider "missteps" that can pose barriers in the therapeutic relationship are discussed.

CHAPTER 13 outlines the top ten life-affirming practices for adults in the lives of trans kids. It summarizes ways that all of us—teachers, counselors, therapists, parents, and others—can create space for trans and gender-diverse youth to safely explore, understand, and inhabit their individual experiences of gender. It offers guidelines to protect and enhance their self-esteem, strategies to help them survive and thrive in the face of internal and external stressors, and ways to partner with them to cultivate hope for the future.

Appendices

Several appendices are located at the end of the book. APPENDIX A provides an overview of legal concerns that can emerge in work with transgender and gender-nonconforming youth and their families. It includes information about legal name changes and changing gender markers on identification documents. It reviews the current state of legal rights and relevant precedent supporting transgender children and adolescents moving through the world in their affirmed gender. Particular attention is paid to respect and access to the same facilities and opportunities afforded their cisgender (non-transgender) peers. APPENDIX B offers an extensive compilation of resources for clinicians, trans and gender-diverse youth and their families, and other service providers. APPENDIX C contains sample mental health letters needed before youth can proceed with hormone therapy or surgeries.

Major changes occurred rapidly during 2016. North Carolina's HB2 law has targeted bathrooms and pushed transgender issues to the forefront in the media and at the water cooler; an Oregon court ruled that non-binary is a legal gender; the U.S. Departments of Education and Justice issued a directive to schools prohibiting discrimination against transgender students, including granting them the right to use the bathrooms and locker rooms that match their affirmed gender; and the U.S. Department of Health and Human Services' final rule on Section 1557 of the Patient Protection and Affordable Care Act explicitly prohibited discrimination based on gender identity and sex stereotyping in any hospital or health program that receives federal funds as well as prohibiting discrimination within most health coverage. Health insurance companies can no longer categorically deny medical procedures simply because the member is transgender or the procedure is related to their gender transition. Yet at the same time, a Georgia judge refused to issue a name change for a transgender man because the judge did not believe it was right for "her" to assume a male name (Bowling, 2016).

In the midst of these exciting and contradictory changes, my goal in working with trans and gender-diverse youth is not focused primarily on gender transition. My most important goal centers around enabling families to create space, love, and support for these children and adolescents to explore and live out their gender identity and expressions freely, without reproach or shame, and for each one of these young people to not be confined by a set of rigid expectations about what is "acceptable" masculine or feminine gender expression or identity but instead to live their whole true selves in each moment in ways that feel authentic to them.

For some young people, this will mean space to express their gender in a wide array of possibilities. It may mean permission for boys to play with dolls or trucks, to wear lavender or navy blue, to decide to be a construction worker or a dancer when they grow up. It may mean girls being free to choose math and science or art and music, playing football or playing princess, wearing combat boots or wearing heels.

Some youth will go beyond gender diversity to express a clear and consistent transgender identity. Their desire will be to transition so that they can live and be acknowledged in the gender they know to be true for them. Other youth will choose neither of these; they are already hurtling beyond the gender binary and daring all of us to catch up with them.

My intention throughout the book is to provide the knowledge and skills mental health professionals, schools, and families need to effectively support these children and adolescents. To do the work of enabling parents to "sit with" gender diversity and not rush toward transition. To teach children and teens to be unafraid to embrace their gender in all its diversity and gain the tools needed to thrive in a world that can sometimes be ridiculing or hostile, and other times amazingly affirming and celebratory. To partner with and empower youth and their families for whom gender transition is the next "right" step. To remember to always hold love as the most important thing.

TRANS
KIDS AND
TEENS

PART 1

Foundations for Understanding Transgender Youth

CHAPTER 1

Talking Trans

Basic Terms and Vocabulary

T HIS SECTION REVIEWS FOUR BASIC CONCEPTS REQUIRED for understanding trans and gender-nonconforming youth. Many times youth or their families confuse or conflate concepts of sex, gender expression, gender identity, and sexual orientation. It is essential to be able to distinguish these concepts so we can understand and support trans youth. This chapter also explores the language trans and gender-nonconforming youth may use to describe themselves and their identities within the context of these basic concepts.

Biological Sex

The first question asked when someone gives birth is, "Is 'it' a boy or a girl?" It is almost as if a child isn't "real" until we know what their sex is. This "sex assigned at birth" is based on our physical bodies. It is a decision the delivery doctor makes based on the appearance of our genitalia. In this sense, sex is about biology; it is about our physical body, our anatomy, or our chromosomal makeup.

For most of us, this biological sex is beyond question. We have a penis or a vagina. We have XX or XY chromosomes. However, this differentiation is not always as clear-cut as we have been taught to believe. One in 2,000 infants (Intersex Society of North America, n.d.) are born with ambiguous genitalia or variant chromosomal combinations that make it impossible for a doctor to clearly determine whether the child is a "girl" or a "boy." The current language to describe this experience is that the child was born with an "intersex condition." The older term, no longer used, was "hermaphrodite."

Historically, when a baby was born with an intersex condition, medical professionals would immediately whisk the infant off and surgically alter their genitals so that they appeared more "normative." This was thought to be essential. Without this surgery, doctors and mental health professionals believed the child would experience ridicule about their physical appearance and likely be confused about their gender identity. Many times the parents were not even informed about this condition prior to the surgery on their infant. In more recent years, parents have been informed about their child's intersex condition, but surgery to alter the appearance of the infant's genitals is still often recommended and considered essential for the child's emotional well-being.

There are two problems with this surgery being done during infancy. The first is that the doctor makes a decision about sex based on the appearance of the infant's genitalia. If the infant has a penis but it is considered "too small" to be a "valid" or "functional" penis, the penis is typically removed and the child is classified as a girl. This decision made at birth by a doctor may not match the child's developing sense of gender identity. As a result, there are intersex adults who were declared girls at birth whose genitals were altered to more closely resemble female genitalia. Yet as they grow up, their gender identity may be male, and the adult man may prefer to have maintained his penis regardless of whether or not it was considered "long enough."

The second difficulty with surgery performed during infancy is that the way the genitals are altered often diminishes that person's ability to experience a rich and full adult sexual life. The removal of erotic tissue during surgery can compromise the person's ability to experience the full sexual pleasure that would have been possible if their genitalia had been left intact.

These factors have led many adults with intersex conditions to advocate that genital surgeries be delayed until a child or adolescent is old enough to make an informed decision for themselves. This allows the child's gender identity to emerge before any decisions about surgery are made and puts these decisions, which may impact sexual satisfaction, within the control of the individual themselves.

With the awareness that significant numbers of births involve intersex conditions, it is clear that biological sex, typically under-stood as unequivocal, is not nearly as binary or unambiguous as often assumed. Cultural messages tell us that you (or your child) are either a boy or a girl. These messages tell us that what distinguishes our sex is the genitals we were born with. Intersex conditions make it apparent that biological sex is more complex. While male and female obviously exist, variations are clearly evident along the sex/gender continuum.

For most people, their internal gender identity matches the sex they were assigned at birth. Most infants assigned male at birth grow up and identify as men. Most infants assigned female at birth grow up and identify as women. For these individuals, their gender identity is aligned with their biological sex. When discussing these individuals who constitute the bulk of the human population, we use the term "cisgender," meaning that their biological sex and their gender iden-tity are aligned (the Latin prefix cis- means to align or line up).

For transgender people, the sex assigned to them at birth dif-fers from their gender identity. There is a mismatch or disconnect between how they were categorized at birth and their emerging gendered sense of themselves. Their gender identity "crosses over" (the meaning of the Latin prefix trans-) their biological sex. Transgen-der women are individuals assigned male at birth but whose gender identity is female. Transgender men are persons who were assigned female at birth but whose gender identity is male.

Gender Expression

In contrast to sex as biological, gender expression is about the ways we express our identities as men or women (or both or neither) to ourselves and in the world. Gender expression is about the ways we communicate our gender to those around us. It can include things like our choice of clothing (masculine, feminine, androgynous); the hairstyles we like; our physical mannerisms, such as the way we walk or talk or move our hands; and whether we wear jewelry, and if so, what kind, and on which body part.

We also express our gender through the activities we enjoy, the roles we assume in our day-to-day lives, or the careers we choose. In white Western culture, there are norms about what is consid-ered acceptable masculine or feminine gender expression. There are activities and careers that are considered "masculine" and others considered "feminine." In some contexts, these expectations about appearance or interests and activities are rigidly enforced, and individuals may be punished for violating the norms.

Gender expression often leads to assumptions about sexual orientation and/or gender identity. A good example of this is the way most children read people. It's the way children determine whether someone is a girl/woman or a boy/man. Children look for clues like the length of a person's hair, the kinds of clothes another child wears, or whether an adult is wearing earrings or makeup. For younger children, these gendered expectations tend to be fixed and not easily altered, even in the face of new information. For example, a young child may have internalized a belief that auto mechanics are men and maintain this belief even after meeting a female mechanic. Despite these assumptions, our gender expression is not necessarily a statement about our sexual orientation or gender identity. It can simply be about how we enjoy looking or what we enjoy doing.

Having grown up in a conservative religious environment where male and female gender expectations were distinct and clear, my first understanding of our inability to "read" someone's identity or orientation by their appearance came during college when I was camping along the coast of Maine. During our first week there, I noticed many women with short haircuts dressed in blue jeans and flannel shirts. I remember thinking, "Wow! There are a lot of lesbians in Maine." As we continued our vacation, I learned that most of these women, whose gender expression would have been considered more masculine, were actually cisgender (not transgender) straight married women who simply bought their clothes at L. L. Bean. The norm for female gender expression in Maine at that time allowed for more "masculine" gender expression than might have been acceptable in other areas in the United States.

Our gender expression is distinct from our gender identity or sexual orientation. The fact that a woman enjoys carpentry or electrical work does not indicate anything about her gender identity or sexual orientation. The fact that a man might wear pink does not tell you whether he is straight, gay, or bisexual, and it does not indicate that he identifies as a transgender woman or feels more feminine than other men. There are cisgender straight women whose gender expression is very stereotypically feminine; there are cisgender straight women whose gender expression is more masculine; and there are cisgender women with androgynous gender expression. The same is true for men within our culture. There is a wide range and variation in the ways we may express our gender as men, women, both, or neither.

At the same time, Western culture does have expectations about what is considered "acceptable" gender expression for men and women. The norms for girls/women are certainly broader than those for boys/men. Young girls have much more latitude for masculine gender expression than do young boys for female expression. If a young girl likes wearing baggy jeans and T-shirts and playing baseball, we even have a fairly affectionate name for that: tomboy. This expansiveness typically narrows upon reaching adolescence. With the onset of puberty, girls are expected to "femme up," grow out of their tomboy phase, and become interested in things that are more stereotypically feminine.

There is no "tomboy" counterpart for young boys. Boys (or men) have little room in white Western culture for any hint of feminine gender interests or expression. A young boy or male adolescent with feminine gender expression is likely to be quickly labeled a "sissy"—a word with extremely pejorative and demeaning connotations meant to enforce acceptable "masculine" behavior and punish any deviations from this standard.

This difference in gender expectations and norms for girls/women and boys/men is rooted in patriarchy, sexism, and misogyny. It evolves out of an underlying belief that no man would want to be anything like a woman—because we all "know" that women are inferior to men, that boys are better (smarter, faster, stronger, more capable) than girls. This kind of sexism and misogyny holds that any man or boy with feminine interests or gender expression is "less of a man" or not a "real" man.

Norms about gender expression vary over time. One hundred years ago in the United States, dresses were the only acceptable clothing for female-bodied people. Women who chose to break this norm were often censured in some way. Yet today women routinely wear pants, even in formal settings. The norms about expressing one's female gender through clothing have shifted over time. Wearing pants today does not bring a woman's gender identity or sexual orientation into question. Similarly, a century ago, pink was considered a men's color. It was considered too strong a color for the "more delicate" sex to wear. While some men wear pink shirts today, pink has overwhelmingly become a "girls' color."

Acceptable norms for gender expression also vary across different cultural contexts. In white Western Anglo culture, it is not considered masculine for men to express emotions other than anger. Beyond that, men are expected to be fairly stoic. They are not encouraged to be verbally or physically affectionate, not given much room for feelings of sadness or grief, and not expected to cry—at least in public.

Socialization about normative or acceptable gender expression begins very early with children. While riding the New York City subway, I sat near a two-and-a-half-year-old boy riding with a young man in his early 20s. They were listening to music together. The young boy had one earphone and his caregiver had the other. At one point, the toddler did what all toddlers do: took the earphone out of his ear and put it in his mouth. His caregiver immediately yelled at him and popped him on the head. The young boy burst into tears and began crying loudly. What I heard next was the young adult man admonishing him: "Stop crying! You're acting like a stupid girl!" Even at two and a half years, this boy was being given the message that boys don't cry, that it's not acceptable masculine gender expression to shed tears.

Adult men in Western Anglo cultures are rarely allowed to physically express their affection for another man. Doing so will get them called a sissy or a "faggot" and may even put them at risk of violence. About the closest white Anglo men get to physical affection is a slap on the butt after scoring a touchdown on the football field. Yet in many Mediterranean and Latin cultures, it's considered perfectly acceptable masculine behavior to be more emotionally demonstrative. In these cultural contexts, men often greet each other with an embrace or even a kiss, and this is considered acceptable masculine gender expression. So our norms about masculine and feminine gender expression, our rules about what is considered acceptable, vary across both different historical time periods and different cultures.

Gender Identity

Gender identity reflects our own internal sense of who we are as a man or woman. For some people, this identity might be both man and woman or neither man nor woman. In contrast to our "sex" assigned at birth, gender identity is our internalized understanding of who we are. Sex is about our bodies, our biology, the secondary sex characteristics that emerge with puberty. Gender identity is about what's in our mind. It's about how we think of ourselves as male or female, both or neither.

The term transgender is often used as an umbrella that includes all gender-nonconforming people. It is also used more narrowly for those transgender people who transition from their assigned sex at birth to their identified gender. An older term used for the latter group is transsexual. This word was coined within psychiatric circles and carries a strong connotation of mental illness and psychological deficiency.

Given these origins, transsexual is less often used today. Just as gay and lesbian people rejected the term homosexual because of its psychiatric origins, transgender people have largely rejected the term transsexual and have chosen transgender to describe themselves. The use of transgender reflects the way trans communities are embracing more positive and empowering language to define who they are.

There are some persons who continue to use the word transsexual to describe themselves. This choice often reflects a feeling that their identity as male or female and their choice to transition is at risk of erasure as the transgender umbrella continues to broaden, encompassing both people who transition and those who identify as nonbinary, gender-nonconforming, or gender-fluid.

The transgender umbrella also includes cross-dressers. These are generally cisgender men who value being able to express feminine aspects of themselves. This may mean dressing "as a woman" might, wearing makeup, styling their hair in more traditionally feminine ways, or wearing a wig so that their feminine or female self is visible in different settings in their lives. For them, cross-dressing and presenting as female is distinct from being a gay man or a transgender woman. It is an aspect of their gender expression and not necessarily an indication of their sexual orientation or gender identity. Most men who cross-dress identify as (cisgender) men; they do not identify as female, and they do not generally wish to transition and live as a woman.

Historically, individuals who cross-dressed were called "transvestites" (coined by Magnus Hirschfeld in the early 1900s). It was believed these men cross-dressed because of the sexual excitement this generated in them. It represented dysfunctional psychosexual development within childhood or adolescence and was characterized as a mental illness (transvestic fetishism). Given the pejorative psychiatric connotation, the term transvestite is rarely used within trans communities today.

Derogatory views about cross-dressers reflect the earlier discussion about how little room there is for male-bodied people to demonstrate any "feminine" gender interest, expression, or aspects of themselves. Men who cross-dress and wear feminine clothing break these rules and historically have been stigmatized and penalized for these "transgressions" against masculinity.

The penalties for men who express femininity or female selves are much more severe than what women typically encounter today as "tomboys" or "butch" women (though there are settings in which more masculine gender expression among women is prohibited and punished).

Individuals who "cross-dress" for specific purposes, typically entertainment, may refer to themselves as "drag queens" (in the case of men who perform as women entertainers) or "drag kings" (female-bodied persons who perform as male entertainers). In this context, "doing drag" is something anyone might do regardless of their sexual orientation or gender identity. Doing drag has a long history within theater arts and typically is more about performance and art than identity.

People who identify as gender-queer experience their gender identity as more fluid. Their gender identity does not neatly fit into one of the two binary boxes labeled male or female. The word largely originated among younger people in urban areas who reject the assumption that we are only either male or female. They claim a space along, or even beyond or outside, the continuum of maleness and femaleness. Some gender-queer people see themselves as both male and female. Some identify as neither male nor female. Some believe the categories of male and female are not large enough to encapsulate all of who they are. And others believe the boxes of male and female are simply irrelevant to their own sense of themselves. Various words gender-queer people might use to describe themselves include gender-fluid, gender-variant, gender-expansive, or gender-diverse. Bigender is typically used by those who identify as both male and female. The term agender may be used if neither category of male or female fits the individual. Some youth use pangender to indicate their identification with all genders (again, broader than a male/female binary construct).

It is evident that the language trans people use to describe themselves is rapidly evolving. It is also evident that many people in the trans community, and particularly many young people, are moving beyond binary constructs for understanding gender identity and instead embracing more complex and fluid ways of experiencing themselves (Ehrensaft, 2016).

Transgender people who identify as male or female and choose to transition and live in their identified/true gender generally use gendered pronouns, such as he/him or she/her, to refer to themselves. Individuals with a more fluid gender identity or a bigender or agender identity often choose gender-neutral pronouns such as "zie" and "hir." Individuals may also use the plural pronouns "they" and "them."

Mental health professionals must respect a client's choice of name and pronouns. Some young people will disclose their preferred name and pronouns immediately. Whether someone is already out as transgender or comes out during their work with you, their birth name may still be their legal name. Even when this is true, it is considered best practice to ask what name and pronoun they would like you to use. It is also important to be cognizant that the choice of name and pronouns may evolve over time among young people exploring their gender identity and expression and among those whose identity or expression is more fluid.

Continuing to use a young person's birth-assigned name and associated pronouns when they have requested the use of their "new" name and pronouns is disrespectful and both denies and invalidates that individual's identity. It communicates that you do not see them for who they are. When someone continues to use male pronouns for a trans woman, it communicates an underlying message that they do not believe she is "really" a woman. It sends a message that in their eyes she is, and always will be, a man.

Sexual Orientation

It is essential to differentiate between gender expression, gender identity, and sexual orientation. Sometimes people conflate sexual orientation and gender identity. They think being gay equals being transgender and being transgender is the same as being gay. In reality, these are two distinct aspects of who we are as human beings. Sexual orientation is about who we are attracted to; it's about who we think is hot. It's about our physical and emotional attraction to other people, and whether we tend to be attracted to people of the opposite sex/gender or people of the same sex/gender. All of us—cisgender or transgender—have both a sexual orientation and a gender identity. We have an internal sense of who we are as men/women/both/neither, and we have an understanding of our sexual and emotional attractions. These two concepts reflect different aspects of our being.

A young trans woman who likes other women may identify as lesbian; a young trans man who is attracted to other guys may identify as gay; young trans women attracted to guys may identify as straight, as may young trans men who are attracted to women. A youth attracted to people of both genders may identify as bisexual.

Other youth identify as pansexual, an orientation typically broader than simply being "bi" or attracted to either/both men and women. Youth who identify as pansexual are typically attracted to a range or type of gender expression and not necessarily to a specific sex or gender or specific "body parts." For example, if a young cisgender or transgender woman identifies as pansexual, she may be attracted to people of all or any gender expression. Or she may be attracted to masculine gender expression, and this attraction could include cisgender guys, trans guys, or butch lesbians. What is important to her in this case is another person's masculine energy, appearance, or gender expression. Their specific body parts (breasts, vagina, penis) are not the primary attraction. The same can be true for transgender men—embracing a pansexual identity can describe an attraction to a particular gender expression (masculine, feminine, both, neither) rather than a desire for intimacy with someone whose physical body reflects normative sex or gender assumptions.

The acronym "LGBT" is often used to abbreviate "lesbian, gay, bisexual, and transgender." Sometimes the acronym will read "LGBTQ," where the "Q" stands for "Queer." In work with youth the "Q" may also stand for youth who are "Questioning" or exploring their gender identity and/or sexual orientation. The acronym is also sometimes written as "LGBTQI" where the "I" stands for "intersex." Beliefs about the inclusion of intersex vary among people with intersex conditions. Some individuals living with an intersex condition consider this (being intersex) part of their identity and thus include the "I" in "LGBTQI." Other persons understand their intersex experience as a medical condition (like any other medical condition) and do not view it as part of who they are or their identity.

Many younger lesbian and gay people (especially in urban areas) have incorporated the word Queer into the LGBT acronym (LGBTQ). It is also used on its own to describe someone's identity. Historically, queer was a derogatory epithet hurled at lesbian and gay people with the goal of demeaning them. Many older lesbian and gay people still find the word offensive because, when they came of age, being called queer was a slur used in the context of verbal harassment or even physical violence.

In recent years, instead of allowing others to disparage them by calling them queer, many young people have reclaimed the word to express their pride in themselves and their community. In this sense, Queer often has an "in-your-face" political edge, as in the slogan "I'm here. I'm Queer. Get used to it." It reflects the LGBT community's insistence on being seen and accepted for who they are, rather than being invisible or silent as was often true in the past. Queer is used as part of the LGBTQ acronym and can be used independently as an umbrella term for the whole spectrum of people within LGBT communities. In this sense, it can speak to either sexual orientation or gender identity or expression or both.

Within the context of this book about trans and gender-nonconforming youth, I use the term transgender to describe those youth whose gender identity does not align with their assigned sex and desire to transition so that they can live as the gender they understand themselves to be. I will alternately sometimes shorten transgender to trans. When I discuss these young people who intend to or do transition, I use the language affirmed gender to reflect their understanding of their gender identity (as opposed to the sex they were assigned at birth). Children and adolescents who have transitioned either socially or medically are now living and presenting to the world in their affirmed gender (and not their birth-assigned sex).

The terms gender-variant and gender-nonconforming have been used to describe children and adolescents whose gender expression varies from what is stereotypically expected from boys or girls.

Both of these terms imply that the young person's gender identity or expression is in some way abnormal. In contrast, I use gender-diverse to describe children who express their gender in (diverse) ways that are not reflective of a binary gender construct. These children do not necessarily intend to transition, though at times a child whose initial or present gender expression is more fluid or nonconforming may later come to identify as transgender and transition. These dynamics and varying narratives will be explored more fully within the remainder of the book.

CHAPTER 2

Gender Diversity and Gender Dysphoria

For Reflection

What is your earliest memory of gender difference?

How has your family shaped your understanding of gender?

Can you remember a time when you were reprimanded for behavior that was perceived as "gender-inappropriate?"

What did the experience feel like? What was your response?

ALMOST ALL TRANS PEOPLE CAN RECALL BEING REPRImanded for behavior that was perceived as "gender inappropriate"—behavior or interests that did not match what was normative or considered appropriate for their birth-assigned sex. In the course of leading trainings around trans and gender-fluid or gender-diverse individuals, I discovered many cisgender people have had similar experiences. As noted in Chapter 1, norms about gender expression are often rigidly enforced; in many families, any deviation is immediately reprimanded.

Reflecting on these questions can help us identify some of the ways our families and communities shaped our beliefs about gender identity and expression, as well as moments when our behavior may not have appropriately lined up with the expected gender norms.

Those of us who identify as cisgender have not often had to think about how we arrived at our gender identity; it typically seems completely essential—we have always been this way—rather than also being socially constructed.

Developing a greater awareness of how gender was formed and functioned within our lives is a starting point for understanding the developmental process of trans and gender-diverse youth. Thinking about moments when our gender expression was corrected, reprimanded, or even punished—or when we saw this happen to another child or adolescent—can help us emotionally connect with the impact of these all-too-frequent moments in the lives of most transgender people, including children and youth.

This chapter begins with a discussion of gender diversity among children, including existing research about long-term trajectories and outcomes. Historical beliefs about gender-nonconforming behavior and models of treatment are reviewed alongside contemporary best practices. The chapter reviews the history of the gender identity "disorder" diagnosis within the Diagnostic and Statistical Manual of Mental Disorders (DSM) alongside conversations within the medical and transgender communities that led to the shift in nomenclature to "Gender Dysphoria." This section concludes by outlining the criteria for Gender Dysphoria within the current DSM-V (American Psychiatric Association, 2013).

The previous chapter defined gender expression as the many different ways we express our sense of ourselves as men, women, both, or neither. We noted the way different historical time periods and cultures have held varying norms about acceptable gender expression or behavior for men and women. Within white Western culture, "non-normative" gender expression has often been cause for concern among both parents and mental health professionals.

Childhood Gender Diversity

Most children are aware of their birth-assigned sex, gender, and normative gender expression expectations by ages two to three years (Grossman & D'Augelli, 2007). Most toddlers know whether they are girls or boys and begin using gendered pronouns around age three. However, children may not understand the notion of gender constancy until age six to seven years—meaning that before this age, children frequently believe sex/gender is determined by the type of clothing someone wears or their haircut or hairstyle (Egan & Perry, 2001). Short hair means you are a boy; long hair means you are a girl—regardless of other physical characteristics or attributes. Children at this age may believe that gender can change by changing external things like hair or clothes—that is, if you are a girl (with long hair, of course) and cut your hair short, you become a boy.

Given that most children are aware of their gender by age two to three years, it is not surprising that children at this age may already display gender-diverse behavior, such as preferring clothes, toys, and games typically associated with the other sex or prefer to play with other-sex peers. Beyond diverse gender expression, children as young as toddlers may express the wish to be the other sex or even assert a gender identity that differs from their birth-assigned sex. They may also express unhappiness with their physical sex characteristics and functions. For some children, this unhappiness can be persistent and severe. In other children, these characteristics may be less intense or only episodically present (Cohen-Kettenis et al., 2006; Knudson, De Cuypere, & Bockting, 2010; Malpas, 2016).

GENDER-DIVERSE BEHAVIOR AND EXPRESSION AMONG CHILDREN

WITHIN BOYS	WITHIN GIRLS
Wanting to wear a dress	Preferring boys' activities, games, sports
Liking "girl" colors and fabrics	Wanting short hair
Wanting long hair	Preferring no makeup or jewelry
Wanting to paint toenails or fingernails	Preferring baggy clothes/pants vs. dresses/skirts
Preferring toys/activities typical for girls	Reducing/eliminating appearance of breasts
Wanting a nongendered nickname	Wanting a nongendered nickname

In children assigned male at birth, gender-variant behavior can include wanting to wear dresses, liking colors and fabrics typically associated with girls, desiring long hair, wanting to paint their finger-nails or toenails, preferring toys or games generally associated with girls, or wanting to use a gender-neutral or feminine nickname. In children assigned female at birth, gender-variant behavior typically includes wanting to dress like a boy; preferring short, boyish hair-styles; reluctance to wear makeup or jewelry; attempting to reduce or eliminate the appearance of breasts; or desiring to use gender-neutral or masculine names.

The above interests and behaviors defined as gender-noncon-forming clearly reflect stereotypical expressions of masculinity and femininity. Not all girls or boys, transgender or cisgender, fit these stereotypes, nor should they be compelled to do so. However, psychi-atry has historically defined "gender variance" as expression that var-ies from stereotypical standards. Gender expression that conforms to stereotypical expectations has been defined as "normative" (and "normal"). Gender expression that varies from these norms has been viewed as "gender-variant."

As previously discussed, Western culture allows much more lat-itude for girls to express interests or behaviors generally associated with boys. Consequently, gender-variant behavior among boys has aroused much more concern than gender-nonconforming behavior among young girls. Most research studies have historically focused on gender variance among boys, and treatment interventions were typ-ically designed to correct non-normative gender expression among children assigned male at birth (Davenport, 1986; Green, 1987; Green & Fuller, 1973; Rekers, 1972; Zuger, 1978).

For much of the 20th century, gender-variant behavior among young boys and male adolescents was considered a precursor to the emergence of homosexuality in adulthood. Homosexuality was not removed from the DSM until 1973. Prior to this, homosexuality was understood as a mental illness in need of treatment that would at minimum change same-sex behavior, if not eliminate same-sex attraction and desire. Any indication of feminine gender expression among young boys was immediately targeted for corrective treat-ment (sometimes called the "therapeutic approach") with the belief that the young boy suffered from gender confusion that needed to be treated in an effort to ensure the young boy did not become an adult homosexual man. Clinical interventions aimed to correct the young boy's gender-nonconforming (feminine) interests and behaviors and replace them with gendered expression that was more normatively masculine (Schwartzapfel, 2013; Zucker, 2005; Zucker & Bradley, 1995; Zucker, Wood, Singh, & Bradley, 2012). The following vignette reflects this approach.

In our first appointment, both parents related that Joey had objected to being called a boy from a young age. As young as three years old, Joey would wrap a big towel around his head after a bath and parade around his bedroom showing off his "long, flowing hair." When he began attending preschool, Joey frequently asked his mother, "Why do people keep calling me a boy? I'm not a boy! I'm a girl." Joey often fussed about getting dressed in the morning because he didn't like the clothes his parents had bought for him. He wanted to wear a dress like his girl cousins.

The parents had been seeing a psychologist for a year when they called to request an appointment with me. At this time, Joey was six years old. The psychologist believed gender-variant behavior among young boys was psychologically unhealthy. He believed it would lead to gender confusion as well as other mental, emotional, and social difficulties as an adolescent and adult if it was not corrected now. His treatment approach required that the parents insist Joey act "like a boy" and immediately "correct" any non-normative (feminine) gender expression they witnessed. This correction included removing any toys that were not traditional boys' toys and getting rid of any clothing that was in any way feminine. It meant prohibiting social interactions with girls Joey's age and allowing only male playmates. When Joey played at home or with friends, things like playing "house" or "dress-up" were forbidden. If Joey said anything about "being a girl," the parents were to respond by saying, "No, Joey. You are a boy."

Increased male attention and role modeling were recommended. Joey's time with his mother was minimized, and his father was advised to teach him to play baseball and football and take him to movies that reflected normative masculine figures, such as Batman or Spiderman. If Joey expressed interest in "girl things," the parents were counseled to remind Joey that boys didn't like these things. They were told to reinforce normative masculinity with messages like "Pink is for girls" and "Boys don't get their nails painted."

Joey's parents stringently followed this protocol. Over the course of the year, their reprimands did succeed in altering Joey's behavior but seemed to have little impact on his underlying feminine interests. Of greater concern when they came to see me was that Joey was becoming anxious, withdrawn, and unhappy. Insisting that Joey "act like a boy" was increasingly precipitating arguments, after which Joey withdrew to his room and refused to talk to anyone. In the months prior to our first appointment, Joey had been having emotional "meltdowns" most mornings, insisting that he would not wear pants to school anymore.

Clinical approaches that demand and enforce normative gender expression are highly problematic (Brill & Pepper, 2008; Ehrensaft, 2012; Wallace & Russell, 2013). These corrective approaches send the message that what you like, and even who you are, is unacceptable. Consequently, these approaches lead to internalized shame about the child's identity. When we compel Joey to act like a "normal boy" despite his ongoing objections, we send the message that we (parents, mental health professionals) know who he is better than he does. We suggest that his understanding of reality is not accurate. When we persist in demanding gender-normative behavior, even when it is it apparent that the child is increasingly distressed, we risk precipitating severe emotional distress and hopelessness. Without validation and support from the adults in their lives, even young gender-variant children can become acutely depressed and suicidal.

Fortunately, a growing number of mental health practitioners who work with children and adolescents have come to understand that what has been called gender variance is simply a manifestation of gender diversity (Brill & Pepper, 2008; Ehrensaft, 2012, 2014; Lev, 2004; Menvielle, 2012; Pyne, 2014a). The concept of gender diversity holds that there are an infinite number of ways people (and other living beings) express themselves and that these varying gender expressions are simply part of our diversity as human beings. Gender diversity posits that there is no single, or right or wrong, way to be a man or woman.

Gender-nonconforming or diverse behavior among children or

adolescents is not abnormal, even if it is not the norm statistically. While there are numerically more children whose gender expression conforms to normative gender expectations, this does not mean that gender variance or diversity is problematic. It simply reflects the many different ways human beings express themselves in the world.

A statement by the board of directors of the World Professional Association for Transgender Health (WPATH, 2010) indicates that "the expression of gender characteristics, including identities, that are not stereotypically associated with one's assigned sex at birth is a common and culturally diverse human phenomenon [that] should not be judged as inherently pathological or negative" (p. 4). Through the lens of more contemporary approaches, gender variance or diversity is not, in and of itself, a psychiatric illness requiring correction or treatment. Furthermore, treatment approaches that aim to change a person's gender identity and expression to become more congruent with their birth-assigned sex have been unsuccessful (Gelder & Marks, 1969; Greenson, 1964), particularly in the long term (Cohen-Kettenis & Kuiper, 1984; Pauly, 1965). As a result, corrective or reparative treatment is no longer considered ethical.

There are two significant difficulties with perceiving gender non-conformity as pathological. The first is that believing that non-normative gender expression leads to homosexuality reflects a conflated understanding of gender expression, gender identity, and sexual orientation. It fails to recognize these as distinct aspects of our identity, as described in Chapter 1. Second, this lens clearly presumes that there is something "wrong" with homosexuality. It implies that if a child grew up to identify as gay, lesbian, or bisexual, this would be problematic.

Gender-diverse behavior among young children is not necessarily an early expression of same-sex sexual attraction or an early expression of transgender identity (Drummond, Bradley, Peterson-Badali, & Zucker, 2008). Many children who manifest gender-nonconforming or diverse behavior do not grow up to identify as transgender adults. Even if their gender diversity continues into adulthood, this may not be reflective of their gender identity. For example, a child assigned male at birth with diverse expression in childhood may grow up to fully identify as a man, yet continue to express their masculinity in ways that some might consider more feminine. Early long-term studies of prepubertal children (generally boys) who presented for assessment of gender dysphoria found that the dysphoria persisted into adulthood for only 6% to 23% of children (Cohen-Kettenis, 2001; Zucker & Bradley, 1995). Many of the boys in these studies identified as gay by adulthood rather than transgender (Green, 1987; Zucker & Bradley, 1995; Zuger, 1984). More recent studies that include girls suggest that gender dysphoria persists into adulthood for among 12% to 27% of children (Drummond et al., 2008; Wallien, 2008).

When adolescents present with gender dysphoria, they are much more likely to continue to identify as transgender into adulthood. In one follow-up study of 70 adolescents diagnosed with gender dysphoria and given puberty-suppressing hormones, all continued with further medical transition steps, beginning with feminizing or masculinizing hormone therapy (de Vries, Steensma, Doreleijers, Cohen-Kettenis, 2010). Some of these adolescents transition and live in their affirmed gender as adults; other youth may identify as gender-queer, gender-fluid, or gender-expansive and not necessarily gender transition. Regardless of their path, most young people who come out as transgender during adolescence continue to identify as trans into their adult lives.

With an understanding of gender variance as gender diversity, treatment approaches for trans and gender-nonconforming youth have begun to radically shift. Contemporary best practices recommend that clinicians and parents create "space" for a child's gender diversity and not attempt to correct or punish their self-expression (Bernal & Coolhart, 2012; Brill & Pepper, 2008; Ehrensaft, 2011, 2012, 2014). These newer approaches stress the importance of validating and affirming a child's sense of themselves as opposed to denying or punishing their understanding of their own interests and/or identities.

The goal of affirming treatment protocols is to raise these young people with a strong positive sense of self and as little shame as possible about who they are or how they are perceived— though some internalized shame may be unavoidable in a world that still rigidly enforces gender conformity. Like those with any difference from what is considered normative in our society, gender-diverse youth may encounter disapproval, stigma, or discrimination in the outside world. However, affirming family, neighborhood, and school environments often counter and diminish the negative impact of this marginalization and its concomitant mental and emotional risks

(Pyne, 2014b; Wallace & Russell, 2013). Having those close to them validate and support their gender identity or expression increases these individuals' chances of becoming healthy, happy adults (Simons, Schrager, Clark, Belzer, & Olson, 2013).

The shift toward affirming the diversity of children's gendered self-expression is not just good news for transgender and gender-diverse youth; it is good news for all young people. Embracing the reality of gender diversity enables all youth to explore, express, and celebrate who they are without shame or punishment.

Gender Diversity or Mental Illness?

The Diagnostic and Statistical Manual of Mental Disorders (DSM) is a compendium of psychiatric diagnoses recognized by the American Psychiatric Association (APA). DSM-5 (the fifth edition) was released in May 2014 following an extensive review of recent research studies (APA, 2013). These studies were evaluated within work groups focused on specific diagnostic sections. The existing diagnostic criteria (DSM-IV-TR) were reviewed alongside more recent research conclusions (APA, 2000). The work groups then revised existing diagnoses or in some cases developed criteria for new diagnoses to be included in DSM-5.

As mentioned earlier, homosexuality was removed from the DSM in 1973. Gender identity disorder (GID) was included for the first time within DSM-III in 1980. This diagnosis was continued in DSM-IV and DSM-IV-TR. Some transgender people believe the inclusion of gender identity disorder in 1980 was linked to (or precipitated by) the removal of homosexuality seven years earlier (Lev, 2013). With the more conservative psychiatric establishment no longer able to diagnose gay and lesbian people (and especially gay men) as mentally ill, concerns about gender-variant behavior in male youth emerged as a way to "prevent" the development of homosexuality and transsexuality—given that gender variance and same-sex orientation were often conflated (Zucker, 1985). Inserting gender identity disorder as a psychiatric diagnosis in 1980 was in part motivated by homophobia and created a continued path for penalizing feminine gender expression (and possible gay identity) among boys and men (Pyne, 2014a). It also led to significantly increased stigma and marginalization of transgender people.

At the root of this stigma is the fact that gender dysphoria (and its predecessor, gender identity disorder) is a psychiatric, not a medical, diagnosis. The fact that the diagnosis is located within the DSM labels it as a mental illness. Consequently, all transgender people who desire to medically transition must assume the stigma of being diagnosed as mentally ill. Medical doctors require that this diagnosis be made by a licensed mental health professional prior to the onset of hormone therapy and any trans-related surgeries. The diagnosis is also required when seeking health insurance coverage for these medical procedures. This was true for DSM-III and DSM-IV when the diagnosis was termed gender identity disorder, and it remains true with the shift in language to gender dysphoria in DSM-5.

During the review process leading up to the publication of DSM-5, the work of the APA group assigned to the DSM-IV section on sexual disorders (which included gender identity disorder) was highly contentious within the transgender community (Schwartzapfel, 2013; Tosh, 2011; Wingerson, 2009). Justifiably, most transgender people strongly object to being diagnosed as mentally ill simply for being "gender different." The process of transitioning typically facilitates greater psychological health and well-being among transgender individuals—the opposite of what a psychiatric diagnosis suggests (de Vries et al., 2010; Spack et al., 2012). Transgender individuals do experience higher rates of mental health diagnoses, such as depression and anxiety, than does the general public. However, this increase is correlated to enacted and felt stigma, as predicted by Meyer's (2003) Minority Stress Model, and not their gender dysphoria (Bockting, Miner, Swinburne Romine, Hamilton, & Coleman, 2013).

Because this psychiatric diagnosis is necessary to access transition-related medical procedures (like hormones and surgeries) and obtain health insurance reimbursement for these procedures, eliminating the gender dysphoria diagnosis altogether could limit trans people's access to medical interventions. However, many transgender people argue that this diagnosis should be classified as medical rather than psychiatric. Most medical conditions are less stigmatizing than being labeled mentally ill. Beyond the negative impact of this diagnosis for the self-image and self-esteem of transgender people themselves, continuing to classify it as a psychiatric illness sends a message to the general public that being transgender is still aberrant and pathological—and thus open to discriminatory behavior and legislation.

There are some ways the shift in nomenclature to gender dys-phoria reflects an improvement over the language of gender identity disorder (DSM-III and DSM-IV). One significant change in DSM-5 is that gender dysphoria now forms its own section in the manual. Previously, gender identity disorder was included in a section titled "Sexual and Gender Identity Disorders" (APA, 2000, pp. 258–259). This section included various sexual dysfunction diagnoses, such as male erectile disorder, female sexual arousal disorder, and premature ejaculation. The section also included paraphilias, such as exhibition-ism, fetishism, pedophilia, sexual masochism or sadism, voyeurism, and transvestic fetishism (defined as sexual fantasies, urges, or behav-ior involving cross-dressing among heterosexual men). The section concluded with gender identity disorder (GID) and "Gender Identity Disorder Not Otherwise Specified" (not meeting the full diagnostic criteria) (APA, 2000, pp. 259–261). The change in how sections are divided means that the gender dysphoria diagnosis in DSM-5 no lon-ger carries the implication that gender identity is a sexual dysfunc-tion, perversion, or fetish.

Eliminating the nomenclature "disorder" (DSM-IV) and replacing it with "dysphoria" (DSM-5) may diminish some of the stigma associ-ated with the prior language. DSM-5 defines gender dysphoria as the distress that can accompany the dissonance between an individual's affirmed gender and their assigned sex/gender. DSM-5 acknowledges that not all transgender individuals experience distress, though lack of access to desired physical interventions (hormones and/or surgery) may precipitate distress (APA, 2013, p. 451).

This acknowledgment means that not all transgender and gen-der-nonconforming persons must, or should be, diagnosed with gender dysphoria (though the diagnosis remains necessary for med-ical procedures and insurance reimbursement). Furthermore, the nomenclature in DSM-5 defines the dysphoria (or distress) as the clinical problem, rather than one's transgender identity itself being the precipitant for the diagnosis (such as in gender identity disorder, DSM-IV).

In another groundbreaking shift, DSM-5 defines gender identity as a category of social identity that refers to a person's identification as a man, woman, or occasionally, some category other than man or woman (APA, 2013, p. 451). With this language, DSM-5 moves beyond historical gender classifications and acknowledges that some gender identities may not fit these traditional binary constructs. Further, DSM-5 differentiates between the gender assigned at birth and one's experienced or affirmed gender, acknowledging the latter as a real and valid phenomenon.

In this sense, DSM-5 reflects the gender-diverse reality that not all human beings identify as men or women—that there are youth and adults for whom these mutually exclusive categories do not fit or match their understanding of themselves. For these individuals, checking one box under sex or gender does not work; it does not accurately encapsulate the complexity of their identity. It acknowledges that some youth (and adults) may identify as both male and female, or neither male nor female, or some gender entirely different from male and female. This new possibility is clearly indicated by the assertion that dysphoria and distress are not limited to one's sense of being the other gender, but may include a desire to be of an alternative gender different from one's assigned gender (APA, 2013, p. 452). This is good news for transgender people and makes a significant contribution to depathologizing trans and gender-diverse youth's and adults' experiences in society.

DSM-5 describes transgender people as a "broad spectrum of individuals who transiently or persistently identify with a gender different from their assigned or natal gender" (APA, 2013, p. 451). This language is significant on two levels. First, this definition is broader than earlier versions that viewed gender identity disorder as applying only to the segment of the population that might be described as "transsexual" (meaning those trans people who desire to gender transition). Second, the inclusion of "transiently" posits a fluidity to our gender identities that was not acknowledged in previous editions of the DSM. This new conception suggests that identifying with a gender different from one's assigned or natal gender might "ebb and flow;" it suggests that our gender identities are not inherently static, but may be fluid and even fluctuate across the lifecycle.

Seventeen-year-old Jase described themselves (the plural pronoun reflects the teen's word usage) as gender-fluid. They did not want to be confined by either male or female stereotypical norms for gender expression or identity. As they put it, one day they might arrive at school dressed "like a girl," while later that week they might show up in baggy jeans with matching "Jordans" and a backward ball cap.

These fluctuations in presentation reflected their experience of a more fluid gender expression and identity.

Historically, Jase's self-identified gender fluidity would have been viewed as inherently unstable and unhealthy (Zucker, 1985; Zucker et al., 2012). The mental health profession would have understood Jase's sense of self as a reflection of gender confusion, or immature gender and sexual development (with sex, gender, and sexual orientation conflated). However, many youth today are deconstructing the traditional binary gender system (Kuklin, 2014). They challenge the historical understanding that there are only two genders, as well as the belief that sex and gender are synonymous.

Speaking to this notion of gender fluidity, the Standards of Care (SOC) assert that "gender nonconformity is not the same as gender dysphoria" (WPATH, 2012, p. 5). With this, the SOC acknowledge (as does DSM-5) that only some gender-diverse people (including children and youth) experience dysphoria (distress) at some points in their lives, while others may never experience this type of cognitive or emotional distress. The diagnosis of gender dysphoria no longer necessarily reflects the experience of all transgender youth or adults (as opposed to the understanding about gender identity disorder within DSM-IV).

DSM-5 rightly acknowledges that diverse gender expression and gender dysphoria are associated with high levels of stigmatization, discrimination, and victimization. However, this stigma is perpetuated by the assertion that these experiences lead to a negative self-concept, increased rates of mental disorder comorbidity, school dropout, economic marginalization, and social and mental health risks among transgender individuals (APA, 2013, p. 458). Identifying with a gender other than the sex one was assigned at birth, or expressing one's gender in diverse and nonstereotypical ways, does not automatically or necessarily lead to the negative repercussions listed in DSM-5. While many transgender and gender-diverse people do encounter stigma and discrimination, these experiences do not always lead to poor mental, emotional, and social outcomes.

In contrast, many studies highlight the tremendous resilience of trans and gender-diverse people (Singh, 2013). Transgender and gender diverse youth who grow up in affirming and supportive environments typically demonstrate a positive sense of self and thrive emotionally, socially, and academically (Wallace & Russell, 2013). Less stigmatizing would be a recognition that these emotional and social struggles, when present, reflect the effect, or consequences, of transphobia and rigid binary gender norms as opposed to the result of gender diversity or dysphoria itself (Meyer, 2007).

Despite the positive impact of the movement from gender identity disorder to gender dysphoria, the inclusion of the diagnosis within DSM-5 continues to inherently classify gender difference or gender diversity as a psychiatric illness. Consequently, the diagnosis continues to stigmatize trans identities and experience, and it remains true that all transgender people seeking transgender-related medical treatment must be diagnosed with gender dysphoria, and thus be labeled with a psychiatric illness.

Criteria for Gender Dysphoria Diagnosis

DSM-5 separates the diagnosis for gender dysphoria into two sections differentiated by whether the distress occurs among children (302.6/F64.2, "Gender Dysphoria in Children," p. 452) or among adolescents and adults (302.86/F64.1, "Gender Dysphoria in Adolescents and Adults," pp. 452–453). The first, solely numerical code is from DSM-5; the second diagnostic code with an "F" followed by a number represents the ICD-10 coding for gender dysphoria (World Health Organization, 1992).

The first section of the diagnosis describes symptoms that reflect the incongruence between an individual's birth-assigned sex and their affirmed gender. The experience that one's gender does not match one's birth-assigned sex is at the core of a gender dysphoria diagnosis. For both age groups, the identified symptoms must be present for at least six months before the diagnosis can be made.

The second part of the diagnosis stipulates that this internal dissonance must lead to "clinically significant distress" or impairment in areas of social, educational, or occupational functioning. The inclusion of the second requirement acknowledges that not all young people presenting with symptoms listed in the first criterion necessarily meet the requirements for a diagnosis of gender dysphoria. The diagnosis is indicated only when their level of distress impairs their ability to function effectively.

Gender Dysphoria in Children

DSM-5 lists eight possible symptoms children might experience. At least six of these symptoms must be present, and one symptom must be the child's (1) strong desire to be of the other gender or a belief that they are in fact, the other gender (or some alternative gender other than their birth-assigned sex). Other possible symptoms include (2) a strong preference for clothing reflective of the child's affirmed gender (rather than their birth-assigned sex); (3) a strong preference for assuming roles in play that match the child's affirmed gender; (4) strong rejection of toys, games, and activities typically associated with the child's birth-assigned sex, or a strong preference for toys, games, or activities typically associated with the child's affirmed gender; (5) a strong preference for playmates of the affirmed gender; (6) strong dislike of one's sexual anatomy; and (7) a strong desire for the primary and/or secondary sex characteristics reflective of the child's affirmed gender.

The symptoms reflect the "marked incongruence" between a child's birth-assigned sex and their affirmed gender. The inclusion of the descriptor "strong" indicates that the diagnosis is applicable only when a child expresses more than a casual interest or preference. Additionally, the required minimum of six symptoms must be present for at least six months and must lead to a clinically significant level of distress, or impairment in school, occupational, or other important areas of functioning.

Gender Dysphoria in Adolescents and Adults (302.85, DSM-5, pp. 452-453)

DSM-5 lists six possible symptoms that adolescents and adults might experience, with at least two symptoms being required for the diagnosis to be made. As with children, the symptoms reflect the "marked incongruence" between an adolescent's or adult's birth-assigned sex and their affirmed gender. Similarly, the symptoms must persist for at least six months and must lead to clinically significant levels of distress, or functional impairment in social, educational, or other important areas.

The symptoms for adolescents and adults include (1) significant dissonance between one's affirmed gender and one's primary and/ or secondary sex characteristics (or anticipated secondary sex characteristics), (2) a strong desire to be rid of (or prevent the development of) the primary and/or secondary sex characteristics reflective of the birth-assigned sex, (3) a strong desire to have the primary and/ or secondary sex characteristics of the affirmed gender, (4) a strong desire to be the affirmed gender (or an alternative gender different from one's birth-assigned sex), (5) a strong desire to be perceived and treated as one's affirmed gender (or alternative gender different from one's birth-assigned sex), and (6) a strong conviction that one experiences feelings and reactions normally associated with one's affirmed gender (or alternative gender different from one's birth-assigned sex).

There are two possible specifiers that can be used with this diagnosis. The first indicates the presence of an intersex condition ("with a disorder of sex development"). The second possible specifier ("post-transition") can be used when an individual is living full-time in their affirmed gender and has taken (or is about to begin) some aspect of their medical transition (feminizing or masculinizing hormone treatment or gender-confirming surgery (DSM-5, p. 453).

As indicated above, one's affirmed gender is not limited to the opposite gender but can be an alternative gender different from one's birth-assigned sex. This critical shift within DSM-5 acknowledges the reality that not all transgender people fit within a binary paradigm existence or choose a medical transition. DSM-5 recognizes that there are people who may identify as gender-diverse and yet also experience clinically significant distress as a result of the dissonance between their birth-assigned sex and their more fluid gender identity or expression.

DSM-5 describes two possible trajectories associated with a gender dysphoria diagnosis—early onset (childhood) or late onset (puberty or adulthood). Early-onset gender dysphoria begins in childhood and may persist into adolescence and adulthood, or the dysphoria may end at some later point. Late-onset gender dysphoria occurs in the context of puberty or adulthood. Some adolescents with late-onset gender dysphoria may recall wanting to be of another or the other gender during childhood but did not acknowledge this to anyone. Other adolescents and adults may not recall earlier gender dysphoria.

Historically, the acceptable narrative for transgender people required an awareness of gender dysphoria as a child. In recognizing the possibility of late-onset dysphoria, DSM-5 acknowledges the reality that some adolescents (and adults) may not recall earlier gender dysphoria and may not have verbalized or manifested the associated symptoms. When the latter is true, many parents are surprised to hear about their adolescent's gender dysphoria or their longing to live in their affirmed gender. The fact that these parents did not see it (the trans identity) coming may lead them to suspect that their adolescent's reported trans identity is not valid or "real."

Many clinicians as well believe that the onset of gender dysphoria always occurs during childhood and are unfamiliar with late-onset gender dysphoria. Consequently, they too may have difficulty believing the teen's recent report of gender dysphoria or announced transgender identity and possible desire to transition. Both parents and mental health providers sometimes view late-onset gender dysphoria in adolescents as a phase or developmentally normative identity exploration that will desist over time. If so, they may not allow the adolescent to transition—even socially, when there are no irreversible medical interventions.

The next chapter addresses these decisions more fully. It discusses how to screen for gender dysphoria, outlines what should be included in an assessment among children and adolescents, and presents strategies for gathering this and evaluating information.

CHAPTER 3

Trans Kids in Therapy

HERE ARE SEVERAL WAYS ISSUES OF GENDER IDENTITY and expression and transgender identity can emerge within the context of more general counseling, youth work, clinical treatment settings. One way is that the young person and/or parents come in specifically to address these issues. When a younger child evidences gender-nonconforming interests, behavior, or expression, parents may have questions or concerns about these interests or behavior and initiate contact with a therapist to discuss their concerns. Frequent questions from parents at this stage include "What does this mean?" and "How should we respond to or handle this [at home, daycare, kindergarten, or elementary school]?"

With a preschool-age child, the concerns will largely focus on what the gender-variant behavior means and how to respond to it within the context of home and family. For example, Tonya called me very upset about her two-and-a-half-year-old son, who always wanted to play with his four-year-old sister's dolls. She worried about what this meant but didn't want to be punitive with her son. Her husband thought she should redirect their son to more gender-normative toys, like his trains and trucks. Their questions about how to handle their son's behavior had begun to affect their marriage.

Other times, gender-variant behavior will not raise concerns or precipitate a call to a therapist until the child begins moving out into the world. Interests and behavior that parents may have been largely unconcerned about at home may begin to attract attention and questions from daycare workers or preschool or elementary school teachers. These childcare personnel may suggest that the parents seek consultation about their child's gender-nonconforming behavior.

Another possible spark for seeking a therapist may occur when a younger child is making statements about being a gender other than the sex assigned at birth. For example, in the vignette about Joey in Chapter 2, the parents told me that "he" frequently asked them, "Why do people keep calling me a boy? I'm not a boy! I'm a girl." Here the primary concern may be the child's self-assertions of being a gender other than their assigned gender as opposed to, or in addition to, the emergence of gender-nonconforming interests and behavior.

Sometimes when a young child displays gender-nonconforming interests or behaviors or makes self-assertions about being a gender other than the one assigned at birth, parents worry about whether or not this indicates the presence of emerging developmental difficulties or mental illness. These concerns about mental health problems may also be true for parents whose child comes out as transgender during adolescence. Parents may suspect an identity disturbance in their teen. Fears about mental illness are often exacerbated when a teen is depressed, anxious, or engaged in self-harming or self-destructive behaviors. In these situations, parents may view the announcement about being trans as part of their adolescent's depression or anxiety rather than the emergence of a freestanding transgender identity.

When gender-nonconforming expression or trans identity emerges (or emerges more clearly) in preadolescence or during adolescence, parents often contact a therapist shortly after their child comes out to them as transgender or gender-diverse. At this stage, parents are often looking for information about gender identity in children and adolescents. For many parents, gender identity and being transgender is still a new concept. Most parents are not personally acquainted with transgender people. The only trans people they know may be through the media. As a result, their impressions and knowledge may be limited, skewed, or inaccurate.

Parents who support their child's gender identity or varying gender expression and are open to allowing their child to socially transition may contact a therapist looking for guidance about this process. They may want help in thinking through the possible ramifications of their child's social transition—how it may affect the child's peer relationships, opportunities for play dates with young children, and the parent's interactions with neighbors and other parents. They may need information about dealing with the child's or teen's teachers and school administrators, or they may have initiated these conversations and need the therapist to function as an advocate for them and their child (Chapter 9 addresses schools). These parents need help in locating resources for their child, such as medical providers or trans youth groups.

As a therapist, there have been times when my first contact was with the adolescent, who may or may not have come out to their parents. They typically find me by researching trans-affirmative therapists online and then contact me to ask if I am willing to see them and/ or their family. There are ethical cautions and, in some jurisdictions, legal prohibitions about working with a minor. Clinicians need to be clear on what the laws in their state say about a minor's right to access mental health services without parental consent and abide by these.

At the same time, when an adolescent contacts me directly, I believe I have an ethical responsibility to assess their safety. I ask whether or not they have come out to their parents and, if so, what the response has been. If they have not come out, I explore their concerns about sharing their trans identity with their parents. I ask whether they have discussed seeing a therapist with their parents and if the parents would support this.

I have found it important to ask for the parent's name and address or phone number. In doing this, I walk a line between assuring the youth of as much confidentiality as possible and letting them know that my primary concern (and legal responsibility) is their safety and that this means I will contact their parents if I feel they are in danger of harming themselves or someone else. I discuss what is possible in terms of our contact, given their age and the laws about counseling minors in that state. In this sense, I want to be as up front with the teen as possible.

In assessing for safety, I ask if they have experienced or are currently at risk for abuse (physical, emotional, verbal, sexual) or violence from family, peers, or others in their life. I screen for depression, self-harming behavior, and suicide ideation, plans, or attempts. If the teen refuses to provide their parents' contact information and seems at risk, I attempt to gather other information—such as the school they attend or a teacher's or guidance counselor's name—that might help me contact a responsible adult. I also work with the youth to contract for safety, such as agreeing to reach out to a responsible adult if they feel they cannot talk with their parents. When possible, I provide information about local or online hotlines and other resources.

There have been a few occasions when I had some concern about crossing a line and engaging in therapy when the state required parental consent for mental health services. In these situations, I weighed this concern alongside my legal and ethical responsibility to ensure a young person's safety. I document phone contacts just as I would an in-person counseling session so that there is a record of what was discussed, any recommendations I made, and any actions I took following the call.

When Gender Identity or Expression Is Not the Presenting Concern

A second way that gender expression or identity issues may become the focus is when these concerns emerge in the course of work with a child or adolescent when this was not the presenting issue. Sometimes this happens indirectly, such as when the young person initiates the conversation by raising questions, fears, or concerns about their own gender identity or expression. They may acknowledge wondering if they are transgender. I have also had teens raise these issues by discussing peers who identified as transgender or gender-diverse. In cases like these, the adolescent may not directly come out as trans or gender-diverse but may want to explore these identities with the therapist or find out what the therapist thinks about transgender people. This may be an attempt to determine whether or not it is "safe" to discuss being trans or gender-diverse with the therapist, how much the therapist knows about transgender people and youth, or whether or not the therapist will "get" it or them.

Questions or discussion about trans and gender-diverse youth may flow from other issues the therapist and the youth have been working on, or they may be completely independent of recent or current work. There are also times when these topics emerge as a result of a young person directly coming out to the therapist as trans and gender-diverse. The latter part of this chapter provides guidelines for clinicians on how to respond when a young person comes out as trans or gender-diverse to them.

In terms of screening new clients, it is part of my practice to incorporate a brief question about gender/gender identity/expression into my intake process with all young people. I recommend that all youth workers and mental health providers do this. It is important to ask this question with all youth, not just those who look gender-different or you think may be transgender.

Asking a question about gender identity/expression provides an opportunity for young people to come out upon intake as trans or gender-diverse or to acknowledge having questions or concerns about their gender identity or expression. The language you use can either open or close the door for disclosure. If you simply assume a young person's gender identity or use language such as "Are you male or female?" you communicate that you see only two options for sex/gender. Even when young people do not immediately engage in this conversation, including a question within your intake signals that you know trans and gender-diverse people exist, it signals that these are topics you are willing and unafraid to discuss, and it signals your affirmation of trans and gender-diverse youth (provided that you ask this question in an affirming way). Messages like this open the door for youth to initiate conversations at a later time.

One suggestion for making these conversations easier is to make a brief normalizing statement about gender and gender identity during the intake, followed by a question that can be answered without requiring the young person to directly declare a transgender identity. I ask these questions in the context of general questions typically included in an intake—racial/ethnic identity, immigration status, school grade and interests, extracurricular activities, whether they are dating/in a relationship, etc.

Here is one way this might sound:

WORKER: *People have different ways they experience their gender. For many people, their gender identity matches the sex they were assigned at birth. For other people, their own sense of themselves may not exactly line up with how they were assigned at birth. You might think I know, but I ask everyone, "What sex were you assigned at birth?"*

YOUTH: *(Typically says male or female.)*

WORKER: *Have you ever felt differently or had any questions about whether that gender identity fits for you?*

In some settings, it may work to directly ask how a youth identifies in terms of their gender or gender identity (e.g., "What words would you use to describe your gender identity?"). You might offer several choices about how people identify. I might again begin with a normalizing statement such as, "People identify different ways in terms of their gender—sometimes as a man, a woman, transgender, or gender-fluid. Sometimes they use other language. How would you describe your gender identity?"

Sherer, Baum, Ehrensaft, and Rosenthal (2015) suggest that screening questions like the following can open the door for discussion about gender identity or expression.

> **WHEN INTERVIEWING PARENTS OF YOUNG CHILDREN:**
> Do you have any concerns about your child's sexual or gender development that you'd like to discuss today?
>
> **WITH CHILDREN OF ALL AGES:**
> Do adults or other children ever pick on you for how you express being a boy or a girl?
>
> Some of the children I work with sometimes wonder if they're more like a girl or boy inside, or something else entirely. What has this been like for you?
>
> Do you ever feel the people around you have gotten it wrong about you being a girl or a boy?
>
> **WITH ADOLESCENTS:**
> During puberty, your body experiences many different changes. All of this is completely normal but can be confusing. Some of the young people I work with feel as if they're more of a boy or a girl or something else inside, while their body changes in another way. What has this been like for you?

Similar concerns arise in thinking about how to ask questions about sexual orientation. How a question is phrased can determine a young person's response. As suggested regarding questions about gender and gender identity, it is essential to assess whether the language you use opens or closes the door for a young person to "come out" as gay, lesbian. bisexual, pansexual, etc.

If you ask a boy or young man whether he has a girlfriend, you have closed the door to him coming out to you as gay, bi, or pan because you communicated that you assume all boys and men are straight. The same occurs if you ask a young woman if she has a boy-friend. Your assumption that she is straight creates a hurdle that she will have to "jump over" if she wants to discuss a non-heterosexual orientation—either at that moment or sometime later. It sends a message that you do not acknowledge that gay, lesbian, bi, and pan youth exist and/or that you are uncomfortable discussing, or even disapprove of, attractions that are non-heterosexual.

A better way to ask these questions is:

Are you involved with anyone?
Is there someone special in your life?
Are you dating anyone? (If the youth says yes without indicating a gender, you can open the conversation further by responding, "Tell me about them.")

You can also ask about sexual orientation directly. Some examples for wording this include:

WORKER: *How would you describe your sexual orientation? This wording leaves it totally open for the young person to use their own language and words to describe themselves.*

WORKER: *People describe their sexual orientation in different ways— gay, straight, lesbian, bisexual, pansexual. Do any of these words describe your orientation (or attractions)? Or would you use another word to describe yourself? This language offers the youth several examples of how they might describe their attraction. However, you should be prepared for a young person to say they do not use or like "labels." Many young people increasingly view labels as constraining, as "boxes" that preclude or limit more fluid choices or ways of being in the world and in relationship.*

Conversations about gender identity and expression may emerge in the context of family therapy when this is not the presenting issue. A parent or sibling may raise the issue, or the young person themselves may initiate the discussion. The topic may be raised directly (e.g., a teen announcing they are trans), or it may emerge more indirectly (e.g., a young child correcting the pronoun or name I used for them, or a parent asking what I think about children who gender

transition or how I think parents should respond to gender-nonconforming behavior in children and teens).

One family originally sought me out to have a safe place where the
parents and children could discuss one parent's (Dwayne's) alcoholism and fairly recent recovery and sobriety. Both Thomas and
Dwayne knew this experience had been stressful for their children
(ages 4, 6, and 11) as well as themselves. Some sessions occurred
solely with the parents, and others involved the entire family.

One tool we used to help decrease the children's anxiety about discussing what it had been like before their parent
stopped drinking was for each child to bring a favorite object—a
toy, doll, stuffed animal. I was aware that their four-year-old son
always brought a cloth girl doll with curly hair—sometimes two
dolls. Over the course of our work, I noticed that Thomas seemed
uncomfortable when their son was playing with his dolls during
our sessions. On one occasion, it was simply Thomas's nonverbal expression that I noted; a second time, Thomas motioned for
their son to put the dolls away under his chair.

Shortly thereafter in a meeting with the parents, I shared my
observations and asked whether Thomas thought my sense that he
had been uncomfortable was accurate. It was an intentional choice
to raise this observation with the parents separate from their children. I wanted the parent(s) to feel comfortable openly exploring
their feelings with me and not feel constrained by the presence of
their children. I was also unsure how the parent(s) would respond; I
wanted this to come out in my presence rather than risking that the
children might hear what could be perceived as a negative feeling
toward them or toward "boys who like girls' things."

Initially, Thomas denied any discomfort. Without challenging his response, I reflected on some of the ways that both boys
and men in our culture experience little room for varied gender
expression that in any way hints at femininity, and offered my own
sense of how this limits us as men. I shared my experience on
the subway of watching the two-year-old boy be scolded for crying "like a stupid little girl" and asked if either of them had ever
been reprimanded for saying or doing something "too feminine."
Dwayne responded by sharing several occasions when his father

had punished him when he caught Dwayne playing with his mother's makeup or trying on his older sister's clothes.

From here, we began over time to discuss ways that gay men in particular are stigmatized as being less than "real men," stereotypes of lesbian and gay people as bad parents, myths that gay men are predators who recruit children into being gay, and the (erroneous) belief that children raised by gay and lesbian parents become gay themselves. The more we discussed these challenges, the more open both Dwayne and Thomas became about how these dynamics impacted them as parents, including their periodic fears that others would judge them if one of their children grew up to be gay. While Thomas was not originally conscious of his discomfort with his son's choice of dolls as a favorite toy, we were gradually able to connect the dots between that discomfort and the stigma he and Dwayne experienced as young boys and later as adult gay men.

This vignette illustrates that work with young gender-diverse children often focuses as much, if not more, on the needs of the parents. At times, their questions, concerns, or fears predominate. In this family, the four-year-old son was doing well, and it was the parents who needed information about childhood gender identity and development as well as the opportunity to explore how their own family-of-origin experiences and internalized societal myths about gay men might be impacting their views as parents. Later chapters on work with families explore these challenges in more detail.

Gathering a Psychosocial and Gender History

Any assessment of a child's or adolescent's gender/gender identity/expression should incorporate all the areas that would be included in a more general assessment in addition to gender-specific questions. A full psychosocial assessment should include the following areas:

- Background and demographic information
- Education and/or employment history, including volunteer experiences
- Psychiatric/mental health history, diagnoses, and treatment history

- Alcohol, tobacco, and other drug use (history and current use) and treatment history
- Family history and current support
- Peer and social support
- Physical health status (history and any current concerns/conditions)
- Trauma and/or abuse/neglect history
- Gender history and present gender identity
- Current degree of gender dysphoria
- Body image concerns
- Sexual orientation, sexual history, and current activity
- Future concerns that might emerge if the young person comes out as trans or gender-diverse or begins a gender transition (e.g., housing, changes in relationships with family and/or friends, the young person's expectations about physical changes with transition, etc.)
- Safety assessment, including family, peers, experiences of bullying, and self-harm
- Strengths and resources
- Assessment of whether the young person meets the criteria for gender dysphoria as outlined in DSM-5

It is useful to screen for depression and anxiety in the mental health assessment, as trans youth are at high risk for both diagnoses (Almeida, Johnson, Corliss, Molnar, & Azrael, 2009; Diamond et al., 2011; Grossman & D'Augelli, 2007; Mustanski, Andrews, Herrick, Stall, & Schnarrs, 2014). Victimization, multiple stigmas, and lack of social support have been shown to lead to increased depression, and rates of depression are higher among trans youth of color (Almeida et al., 2009; Nemoto, Bödeker, & Iwamoto, 2011; Travers et al. 2010).

Diamond et al. (2011) as well found that one prominent risk factor associated with adolescent depression and suicidality is the quality of the adolescent–parent relationship. In particular, parental criticism, emotional unresponsiveness, lack of care and support, and rejection contribute to increased depression, suicidal ideation, and suicide attempts (Connor & Rueter, 2006; Kerr, Preuss, & King, 2006).

Though the etiology is not yet understood, there is a growing body of research that documents a higher co-occurrence of gender dysphoria among youth with autism spectrum disorders (ASDs) (de Vries,

Noens, Cohen-Kettenis, van Berckelaer-Onnes, & Doreleijers, 2010; Jannsen, Huang, & Duncan, 2016; Strang et al., 2014; Van Schalkwyk, Klingensmith, & Volkman, 2015). In the Jannsen et al. (2016) study, youth with an ASD diagnosis were 7.76 times as likely to indicate that they "wished to be the opposite sex" than were the comparison group.

Given this association, it is important to screen for gender dysphoria among youth with ASDs and to screen for autistic symptoms among youth with documented gender dysphoria. At the same time, mental health professionals need to be cautious not to assume that a stated wish to be the opposite sex dictates a diagnosis of gender dysphoria, as there is some indication that gender development among youth with ASDs is fluid and complex (Best, Minshew, & Strauss, 2010; Deruelle, Rondan, Gepner, & Tardif, 2010; de Vries, Noens, et al., 2010). Because of the obsessive and compulsive aspect of ASDs, these young people may be insistent about transitioning but oddly unconcerned about the social adjustment involved, given their difficulties with social cues (Bockting, Knudson, & Goldberg, 2006).

Therapists need to conduct a safety assessment with all youth, and especially with trans and gender-diverse youth. This includes determining whether the young person is experiencing any type of abuse or neglect, any self-harming behaviors, or any suicidal ideation, intent, or plan. The HEEADSSS interview offers an excellent assessment tool that explores key areas of an adolescent's life (Klein, Goldenring, & Adelman, 2014). The acronym stands for each of the areas covered in the assessment: **H**ome environment, **E**ducation and employment, **E**ating, peer-related **A**ctivities, **D**rugs (including alcohol and tobacco), **S**exuality (including relationships and sexual intimacy), **S**uicide/depression, and **S**afety from injury and violence.

Therapists can discuss these assessment areas with many older children and most adolescents. With children, it is important to also explore these areas with the parents or guardians, as the adults can typically provide greater detail or answer questions a child might not understand or be able to express. Parents are generally able to describe a child's early gender interests, expression, or gender-variant self-assertions.

It is useful for therapists to explore these areas with parents of teens as well, although their ability to do this may depend on the context of their practice setting. It is possible that a parent's experience of their child or adolescent in terms of gender identity may vary from the young person's experiences and sense of themselves. When this is true, it is possible that the young person's internal sense of themselves was not apparent to those around them. It could also be that the young person's description of their interests and/or behavior occurred primarily with peers and not within the family.

Sometimes a mental health provider or parent may worry that raising questions with young people (especially young children) about gender identity or expression will "cause" the young person to think or believe they are transgender—that asking these questions will introduce areas the child has no knowledge about or has never considered before. Parents or clinicians may worry that discussing gender identity or expression will lead older children and adolescents to "research" these topics, look for stories of transgender youth or adults, and watch videos online of young people in the process of gender transition—again potentially encouraging them to question or believe they might be transgender as well.

These fears are not founded. While we do not fully understand why some people are cisgender and others are transgender, children and adolescents do not "become" trans or gender-diverse simply by talking about gender identity or expression or watching or listening to the stories and experiences of trans and gender-diverse youth.

For some young people it is sufficient to be referred to an affirmative counselor or therapist with basic knowledge of trans and gender-diverse issues. When there are more complex concerns or needs it is better to refer youth to mental health professionals with significant training and experience in gender identity and expression among children and adolescents.

Guidelines developed by the National Resource Center for Permanency and Family Connections (Mallon, n.d.) suggest that when a young person simply has questions about gender issues or is exploring their gender identity or expression, counseling by a nonspecialist, coupled with referrals to age-appropriate community resources, is generally sufficient. In these situations, the role of the mental health provider often includes normalizing the young person's thoughts and feelings; discussing the wide range of ways people may express their gender and name their gender identity; exploring any fears, anxieties, or concerns the young person might have; and identifying constructive ways to navigate possible societal stigma—whether external or internalized.

Helping transgender young people connect with and utilize community peer supports and online resources can effectively serve to reduce isolation. These might include school Gay–Straight Alliance (GSA) clubs, local community LGBTQ youth groups or programs, or online forums such as the Gender Spectrum Lounge or a Trans Youth and Family Allies (TYFA) teen online chat group. In this type of situation, mental health providers with basic knowledge of gender identity and expression and relevant adolescent resources are often able to facilitate the young person's gender exploration and respond to questions the youth may have.

In contrast, there are other scenarios when it is best for the provider to refer the child or teen and their family to a clinician who specializes in work with trans and gender-diverse young people. In some situations, this may be a referral for a gender evaluation, after which the initial clinician may be able to continue providing ongoing care with consultation from a gender specialist. When the original provider has little expertise with gender identity or expression, the young person may benefit from being transferred to a gender specialist for ongoing treatment.

Mallon identifies four situations when evaluation by a mental health clinician specializing in gender identity is recommended (Mallon, n.d.). These include when a child or adolescent:

- presents with a level/intensity of distress about gender issues such that their physical, mental, and/or emotional health and well-being, relationships, or school/work are negatively affected;
- expresses feelings of gender dysphoria, an aversion to aspects of their body associated with sex/gender, or discomfort with their current gender identity or expresses a desire to live as a gender other than their birth-assigned gender;
- is compulsively cross-dressing or pursuing validation of gender identity (e.g., through compulsive sexual or online encounters); or
- has a coexisting or preexisting condition that complicates evaluation of gender concerns (e.g., schizophrenia or other thought disorder, personality disorder, or cognitive disability due to injury or developmental disorder).

Additional situations where I recommend referral to a gender specialist include when a child or adolescent:

- presents with clinical depression and/or suicidal ideation or attempts that may be related to their gender dysphoria and/or desire to begin transitioning, or hopelessness that gender transition may/will never be possible for them;
- is a member of a family that is rejecting of their trans or gender-diverse identity/expression and has not altered this stance despite education about gender identity/ expression and the risks that come with family rejection (in this case, it is important that the gender specialist also be trained in family therapy); or
- indicates (or you suspect) that they have already begun medical transition steps without appropriate medical care and/or parental/guardian knowledge or consent.

In the last instance, each of the actions below represents significant risk to the youth:

- Taking cross-gender hormones when not under the care of a primary physician/endocrinologist
- Obtaining hormones "on the street" or online
- Receiving silicone injections from nonmedical providers (e.g., from friends or other trans persons; this is particularly a concern with lower-socioeconomic-status young trans women, who use these injections to access a more feminine figure, such as [larger] breasts or hips)
- Sharing needles when injecting hormones or silicone

It can be helpful to think about where the transgender child or youth (and their family) is in the process of gender exploration, coming out, or desire to transition, alongside what services might be necessary at each stage. One way to conceptualize the stages of the young person's gender process is as follows:

CONFUSION AND/OR EXPLORATION: At this moment in the therapeutic process, a child or adolescent is confused about their gender identity, has questions about gender identity and gender expression, or is exploring different ways they may want to, or feel comfortable, expressing their gender or experiencing or naming their gender identity. As stated previously, a youth worker or clinician with basic knowledge about gender/gender identity/gender expression is often able to facilitate these conversations and explorations as well as provide gender education and help the young person make connections to supportive peers.

TRANSITION: This can include making the decision to transition, taking the first steps of coming out and socially transitioning, or making initial adjustments to life in the affirmed gender/expression. These tasks require the provider to be informed about local resources, such as medical providers for hormone therapy or attorneys who can assist with a legal name change.

POST-TRANSITION: There are various ways people might define "post-transition." Historically, this was defined by "full transition," which meant genital surgery. From my perspective, this term is also valid when the child or adolescent has been living in their affirmed gender for some time and has successfully navigated this shift in their day-to-day lives—for example, in school, extracurricular activities, their faith community, etc. At this point, the gender work may become less intense and the young person may primarily need supportive counseling. However, there may still be significant pieces to address like dating, body image, or ongoing dysphoria that can require a clinician with greater experience to explore these concerns and intervene effectively.

Transgender and gender-diverse adolescents often have many questions about how to navigate social situations, such as whether or not, or when, to come out as trans if they are attracted to someone, or how to be sexually intimate when their body parts do not match their affirmed gender. Being able to effectively address these concerns requires more than just sensitivity. It is essential for the clinician to have a breadth of knowledge about transgender people and their lives. This includes things most cisgender people, including mental health providers, have not had to consider, such as the frustration a trans adolescent may feel about having to potentially come out every time they want to make out.

Another time when some mental health providers may want to refer out occurs when they feel competent supporting the parents but not working with the child or teen. Or the reverse may be true: A clinician may have significant expertise in working with trans and gender-diverse youth but have little training in work with families—or perhaps be uncertain of how to work with particular families, such as a family that is highly rejecting of their child's gender identity or expression.

Information and Referrals Families Need

- Education about trans identities and how these differ from sexual orientation; education about cultural norms of gender and gender expression
- Information about physical transition: puberty blockers, feminizing and masculinizing hormone therapy, surgeries
- Info about support groups and organizations for trans youth and their families; introductions to other parents with transgender children
- Names of service providers: Trans- and gender-diverse-knowledgeable and -affirming pediatricians, nurse practitioners, physician's assistants, pediatric endocrinologists, psychiatrists, schools, lawyers.

If you are unfamiliar with these resources in your community, helpful places to begin locating them include LGBT centers, trans activity and support groups (adult transgender groups may be aware of resources for transgender children and teens), and your nearest chapter of PFLAG (Formerly "Parents, Families, and Friends of Lesbians and Gays" www.pFlag.org).

Working With Gender-Diverse Young Children

There is considerable controversy within the medical and mental health arena, as well as within the general public, about the issue of young trans children making a gender transition. Much of this is rooted in the reality that we do not yet have a valid and reliable way to determine which gender-diverse children will continue to identify as transgender as they move into their adult lives, as opposed to those children whose varied gender interests and expression will become normative as they move through puberty. We cannot reliably predict which children will want to transition from their birth-assigned sex so they can live in their affirmed gender with the associated medical interventions and changes, as opposed to those who will decide over time that they are comfortable living in their birth-assigned sex.

In response to this controversy, some mental health professionals have carved out "camps" that represent their treatment approach when working with gender-diverse young children in particular (as opposed to adolescents). The "correct and redirect" camp, as described in Chapter 2, reflects the historical belief that gender-nonconforming or variant behaviors should be immediately corrected and the child redirected to more normative gender expression (Lament, 2014).

A second camp might be called the "wait and see" group, where mental health professionals coach parents to create space for the child to explore and express their gender. This approach is careful not to anticipate or project a particular outcome. While professionals working within this framework would not preclude a young child from socially transitioning, neither would they encourage this step. The primary emphasis is focused more on slowing the pace to observe the evolution of the child's gender identity over time rather than moving quickly toward a social transition.

More recently, many professionals have embraced an affirming, even celebratory approach to work with gender-diverse children. The shift in nomenclature from gender-variant or gender-nonconforming to gender-diverse, gender-expansive, and gender-independent reflects this newer framework. Working within this context encourages families to go beyond simply making space for their child's exploration and instead to affirm the full range of their child's diverse gender expression. Neither parents nor children are required to justify their affirmed gender; it is understood that even young children are fully capable of recognizing and naming their gender identity, whether trans or cisgender.

I suspect I stand somewhere between the "wait and see" approach and the "affirm and move forward" approach. Recognizing that not all gender-diverse children grow up to identify as transgender, I am cautious not to rush a child toward social transition or to allow a parent to rush their child. I believe it is important to spend some time exploring the child's historical and emerging gender expression and self-understanding of gender identity with both the young person and their parents—although the specific length of time for this exploration varies with each child's particular needs and context.

Simultaneously, I am fully committed to a stance that rejects gender shaming of children. I am convinced that if young children can know that their gender matches the sex they were assigned at birth—and my granddaughter had no questions about being a girl by the age of two, when she spun and twirled around the living room in her princess dress—then transgender children can be equally clear about their affirmed gender identity. Regardless of the final outcome of their gender identity in adulthood, all children deserve the space to freely explore and express their gender in diverse ways without shame, and with the understanding that both our gender expression and gender identity are more fluid and evolving than static and settled.

It can be challenging for parents to remain in the moment with a child's gender fluidity or non-normative gender expression—to stay in this "in-between-genders" place rather than moving toward the clarity of a gender transition. Most people are uneasy around gender fluidity. They feel unsettled when they are unable to decide whether someone is a man or woman. Being able to confidently put someone in a recognized gender box makes us much more comfortable.

I know this from personal experience. My hair was cut short prior to my transition, and I wore the same suits and ties I wear today. From the other end of the subway car, people were not always able to determine my sex/gender. Their discomfort was clear in the ways they stared at me, moved away from me, sometimes whispered about me, or even moved their children further down the bench from me. I am keenly aware that the world is far more comfortable with my male appearance today simply because they are confident they know which gender box I belong in.

As difficult as it can be for a parent to navigate the emotions involved in having your son become your daughter, I think it's sometimes more difficult to be the parent of a son whose gender expression is feminine yet does not identify as a girl or socially transition to live as a young woman. The in-between places can be hard to sit with emotionally.

Parents sometimes experience a greater degree of fear about the potential for ridicule, bullying, and violence when their children remain gender-diverse rather than transitioning to live in a seemingly clear gender box. Gender-nonconforming boys in particular are at high risk of bullying due to their feminine gender expression. In the long term, the risks of bullying and violence may diminish when a child transitions and moves through the world as an increasingly gender-conforming girl. There are still the initial challenges and responses of others to face regarding a child's disclosure and social transition. But in most situations, the reactions of other people— extended family, neighbors, classmates, coworkers—blow over within a few months and life returns to a new normal, with the parents now parenting a daughter instead of a son.

When working with young children and their families, I begin by taking a thorough family history. Beyond the usual areas of family history and functioning, this includes a detailed history of the child's gender-diverse interests and expression as well as any feelings of unhappiness about their bodies and how they function or any self-assertions that their gender identity differs from their birth-assigned sex.

In light of research suggesting that many children with gender-diverse expression do not go on to identify as transgender adults, I rarely move quickly toward social transition with a young child. While there is a fair amount of critique of earlier studies, we still do not have research that indicates a more persistent transgender trajectory among young gender-diverse children.

Since gender identity and gender expression are distinct aspects of ourselves that are sometimes conflated within families and the larger society, it is important to explore whether the child's gender-diverse presentation reflects their preferred gender expression, or whether this presentation is more reflective of an established or evolving affirmed gender identity. Despite the major gains of feminism during my lifetime, societal messages and expectations about gender-"appropriate" interests and behavior can still sometimes be incredibly rigid.

In this early phase of exploration, I want to ensure that a young child assigned male at birth has not internalized a message suggesting that he must be a girl simply because he likes girls' things. This desire is not limited to gender-diverse children; it is relevant for all children. It is almost impossible not to internalize some of the societal messages that permeate our culture—whether these messages are positive and helpful or oppressive and destructive. Even as adults, these messages continue to impact us. Children are particularly impressionable, as the following vignette suggests.

Early one morning, near the beginning of her year in first grade, our youngest daughter was on my lap. We were being silly and laughing, talking about her favorite cartoon. Out of nowhere, she said, "Daddy, the boys who make the rules at school say girls can't play with boys' toys."

I was stunned. My mind began to race. How is it that as early as first grade, she'd figured out that it's the boys who make the rules? Who told her this? I grew incensed. This is not what I want my daughter to believe! This is not the world in which I want her to grow up!

Before I had a chance to corral my thoughts and compose a response, she went on. "But Daddy, we believe girls can play with anything, don't we?" I sighed with relief and answered, "Yes. Yes, we do. Your mom and I believe girls can be anyone or anything and girls can play with any toys they like." At least for the moment, we had managed to override the gender-normative messages.

It is the pervasiveness and persistence of gender-normative messages that encourages me not to rush our explorations with younger children.

Sam (age seven when his parents came to see me) and I spent a lot of time exploring all the different ways there are to be a boy. We read books together about boys who like girly colors, books about boys who like girls' toys and games, and books about boys who like girly things. We read books about girls who want to be policemen and firemen when they grow up. We drew pictures of boys in dresses and princess gowns. We wrote stories together about boys who sang and danced in musicals. We watched My Fair Lady and the "Evil Like Me" scene from Descendants over and over again.

The overriding message was that boys can be anyone they want to be and can like any kind of clothes, toys, songs, or games. We affirmed that there is no one right way to be a boy and that people who say boys have to like boy colors or boy toys or boy games are wrong. We looked at pictures of boys and men wearing pink shirts, frilly or ruffled shirts, or bright yellow jeans. We looked at male ballet dancers, men who perform in Broadway musicals, pictures of gay men performing drag.

In the spring of that year, I saw a young adult man in New York City standing on the street in his commencement gown. His appearance was gender-normative—with the exception of the most amazing neon pink hair. Thinking about how much Sam loved the color pink, I went up to the young man and asked if I could take his picture. I shared that I was working with a seven-year-old boy and that I wanted him to see that he could have pink hair when he grew up too if that's what he wanted. All of this was to ensure that Sam knew that the "boys who make the rules" and say boys can't play with girls' things are wrong. It was essential to ensure that Sam understood that he didn't need to be a girl simply because he liked girls' things.

The work of watching and waiting focuses on exploring the range of ways children can delight in expressing their gender and creating space for the child to be who they are without any presumptions by parents or professionals about the outcome in the sense of whether the child's gender diversity is about gender expression or may signal an emerging transgender identity. The goal in this stage of the work is affirming the child's sense of self in the world, however their gender identity might evolve over time.

Clarity about shifts in the direction of the work begins to coalesce if the child more clearly and consistently asserts a gender identity other than the sex they were assigned at birth. At this stage, it is important to move out of watching and waiting and more fully affirm and support the child's ability to live their affirmed gender in the world. If the adults do not make this shift, continuing to focus on gender exploration ceases to be affirming and runs the risk of communicating to the child that they do not really know who they are, that they are not capable of knowing their own gender identity, or that they must justify or prove their gender identity—sometimes beyond a shadow of adult question—in order to simply be who they are in the world.

This is the tension many transgender people have with how the psychiatric establishment approaches gender dysphoria. There is a long history of trans people being forced to defend themselves, to justify their identities in order to be diagnosed with gender identity disorder and allowed to transition. Too many questions to a young child about whether they simply like girls' toys or really feel like a girl, or how they know their gender is different from their biological sex, can begin to feel to the child as if they are being asked to justify their affirmed gender.

The questions themselves can even border on shaming a child or their parents. Insisting on knowing why "he" thinks he's a girl, or trying to understand what caused his belief that he is a girl, smacks of trans-prejudice. The underpinning for these questions suggests that there is something aberrant about being assigned male at birth and yet knowing you are a girl.

This line of questioning is strikingly similar to what occurred 10 to 20 years ago when an adolescent came out as gay or lesbian. Mental health professionals wanted to know how they developed same-sex attractions. Lesbian and gay clinicians and activists countered that we did not ask heterosexual individuals why they were attracted to opposite-gender partners. We didn't look for things in their family life or social context that might have made them straight. We only did that with people considered non-normative.

Similarly, we don't ask gender-conforming children how they know they are a girl or a boy; we simply accept that they know this. We don't explore what in the child's environment might have contributed to the fact that their affirmed gender is aligned with the sex they were assigned a birth. Wanting to know "why" or "how" a child is the way they are carries an implicit message that there is something wrong with that child or adolescent, that something inside the child is not only different but also defective. This is the balancing act of exploring gender expression, watching how this may or may not evolve into or reflect an affirmed gender identity, and being continuously attentive to ways we might communicate shame or undermine a child's sense of self.

Spending time exploring the wide range of ways a boy can express his gender was not about trying to change Sam's true gender identity. It was about ensuring that Sam knew there were many ways to be a boy. It was about countering the gender-conforming messages that might have communicated to Sam that he could not be a boy if he liked feminine things.

This exploration about gender expression was balanced alongside education about transgender people. Sam and I talked about how some children are born in little boys' bodies but know in their hearts they are really a girl. We learned that doctors can help them become a girl as they grow up. We met as a family, and Sam's parents assured him they loved him whether he was a boy or a girl. Throughout this time, I was careful never to suggest that Sam did not know who he was but at the same time to create an affirming space that would allow Sam to assert his gender identity for when he was ready to do so. It is critical that a child's knowledge of, and confidence about, their affirmed gender emerge directly from the individual child and not from the parents or the clinician.

More and more trans adolescents are challenging and literally deconstructing our binary understanding of gender. They are rejecting the notion that there are only two genders in the world. And as noted in the introduction, in June 2016, an Oregon judge ruled that nonbinary is a legal gender, allowing the individual who filed the suit to define themselves outside a binary construct of gender identity. When I reflect on these experiences with adolescents, it leads me to ensure that young gender-diverse children understand that gender does not need to neatly fit into one of two boxes; it can be diverse; it can be fluid. Staying in your birth-assigned sex or transitioning to the opposite box are no longer the only options.

When young children assert that their affirmed gender differs from their birth-assigned sex, this more clearly suggests a transgender identity rather than diverse gender expression. When a child continues or persists in asserting this affirmed identity, the likelihood that they are transgender increases. However, even in these situations, it is still important for the clinician to obtain a full history and picture of the family, including a history of the emergence of their child's gender expression and gendered self-assertions. It is still important for the clinician to spend time working with the child and the parents to observe the clarity of the child's self-assertions as well as to ensure that both the child and their parents are prepared for the social transition. These tasks are discussed further in the next chapter.

When working with children whose transgender self-assertions are clear, consistent, and persistent, it is critical for therapists to closely and continually assess the level of dysphoria the child is experiencing. It is important to explore how this distress is impacting them and what strategies they use for managing the dysphoria. The distress associated with gender dysphoria can rise to a level where it presents significant risks in terms of the child's safety and well-being. Gender dysphoria can contribute to depression, and the challenges of navigating it often precipitate increased anxiety. If a child begins to feel overwhelmed, the risks for self-harm increase and must be addressed.

This too, is a balancing act—ensuring that the child and family are ready to socially transition, yet not delaying so long that the young person's experience of dysphoria intensifies beyond their ability to manage it. There are times when an increased degree of distress can push forward the timeline for social transition, or even early medical transition steps with adolescents. The protocol for assessing readiness will be presented in the next chapter.

CHAPTER 4

When a Young Person Comes Out

Disclosure and Social Transitions

> ### For Reflection:
> ### Coming Out as Transgender
>
> - Imagine telling your family you are a different gender, a gender other than the one you were assigned at birth and how they have always known you. Imagine telling them that you are going to begin using a new name and that you want them to use this new name and use new pronouns that match your new/true gender identity. What feelings come up for you as you imagine this scenario?
>
> - Imagine telling your friends about your impending gender transition.
>
> - Imagine telling your colleagues.
>
> - Imagine telling the young people with whom you work. Their parents.
>
> - How might these different people/groups of people respond?

THE CONCEPT OF "COMING OUT" EMERGED AS LESBIANS and gay men began to be more visible within American society. It was embodied in phrases like "Come out! Come out—wherever you are!" and the 1987 March on Washington slogan "No matter how far out of the closet you are, there's always another step." It was rooted in the metaphor of lesbians and gay men historically being "in the closet," meaning very few people in their lives, often even family, were aware of their sexual orientation or intimate partnerships.

The call to come out challenged lesbians and gay men to be more open about their lives and their loves; to introduce their partners to their families, friends, neighbors, and coworkers; to be unafraid to authentically be their whole selves and no longer hide parts of who they were. The challenge to come out became the cornerstone of the mainstream lesbian and gay rights movement during the 1980s and 1990s. The belief was that the more heterosexual people knew gay and lesbian people as their family members, neighbors, and coworkers, the more this familiarity would decrease the sense of gay people as "other" or different, and thus abnormal or deviant. This would lead to increased acceptance of lesbian and gay people and pave the way for a movement toward equal rights.

There are different ways to conceptualize "coming out." Many people, including parents and clinicians, view coming out as an "event"—the act of self-disclosing or telling someone about your sexual orientation or gender identity. Though this lens, we can envision concentric levels of coming out. The inner circle represents coming out to oneself—the process of coming to realize that one's sexual orientation or gender identity varies from the norm, and then naming one's identity (e.g., gay, lesbian, bisexual, transgender, gender-queer). For some people, coming out to oneself is the endpoint of their process. They may never disclose their gender identity or sexual orientation to other people.

Many trans people move out from this inner circle and share their identity with a few close family members or friends. Other trans people continue to come out socially with a wider circle of family, friends, and/or neighbors. Another circle might represent coming out within institutions or organizations, such as at school or work, in a faith community, to a sports team, or to a neighborhood civic group. An outermost circle might represent transgender people who are public figures, "out" in every area of their lives—celebrities, athletes, authors, artists, people who speak and train about LGBTQ concerns.

The "event" of coming out involving any of these circles can occur anywhere along the life cycle. The focus in this book is on children and adolescents coming out as transgender or gender- fluid/gen-der-queer/gender-diverse. But trans people also come out as young adults, middle-age adults, and older adults.

Lev (2004) developed a six-stage "transgender emergence" model, which posits that the process of developing an authentic self for trans-gender people involves moving through an experience of emergence— of realizing, discovering, identifying, or naming one's gender identity.

The first stage is Awareness, the internal realization that one is transgender. This is followed by a period of Seeking Information and Reaching Out to other transgender people. The third stage is Disclo-sure to Significant Others, followed by Exploration About Identity and Self-Labeling. The key issue in this stage is resolution of one's gender dysphoria and acceptance of one's gender identity. Stage five focuses on Exploration of Transition Issues, including consolidating one's gender presentation and making decisions about possible body modification. Stage six is called Integration and Pride: Acceptance and Post-transition Issues. It is important to acknowledge that these stages are not linear and that not all trans and gender-diverse youth move through each stage.

While not all trans people choose to transition, all face the process of coming to terms with their variant gender identity. In this sense, coming out is an adaptive process made necessary by a binary gender system that assumes everyone's birth-assigned sex and gender identity are identical. The experience of coming out is also shaped by many other aspects of a trans person's identity, including race, ethnicity, cul-tural background and norms, class access, and ability/different abilities.

When a Young Person Comes Out

When a young person comes out to you as transgender or gen-der-fluid, it is important to ask questions that demonstrate under-standing, acceptance, and compassion. These might include:

- Has this been a secret you've had to keep, or have you been able to tell anyone else?
- Do you feel safe in school? At home? Supported by the adults in your life?
- Do you need help of any kind? Resources? Someone to listen?

It is essential to appreciate and acknowledge the young person's courage in sharing about their gender identity or expression and to be a role model of acceptance. With trans and gender-queer youth, validating the young person's gender identity and expression by asking about, and then using, their identified name and pronouns—at least in the context of your individual relationship with them—does much to communicate acceptance and support.

The most important thing you can do when a child or young person comes out to you as trans or gender-diverse is to listen. You may be the first person they have told. You may be the first person who has been accepting and affirming. You may be the first person who validates their identity by asking if there is a name they prefer other than their birth name. Asking open-ended, affirming questions about their experience/journey/feelings, followed by active listening without judgment, is essential.

The fact that an adolescent comes out to you does not necessarily mean they are ready to be out with others in their lives. There are some instances where disclosure may be necessary, such as when there is self-harm or when the young person is being threatened, harassed, or bullied. Even in these situations, I am cautious about disclosing the young person's gender identity. I always ask whether this disclosure is absolutely necessary, or if it is possible to address the risks without disclosing their gender identity.

One adolescent I saw who was not yet out to his parents about being a trans guy was experiencing significant depression. I needed to refer him for ongoing psychotherapy with a clinician experienced in working with gender identity and expression. In this case, I was able to discuss the depression with their parents, including the urgency of further assessment and treatment, yet not go into detail about potential triggers. In other situations, I am able to acknowledge that a young person had questions about their identity without sharing that this involves gender identity or expression.

When disclosing a youth's trans identity seems essential, I make every effort to discuss this need with the young person directly. The rare exception occurs when there is a potential life-threatening emergency. I want the young person to know I am disclosing their trans identity, and I want them to know why I believe this is necessary. In some situations, I have worked to prepare the young person so that they can directly share this information about themselves.

Decisions About Coming Out to Others

If a trans young person comes out to you, there may be conversations about the possibility of coming out to others in their life. This might include their parents and other family members or teachers. It might include exploring how their friend(s) might respond. Some suggested questions to think about and explore with the young person include:

1. Has the trans or gender-diverse youth thought about where and when to come out to their parents/family? What does the young person imagine their responses might be? Has their family/parents ever discussed transgender people or issues? If so, what was the conversation like? Are there any other trans family members? Any lesbian, gay, or bisexual family members? Who in their family might be more likely to be accepting? Who might be less likely?

2. How would the trans or gender-diverse youth handle rejection from their parents? From other family members? What would the young person say or do in that moment (the initial disclosure)? Where would the young person go for support? When possible, especially with younger people, it can be helpful to invite parents or guardians in to meet with you and the young person and plan the coming out to occur with you present to support both the youth and their parents or to field questions and concerns from the parents.

3. When adolescents or young adults plan to come out on their own, it is always important to make a safety plan— meaning where will the young person go (literally) if their safety is at risk? If there is a threat of physical violence? If the level or intensity of verbal or emotional violence is overwhelming? If the parents or caregivers tell the young person to leave the house or not come home? It is critical to identify a person and place the youth can go to after coming out if necessary. This might be an extended family member or friend of the family they trust, a friend's home, or a neighbor. In some instances, when the teen knew when they planned to tell their parents, I have

given them permission to call me afterward to check in about how the disclosure and conversation went.

4. Does the trans or gender-diverse youth feel shame about their gender identity, and, if so, how might such shame influence the experience of coming out to others? Is it important to for them to explore/address/work through/let go of these feelings prior to coming out? Is it important to build a stronger positive sense of self before coming out to someone/some group?

5. What are the pros and cons of coming out to various friends? How will the young person respond if a friend asks questions about being trans, including personal questions? How will the young person respond if a peer makes fun of them, harasses them, or bullies them? What if the peer tells others they are trans and/or gender-diverse? Is the young person ready for this possibility? It is important to discuss the fact that once we disclose this information, we are no longer "in control" of it. The friend we tell may tell others, even if they promise not to. Young people need to think about how they might handle this possibility or whether they are prepared for it to happen.

6. When a young person is planning to come out—whether with family or friends—it can be useful to role-play these conversations with the youth. This can help the young person become clear about what they want to say and how they want to say it. You can also role-play different scenarios. What kinds of questions might a parent or friend ask? How will they answer this question? You can role-play a parent or friend being accepting or not accepting, giving the youth a chance to prepare for either response.

Beyond the Initial Disclosure

It is critical to understand that "coming out" as a disclosure about one's trans identity does not have an endpoint. There is never a time when a trans person will "finish" coming out. Even post-transition, there are new moments where trans people, youth included, face decisions about whether or not to come out about their trans history or experience. These moments might occur when a trans youth sees a new doctor, is rushed to the emergency room, begins to develop a more intimate friendship, or engages in dating and sexual intimacy.

Given this, coming out never ends. Each new coming-out occasion can still generate fear and anxiety about the potential response of others. The fact that a 15-year-old came out as trans two years ago does not mean coming out today is "no big deal." Even when a young person is "post-transition" in the sense of being out and living in their identified gender, it is important to explore potential coming-out decisions and associated feelings.

Another important understanding of coming out involves the awareness that it is not just an "event" or disclosure, but also an ongoing "process" of moving from a stigmatized to a more positive and affirming sense of self. When an aspect of your identity is marginalized or stigmatized, it is almost impossible not to internalize some of these negative views about your identity.

Trans children and adolescents often grow up knowing that others perceive trans or gender-different people as weird, abnormal, deviant, wrong, or sinful. As a result, trans and gender-diverse youth may internalize a sense that there is something "wrong" or "bad" about who they are. They may experience a sense of shame or guilt about their identity.

Trans and gender-diverse youth may have heard messages suggesting that trans people are failures, mentally ill, and unhappy. They may have been told they will never be able to obtain a job or find someone to love them. They may have been told that ridicule, harassment, and violence is inevitable. They may have come to believe they will never be accepted because they will never be a "real" man or woman. These messages can create a pervasive sense of hopelessness about their future possibilities and life.

As a result, coming out is more than simply announcing your trans and gender-diverse identity. It necessitates recognizing these shaming internalized beliefs and engaging in a process of recovery. This begins with identifying these beliefs, sometimes exploring where these beliefs may be rooted, and expressing and working through the associated feelings of shame, guilt, fear, or hopelessness about your identity and/or your future. Many trans and gender-diverse youth can benefit from clinical support in successfully navigating this process. Cognitive behavioral therapy (CBT) interventions can be particularly useful in exploring and altering these internalized negative beliefs.

Trans and gender-diverse youth need to learn the "facts" about transgender people and their lives. They need to read, listen, and ideally meet trans and gender-diverse people who are living happy, productive, meaningful lives in elementary, middle, or high school, in college, and as adults—depending on the trans or gender-diverse youth's own current developmental stage. These connections to others who are "like them" are powerful antidotes to internalized shame and hopelessness. Experiences of community can sometimes accomplish more toward recovery from internalized shame than hours of one-on-one psychotherapy.

Finally, it is important to note that some young people may no longer perceive "coming out" as relevant. In their minds and experiences, they may have "always" been out, or they may have come to understand their transgender identity early on in a more developmentally appropriate and natural way. As a result, there may have been very little time when they were "in the closet" and hiding this aspect of themselves. However, given that gender identity is typically formed earlier than one's awareness of sexual orientation, many trans adolescents still have a process of coming out to either themselves or others or both.

As society becomes more aware of gender identity and more accepting of young people whose gender identity may not line up with their assigned gender, the need to "come out" may become increasing less relevant for trans and gender-diverse children. These children will become aware of, and disclose, their trans and gender-diverse identities much earlier than was true in previous generations. In some ways, this has begun to occur. With decreased stigma and increased societal acceptance, these young people will not face the same coming-out "process" of unpacking their internalized shame about being trans or gender-diverse. They will be able to come of age with a positive sense of self from early on in their lives.

Transitioning

Transitioning is the term used to describe the process of transgender youth shifting from being seen in the world in their birth-assigned sex to moving through the world in their affirmed gender. The term social transition describes the process where a transgender young person begins to live in their affirmed gender without any medical interventions. Medical transition typically includes hormone therapy or surgeries. A young person's transition may or may not include these medical steps.

Sometimes people erroneously use the term full transition to describe transgender people who have had hormone treatment and both top and lower surgeries, implying that any step short of this is not a complete transition. The truth is that trans youth and adults make varied choices about the steps in their transition for many different reasons. Some youth may be able, and choose, to simply transition socially. Others may choose hormone therapy but not have one or either surgery. It is critical to understand that none of these choices invalidate a transgender youth's affirmed gender identity. As outlined in the first chapter, their affirmed gender is a function of their knowledge of who they are, not the medical choices they make.

This chapter presents the different aspects of social transition (with no medical interventions). It begins with a discussion of readiness to begin transitioning in terms of both the child or adolescent and their family. The tasks typically involved in a social transition are outlined (e.g., legal name change, being recognized in one's affirmed gender at school), along with suggestions about how these can be accomplished. Chapter 5 focuses on about medical transitioning, including the possible use of hormone blockers, feminizing or masculinizing hormone therapy, and different types of gender-affirming surgeries. The specific tasks involved in a social transition and the appropriate or possible medical steps vary depending on the age of the young person.

Social Transition

The process of gender transition generally begins with a "social" transition where the young person begins to live part time or full time in their affirmed gender (as opposed to their birth-assigned sex). Social transition is about how we move through the world and present to those around us. It typically involves steps such as a name change and a shift to pronouns that more closely match the young person's affirmed gender. Social transitions are fully "reversible"; there are no medical interventions at this stage. If a young person socially transitioned and later decides they are comfortable returning to their birth-assigned sex, they can fully do so. Social transitions generally precede medical interventions such as hormones or surgeries that can be irreversible, offering additional time and lived experience for young people in their affirmed gender identity.

The decision for a child or adolescent to begin presenting in their affirmed gender is always momentous, both in its significance and in the tasks involved for youth and their families. One of the roles of mental health practitioners—after completing an assessment about whether the young person meets the criteria for gender dysphoria—is to help the youth and the family decide when the time is right to begin a social transition.

Assessing Readiness: Guidelines for Practitioners and Parents

Does the young person understand the differences between biological sex, gender identity, gender expression, and sexual orientation?

Are they aware of the wide range of gender identities and gender expressions that are possible?

Are they clear and/or certain about their affirmed gender/gender identity?

Has their understanding of their affirmed gender been consistent over some period of time?

Are they prepared to navigate the steps/tasks involved in a social transition?

Do they have the information they need, such as the tasks involved in different steps, or what is possible/not possible in a social transition?

Are they prepared to come out to siblings, extended family, peers, school personnel, or other adults in their lives?

Have they thought through what they will say and how they want to disclose? Have they decided whether to have one-on-one conversations or use email, Facebook, Instagram, Twitter, etc.?

Are they emotionally ready for self-disclosure, such as having a strong enough sense of self?

Have they thought through possible reactions or responses they may receive, what questions people might ask, and how they can/want to respond?

Have you and the young person made a plan for any possible safety concerns?

Does the young person have the support they need to successfully navigate this transition, especially family support but also that of friends, a trans or LGBTQ youth group, extended family, or a teacher?

Determining the right time to begin a social transition involves assessing the young person's clarity and consistency of their affirmed gender, the readiness of their family members, and often, the readiness of external organizations, such as schools, youth programs, or faith communities. There is no single universal timeline for all transgender youth. A therapist cannot dictate a universal set number of sessions before determining whether a young person should begin to socially (or medically) transition. A parent or teacher cannot establish the timeline in isolation. While there are useful guidelines to consider, the timing of beginning transition is an individual one made in conjunction with the youth, their family, and their mental health provider.

Some children and teens have known their affirmed gender for many years; some parents have also known (or suspected) their child's affirmed gender. When these families first come to therapy, some may have already participated in trans youth or parent support groups. They may have already seen an affirming thera-pist at some point. They may have already disclosed their child's affirmed gender with extended family members and obtained their support. In these situations, both the parents and the young person may be ready for the youth to socially transition at school and other community settings. With these young people and their families, work with the mental health practitioner gener-ally involves completing a gender assessment as outlined in the previous chapter and then exploring the various tasks involved in beginning to transition.

In other situations, the young person may have only recently begun their gender exploration or disclosed their transgender identity to their parents. The process here often necessitates a more in-depth exploration of gender identity and expression before any decision or preparation for the start of a gender transition can be made.

Sometimes young people have known their affirmed gender for some time and are ready to begin their social (or medical) transition, but their parents are not on board with moving forward—as the fol-lowing vignette illustrates.

> When I began to see Jasmine, a 16-year-old trans woman, she was clear about her affirmed gender identity as a woman. Her parents were not. While they acknowledged that Jasmine was not your stereotypical male, they did not believe she was a woman (they used her birth/male name at this point, but I use her affirmed name here in respect for Jasmine's self-knowledge; I will talk more in the chapter about navigating names in family sessions when children and parents are on different pages). The parents did not see Jasmine as feminine and believed her assertion of a trans identity was either a phase or reflective of some underlying issues we should work through in therapy.
>
> The parents brought up an earlier time when Jasmine was fixated on an aspect of her body that bothered her; she talked about it incessantly and pleaded with her parents to pursue a surgical change. This fixation persisted for two years and then dissipated. The parents believed Jasmine's insistence on being transgender reflected a similar phenomenon.
>
> Jasmine walked into our first appointment asking how soon

she could begin hormone therapy (this sense of urgency is reflective of many trans adolescents). Her parents were unwilling to support this step. In fact, they were hesitant about her even beginning to socially transition at school, given their reservations about the "reality" of her trans identity. This difference in perspective brings us to the first step in assessing readiness for transition—social or medical. Both parents and youth need to be on the same page.

My work with Jasmine included exploring how she viewed/understood the history of her gender expression and identity, helping her understand and tolerate her parents' questions and process, and developing strategies to manage her gender dysphoria. I closely monitored any signs of depression that might indicate that her level of gender dysphoria was increasing and posing risks of self-harm, self-destructive behavior (drug or alcohol use, unsafe sexual encounters), or suicidal ideation.

My work with her parents included education about the basic concepts discussed in Chapter 1—the differences among sex, gender identity, gender expression, and sexual orientation—and how these were reflected in Jasmine's narrative and experience. We explored the parents' concerns and fears about their child.

The relationship between the parents was conflictual. The mother believed Jasmine was angry with her father and thus hated men. She believed that this led to Jasmine "not wanting to be a man" and was insistent that I work with Jasmine around this possibility.

I worked with Jasmine and her parents for a year before the parents were comfortable with Jasmine beginning to take an anti-androgen. This medication would shut down the production of testosterone, precluding further development of male secondary sex characteristics—a factor likely to reduce Jasmine's gender dysphoria.

Is the Family Ready for Transition?:

Do the parents/guardians understand the differences among biological sex, gender identity, gender expression, and sexual orientation?

Do the parents acknowledge and support the young person's affirmed gender?

Do the parents have the information they need to support the child's social transition?

Are the parents emotionally ready for an intense wave of self-disclosure about their child's affirmed gender?

Are they prepared to navigate possible reactions, responses, or questions from their own parents or siblings?

Do the parents know what they need to tell the school and what they can legally ask the school to do to support their child? Are they aware of resources, such as education for school personnel or advocacy if needed?

Do the parents have the social and emotional support they need, such as family, a trans parent support group, friends, or a faith community or leader?

Readiness to transition means that everyone has the information they need to effectively move through the transition. This can be education about hormone blockers and feminizing or masculinizing therapy—such as reversible and irreversible effects, the steps to obtaining a legal name change in their jurisdiction, or the names of competent doctors/surgeons.

Readiness means that any concerns parents or youth may have about coming out to various people have been addressed. It includes being prepared to respond to questions people may have and knowing how to respond to possible ridicule, harassment, or bullying—both in the moment and when an adult needs to be informed. Role-playing possible scenarios can be helpful for young people and parents. Identifying helpful literature or videos is also useful for family members and others who want to learn more about trans youth (see Appendix B).

Coolhart, Baker, Farmer, Malaney, and Shipman (2013) offer an excellent clinical tool that provides specific questions that practitioners may ask youth and their families in assessing readiness for transition. The questions are organized around topic areas, such as early awareness of gender, parental attunement to the youth's affirmed gender, school context, sexual/relationship development, and future plans/expectations.

Choosing a New Name

Social transition typically involves choosing a new name that more closely matches the child's or teen's affirmed gender identity and asking others to use the pronouns that match this gender. Depending on the age of the young person and the family's culture and norms, there are different ways the youth or family may choose a new name. Sometimes the child or adolescent themselves chooses their new name, other times parents may choose the name, and sometimes it is a collaborative effort with both the parents and the youth generating possible names and coming to a decision.

Several young people raised by their biological parent(s) have wanted to know, and then adopt, the name their parent had chosen for them if they had been born in their affirmed gender. The new name may have family significance; one young man used his two grandfathers' first names to create his own new first and middle names. New names may start with the same letters, leaving the young person's initials the same. Other times, the new name is completely different from the birth name. Some youth create a unique name or use unique spellings.

Some young people know immediately what name they want to begin using; many have picked out this name as early as childhood. One college student had a brother born when he was 10 years old. His parents planned a particular name for his brother, but a relative named their son born just two months earlier with the same first name, and his parents chose a different name for his brother. The college student recalled being 10 and wishing he could have the name his parents originally chose for his brother. When he and his parents discussed a new name for him, he asked for permission to take the name they had originally planned for his younger brother.

Some youth struggle to find a name they can connect with, a name that feels like "them." They may try out several different names, using them with family and friends over a period of time to decide which one best fits them. I have worked with youth who have chosen a new name and begun going by that name, then some months later decided that name wasn't right and chosen a different name.

Having difficulty settling on a new name does not necessarily reflect ambivalence about gender identity. Few of us get to choose our names; our names are given to us at birth or upon adoption and generally belong to us throughout our lifetime. If you were required to choose a new name today, would you know immediately what name you wanted? Or would it take some time to decide on a new name and become comfortable hearing it from others? Would you simply "pick" any name, or would you try to find one you thought fit who you are? Deciding what name to go by for the remainder of your life, which is almost all of their life for a young person, is not necessarily an easy task.

Sometimes there is debate about who gets to choose a young person's new name—the child or adolescent themselves or the parent(s), as the following vignette reflects.

> One eight-year-old transitioning to live as a girl had several names she had chosen for herself, two of which were names of favorite Disney characters. She talked incessantly about these three names for several weeks. As we discussed her choices, the parents became increasingly upset. Neither was thrilled with the Disney choices. One parent found two of the names completely unacceptable. In addition, the child's birth name held special family significance, while the new names the eight-year-old chose did not. The parents wanted a name that felt comfortable for them and would continue to hold meaning for them and the extended family.
>
> As we talked further, I realized that the parents assumed the choice of a new name should be their daughter's alone and not theirs, or even a joint decision. They wanted to empower her as she was finally able to become her visible self as a girl in the

world. The new name reflected their confirmation of her affirmed gender, and they recognized that she would be using it for the remainder of her life. I applauded this desire on their part as testimony to how much they wanted to support her social transition.

Yet, I also noted that naming a child is typically a parental responsibility that children rarely get to weigh in on. I wondered out loud if perhaps they did not need to entirely relinquish this role as her parents. I encouraged the parents to spend time that week brainstorming and discussing what name(s) they would choose if they were naming their (new) daughter as well as discussing the names she had chosen for herself.

We brought the child in at the end of our time and talked together about the significance of the name her parents had given her at birth. Her parents shared that they wanted her new name to be special for the family as well. We agreed that it was important for her to like her new name, and that it was important for her parents to participate in this choice as they had when she was born because this was a part of her parents' job. When we met again the following week, the parents shared that they had discussed many different names and ultimately settled on one of the names their daughter had chosen for her first name. The parents selected a middle name that held family significance.

A similar conflict emerged between a mother and her 17-year-old trans male son. In this case, he had chosen a new name for himself (Giovanni) and begun using it with friends six months before disclosing his trans identity to his parents. While his parents were supportive of his affirmed male gender, the mother was not happy with the name he had chosen for himself—in part because the name did not reflect their ethnic background. The transgender son insisted on going by Giovanni. His teachers and friends were already used to it. Besides, he was almost an adult; he felt it should be his choice, not hers. The mother adamantly refused to call him Giovanni, and furthermore was vocal about hating it. Over the past few weeks, they had become locked into their opposing positions, and Giovanni had withdrawn.

In working with Giovanni, we were able to acknowledge that at least in part, choosing his own name and a name outside the family's ethnic norms reflected his efforts to individuate from his family. Naming himself, and choosing the name Giovanni, became a way to assert his independence from his parents.

With this understanding, I was able to coach his mother to ease up a bit and take a more relaxed stance about the possibilities of his new name. In a joint session after this, the mother was able to express what was important to her in terms of their cultural connections, and the son was able to verbalize his real desire to choose a name that meant something to him as an emerging young adult.

They each agreed to generate a short list of names to bring back to our next session—without discussing them with each other before this appointment (I was still concerned that this discussion might devolve into an argument and undo the détente just achieved). In the following session, the mother and son took turns sharing the names on their lists and what they liked or valued about each name they had chosen. When the son shared his names, the mother's task was to listen and remain open, and then the son focused on remaining open and listening as his mother shared the names she had chosen. We then took a few minutes in silence for each to identify one to two names from the other's list that they appreciated (we agreed in the spirit of cooperation that they had to choose at least one name from the other's list). Through this process, mother and son were able to agree on his new male name.

Changes in Gender Expression

A social transition may include changes in the ways trans youth express their gender. For example, a young trans boy or teenager may choose clothing that is more identifiably male. He may cut his hair shorter in a more masculine style. A young trans girl may begin wearing more feminine apparel, may grow her hair longer, and may begin wearing jewelry and makeup.

These stereotypical gender expression choices are not true for every young trans boy/man or girl/woman. Just as cisgender young girls may feel more comfortable in jeans and T-shirts, young trans girls/women may express their female gender in ways that may be considered masculine; trans girls can be tomboys too. Gender expression for young trans boys/men is not always stereotypically masculine. Like other boys/men, trans boys/men can be more feminine in their gender interests or expression and still identify as boys/men.

Parents or other adults may question a trans young person's gender identity when their gender expression varies from what society considers appropriately masculine or feminine. The mother of one teenage trans boy questioned whether she could be "sure" he was really transgender after he bought a pink sweater, saying, "If he really is a boy, why doesn't he dress like a boy?" When we discussed this together, the young man said, "I've always liked pink. And even though I'm a guy, I still like pink." He was clear that his gender identity was male, even though others might perceive his gender expression as feminine. His choice of gender expression did not negate his identity as a young man.

Jasmine, the trans-feminine adolescent mentioned earlier, had been going by her female name and pronouns for most of the academic year. She had grown her hair out some, but her clothing choice was much the same "punk" style as it had been before she socially transitioned. She was not a "femme" trans young woman. She was not socially transitioning into the socially acceptable or stereotypical notions of what a woman "looks like." As with the young trans man above, this trans woman's parents questioned her female identity. When exploring her gender expression, she clearly stated her understanding of herself: "I'm an atypical woman, not an atypical man."

As discussed in Chapter 1, gender identity and gender expression are two different facets of who we are—whether we are trans or cisgender. Yet confusion about the distinctions between these two aspects, alongside developmental concerns about adolescent identity exploration, can make it more difficult for parents or professionals to believe that a young person with nonconforming gender expression is truly transgender.

Living in the Affirmed Gender

Some children and youth initially begin living in their affirmed gender on a part-time basis. With young children and teens, this may mean having immediate family use their new name and pronouns. Some adolescents begin their social transition at home, but many come out to friends first. Some may disclose their trans identity within a youth program, and have the peers and/or youth workers there begin to use their new name, before socially transitioning at school. In this sense, a young trans woman or man may be known in their affirmed gender in some settings but not yet in others.

Transitioning part time can be a way to "ease into" the transition, a way to break the process down into smaller steps or to navigate other people's responses in stages rather than all at once. Coming out to peers or a trusted teacher or youth worker, and gaining their acceptance and support, can build young people's confidence for coming out to others in their life, including parents. It can also be a way to "test out" their affirmed gender, to gain a glimpse into what it might feel like to move through the world in this gender. These part-time steps can help prepare a young person for a fuller social transition— mentally, emotionally, and socially.

With young gender-diverse children, as discussed earlier, exploring gender expression at home allows more time for parents and professionals to observe the child's evolving understanding of themselves and their gender. For families with young children whose transgender identity is clear and consistent, social transition typically begins at home. A child assigned male at birth but whose affirmed gender is a girl may wear princess nightgowns to bed or play "dress-up" when they come home from school. They may have girls' toys and books at home but not be "out" as a girl at school or in their neighborhood. The same may be true for a young trans boy.

Living more full time in an affirmed gender generally involves coming out more widely—at school, within faith communities, at after-school programs and activities—and having teachers, other adults, and friends begin to use one's affirmed name and pronouns. Parents have the right to request that schools and other youth programs use a young person's affirmed name and pronouns even if their name has not yet been legally changed.

Since allowing younger transgender children to socially transition is still relatively recent, parents, teachers, therapists, and others may wonder whether this is the "right" thing to do. Past studies of children diagnosed with gender identity disorder and transgender adolescents indicate high risk for mental health problems. Given the historical context, these young people were unable to socially transition as children and spent numerous years living in their birth-assigned sex.

A recent study by Olson, Durwood, DeMeules, & McLaughlin (2016) suggests that when transgender children are able to be who they are in the world (live in their affirmed gender), mental health risks may no longer be a significant problem. The study examined the mental health of prepubescent children (ages 3 to 12 years) who had socially transitioned with their family's support and were living full time in their affirmed gender. In contrast to the high incidence of mental health difficulties reported in other studies, the children who had socially transitioned with the support of their families had developmentally normative levels of depression and only mildly elevated (not clinical or even preclinical) levels of anxiety in comparison to the cisgender comparison group and an earlier comparison group of children diagnosed with gender identity disorder (K. Olson et al., 2016). Possible reasons for slightly elevated anxiety levels might include peer challenges or harassment, navigating the tensions of being "stealth" (meaning not out to others about their transgender history), and/or not having the typical bodies of their peers.

While this study is not conclusive, two smaller studies have also reported positive mental health among gender-diverse young children whose parents supported their gender identity or expression (Hill, Menvielle, Sica, & Johnson, 2010; Kuvalanka, Weiner, & Mahan, 2014). These newer studies offer hope that as trans youth are able to transition at younger ages and live in their affirmed gender, the historical high incidence of mental health disorders will diminish. This study suggests that socially transitioning when young contributes to resilience among trans youth.

The following vignette illustrates the process with a young transgender girl who socially transitioned toward the end of third grade.

> Debbi (birth-assigned male) and her parents began seeing me at the beginning of second grade. We spent significant time exploring her history of feminine gender expression as well as occasional self-assertions that she was, or wanted to be, a girl. During third grade, Debbi began to more consistently assert that she was a girl and wanted to be a girl all the time. She was increasingly insistent about wearing girls' clothes around the house and wanted to wear them to school as well. In the winter, we began

to talk more with Debbi about what a social transition at school might look like.

Her parents had an initial conversation with her teacher, who was well aware of Debbi's feminine gender expression. Over the course of several meetings, both the teacher and school district personnel were completely supportive. The school social worker reached out to consult with me about best practice to ensure that Debbi's experience of attending school as a girl was a positive one. The social worker also wanted to know how to share Debbi's social transition with her classmates. I provided educational material for the school staff to review.

The parents and I continued to assess Debbi's needs—the level of her gender dysphoria, the intensity and consistency of her self-assertion that she was a girl and wanted to be a girl at school, and the school's readiness to support Debbi in her affirmed gender. Our initial thought had been for Debbi to socially transition at the start of fourth grade in the fall. However, her third-grade teacher adored her. Debbi loved the teacher as well and had excelled in her classroom despite persistent and sometimes disruptive gender dysphoria. Given the closeness of this relationship, the teacher suggested that it might be beneficial for Debbi to socially transition in her class that year rather than waiting until the following fall with a brand-new teacher.

As the parents and I discussed her suggestion, it became clear that there were several benefits associated with allowing Debbi to socially transition at school before the end of the year. The teacher's suggestion made sense. It allowed Debbi to come out with the support of a teacher she had known the entire school year—a teacher she loved, trusted, and felt safe with— rather than a brand-new teacher. The parents also knew and trusted the current teacher. Moving up the timeline meant they would not need to plan Debbi's first day as a girl with a teacher they did not know. We were also cognizant of Debbi's insistence on being a girl at school now, as well as the level of intensifying dysphoria surrounding this.

Another benefit to beginning school as a girl in late May was that this enabled Debbi and her classmates to make the transition for a few weeks, followed by summer vacation. When they entered fourth grade in September with a new teacher, neither

Debbi nor her classmates would need to simultaneously navigate new relationships with each other. This seemed less disruptive for everyone. Knowing that the beginning of a new school year with a new teacher was anxiety producing for most children, we suspected Debbi would be less anxious if she was already known as a girl. Rather than facing coming out as a girl and being in a new setting, her only task would be settling into her new classroom.

Chapter 9 presents more information for helping trans youth navigate school and community settings, including what kind of advocacy may be needed.

Updating Legal Documents

Legal Name Change

Name and Gender Marker:

Passport

Social Security

Driver's Permit/License

School Records/Transcripts

College Admission Exam Reports

Birth certificate

Obtaining a Legal Name Change

Over time, many youth (often adolescents, but also younger children) and their families pursue a legal name change so that documents such as school records, camp registrations, or a new driver's license reflect the name that matches the young person's affirmed gender. This ensures that a child's or teen's affirmed name and pronouns are used more consistently. For example, prior to a legal name change, "regular" teachers may be using a child's affirmed name; however, the official school record typically still reflects the birth name. Consequently, a substitute teacher will have, and use, the birth name on the roster. This can embarrass, or even "out," a trans young person. I had one trans 17-year-old who skipped class anytime she saw a substitute teacher in the room because it was so dysphoric to have them use her birth name.

If not completed earlier, obtaining a legal name change prior to beginning college (or any new school) often facilitates the young person's initial adjustment to college life. It allows them to introduce themselves with their affirmed name with teachers and peers, who consequently never know them by anything other than their affirmed name. This means that a trans college student whose appearance closely enough matches their affirmed gender may not have to come out to everyone on campus or discuss their trans history unless they choose to bring this up.

An order from a judge in the family's jurisdiction is required to legally change your name. The petition asking the court to issue the name change is completed by filing the required paperwork. In most settings, these forms can be downloaded from the county courthouse website and can be filed with the county clerk in person or through the mail. If a trans youth is considered an adult in that jurisdiction, they can petition the court themselves. When the name change is for a minor, the parents (or other legal guardian) must petition the court. A fee is generally involved, and some courts require that a lawyer represent you.

In many areas, the family or mental health provider can obtain information about the exact requirements and process within their state or local government from organizations such as PFLAG, local LGBT community centers, or local and state transgender groups. Some LGBT community centers have a pro bono legal name change clinic where lawyers volunteer their time to assist trans youth and adults in filing their name change petitions with the court. These lawyers may also advocate on the individual's or family's behalf when necessary.

As a rule, the court's primary concern is to ensure the name change petitioner is not evading creditors or the criminal justice system. This means that the process of changing your name as a transgender individual should be pro forma. Yet some courts ask invasive questions about a person's gender transition and/or may require additional documentation as to why the name change is indicated or should be granted. It varies by state whether the judge can request confirmation of the DSM gender dysphoria diagnosis in the form of a letter from the transgender person's medical or mental health provider.

The decision to pursue a legal name change is really a decision that belongs between the child or adolescent and their parents. There is no court approval required to name your child when they are born. It is difficult to understand the need for one when you and your child decide to change their name. If gender dysphoria is classified a psychiatric diagnosis, then deciding whether a young person is transgender or not is an assessment between that young person, their family, and their medical or mental health providers. It should not be a decision for the court system to make.

In some locales, the courts require the trans person to publish their name change in a local newspaper. This is not specific to a transgender name change but reflects the courts' concern that an adult may change their name to evade creditors or the criminal justice system. Parents are often able to have this requirement waived to protect the confidentiality of a minor. Some jurisdictions will seal name change records for minors so the information is not accessible to others once completed.

While U.S. courts have increasingly ruled that Title IX prohibiting discrimination on the basis of sex also prohibits discrimination on the basis of gender, there is still no federal law that prohibits discrimination on the basis of gender identity or expression. While some locales have passed nondiscrimination bills, many states have yet to put these protections in place.

Publishing a name change can "out" trans youth or young adults, placing them at increased risk of harassment, discrimination, and/or violence. Without legal protections, being "outed" in the local paper can lead to termination of employment, expulsion from college, or eviction from an apartment. When young adults transition prior to disclosure with their family, publishing their name change can reveal their trans identity before they are prepared to navigate this disclosure. This can lead to psychological and/or financial repercussions, such as increased emotional distress for the youth or a nonaccepting parent discontinuing college payments.

Updating Other Legal Documents

With a court-ordered name change, transgender young adults and parents of trans children and teens are able to have most legal documents reissued to reflect the new name. This includes official school district records, college transcripts, driver's permits and licenses, passports, and social security cards and records.

A court ordered name change does not generally change the male/female gender marker on identity documents. Depending on the document, changing the gender marker can be regulated by the federal government, individual states, or local municipalities. Parents, clinicians, and others working with transgender children and youth must become familiar with regulations in their local jurisdiction for requesting name and gender marker changes. An LGBT-affirmative lawyer can often assist in this work.

School Records/Transcripts

Appendix A (under "Schools") outlines the May 2016 DOC/DOJ directive to all U.S. schools prohibiting discrimination against transgender students. Under Title IX, schools must treat students in a manner consistent with their gender identity even if education records or identification documents indicate a different sex. A parent's assertion that their child's gender identity differs from previous records or representations is sufficient to require that the school recognize that student's affirmed gender.

Passport

Passport documentation is handled on a federal level.. The court-ordered name change allows these documents to be re-issued with the new name. The U.S. State Department no longer requires proof of gender-confirming surgery (lower surgery) for changing the gender marker on passports and consular birth certificates. Instead, documentation of "appropriate clinical treatment for gender transition to the new gender," can be provided by a medical doctor (not a mental health provider). The text for this letter is available on the U. S. passport site and at http://www.transequality.org/know-your-rights/passports

Social Security

While your Social Security card only lists your name and Social Security number – not your gender - the information maintained by the Social Security Administration (SSA) includes name, date of birth, and sex as assigned at birth. Social security documentation is handled on a federal level. Sex-reassignment surgery is no longer required to change gender markers. Specific details about this request can be found on the SSA website and at the **National Transgender Center for Equality** (NCTE) website, http://www.transequality.org/know-your-rights/social-security.

Driver's Permit/License or Other State ID

These are handled on a state level, generally by the Department of Motor Vehicles. Presenting the court-ordered name change generally allows your name to be updated on these documents.

Each jurisdiction sets its own requirements for changing the gender marker (or in some states, refusing to change these markers). In many states a letter from a medical doctor or licensed mental health clinician (sometimes a PhD clinician is required) confirming gender identity will suffice (providers should check the directions on that state's website regarding what specific information is required in your letter). Departments of Motor Vehicles in about half the states have removed surgical requirements for those applying to change their gender marker on their drivers' licenses. (Sample DMV mental health letter in Appendix B).

For young adults, **bank accounts or credit cards** can generally be updated by submitting the request in writing along with a copy of the court ordered name change.

Birth certificate

Birth certificates are more difficult to change than other documents. The requirements to have a new birth certificate issued vary widely by state (some large cities issue birth certificates as well). Many of the 57 state, local and territorial jurisdictions that administer birth certificates require a court order to change or amend them (process of petitioning a judge for an order stating that you are now male or female) and/or a letter from a surgeon certifying sex-reassignment surgery (SRS).

The **National Transgender Center for Equality** (NCTE) website provides information about the specific requirements and laws within each state: **http://www.transequality.org/documents**.

Being outed by your legal documents, or having a legal document that does not match your gender presentation, poses real difficulties, and even dangers, for trans people. At best, it can create confusion, such as for an 18-year-old stopped while driving whose gender presentation does not match their gender marker. In situations like this, the trans youth may be extensively questioned, detained, ridiculed, or even subjected to violence. For trans youth of color, this situation is compounded by the intersections of racism and trans-prejudice.

It is sometimes helpful for a trans young person to have a "carry" letter from their mental health clinician or medical doctor. This letter affirms their transgender identity and explains the possible "discrepancy" between their gender marker and presentation (see sample letter in Appendix C).

While trans-affirming and competent clinical services are critically needed, the issues just addressed reflect areas where parents and professionals can play pivotal roles in advocating local, state, and federal policy changes that ensure respect, privacy, and safety for transgender children, adolescents, and young adults. The next chapter moves from the tasks of coming out and socially transitioning to explore the medical interventions that often follow when a young person's trans identity persists into late adolescence.

CHAPTER 5

Medical Transition

M EDICAL TRANSITION GENERALLY FOLLOWS SOCIAL TRAN-
sition when the child's or adolescent's (transgender) identity
has remained consistent over a period of time and the youth has
demonstrated positive emotional and social adjustment in their
affirmed gender. Medical interventions typically include hormone
therapy and gender-affirming surgeries. The eligibility requirements,
protocols, effects, benefits, and possible risks associated with each
step are presented in this chapter.

For a transgender young person, the first steps in a medical transition may include the use of hormone/puberty blockers at the onset
of puberty, followed at a later age by feminizing or masculinizing
hormone therapy. Historically, hormone therapy was referred to as
"cross-gender" hormone therapy. The newer nomenclature, "feminizing" or "masculinizing" hormone therapy, reflects the acknowledgment that hormone therapy is consistent with the young person's
affirmed gender identity and not "cross-gender."

Surgical aspects of a medical transition may include chest reconstruction surgery for trans men or breast augmentation for trans
women ("top" surgeries) and genital surgeries (lower or "bottom"
surgery) for both trans men and women. (For trans men, the full
nomenclature is "chest reconstruction surgery," not "mastectomy"
or "breast removal.") Young adult trans women who medically transition after their initial puberty is completed may desire other feminizing procedures, such as a tracheal shave, hair removal, or facial
feminization surgery (FFS).

Until recently, few transgender individuals were able to proceed
with any medical aspects of their gender transition before reaching

adulthood. The current version of the WPATH Standards of Care (SOC) suggests that eligibility decisions be assessed on an individual basis by medical and mental health providers in conjunction with the young people and their parents. Both the WPATH and U.S. Endocrine Society SOC specify that feminizing or masculinizing hormone therapy may begin at age 16 (Hembree, et al. 2009 WPATH, 2012). The more recent decision to allow adolescents to begin hormone therapy reflects research findings indicating decreased gender dysphoria and overall positive mental health and well-being among transgender adolescents when they are allowed to begin hormone therapy (Cohen-Kettenis, Delemarre–van de Waal, & Gooren, 2008).

Not all trans or gender-diverse individuals choose what some call a "full medical transition," meaning all of the above steps: hormones and top and bottom surgeries. The choice to complete some but not all steps can be based on numerous factors, such as the degree of an individual trans young person's gender dysphoria about their body, their socioeconomic status or access to health insurance and the financial cost of these procedures, or the presence of health conditions that might preclude medical interventions.

In addition, gender-fluid or nonbinary trans youth may not choose to pursue a medical transition or may choose only some medical steps—such as top surgery and no hormones, or hormones but no surgeries. It is critical to understand that these varying choices do not invalidate the young person's affirmed gender identity, nor do they suggest that their transgender experience or status is any less legitimate.

WPATH Standards of Care (2012)

WPATH is an international, multidisciplinary, professional association whose mission is to promote evidence-based care, education, research, advocacy, public policy, and respect in transsexual and transgender health (WPATH, 2012). This body of professionals works collaboratively to publish the WPATH Standards of Care (SOC). The SOC outline the best medical and mental health practices for promoting optimal care for trans and gender-nonconforming children and adolescents (as well as for adults). These guidelines are rooted in the best available research information as well as professional consensus. The first version was published in 1979, and the current (seventh) version was published in 2012 and is available on the WPATH website (www.wpath.org).

As described in the SOC, the document provides "clinical guidance for health professionals to assist transsexual, transgender, and gender-nonconforming people with safe and effective pathways to achieving lasting personal comfort with their gendered selves, in order to maximize their overall health, psychological well-being, and self-fulfillment. This assistance may include primary care, gynecologic and urologic care, reproductive options, voice and communication therapy, mental health services (e.g., assessment, counseling, psychotherapy), and hormonal and surgical treatments" (WPATH, 2012, p. 1).

In this sense, the SOC provide guidelines for making decisions about when medical transition and the related hormone and surgical treatments are indicated for both adolescents and adults. The guidelines also describe the role of mental health services within the process of gender transition. While some health and mental healthcare providers interpret the SOC in a literal fashion, the document clearly indicates that the standards are meant to be flexible so that they can better "meet the diverse needs" of trans and gender-nonconforming youth (and adults). In this sense, they may be modified by individual health and mental health care providers and adapted within varying cultural contexts (WPATH, 2012, p. 2). While the SOC largely address the treatment of transgender adults, Chapter VI, "Assessment and Treatment of Children and Adolescents With Gender Dysphoria," pertains specifically to medical and mental healthcare for transgender youth.

The material reviewed within this chapter will discuss eligibility criteria in detail and offer suggestions about more challenging decisions involving timing for proceeding with a specific medical intervention. From an overall perspective, mental health providers should always conduct a thorough assessment of the transgender adolescent's mental, emotional, social, and familial functioning prior to any decisions about beginning hormone therapy or accessing surgical interventions. It is also essential to assess the trans adolescent's current living environment, the level of caregiver/parental functioning, and the range and quality of supports available to young people as they begin their medical transition.

In keeping with the understanding of the SOC as flexible in an effort to better meet the varying needs of trans and gender-nonconforming youth, the length of time and/or number of assessment sessions should be determined by the needs of the individual adolescent and the complexity of their history and/or current situation. At the same time, transgender adolescents often experience profound gender dysphoria, as will be discussed in greater detail in Chapter 6. The intensity of their distress can lead to being at high risk for depression, self-harm, suicidal ideation, and other mental health concerns. This reality cautions mental health providers to refrain from delaying the onset of medical transition steps unnecessarily.

Hembree et al. (2009) suggest that it can be helpful to conceptualize medical interventions in terms of the three following categories when assessing adolescent readiness for each area of transition: fully reversible interventions, partially reversible interventions, and irreversible interventions. This framework offers a way for clinicians and families to explore the various types of medical interventions and the permanency of their consequences alongside the degree of consistency and certainty regarding the transgender teen's affirmed gender identity.

FULLY REVERSIBLE INTERVENTIONS include the use of GnRH analogues (colloquially called puberty or hormone blockers) to suppress estrogen or testosterone production and consequently delay the development of secondary sex characteristics that emerge with the onset of puberty. In the treatment of young trans women, occasional alternative treatment options can include progestins or medications (such as spironolactone) that decrease the effects of androgens secreted by the testicles of adolescents who are not receiving GnRH analogues. Continuous oral contraceptives (or depot medroxyprogesterone) may be used to suppress menses among young transgender men. These interventions are fully reversible in that if GnRH analogues are discontinued, the development of adolescent's birth-assigned secondary sex characteristics will quickly resume.

PARTIALLY REVERSIBLE INTERVENTIONS include masculinizing or feminizing hormone therapy that initiates the development of secondary sex characteristics to match the adolescent's affirmed gender. While more detail follows, this means the administration of testosterone for young trans men and an anti-androgen and estrogen for young trans women. Some physical changes induced by these hormone treatments may be reversed through surgery (such as removal of breast tissue that developed while on estrogen). Other changes are not reversible (such as a trans man's voice dropping after beginning treatment with testosterone).

IRREVERSIBLE INTERVENTIONS are surgical procedures (for example, once a trans man completes chest reconstruction surgery, there is no way to reverse the removal of breast tissue; while he could have implants, there is no way to restore breast tissue).

Hormone Therapy

Historically, the first steps in a medical transition have involved masculinizing or feminizing hormone therapy. When transgender men begin testosterone, their bodies start developing male secondary sex characteristics, such as facial hair and a deeper voice. When transgender women begin taking an anti-androgen (testosterone receptor blocker) and estrogen, their bodies start developing female secondary sex characteristics, such as softer skin and breast development. The development of these male and female physical characteristics generally allows trans men and women to be more consistently viewed in their affirmed gender. The first medical transition steps for transgender youth may begin with GnRH analogues at the onset of puberty.

This section provides an overview of hormone/puberty blockers (GnRH analogues) for prepubertal trans youth, followed by an overview of masculinizing and feminizing hormone therapy for young trans men and trans women, respectively. It covers the types of hormones used, the mode of administration, reversible and irreversible physical effects/changes resulting from hormone therapy, and WPATH (2012) standards for beginning each intervention. Guidelines are outlined for conducting an assessment about whether and/ or when hormone treatment is indicated, exploring potential medical, emotional, and social risks and/or benefits, and providing clinical support for parents and young people making these decisions.

Hormone/Puberty Blockers

Medical doctors have used gonadotropin-releasing hormone agonists (GnRH agonists) for about 30 years (Mul & Hughes, 2008). They were developed for use with children whose puberty began well in advance of the usual biological timeline (called "precocious puberty"). These children began developing secondary sex characteristics as early as age five or six when they were not emotionally, socially, or physically prepared for this experience. The medication did just what the name suggests: block puberty, essentially putting it on hold until the child was developmentally and physically prepared for the accompanying physical and emotional changes.

Given that these medications have been in use for 30 years, we have considerable research that documents few side effects. The use of GnRH agonists for suppressing puberty is completely reversible. When GnRH agonists are withdrawn, the child's biological puberty simply resumes.

With transgender children, hormone blockers are typically prescribed for peripubescent youth, or youth in the initial stages of puberty (Tanner stage 2). Puberty is medically categorized into four stages that describe the progression of secondary sex characteristic development. Tanner stage 1 is the pubertal state of a child prior to any development of secondary sexual characteristics (i.e., no pubic hair, no breast development). Tanner stage 2 is the onset of puberty and is defined as the presence of breast budding in cisgender females, the growth of fine pubic hair in males and females, and the increase in testicular volume and thinning of the scrotal skin in cisgender males.

These medications are prescribed to prevent the development of secondary sex characteristics that match the child's birth-assigned sex rather than their affirmed gender. Blockers are generally discontinued in mid to late adolescence. Assuming that the young person's affirmed gender persists, masculinizing or feminizing hormones are begun when the GnRH agonists are withdrawn. This protocol means that the young person will experience a single puberty that matches their affirmed gender.

There are several advantages to using puberty blockers with pre-pubertal trans youth. First, by suspending the development of secondary sex characteristics that match a child's birth-assigned sex and then moving directly to masculinizing or feminizing hormones, there is no need to attempt to later reverse, or undo, the effects of secondary sex characteristics that do not match the young adult's affirmed gender.

For example, if a transgender young woman has already completed her birth-assigned puberty, her voice will have dropped (just as it does in cisgender males). Beginning feminizing hormone therapy after her voice has deepened will not reverse this effect and will not raise the pitch of her voice. As a result, she will go through life as a woman with a deep voice. This may provoke questions from those around her and raise her risk of being perceived as transgender, and trans women who are perceived as trans are at extremely high risk for street harassment or violence. Living with a deep, more male-like voice is also likely to exacerbate her gender dysphoria. Given the irreversible effects of testosterone, the use of puberty blockers at the onset of adolescence can greatly enhance her quality of life as well as her literal safety in the world.

Another benefit of preventing the development of birth-assigned secondary sex characteristics is typically a significant reduction in adolescent gender dysphoria. When faced with the emergence of secondary sex characteristics that are at odds with their affirmed gender, trans youth often experience profound distress. It increases the likelihood that their reflection in the mirror will not match their gendered sense of themselves. It can also feel as if their body is betraying them by becoming someone other than who they know themselves to be.

Many youth who come out in adolescence report not having had a strong sense of gender during preschool, kindergarten, or elementary school. Young children are physically fairly gender neutral. If a six-year-old wears girls' clothes and grows long hair, she will be seen as a girl. If the same child cuts their hair and wears boys' clothes, people will assume he is a boy. It is only with the emergence of secondary sex characteristics such as breasts, facial hair, and a deeper voice that our clothed bodies become more clearly male or female. As a result, gender may not have seemed particularly important for some trans children. It is the onset of puberty and the increased ways they are sexed/gendered in the world that typically precipitate the emergence of adolescent-onset gender dysphoria.

Not all young people come out early enough to begin hormone blockers and prevent the onset of puberty. With youth already in the midst of puberty, endocrinologists may use blockers to halt the progression of birth-assigned secondary sex characteristics. For some trans youth, this may alleviate aspects of their dysphoria, as illustrated by the following vignette.

One 15-year-old trans man had come out to his parents only a few months before calling me. Neither his parents nor I was ready to move forward with testosterone yet. We all felt we needed more time to explore his gender identity as well as some other mental health concerns. At the same time, this young man was experiencing profound gender dysphoria, and concomitantly significant depression and suicidal ideation. The concern about these risks led the parents, the young man, and a pediatric endocrinologist to begin hormone blockers as an interim measure that would relieve dysphoria and thus lower the young trans man's risk factors.

The major benefit for this young man was that blocking his estrogen production shut down menses, a source of profound gender dysphoria for him and most trans male adolescents. Since the medication blocks only the production of estrogen, there are no irreversible effects, as mentioned previously. If the young man had discontinued the blockers, his body would have resumed estrogen production, meaning menses as well as other aspects of puberty. This can "buy time" for parents and professionals who want to further assess the solidity of the young person's trans identity or their adjustment to their affirmed gender if they have socially transitioned. At the same time, some of the distress associated with their gender dysphoria (and thus risk of self-harming behaviors) may be alleviated. In this sense, hormone blockers can offer a first step when adolescents (or their parents) are not ready to begin feminizing or masculinizing hormones.

For young trans women already in the midst of their birth-assigned puberty, GnRH agonists will shut down their bodies' production of testosterone, which generally relieves some of their dysphoria—for example, by decreasing sex drive and frequency of spontaneous erections. Decreasing gender dysphoria simultaneously reduces the risks for major depression, anxiety, and self-harming coping strategies.

For young trans women, like young trans men, the use of hormone blockers offers a longer period of time for gender exploration and ongoing assessment of their evolving gender identity development. Both parents and providers have more time to observe how the young woman experiences her social transition, as well as how she navigates moving through the world as a young woman, without the risk of irreversible effects of anti-androgens and estrogen.

The requirements for adolescents to begin puberty-suppressing medications such as leuprolide as outlined within the WPATH SOC (2012) include the following criteria.

1. A long-lasting and intense pattern of gender nonconformity or gender dysphoria (whether suppressed or
   expressed) has been demonstrated.
2. Gender dysphoria has emerged or worsened with the
   onset of puberty.
3. Any coexisting psychological, medical, or social problems
   have been stabilized sufficiently so they will not likely
   interfere with treatment or compromise adherence.
4. Informed consent has been obtained from the adolescent
   (and legal guardian[s] if the youth is younger than the age
   of medical consent), and parents/guardians are willing to
   support the trans young person during treatment.

Some medical doctors require a written mental health assessment supporting this step prior to initiating puberty-suppressing
medications; other doctors do not require this assessment, as the
effects of the medication are reversible. This letter must be written
by a licensed mental health clinician based on their completion of a
gender assessment, including psychosocial and gender history, and
a diagnosis of gender dysphoria. The Standards of Care (WPATH,
2012) outline what information should be included in these types of
letters; sample letters are included in Appendix C.

Feminizing and Masculinizing Hormone Therapy

Assuming that their affirmed gender remains consistent, the SOC
indicate that feminizing or masculinizing hormone therapy may
begin during adolescence. In many jurisdictions, 16-year-olds are
legal adults for medical decision-making and do not require parental consent. Given that there are irreversible physical changes associated with this intervention, it should be initiated when the trans
young person is firmly grounded in their affirmed gender, both in the
present and moving into adulthood. Ideally, the treatment decision
is made among the adolescent, the family, and the medical provider.

Transgender Men and Testosterone

Masculinizing hormone treatment for transgender men involves taking testosterone. This is most frequently administered through an

intramuscular injection in the buttock or thigh muscles. It can also be administered with a patch or gel. Masculinizing effects tend to occur more quickly with injections. Taking testosterone alone generally shuts down the production of estrogen, though some doctors may choose to use Lupron to shut down production of estrogen before beginning, or in addition to, testosterone.

Beginning treatment with testosterone essentially means entering a male puberty—even if the young person has already completed the puberty associated with their birth-assigned sex. Like a cisgender male adolescent who begins puberty, a young trans man will experience the development of male secondary sex characteristics over time as he begins taking testosterone. Some physical changes occur more quickly, and some only fully develop over the course of several years.

For older trans male youth who have already entered an estrogen-based ("female") puberty, beginning testosterone generally causes menstruation to cease within three to six months. This effect is reversible. If the young man later discontinues testosterone, his body will resume the production of estrogen and menses will resume. As with a cisgender adolescent man, a young trans man's voice will also drop or deepen with testosterone. This voice change often occurs within the first three to six months and is irreversible. If the young trans man stops taking testosterone at a later time, his voice will not return to its original pitch.

Taking testosterone creates additional facial and body hair, though the amount and location varies based on personal and cultural genetic variations and norms. For example, young Korean trans men may not experience significant facial hair growth, given that cisgender Korean men often have minimal facial hair. Other cultural genetic makeups may result in significant facial or body hair.

When cisgender boys begin puberty, it is not possible to predict how much facial or body hair will develop by the end of their adolescence. Even within cultural groups, some cisgender men are very hairy; some have lighter hair growth. Some cisgender men can grow a beard or full mustache; some cannot. The unpredictability of these variations holds true for trans men as well. Family members may make an "educated" guess based on norms within that family history, but individual genetics vary even within families.

The development of additional facial and body hair is irreversible.

If the young trans man discontinues testosterone, the additional hair growth can be removed only through electrolysis or laser treatments. In the absence of testosterone and the resumption of estrogen production, the growth of facial and body hair will decline, but this will not cause existing hair to disappear without intervention.

As in cisgender men, other physical changes that occur with testosterone include skin texture becoming rougher due to pore enlargement. Trans men taking testosterone will gain additional muscle mass without working out—and will develop more muscle mass if they do work out (as do cisgender men). These initial changes—a deeper voice, more muscle mass, visible facial and body hair—form significant male gender markers in our world. Consequently, many young trans men begin to be more consistently read/seen as a man in the world as soon as three to six months after beginning testosterone.

Other effects of testosterone include body odor changes, the clitoris becoming larger, and, typically, an increase in sex drive. Over a longer period of time, body fat redistributes from the hips to the stomach area, and facial bone structure may shift, becoming more typically masculine in appearance. Depending on the trans man's genetics, his hairline may recede over time and lead to male-pattern baldness.

Some trans male youth may think increasing their dose or frequency of testosterone will cause more rapid development of male secondary sex characteristics. This myth frequently circulates online. However, the reverse is actually true. High levels of testosterone can be converted to estrogen, thus defeating the aim of masculinizing hormone therapy.

Hormone Therapy for Transgender Women

Trans women take both estrogen and an anti-androgen. The latter is often called a "T blocker" because it blocks testosterone from attaching to receptors on the target cell and so functionally decreases testosterone activity. The anti-androgen is required because the dose of estrogen required to shut down production of testosterone is too high to be safe. In addition, without an anti-androgen blocking the production of testosterone, trans women would not experience the full effects of estrogen. These hormones are most frequently administered orally, though they can be injected and a skin patch is available.

Feminizing hormone therapy causes a trans woman's face and skin to become softer as her pores become smaller. Over several years, her body fat redistributes itself from the stomach area to her hips, creating a more typical feminine body shape. As mentioned previously, the anti-androgen decreases, and can eliminate, spontaneous erections. Trans women may experience a decreased sex drive. These effects are reversible. If the young woman discontinues the anti-androgen and estrogen at a later date, the production of testosterone will resume, and each of these effects will return to their original state over time.

Estrogen does cause some breast tissue growth, though often only what would be an A or at best a small B cup size. Generally after two to three years, the full extent of breast development possible for a given young trans woman will be apparent. This breast development is irreversible. If the young woman discontinued hormone therapy, the breast growth she experienced would remain.

For trans women who begin feminizing hormone therapy after completing an initial testosterone-based/male puberty, taking estrogen and an anti-androgen does not change the size of an Adam's apple, alter facial bone structure, or reduce height or bone structure/ size. Taking estrogen will not raise the pitch of their voice (given that it would have dropped in the earlier "male" puberty). The anti-androgen and estrogen will slow the growth of additional facial and body hair but will not remove existing facial and body hair. This hair will need to be removed through electrolysis or laser methods.

The fact that "masculine" physical features, such as voice, height, facial bone structure, and size of hands and feet, cannot be reversed after an initial testosterone-based puberty increases the risk that trans woman may be "read" or seen as transgender in the world rather than simply being seen as a woman. In a culture marked by sexism, misogyny, and transphobia, this places trans women at increased risk of verbal harassment and physical violence as they navigate their day-to-day lives in the world. The existing lack of legal protection against discrimination also decreases employment opportunities, can place current employment at risk, and can jeopardize housing stability, contributing to increased homelessness.

Trans women from lower socioeconomic brackets who are unable to financially afford hormone therapy sometimes access hormones on the street or online. In both cases, the purity of the hormone is not assured. Accessing hormone therapy in this manner means it is not medically supervised, thus increasing potential health risks. Trans women purchasing hormones this way may inject together, using shared needles, creating additional health risks.

Some trans women inject silicone for breast and/or hip development. In addition to being illegal, this poses tremendous health risks. As with other substances obtained from a nonmedical source, the purity is unknown. Silicone injections can cause disfigurement and death, generally due to pulmonary complications resulting from immune system reactions. Additionally, silicone does not necessarily remain where injected and may migrate to other sites, causing significant health risks and physical damage. Typically, a more experienced trans woman obtains the silicone and other trans women meet to inject at gatherings often called "silicone parties."

While choices to obtain hormones outside medical supervision or inject silicone oneself may appear self-destructive, it is essential to remember the high risks of discrimination, harassment, and violence that exist for trans women perceived as trans in the world. More than one in four trans persons have been the victims of bias-driven assault. These numbers are significantly higher among trans women and in particular, among trans women of color. In data collected by the National Coalition of Anti-Violence Program (NCAVP) (2015), over half (55%) of anti-LGBTQ homicide victims were trans women and half (50%) were trans women of colwor, despite the fact that transgender people represented only 19% of the total homicide reports (National Coalition for Anti-Violence Programs (NCAVP), 2015). A "normative" feminine figure with visible breasts and hips can enable trans women to be more consistently read as women (rather than as trans women) and thus significantly contribute to their safety when in public.

Given the irreversible effects of testosterone during puberty, the value of hormone blockers for young, prepubescent trans women is unequivocal. Beginning hormone blockers at the onset of puberty or shortly thereafter means that these trans women will not develop male secondary sex characteristics, like a deeper voice or facial hair. They may not grow as tall as they would during a male puberty and their bone structure will typically be smaller and more delicate.

Assuming their affirmed gender identity remains consistent, these adolescent trans women would begin anti-androgens and estrogen in mid to late adolescence. Without the emergence of male secondary sex characteristics, such an individual will likely be more consistently viewed as a woman (as opposed to a trans woman) as she moves into adulthood, greatly enhancing both her mental and emotional well-being and her physical safety.

Feminizing or masculinizing hormone therapy generally continues throughout a transgender person's lifetime. There will never be a time when a trans man's body naturally produces testosterone nor a time when a trans woman's body produces estrogen. Some trans men choose to discontinue testosterone after achieving the desired masculinization, though if they are younger than menopausal age, menses resumes. For both trans men and women, the dosage can be reduced after a hysterectomy, orchiectomy/castration, or gender-confirming surgery. The dose can also often be lowered as trans people age (when hormones levels are naturally decreasing in cisgender men and women).

Additional Thoughts About Hormone Therapy and Trans Adolescents

As mentioned above, the Standards of Care (SOC) indicate that adolescents may begin feminizing and/or masculinizing hormone therapy at age 16, citing the fact that in many countries 16-year-olds are considered legal adults for making their own medical decisions and parental consent is no longer needed (WPATH, 2012, p. 20). At the same time, the SOC do state that the ideal is for this decision to be made in conjunction with the transgender young person, their family, and their medical and mental health providers. Within the United States, laws specifying the age at which a young person can make their own medical decisions without parental consent vary by state. Many states have additional provisions for youth who are homeless or unaccompanied or have been emancipated.

Some medical doctors categorically will not prescribe feminizing and/or masculinizing hormone therapy for trans youth younger than 18 years. At the same time, there are a growing number of medical providers and children's gender centers that may initiate feminizing and/or masculinizing hormone therapy at 14 to 18 years of age. Beginning this treatment at a younger age generally occurs only when the young person's affirmed gender identity has been consistent and they have already been living in their gender identity for a period of time. The specific length of time varies based on the needs of the young person, family input, and recommendations from medical and mental health providers.

As with other medical interventions for transgender youth, medical doctors require a written letter of support from a licensed mental health clinician indicating that the young person meets the criteria for a diagnosis of gender dysphoria and is mentally, emotionally, and socially prepared for this next step. This letter includes a psychosocial and gender history, a diagnosis of gender dysphoria, and a recommendation to proceed with hormone therapy as specified in the Standards of Care (WPATH, 2012); sample letters are included in Appendix C.

With the immense physical changes and development occurring during adolescence, it is generally best to refer transgender youth to pediatric endocrinologists, who hold a greater body of knowledge and expertise around adolescents and their hormonal well-being. The exception may be a reputable adolescent health center or practice where nonspecialty pediatricians are knowledgeable about the medical treatment of transgender youth, including puberty-suppressing and feminizing and/or masculinizing hormone protocols. For trans young adults, a general medical doctor such as an internist or family practitioner can prescribe and monitor hormones if they are familiar with the protocols. However, when additional health concerns or conditions (such as diabetes or a heart condition) are present, referral to an endocrinologist is always advised.

Some medical and mental health providers may be reluctant to prescribe puberty suppressants and/or feminizing or masculinizing hormones to adolescents. This is generally due to concerns about potential health risks or worry that irreversible changes precipitated by the latter could pose a problem if the young person later "changed their mind" and decided they were not transgender.

While these concerns hold some merit, they must consistently be balanced against the risks of delaying medical transition among transgender adolescents. Delay or denial of hormone therapy ensures that the young person's gender dysphoria will continue, and over time the degree of dysphoria will likely intensify. In addition, trans youth who physically appear different from similar-aged peers (e.g., a 17-year-old trans boy whose voice has not yet dropped) may be at higher risk for verbal harassment and/or physical abuse and bullying.

Recent research indicates that the level of gender-related abuse experienced by trans adolescents is strongly associated with the degree of internal psychiatric distress the young people are experiencing (Nuttbrock et al., 2010). In light of this, the SOC emphasize that "withholding puberty suppression and subsequent feminizing or masculinizing hormone therapy is not a neutral option" for adolescents (p. 21). The following vignette illustrates some of the complexities of these decisions about readiness.

Assessment of Readiness for Hormone Therapy

EVAN

Evan was a 17-year old-transgender young man (natal female) with a history of gender dysphoria dating back to early childhood. His parents reported that he had resisted wearing girls' clothes by age six and that most of his early playmates were boys. During the fall of his freshman year in high school, Evan came out to his parents as gay. The following March, he told them he was not really gay but instead transgender and identified as a boy. During late April, his parents brought him to see me for gender evaluation and support.

The parents (mother/father) had been divorced for five years and shared custody of Evan and his brother (three years younger). While their primary residence was with their mother, the two apartments were only blocks apart so that the boys could go back and forth easily. The divorce had been difficult for the family. It had been precipitated in part by the father's addiction. He (the father) was now sober three years and the relationships between all of them had improved. As the oldest child (and perceived daughter), Evan had sometimes been his mother's confidant after the parents separated, and their relationship remained close.

Evan was a bright, articulate, compassionate young man who formed friendships quickly with adults and peers and enjoyed socializing. He was passionate about math and science and wanted to become an engineer. Upon intake, Evan presented with some depression and anxiety. He had a history of cutting behavior (five to six times) prior to disclosing his transgender identification. He had a history of some drug and alcohol use. He had had some difficulty with school performance in the past, mostly in terms of not completing work in a timely manner, and took medication for ADHD. Overall, Evan presented as a relatively high-functioning high school student.

We met regularly beginning in April and into the summer. During this time, I met with his parents separately several times and with the three of them for periodic family sessions. Both parents were supportive of his affirmed gender.

Evan socially transitioned that fall at the onset of his sophomore year at the same small private school he had attended the previous year as a freshman. He successfully came out to his peers and navigated these relationships effectively throughout the academic year.

The following fall, in his junior year, Evan's academic performance deteriorated. He was issued an academic warning at the end of his first quarter. When his grades did not improve during the second quarter, Evan was placed on academic probation. He was failing several classes. His attendance record showed numerous absences and instances of lateness in addition to periodically cutting classes.

Outside school, Evan began to be late and/or miss our appointments and often violated curfew at home. He appeared forgetful (or defiant?) and consistently had an excuse for why things were "not my fault." He often lied about what had transpired when confronted with lateness, poor performance, etc. He appeared not to internalize the consequences of his behavior (e.g., behavior leading to school failure despite many admonitions and warnings during the first two marking periods).

During our sessions and family sessions, when Evan was confronted about his poor academic performance, he repeatedly insisted he was back on track and was up-to-date on all his homework and studying regularly. He consistently promised not to be late again.

In the following weeks, Evan alternated between feelings of failure and low self-worth and other moments of denial while still insisting that everything was fine. Evan had begun taking Lupron (hormone blocker) about four months before to decrease his gender dysphoria. The plan had been for Evan to begin testosterone that spring. When his school performance began to deteriorate, his parents and I talked with Evan about the need to get back on track at school in order to continue with this timeline. The frame for this was that if Evan was doing well in school and life, this was a sign that he was responsible enough and ready to begin masculinizing hormone therapy. If he was not able to be responsible at school, this might indicate that Evan was not mature enough to navigate responsible maintenance of hormone therapy.

Unfortunately, Evan continued to do poorly and was expelled from the school in February (of his junior year). At that point, it seemed unclear whether Evan should begin testosterone in the near future or wait until his behavior/performance improved and his academic situation stabilized. His parents were very angry about his poor academic performance and now expulsion as well as his repeated failure to take responsibility for his choices and actions. In our most recent session, Evan disclosed that he had had an episode of cutting during the past week and reported significant anger toward himself.

REFLECTION QUESTIONS FOR PARENTS OR PROFESSIONALS:

1. What thoughts do you have about what might be going on for Evan? Do you have any hunches about what may have contributed to his poor school performance and failure to take responsibility this year?
2. At this point, what position would you take in terms of the original plan for Evan to begin testosterone within the next one to two months? What factors would go into your decision? What do you see as the possible benefits or risks of Evan starting or delaying testosterone treatment?
3. How do you feel about permission to begin masculinizing hormone therapy being linked to Evan's ability to "be responsible?"
4. Describe your intervention plan at this point. With Evan? With the parents? With the family as a whole? What do you think the next steps should be?

Deeper Exploration

This vignette illustrates the complexity of decisions surrounding the onset of hormone therapy with transgender adolescents. While the SOC provide guidelines, there is no single "measuring stick" to pinpoint exactly when a teenager is ready for this next step in their transition. Taking testosterone, or an anti-androgen and estrogen, does require some ability to be responsible—at minimum, adherence to the prescribed dosage and medical follow-up appointments. It can be challenging to weigh existing risk factors, such as the degree of the trans adolescent's current gender dysphoria and how well they are managing this.

The SOC suggest that other aspects of a young person's life should be relatively stable. Any mental health conditions should be resolved and stable enough so as to not interfere. However, this must often be balanced alongside the risks of delaying medical interventions. While we initially framed the onset of masculinizing hormone therapy as an affirmation of Evan's ability to be responsible at home and school, this plan did have its risks. What if the fact that Evan was not doing well in school was linked to his gender dysphoria? Might Evan, in fact, do better in school after beginning hormone therapy? How do you, along with his parents, discern these factors? How do you sift through these concerns to arrive at an appropriate decision?

In this particular situation, the parents and I did come to the decision that Evan should begin taking testosterone as planned that spring. We agreed that it was not appropriate or effective to link beginning hormones to Evan's behavior or performance. We identified that beginning testosterone was about Evan being more fully himself in his own body and within the world, and that it was not healthy to link this with his performance. We became clear that we did not want to send the message to Evan that "you can only be yourself if you do well"; we did not want to predicate his ability to be himself on what he did or did not do. If we believed Evan was a young man, then he should be able to be that young man to the fullest extent possible—regardless of whether he was currently being a responsible young man (as his parents or I might define this). As a result, we revised our initial plan and Evan did begin testosterone that spring. In addition to illustrating the complexities of these decisions, this vignette highlights the need to be willing to periodically reevaluate and revise the original plan.

Early Transition

Gender transition is an inherently public act. There is no way to transition in private. It is important for mental health providers to grasp the fact that as difficult as it is to manage the gender dysphoria prior to coming out as transgender, the visibility inherent in the early stages of medical transition can be equally challenging. Everyone in their day-to-day life is able to observe the physical changes as they occur—neighbors, grandparents, the bus driver, the guy at the corner deli, all of the parents' friends.

Another challenge in the early stages of masculinizing or feminizing hormone therapy is being read half of the time as a woman and the other half of the time as a man—and not being able to predict how you are going to be read in any given situation. Most transgender adolescents arrive in my office ready to transition and begin hormone therapy a month ago. The degree to which their gender dysphoria has been intensifying is often what precipitates coming out to their parents. From their perspective, it feels like they have been living with this distress for so long (and they have) that they simply cannot tolerate it one minute longer—especially now that the news is out.

When they begin hormone therapy, they want to be consistently seen in their affirmed gender overnight. By this point, teenage transgender boys don't ever again want to hear anyone say to their mother, "What a beautiful daughter you have." Young transgender women don't want to be "Sir'd" when they pay for hair products anymore. But given the fact that the physical changes happen over time, when transgender youth first begin hormone therapy, they are likely to be misgendered frequently (misgendering involves not using someone's affirmed name or pronouns or describing trans men as women or trans women as men). Surviving this stage of the process, in which they still are not consistently being seen for who they are, is emotionally painful and draining as well as hard on their self-esteem.

These struggles with how others perceive them occur alongside the trans adolescent's own internal dysphoria and growing impatience to see their affirmed gender's secondary sex characteristics in themselves. Here, too, there is the dynamic that the young person has lived with this distress for so long, lived with their current physical appearance not feeling right, that it feels impossible to tolerate it any longer. Given this, it's not surprising that once beginning masculinizing or feminizing hormone therapy, many trans youth are out of bed every morning in front of the mirror to see if their body has changed any overnight.

Surgical Interventions

Top Surgery

Many transgender adolescents and young adults may want to pursue what is colloquially called "top surgery." For trans men, "chest reconstruction surgery" (not "mastectomy" or "breast removal") involves not only removal of breast tissue, but also the contouring of the chest to ensure a male appearance. Trans men with smaller breasts are often able to have a less invasive chest surgery called keyhole or drawstring. In these two procedures, the nipple generally remains attached to the body while breast tissue surrounding the nipple is removed. The fact that the nipple is not fully disconnected typically allows for greater nipple sensation post surgery.

Transgender men with larger breasts have a procedure called double incision. In this surgery, the nipple is detached while the breast tissue is removed and the areola is resized for a more masculine appearance. The nipple is then regrafted on. The need to completely detach the nipple (and its nerve endings) generally leads to minimal nipple sensation post surgery. More recently, the "button hole" technique (as opposed to the keyhole technique described above) has enabled larger-chested trans men to have breast tissue removed without fully detaching the nipples, thus preserving significant sensation post surgery. Top surgery for transgender men is generally performed on an outpatient basis unless there are other significant medical concerns that warrant closer post-surgical observation and a hospital stay.

Top surgery for transgender women includes breast augmentation using silicone or saline implants. While estrogen causes some breast growth (generally over a two- to three-year period), the growth is often relatively small, approximately an A or small B cup size. Like cisgender women, trans women vary in their preferences about the size of their breasts. Some women—trans and cis—may prefer smaller breasts; other women—trans and cis—may prefer larger breasts. The degree to which a transgender woman feels comfortable with the breast growth she experiences while taking estrogen plays a role in her desire for top surgery.

Breast augmentation surgery both increases breast size and enhances shape. Implants may be "round" or "teardrop" (anatomically shaped) and may be textured or smooth. Like top surgery for trans men, breast augmentation is generally performed on an outpatient basis.

On a personal level, top surgery decreases gender dysphoria in two ways. The first is that when a transgender woman looks in the mirror and sees that her chest is flat, it is extremely challenging for her to see herself as a woman—despite how strong her internal sense of herself may be. When she tries on clothes, she wants to be able to see her breasts—not just feel them in her mind. The same is true for a transgender man. When he has to wear a tie, he wants it to lie flat on his chest—not bulge out and then curve back in. When he's wearing a T-shirt and catches a glimpse of himself walking by a shop window, he expects his chest to be flat. When it is not, he generally experiences gender dysphoria—sometimes profoundly so.

Second, all human beings share a basic human need to be seen for who we are by those around us and to have our identities validated by them. Transgender youth are no exception. After they have endured many years of being "misgendered," typically, top surgery significantly contributes to their ability to have others in the world see and acknowledge them in their affirmed gender. In an early study examining the lives of transgender men, Devor (1997) highlighted the insight that "each of us has a deep need to be witnessed by others for whom we are, and each of us wants to see ourselves mirrored in others' eyes as we see ourselves" (p. 46).

However, this ability to be recognized in one's affirmed gender as one moves through the world goes beyond simply decreasing gender dysphoria. Top surgeries contribute to a young trans person's emotional and physical safety in the world. When we see someone on the street whose attire or hairstyle or cut is androgynous, having a flat chest is a major way we determine whether they are "male."

In the same way, visible breasts are a primary way people perceive someone as female. Consequently, top surgery (typically coupled with hormone therapy) greatly increases a trans woman's or man's ability to consistently be "read" or seen for who they are in the world—to be recognized in their affirmed gender. As discussed previously, being seen in your affirmed gender—and not "read" or "called out" as transgender—is perhaps the most critical factor that determines whether a young transgender man or woman is free from verbal harassment and physical and violence—even murder—in private and public settings.

The realities of sexism and misogyny place young trans women (and young trans women of color even more so) at particular risk of "street" harassment and violence. Trans women can be perceived as threatening to some straight cisgender men and their masculinity and/or heterosexuality. After assaulting or murdering a transgender woman, some men have claimed they could not be held responsible for their rage when they "discovered" she was transgender. Their justification was that they had been "deceived." For these straight cisgender men, their attraction to a trans woman challenges their heterosexuality. In their minds, she is not really a woman, which then raises the untenable possibility (to them) that they were attracted to a man.

The pervasive impact of trans-prejudice, racism, and sexism on the lives of transgender youth, particularly poor trans youth, homeless transgender youth, and trans youth of color, underscores the reality of Judith Butler's (2004) analysis that (human) lives are

> supported and maintained differentially, that there are radically different ways in which human physical vulnerability is distributed across the globe. Certain lives will be highly protected, and the abrogation of their claims to sanctity will be sufficient to mobilize the forces of war. And other lives will not find such fast and furious support and will not even qualify as "grievable." (p. 24)

Essentially Butler posits that not all lives count as human, or that some lives count as more fully human and worthwhile than do others. In this schema, trans lives and gender-nonnormative lives count less than cisgender, gender-normative lives do. The ways in which some lives are not even grievable particularly impacts trans women, trans people of color, and poor trans people, who are already marginalized in other aspects of their identities. Being a young transgender person compounds these risks and realities. From this understanding alone, top surgery should always be considered medically necessary for transgender individuals, including young trans people.

Despite these benefits, top surgeries are typically not performed before a young person reaches the age of majority. There are a limited number of surgeons in the United States who will perform top surgery at 16 to 17 years of age—generally when the young person has socially transitioned earlier and their affirmed gender has remained consistent. The SOC suggest that trans men younger than 18 years of age should ideally have lived in their affirmed gender for a period of time and have been taking testosterone for one year prior to obtaining chest surgery. Parental consent is required for all surgical procedures for minors.

Like hormone therapy, top surgery requires a letter from the young person's doctor and/or licensed mental health practitioner or therapist (see sample mental health letters in Appendix C). There is no single universal timeline for top surgeries for transgender adolescents. Decisions about eligibility and timing must be flexible and individualized in accordance with the needs, risks, and benefits of each specific young person.

Some parents and/or medical and mental healthcare providers may be reluctant to permit top surgery for transgender adolescents younger than 18 years. However, it is important to note that from the trans youth's perspective, obtaining this surgery prior to beginning college or entering the work world in a full-time manner may be very important. Again, the importance may be in terms of alleviating internal gender dysphoria and/or it may impact their ability to navigate college or employment without encountering harassment and discrimination.

Genital Surgeries

The historical definition of "sex reassignment" surgery by the medical establishment was genital surgery. It was this specific surgery (and not hormones or top surgery) that determined whether or not a person could legally be considered a man or woman in their affirmed gender. The gender marker on most legal documents could not be changed without documentation of genital surgery. This required a letter from the surgeon and, in some states, an actual copy of the operating room report as well to ensure the authenticity of the letter.

The United States passport and social security agencies eliminated the genital surgery requirement several years ago.

Within the larger world as well, whether or not a person has had "the surgery" (genital surgery) is typically the benchmark of gender transition. Without lower surgery, trans men and women are often not classified as "real" men and women. For example, when one trans woman came out publicly, someone else tweeted that she would never consider the trans person a woman until "she has her pee-pee removed."

This question about whether or not a transgender person has had genital surgery is a highly intrusive and personal question about their body. Before I came out as trans, I never had an acquaintance—let alone a stranger—ask me what my genitals looked like, but trans youth and adults, and I, get asked that question all the time. Beyond the intrusiveness, the question carries the implication that the questioner wants to know whether you are a "real" man or woman yet— clearly suggesting that the shape of our bodies is the sole determinant of what it means to be a man or a woman, as the above tweet reflects.

Given the cost of this surgery and the historical denial of health insurance coverage for trans-related surgeries, establishing the bar at genital surgery meant that many transgender people were unable to have the gender markers updated on their identification documents. This often "outed" them against their will in situations when identification was required, such as seeking employment, being stopped by the police, or traveling internationally. In addition to the emotional discomfort and dysphoria experienced in these situations, such disclosures risked the trans person's safety in some settings. When you are traveling internationally and your gender presentation does not match the gender marker on your passport, you may be subject to suspicion, ridicule, invasive questions and searches, harassment, or even violence.

Among transgender youth and others in the larger trans community, more recent nomenclature for genital surgery includes "gender-affirming" or "gender-confirming" surgery. Both phrases dispute the belief that one's sex is being changed or "reassigned." In contrast, the transgender person's gender is simply being confirmed or affirmed through these medical procedures. The terms "bottom" or "lower" surgery" are often used informally within trans communities.

As discussed earlier, transgender youth experience differing degrees and types of gender dysphoria regarding their body parts. As a result, they make varying decisions about the importance of particular surgical procedures. Still, for many trans youth and young adults, lower surgery can significantly decrease gender dysphoria and enable them to be more fully the gender they know themselves to be regardless of the genitalia present at birth.

Even though the Standards of Care (WPATH, 2012) indicate that genital surgeries should be performed only after the age of consent as an adult, it is important for mental health providers to be knowledgeable about these procedures when working with adolescents. Both youth and their families often want to know what is possible as the young person moves into adulthood.

Transgender Men

Genital surgery for trans men involves one of two procedures: metoidioplasty or phalloplasty. Metoidioplasty (sometimes called a "meta") involves "releasing" the clitoris, which has become enlarged as a result of taking testosterone. This procedure creates a small phallus (about 4 to 6 cm) from the enlarged clitoris, which is then covered with adjacent skin. The metoidioplasty can be performed with or without urethral lengthening. Lengthening of the urethra allows trans men to void standing up. Penetration during sex is not generally possible with a metoidioplasty given the small size of the penis.

Phalloplasty creates a "standard-size" phallus using a skin graft, generally taken from the outside of the thigh, the back, or the radial forearm. Having a more "normative"-appearing penis can not only reduce dysphoria but also make being "outed" in settings like restrooms or locker rooms less likely. Urethral lengthening typically accompanies a phalloplasty, enabling urination while standing. Roughly 9 to 12 months after the phalloplasty is completed, penile implants can be inserted that allow for penetrative sex. These implants can be semi-rigid or inflatable. Both transgender men and surgeons typically have preferences for the type they recommend. Scrotoplasty, with the insertion of testicular implants, can accompany both metoidioplasty and phalloplasty. Both lower surgeries require a hysterectomy.

Some transgender men choose to have a hysterectomy even if

they do not intend, or are unable, to have a metoidioplasty or a phalloplasty. While the internal organs are not visible body parts, the removal of what are typically considered female organs can relieve aspects of gender dysphoria for some trans men. There is also some research suggesting that having a hysterectomy after three to five years on testosterone may reduce certain cancer risks, although the evidence is not conclusive (Gorton, Buth, & Spade, 2005). A hysterectomy also stops the menstrual period and allows for time off testosterone shots without concern that menstruation will resume.

In the past, many trans men did not believe bottom surgery was worth pursuing. Without health insurance coverage, the cost was prohibitive for most trans men. Further, the penis created by early surgical techniques was rarely realistic enough to feel gender-congruent for trans men. The resulting penis at that time was minimally sensate, and penetrative sex post lower surgery was not as pleasurable as most trans men had anticipated or hoped. The lack of adequate resemblance to a cisgender man's penis meant trans men often still did not feel safe or comfortable disrobing, or being in underwear or tight swim trunks, around cisgender people. Before more recent surgical advances, there was a high risk of postsurgical complications, with most resulting from the complexities of lengthening the urethra.

Phalloplasty techniques have greatly advanced in the past five to eight years across all indices—physical appearance, sexual satisfaction and pleasure, and reduction of postsurgical complications. Microsurgical advances have enabled surgeons to connect nerve endings within the erotic clitoral tissue to the nerve endings within the skin graft. This allows the formation of a penis that is more sensate and more capable of orgasm and sexual pleasure than was possible earlier. In addition, these surgical advances have resulted in significantly decreased complication rates.

Older pessimistic beliefs about lower surgery for trans men persist in many places. They can still be easily found on the Internet, where many trans men seek information today. In working with trans male adolescents, it is important to be able to correct these impressions and provide, or direct them to, more current and accurate information about these surgeries. For youth and their families as well as providers, one direct source of accurate information can be found at the growing number of transgender conferences emerging throughout the United States (see Appendix B). Many surgeons regularly present the surgeries they perform and the specific techniques and procedures utilized at these events. Additional invormation is also often located on their websites

Transgender Women

The standard genital surgery for transgender women is called vaginoplasty. The testicles are removed and the scrotal skin is used to create the labia majora (labiaplasty). The penile tissue is then inverted and used to construct the vagina, while the clitoris is constructed using erotically sensate tissue from the glans penis. The urethra is then shortened and positioned like that of a cisgender woman.

The fact that the vagina and clitoris are constructed from erotically sensate penile tissue as well as the consistent enhancement of techniques developed over time enables most transgender women to experience sexual satisfaction and pleasure post genital surgery. When surgery is performed by a knowledgeable and competent surgeon, the aesthetic appearance post surgery reflects no difference between transgender women and cisgender women. A transgender woman's sexual partner would not become cognizant of her trans history simply based on the appearance or functionality of her genitals.

Largely due to the cost of vaginoplasty (and historical absence of insurance coverage), some transgender women choose to have an orchiectomy rather than vaginoplasty. This procedure involves removal of one or both testicles. The penis and scrotum are left intact. The removal of the testicle(s) reduces testosterone production and consequently can be helpful in alleviating gender dysphoria for some transgender women.

The earlier discussion of feminizing hormone therapy noted that estrogen does not reverse all the secondary sex characteristics accompanying a male puberty. Consequently, additional medical or surgical procedures may be sought by trans women who want to be more consistently viewed as women in the world. These can include a tracheal shave to reduce the size of an Adam's apple, removal of facial or body hair through electrolysis or laser treatments, and/or facial feminization surgery (FFS) to achieve a more feminine facial appearance. There are some surgical approaches to voice feminization, but more typically trans women (or men) seek coaching around tone and pitch from a vocal therapist knowledgeable about the needs of transgender individuals.

The importance placed on gender-confirming surgeries varies among transgender women and men. In part, this is rooted in the different ways trans people may or may not feel comfortable with specific aspects of their bodies and body parts as well as their physical and sexual intimacy. For some trans men and women, these surgeries significantly reduce gender dysphoria and allow the trans man or woman to move more comfortably in their bodies and in the world. For these individuals, lower surgery is essential to their overall mental, emotional, social, and physical well-being.

Genital surgery may be less crucial for other trans men and women. It is critical to note that the varying importance of pursuing lower surgery is not indicative of whether a young trans woman or man is "truly" transgender. Instead, these different choices simply reflect the diverse ways human beings navigate their personal bodily comfort and pleasure.

As indicated earlier, the SOC indicate that genital surgery should not be performed until a transgender young person reaches the legal age of majority to give consent for medical procedures within their locale. The SOC also suggest that the youth live continuously in their affirmed gender for at least one year prior to obtaining lower surgery and are careful to note that turning 18 years old does not, in and of itself, suggest that lower surgery is recommended. Instead, the decision about eligibility and readiness should be determined based on numerous factors, including the young adult's functioning, current familial and social support, and overall well-being.

Moving from one aspect of transition to the next should generally include time for adolescents and their parents to fully assimilate the effects of earlier interventions. Recommendations about the length of time lived in their affirmed gender, as well as the usual sequence of beginning with hormone therapy, followed by top surgery, and then potentially lower surgery, are not meant to be prescriptive for all transgender young people. The primary goal underlying these considerations within the SOC is to ensure that trans youth have the opportunity to experience living in their affirmed gender both internally and socially prior to making decisions involving irreversible physical changes. As with other steps within a medical transition, the SOC clearly state that the guidelines must be applied with an eye to the specific needs, goals, and context of each transgender young person.

Access to Transition-Related Medical Care

The Internet has significantly increased the amount of information available to trans youth and increased access to trans-knowledgeable and affirming medical and mental health providers. Trans youth today are likely to arrive in a therapist's office having extensively researched how to transition. They have often watched videos and read blogs of young trans men and women recording their hormone treatment experiences, including their "progress" on a weekly or monthly basis. They may have communicated with trans youth across the United States and around the world. This increased access decreases isolation, contributes to trans youth coming out at younger ages, and provides greater knowledge of what is possible for trans youth today.

At the same time, not all information available on the Internet is accurate. It is important to evaluate what transgender young people have learned about the various aspects of medical transition to ensure that their beliefs reflect current medical information. Trans adolescents, family members, and others may have misinformation about various medical procedures, protocols, benefits and risks, and possible results.

Depending on laws for parental consent, age plays a significant role in regulating access to medical transition among adolescents. In families who are rejecting, trans youth may not be able to access medical care until they reach adulthood. Even after reaching the legal age for making medical decisions, many young adults remain dependent on their families for health insurance and financial support. Medical providers and/or parents who believe transgender identity is a psychiatric illness often impede transition among youth and may insist that the young person attend reparative therapy designed to "cure" their transgender identity.

Location can play a key role in determining who has access to trans-knowledgeable or affirming health care. Very few medical or nursing schools incorporate education about the needs of transgender youth. Consequently, in many locations there are few trans-knowledgeable or affirming healthcare providers. This goes beyond the provision of transition-related care, such as hormones and gender-confirming surgeries, to encompass general healthcare for transgender youth. For example, most healthcare providers think about gynecology in terms of women. Many are unaware that all people with vaginas need regular gynecological exams, including trans men if they have not had a hysterectomy.

In areas without trans-competent adult medical providers, doctors may lack knowledge about protocols for trans youth or simply be unwilling to provide hormone treatment for youth, including puberty blockers. The geographic distance and consequent isolation of many transgender youth and their families in rural communities can also form a barrier in locating and accessing medical care.

Socioeconomic status and lack of access to health insurance covering trans-related medical care often limits the ability to medically transition. Historically, health insurance has excluded any trans-related medical treatment. In particular, this has applied to hormone therapy and surgeries associated with medical transition. However, many health insurance plans have denied coverage for medical care that was completely unrelated to transition after they learned a member was transgender.

While the out-of-pocket cost for testosterone and estrogen is affordable for many working- and middle-class families with trans youth, hormone blockers are very expensive. Trans-related surgeries are generally not financially accessible without health insurance coverage. Top surgery typically costs $8,000 to $10,000 out of pocket. Genital surgery for trans women may cost $20,000 to $40,000, and it may cost as much as $80,000 to $100,000 for trans men. While some young adults or families may find the money to pay for top surgery, most simply cannot afford lower surgery without insurance coverage.

Lack of health insurance coverage for transgender individuals is rooted in stigma. Hormone treatment is regularly covered for cisgender people (e.g., menopausal cisgender women or older cisgender men with decreased testosterone levels). Transgender people are often denied surgical procedures routinely available to cisgender people. For example, most insurance policies cover chest surgery for cisgender men with gynecomastia, even though this procedure is largely about the man's emotional sense of "gender congruence" and not a physical health risk.

In the past 5 to 10 years, more health insurance policies have begun to include trans-related medical care, generally in larger corporations and educational institutions who are able to write their own policies. A few states have mandated this coverage from both private and public insurers. However, the vast majority of trans youth across the U.S remained unable to access transition-related medical treatments that WPATH (2012) considers medically necessary for transgender people. Youth in child welfare and juvenile justice have routinely been denied trans-related medical care.

However, in May 2016, the U.S. Department of Health and Human Services (HHS) issued a document with final regulations clarifying many aspects of the 2010 Affordable Care Act (ACA). These guidelines are clear that discrimination against transgender people within healthcare is no longer legal. All health insurers receiving federal funds—most private insurers, state Medicaid, the Indian Health Service, and CHIP (Children's Health Insurance Program) programs—must now provide transgender-related medical care in the same way they cover any other medical care. Insurers are no longer legally able to categorically deny a medical procedure simply because the member is transgender or because the procedure is related to a medical transition (National Center for Transgender Equality, 2016). While other factors continue to limit access to medical care for transgender youth, health insurance coverage is becoming less of a barrier in light of the HHS ruling.

CHAPTER 6

Transgender Adolescents

Development of Transgender Identity

IN A RECENT STUDY ON IDENTITY DEVELOPMENT AMONG male-identified transgender youth, Pollock and Eyre (2012) found that the initial stage of adolescent trans identity emerged as the young people experienced an evolving sense of their own male gender. The young trans men described their growing understanding of themselves as being shaped by the onset of puberty and their emerging sexuality as well as interactions with peers and discovering the stories of other transgender individuals.

This was followed by a moment when they recognized their own transgender identity (the second stage of trans identity development). In the third stage, the young men moved from this more internal process out into the external world. The developmental tasks revolved around a period of social adjustment when they were integrating their male identity and exploring new ways of interacting with the world around them.

During trainings, I am often asked, "Why there are so many more transgender children and adolescents today than before?" Part of my response is that I don't necessarily know that there are more transgender youth than there were in the past; perhaps transgender people simply feel safe enough today to come out at younger ages than they did in the past.

Most transgender adults today report having at least some sense of being different as a child, and many suspected, or knew, this difference was about their gender somehow not fitting their birth-assigned sex. With the increasing visibility of transgender children, adolescents, and adults in the media and so many of their stories being recorded on social media, trans youth are more likely to be able to name what feels different about them. In fact, for Pollock and Eyre's (2012) participants, learning about the existence of other FTM transgender people was a critical link in recognizing their transgender identity. When they learned about the existence of other transgender people, they recognized themselves. This recognition can occur at much younger ages today, whereas in the past, trans people were largely invisible.

Another change that contributes to transgender adolescents coming out is the fact that historical representations of transgender people reflected deviance and criminality. As discussed earlier in the context of psychiatry, transgender identity was abnormal and deficient. Even more, it was a mental illness, and this is how transgender people were portrayed in the media. "Successful" transgender adults who lived engaged and fulfilling lives were largely "stealth." Media portrayals were the only ones most youth and adults generally saw. The few visible trans people tended to be those outed by the psychiatric or criminal justice system as people who lived unhappy and tragic lives. Today, trans youth have access to many more narratives of the possibilities of transgender life. They are able to see transgender people with families and careers, enjoying their lives.

The Emergence of Trans Identity in Adolescence

As discussed earlier, young children with diverse gender expression may or may not identify as transgender when they grow up. In contrast, youth who come out as trans during adolescence typically continue to identify with their affirmed gender into adulthood. In one study of 70 young adolescents given puberty blockers to alleviate their dysphoria, all youth continued to identify with their affirmed gender and began masculinizing or feminizing hormone therapy at a later date (de Vries, Steensma, Doreleijers, & Cohen-Kettenis, 2010).

The onset of puberty leads to the development of greater gender consistency among young people. There is an increasing understanding that who you are now in terms of gender is who you will be as an adult. This is one reason trans identity often emerges more clearly in adolescence as opposed to gender variance or gender diversity. Young children who were more gender-diverse may begin to identify as transgender when they enter adolescence.

As discussed earlier, gender is not always a central identity for young trans children. Some youth report not thinking about gender much until adolescence. Other gender-diverse children imagine they will become the gender they identify with when they grow up rather than their current birth-assigned sex.

When I asked Tommy, a 14-year-old trans boy, to tell me about his experience of gender when he was younger, he said, "You know how on your birthday, you have a cake with candles? And you're supposed to make a wish before you blow out the candles and if you blow them all out, the wish will come true? Well, every year my wish was to wake up in a boy's body, but it never happened." Even at 14 years, the tone in his voice as he described this suggested he was still astonished that his wish never came true.

For Tommy and other prepubertal trans youth, as secondary sex characteristics begin to develop for their peers and themselves, the reality of becoming an adult man or woman, as defined by their birth sex, becomes suddenly undeniable.

It is difficult, if not impossible, for most cisgender therapists to comprehend the degree and intensity of these feelings for transgender adolescents. When young transgender boys look in the mirror and see breasts developing, their gender dysphoria shoots through the roof. It becomes almost impossible to get dressed to go to school in the morning because none of their shirts fit right. No matter what they do, those breasts are visible to others. This is why transgender teenage boys bind their chests—with binders made for this purpose if they can afford them; if not, they use Ace bandages or duct tape. The horror of beginning to menstruate is almost unimaginable.

The stakes are no less high for teenage transgender women. Watching their peers develop facial hair, hearing their own voice start to crack, waking up to a wet dream—each of these experiences creates a sense of overwhelming anxiety and panic. The changes occurring in their bodies are completely out of their control. There is nothing they can do to stop a spontaneous erection from occurring.

The panic that accompanies this crisis contributes to elevated risk among transgender adolescents. Facing an adult life in the world as someone you do not recognize places these teenagers at high risk of drug and alcohol use, self-harming behavior, eating disorders, and other behaviors in an effort to manage their anxiety and block out what is happening to their bodies and their lives (Almeida et al., 2009; Diamond et al., 2011; Grossman & D'Augelli, 2007; Mustanski et al., 2014).

Alongside this internal dysphoria and distress are the pressures trans youth encounter to present themselves in gender-normative and expected ways—for teenage girls to look and act like girls and teenage boys to look and act like boys in ways that align with their birth-assigned sex. As discussed earlier, while there is a certain latitude for young girls to be tomboys, as they reach adolescence they are expected to feminize their appearance and behavior and start becoming young women. In a heteronormative culture, this means teenage girls are supposed to become interested in makeup, jewelry, and getting their nails done. They're supposed to begin noticing boys and caring about what they think. Navigating these enforced social norms unquestionably creates tremendous discomfort for male-identified transgender yout.

Female-identified transgender teens move into adolescence where expectations about masculinity suddenly intensify. In our world, teenage boys are unequivocally men. Real men are supposed to be strong and independent, capable of taking care of themselves and the women around them. Real men walk and talk and dress like men. Real men no longer need others for emotional support. While there has never been much room for their femininity, the consequences of this escalate in adolescence. Masculinity is enforced verbally and physically. Any trace of femininity leads to punishment by other men.

In this increasingly gendered environment, transgender teens are forced to develop a false self in order to survive. Moving through the world in this false self means that they are not visible or seen by others. No one, not even those closest to them, really knows them. This, in and of itself, creates a tremendous sense of isolation for transgender youth. They are present, but not fully present. They may have friends, but the friends' acceptance cannot fully be trusted because they know the friends do not really know them. The same is true for their family. This false self must be maintained at all costs.

During this period when the teen is closeted about their affirmed gender, sometimes this false self is manifested by becoming unusually and even intensely gender-conforming. The adolescent may assume a hypermasculinity or hyperfemininity that can serve a number of functions. This extreme gender conformity may represent an attempt to align with their birth-assigned sex in an effort to fit in with peers. It may represent one final attempt to become the gender they understand others expect them to be. In this context, the teen may say to themselves, "Let me try one more time to be a girl/boy. Maybe I just haven't tried hard enough before. If I can't make it work, at least I'll know I tried hard enough." In other cases, the gender conformity can serve to deflect harassment and bullying that the teen has experienced as a result of their diverse gender expression. This period of hyperconformity often confuses family members and professionals when the teen later comes out as transgender.

Coming out alleviates some of the internal stressors a trans adolescent experiences. They no longer need to rigidly maintain a false self. If there is some familial and peer support, they are able to begin expressing their affirmed gender through hairstyle, dress, and mannerisms. They can begin going by a name and pronouns that match their affirmed gender—at least with peers, even if parents are not quite there yet.

However, many transgender teenagers do not experience the support of their families, or even peers. Parental rejection takes a tremendous toll on transgender teens. All of us want the people who brought us into this world to love and accept us. Rejection never feels good. Parental denial—when parents refuse to acknowledge or simply ignore their child's trans identity—can be just as painful. The consequences for transgender adolescents in these situations are clear. They are much more likely to abuse drugs and alcohol, drop out of school, engage in risky sexual behaviors, or attempt suicide by the time they are young adults (Diamond et al., 2011; Grossman & D'Augelli, 2007; Ignatavicius, 2013; Ryan, Huebner, Diaz, & Sanchez, 2009).

In addition, transgender adolescents are at high risk for harassment and bullying from other teenagers (Grossman, D'Augelli, Howell, & Hubbard, 2006; Grossman, D'Augelli, & Salter, 2006; Sausa, 2005). Even when there is no overt harassment, trans youth often encounter unsupportive school settings where teachers refuse to use their affirmed name and pronouns or they are forced to use the restroom that matches their birth-assigned sex. While these microaggressions do not rise to the level of overt bullying, they nonetheless contribute to the inherent stressors trans and gender-diverse youth face.

Microaggressions can be defined as "everyday verbal, nonverbal, and environmental slights, snubs, or insults whether intentional or unintentional, that communicate hostile, derogatory, or negative messages to target persons based solely upon their marginalized group membership" (Sue, 2010a, p. 3). These messages invalidate the experiential reality of trans and gender-diverse youth, demeaning them and communicating that they are lesser human beings. Further, these messages often stigmatize the young person in the context of their peers. Numerous studies indicate that while microaggressions may seem less harmful than more overt aggression, they can have a powerful impact on the psychological well-being of marginalized persons and groups (Sue, 2010a, 2010b; Nadal, 2013).

In a recent study of transgender persons, many participants reported experiencing anger, frustration, sadness, belittlement, and disappointment in the face of microaggressions. Participants expressed how these experiences negatively impacted their interpersonal relationships. Many described these incidents with words like "taxing" or "exhausting," indicating the emotional toll these microaggressions had on their psychological well-being (Nadal, Skolnik, & Wong, 2012).

The fact that these incidents are often "small acts" does not diminish their cumulative effect and demeaning impact and power.

Types of microaggressions that transgender and gender-diverse students typically encounter include denial of their sense of self (their affirmed gender) by continuing to use the birth-assigned name (or legal name) when the trans student has requested the school use their affirmed name, or refusing to use the pronouns that match the student's affirmed gender. Other microaggressions within educational settings include negative language or comments about transgender people, endorsement and/or enforcement of gender-normative culture and behaviors, viewing transgender people as abnormal or deviant, denying the reality of transphobia, physical threat or harassment, and bullying.

The way transgender students are frequently denied bodily privacy reflects another aspect of routine microaggression. Cisgender adults and peers often feel they have permission to ask intrusive personal questions about the trans youth's body, such as, "Do you have a penis or vagina? Are you on hormones? Have you had 'the surgeries' yet?" These personal questions about someone's physical body are not asked of non-transgender youth or adults.

More systemic microaggressions can be rooted in policies that insist that transgender students use the restroom of their birth-assigned sex rather than that of their affirmed gender—sometimes long after the student has transitioned and no longer even "looks like" their birth-assigned sex. When sustained over time, these experiences of microaggression and overt bullying can put trans teens at high risk of isolation from peers, depression, and other mental health concerns (Almeida et al., 2009; Nemoto et al., 2011; Nuttbrock et al., 2010).

Risk Factors

Risky behaviors typically emerge as a strategy for managing the stress associated with gender dysphoria, lack of family acceptance and support, rejection by peers or social isolation, or bullying. Engaging in alcohol and other drug use can alleviate the anxiety or depression generated in the face of these internal and external stressors. Getting high can take the edge off the heightened pressures transgender adolescents feel to fit in with peers. Drinking can lessen the social anxiety caused by trying to ensure people believe your false self is authentic. Getting high and drinking help transgender teens manage their gender dysphoria in moving through the world. They can make it possible to feel comfortable enough to be intimate with one's boyfriend or girlfriend.

Self-harming behaviors are another tool that can help trans teens manage anxiety and depression. The real pain they experience from cutting diminishes the pain felt earlier at school when another student called them a "he-she." Isolating in their room and scratching their arms until they bleed validates the pain they felt in the kitchen when their mother told him, "I don't care what you think. You're my daughter. You were born a girl and you will always be a girl—no matter what you try to do to change that."

Many clinicians are unaware of the development of eating disorders as a strategy for body modification among transgender youth (Goldberg & Ashbee, 2006). Grossman and D'Augelli (2007) define gender dysphoria as a "strong and persistent (long term) discomfort and distress with one's birth sex, gender, and anatomical body." They go on to note that, given this, "body esteem—especially how one feels about one's appearance and weight, and perception of how others think of one's body—assumes importance" (p. 528).

If an adolescent trans boy overeats or binges and becomes fat, his breasts may be less obvious. Overweight, and dressed in baggy jeans and bulky sweatshirts, he may finally be recognized as a guy. Alternately, he may starve himself to become too thin to be seen as a girl anymore. If he loses enough weight, there's the added bonus of menstruation ceasing. For young trans women, that thin, no-hips shape is a dead giveaway for a man. Added body weight can make them appear more femininely shaped. This lessens the daily harassment on the street. It is more likely that they will be read as a woman by the man on the other side of the street and arrive home safely.

Transgender students report the lowest feelings of safety at school (Greytak, Kosciw, & Diaz, 2009). Because they are at increased risk for being the target of verbal or physical bullying at school, transgender youth are more likely to be absent from school, experience diminished academic performance, or drop out before high school graduation (Greytak et al., 2009).

Transgender youth are more likely to engage in compulsive and/or risky sexual behaviors, often as a way to have their affirmed gender identity validated (Garofalo, Deleon, Osmer, Doll, & Harper, 2006). "If you are attracted to me, I must be a beautiful young woman. You must see me as a woman. You see me as a desirable woman." While this validation might feel good for any heterosexual young woman, for young trans women it is a validation of their identity as women. Someone in the outside world believes them. Someone recognizes and acknowledge their true self. The need for this kind of validation increases when trans youth experience rejection from family and peers.

When parents or other caregivers deny a transgender adolescent's affirmed gender identity or refuse to allow the young person to socially or medically transition, some youth run away from home or find themselves thrown out of their homes. Most studies indicate that approximately 20% to 40% of homeless youth identify as LGBT, with transgender youth being disproportionately represented among this population (Durso & Gates, 2012; Shelton, 2015). An estimated two thirds are youth of color (U.S. Department of Health and Human Services, 2014). The most frequently cited factor that led to being homeless was family rejection because of sexual orientation or gender identity.

In the face of rejection, and many times ridicule and abuse, some trans youth can no longer tolerate the manifestations of this rejection and self-initiate leaving home. They may want to disconnect before the final rejection of being thrown out occurs. Some teens feel the need to seek relief by escaping for a time. Other trans youth leave rejecting and abusive homes because they want something better for themselves or to find a community where they can safely be themselves.

Nearly three quarters of trans youth experience verbal abuse from their families. More than one quarter report that they have been slapped, beaten, or hit very hard. Thirteen to twenty percent report being punched, kicked, or pushed very hard (Grossman & D'Augelli, 2007). Young trans women (typically perceived early on as gender-variant boys) were at highest risk for physical abuse within their homes (Koken, Bimbi, & Parsons, 2009). Studies indicate a significant correlation between more verbal and physical abuse and suicide attempts (Grossman & D'Augelli, 2007; Ryan et al., 2010).

Nearly one-third of homeless LGBT youth have experienced some kind of physical, emotional, or sexual abuse while still living at home (Durso & Gates, 2012). Given these statistics, it is not surprising that homeless transgender youth experience lower levels of physical and mental health compared to other homeless youth (Durso & Gates, 2012; U.S. Department of Health and Human Services, 2014).

Another factor contributing to increased homelessness among transgender youth is the discrimination they frequently encounter in the areas of obtaining and maintaining employment and finding stable housing. Most transgender youth who are homeless encounter significant difficulty accessing trans-competent and affirmative health care. Being unemployed and unable to obtain employment due to discrimination, coupled with homelessness, severely limits access to education among transgender youth—a factor that only perpetuates their homelessness. For homeless youth, generally unemployed, the costs associated with obtaining required paperwork frequently delays or precludes their being able to legally change their name and identity documents. This in turn increases opportunities for further marginalization and discrimination (Shelton, 2015).

Given the extent of these internal and external stressors, it is not surprising that trans youth are at increased risk for suicidal ideation and attempts (Almeida et al., 2009; Diamond et al., 2011; Kelleher, 2009). Suicide risks are higher among trans youth who have been victimized, bullied, and harassed or have experienced parental or familial rejection (Grant et al, 2010; Diamond et al., 2011; Nuttbrock et al., 2010). In one study, 45% of transgender youth reported thoughts about suicide and 26% had attempted suicide (Grossman & D'Augelli, 2007). In the face of these compounding risk factors, clinical interventions must focus on strengthening coping skills and resilience with transgender youth.

Resilience

Despite these stressors and very real risk factors, most transgender adolescents are incredibly resilient. The Merriam-Webster Online Dictionary defines resilience in two ways: the ability to become strong, healthy, or successful again after something bad happens; or the ability of something to return to its original shape after it has been pulled, stretched, pressed, or bent (Resilience, n.d.).

Take a moment to reflect on the courage it takes to announce to the world that you are not who everyone perceives you to be, that your true gender identity does not match the sex you were assigned at birth or the gender others have known you to be. Imagine the risk involved when a transgender child or adolescent defines themselves in opposition to what has always been assumed to be true about their identity, in opposition to what they have always been told is true about who they are. Consider the internal sense and strength of self required to affirm and maintain your understanding of yourself in the face of others' persistent denial of your truth.

I see this resilience every day in my clinical practice—the way a high school freshman navigates coming out in the middle of her school year; the way a young trans man negotiates his first year in college where he is stealth; the way a 17-year-old trans woman shows up every day for work at a large clothing store prior to obtaining her legal name change even though the job roster continues to list her birth name and regularly outs her as trans; the 13-year-old trans boy who adamantly insists his father find him a new therapist because his previous one knew little about gender identity and dismissed his questions and concerns; the unemployed 21-year-old trans woman so determined to see a transgender therapist that she kept calling her managed care Medicaid insurance company until they finally agreed to sign a single-case agreement with me so she could afford to see me for therapy.

In contrast to earlier experiences of internalized shame, resilience among transgender youth is enhanced as they acquire a sense of pride in their identity. For trans youth of color, this includes developing pride in each aspect of their identity—both race and gender (Singh & McKleroy, 2011). In a study of emerging young adults, Woodford, Paceley, Kulick, and Hong (2015) noted that as Queer identity is strengthened and becomes more salient, anxiety symptoms decrease.

Peer relationships are important for all adolescents. Social support, including having supportive and accepting friends and access to trans-friendly groups and activities, is a strong facilitator of resilience among transgender adolescents (Budge, Adelson, & Howard, 2013; Liu & Mustanski, 2012; Mustanski, Newcomb, & Garofalo, 2011; Singh & McKleroy, 2011).

When transgender youth come out, surrounded by love and acceptance, stressors and concomitant risk factors generally diminish. There is still the challenge of negotiating who you are in the world—of your body not looking like it should, of others knowing you are transgender—but when those closest to you support you, these stressors become more manageable. This is reflected in the fact that trans adolescents growing up in accepting families experience fewer risk factors and greater mental and emotional well-being as they move into young adulthood (Bouris et al., 2010; Needham & Austin, 2010; Ryan et al., 2010; Simons et al., 2013; Singh & McKleroy, 2011).

Gender-Diverse and Nonbinary Youth

Gender-diverse and nonbinary youth face certain challenges that can differ from those encountered by trans youth who gender transition. Virtually every time we fill out an application, we are asked to check male or female. There are no other choices. When you lined up along the hallways to use the bathroom in first grade, it was boys on one wall and girls against the other. There were no other choices. Trans youth who identify as nonbinary are forced over and over to make a choice when neither choice adequately represents their identities. This means confronting the message on a daily basis that you don't fit in—anywhere.

Not only do you not fit in; you do not even really exist. Not on your driver's license. Not on your college or job application. There is simply no way for nonbinary youth to check a box that reflects who they are.

Given that gender is ubiquitous in our society, people gender us constantly. While it has begun to change, much of the time when we interact with customer service personnel, we are "Sir'd" or "Ma'am'd." The outcome of this for nonbinary youth is that they are continually being misgendered. This contributes not only to a feeling of not fitting in but also a profound sense of being invisible in the world. If there is no language, no pronouns, that adequately reflect who I am, then I am invisible. There is no way to address me; "Mr.," "Mrs.," "Ms." do not describe who I am. There are no pronouns that work adequately when you discuss my progress in a teacher's meeting—"he," "she," but not me.

Given that their identity is neither male nor female, some nonbinary youth use more recent gender-neutral pronouns, such as "zie" for he or she and "hir" for him or her. Some nonbinary youth use plural pronouns, like "they," "them," and "theirs." Other youth prefer not to use pronouns at all and simply use their name.

Nonbinary youth often find themselves not taken seriously by adults. They are frequently told they are "just confused" about gender, or that there simply are only two genders and sooner or later they will have to accept this. They are told you can play around like this while you're in high school, but once you get into the real world, you'll have to choose one gender or the other. They are told, "People in the work world are not going to play along with your little gender pronoun games." Adults, even medical and mental health providers, may ask, "Why do you have to make things so complicated [for me]? Why can't you just choose a box?" Or, they are sometimes admonished for "just being difficult."

The gender-fluid or nonbinary adolescents and young adults with whom I work struggle not so much with themselves and their own identities. Instead, they struggle with how to live in a world constructed and still operating around a binary gender system—a system that does not acknowledge their existence and insists on putting them in a binary box despite the lack of fit. While they have claimed a place underneath the large trans umbrella, most of these young people do not want to gender transition in the traditional sense of moving from their birth-assigned sex to living in the opposite/their affirmed gender. Instead, they simply want a world where gender matters less or doesn't matter at all. They want a world where there are multiple genders, or no gender. Despite this, we have often had conversations where they grappled with whether or not to gender transition simply because it would be easier to live in the world as a young man or young woman rather than as someone who is gender-fluid or nonbinary.

As mentioned previously, in June 2016, a judge in the Circuit Court in Multnomah County, Oregon, ruled that nonbinary is a legal gender and that individuals may use nonbinary as a legal sex classification rather than choosing male or female (Mele, 2016). This may be the first step in our lifetime toward the world these nonbinary youth envision.

Trans Youth of Color

While all transgender youth encounter moments of discrimination or marginalization as they move through the world, trans youth of color routinely experience multiple facets of stigma and marginalization. For example, a white transgender young adult or a white nonbinary teenager may not be hired for a job because of discrimination against transgender people. Yet, a Black or Latino transgender adolescent may encounter discrimination in terms of their trans identity, their racial identity, or both. A 17-year-old African American trans woman may experience negative stereotyping or stigma on three levels—her racial identity, her transgender identity, or her gender as a woman. In situations like this, it may be difficult or even impossible for a transgender young person to determine which aspect of their stigmatized identities resulted in the discrimination or marginalization.

The salience of different aspects of a transgender youth's identity can vary based on the immediate context. For example, an African American transgender male college freshman who transitioned during high school may no longer experience routine discrimination due to his transgender identity. Being seen consistently as a man at this point typically renders his transgender history or identity invisible.

Yet his racial identity is never invisible, leaving him open to ongoing experiences of racial microaggressions, stigma, and discrimination. Being consistently read as a young man in the world, he can choose to be stealth with peers, but he cannot choose to be stealth as a black man. Forced to continually navigate both racism and transphobia in the context of the dominant culture, transgender youth of color often face day-to-day realities that vary significantly from the lived experiences of white transgender children and adolescents.

Transgender youth of color often also experience racism within LGBTQ communities. Historically, and often even today, the visible LGBT community has been predominately white. White LGBT individuals experience white privilege in a white dominant culture the same way white cisgender individuals experience privilege around racial identity. White LGBT individuals are socialized in an environment that is rife with negative images and stereotypes about people of color. Given this, systemic racism and personal racial prejudice can be just as prevalent within LGBT communities as they are in the larger culture.

The impact of this can be particularly difficult for trans youth of color. Attending a transgender adolescent support group may mean feeling incredibly accepted and included in some ways. However, if the group is predominantly white, the young person may feel out of place and disconnected in terms of racial identity. Their peers may relate to the shared struggles as trans youth, but not to the added dynamics of intersecting racism.

White group facilitators or program directors frequently do not address intersectionality within the context of transgender youth. Consequently, these challenges go unaddressed for trans youth of color, increasing their sense of isolation. Unaddressed internalized racism among white-identified mental health professionals means that encounters with stigma or marginalization may be just as frequently perpetrated by adult youth workers and mental health providers, even if unconsciously or unintentionally.

Simultaneously, the nature of systemic racism means that marginalization and discrimination are typically embedded within program planning, structures, and governance. Consequently, many trans youth of color experience the same degree of racism within LGBT and trans settings as they do in the larger world.

Homophobia and Transphobia Within Racial/Ethnic Communities

For people of color, their family and larger racial ethnic community often serve as significant sources of support for navigating the realities of racism in the world. As children grow up, their families socialize them and prepare them with the tools needed for staying safe in the world and not internalizing the negative attitudes and beliefs of the dominant culture.

This is generally not the case for transgender youth of color, in terms of their trans identity. While they may experience support around their racial identity, they may encounter prejudice and discrimination around their transgender identity. In accepting families of color, there are ways parents connect the dots between encounters with trans oppression and their lived experience of racial oppression. These connections form a strength they are able to offer their trans children and adolescents. While the information and vignettes in this book and others can be helpful, most parents do not share the same lived realities of navigating trans-prejudice or discrimination.

Communities of color are not more transphobic than white communities. There are individuals and families within all racial/ethnic communities that do not understand the differences between biological sex, gender expression, gender identity, and sexual orientation. Many times, family rejection may be rooted in this lack of education and accurate information can facilitate greater understanding and acceptance.

Lack of family acceptance of transgender youth of color may also be rooted in fear. While white parents also worry about their children's life possibilities and safety, there is an added dimension when the young person experiences discrimination and stigma in terms of both racial and gender identity.

Another dynamic trans youth of color encounter is the phenomenon of being perceived as representing their entire racial group. When a person of color does something that is perceived as wrong, their choices and behavior are frequently seen as typical of their entire racial/ethnic community. For example, when an African American teenager is arrested for drug possession or vandalizing property, their actions are often viewed by the white dominant culture as proof that all black teenagers are drug addicts or delinquents. Yet when a white adolescent is arrested for burglary or a white young adult enters a church and murders nine adults during Bible study, the cloak of white privilege means that the individual white young person's actions are never viewed as representative of white people as a whole.

The systemic reality of these dynamics places a higher burden on youth of color to not act in ways that could reflect badly on their racial community. Both trans youth and their families struggle with how these higher expectations impact them. This pressure can add to the challenges of coming out for transgender youth of color and sometimes delays their coming out. As a whole, youth of color are significantly less likely to have disclosed being LGBTQ to their parents. In one study, while about 80% of white youth were out to parents, only 71% of Latinos, 61% of African Americans, and 51% of Asians and Pacific Islanders (APIs) had shared their identities with their parents (Grov & Bimbi, 2006). What appears to be rejection by families of color may be an embedded struggle around the ways a trans youth's gender identity might negatively reflect on the larger racial minority community or compound the family's experiences of discrimination and oppression in the world.

Within immigrant families, rejection of transgender children and youth can intersect with the challenges of acculturation processes. Adults tend to be more strongly tied to the culture of origin, while adolescents are typically more acculturated to white American norms and customs. In this context, parents may object to their children's growing Americanism and view being transgender as a white American phenomenon. Education about gender identity and trans youth may not be enough in these situations. Mental health providers and families must also explore the intersections between the needs of the transgender young person and how a seeming lack of acceptance and support may be precipitated by perceived benefits and negative consequences of acculturation.

While much of white, Anglo culture places a high premium on individualization and self-actualization, other cultural groups prioritize familial and communal values. In the latter context, the needs of the family or group may override the needs of one individual member of that group. Valuing the larger unit over the needs of an individual is particularly reflective of many Asian and Latino families and communities. The conflict between the dominant white U.S. culture and ethnic community values can cause trans youth of color to feel torn between these two systems.

When trans youth come out within communities that place a greater premium on the family over the individual, the young person may be perceived as rejecting their ethnic heritage. The compounding nature of societal prejudices toward ethnic minority groups and transgender people may contribute to trans youth delaying their disclosure and/or cause family members to remain silent about a child's disclosure and refrain as long as possible from sharing this information with anyone outside the immediate family. Within Latino cultures, the key role of machismo alongside traditional Roman Catholic beliefs can play a particular role in female-identified trans youth denying their affirmed gender and/or delaying disclosure to family members (U.S. Conference of Mayors, 1996).

The way negative beliefs and attitudes toward trans people can reflect on families may precipitate questions about what parents did to cause this in their children. As a result, within Asian American and Pacific Islander communities, trans youth may feel they have shamed their family by diverging from normative cultural expectations about biological sex and gender identity as well as norms of marrying and having children (Wade, 1991).

Higher Risk for Discrimination, Harassment, and Violence

Each of the above dynamics plays a role in whether a transgender young person of color comes out, how "out" they choose to be, and/or the repercussions of being out as transgender. White trans youth generally experience only one marginalized identity; this means greater privilege to be openly transgender with fewer risks of harassment, police surveillance, and transphobic violence. Intersecting and compounding experiences of oppression place trans youth of color at much higher risk for external stressors and isolate them from numerous avenues for obtaining affirmation and support (Garofalo et al., 2006). Transgender women of color consistently face the highest rates of violence and abuse (NCAVP, 2015).

GLSEN's biennial National School Climate Surveys consistently indicate that transgender youth are harassed and assaulted at higher levels than their non-transgender peers. Almost all transgender students were verbally harassed (e.g., called names or threatened) during the 2013 school year because of their sexual orientation (89%) and their gender expression (87%) (Kosciw, Greytak, Palmer, & Boesen, 2014). Over half had been physically harassed (e.g., pushed or shoved), and many trans students had been physically assaulted (e.g., punched, kicked, or injured with a weapon) in school that year because of their sexual orientation (28%) and their gender expression (26%). While transgender youth of color are harassed for their gender identity and expression as often as the general transgender population, the additional reality of hearing racist language from school staff (54%) and fellow students (23%) puts additional stress on transgender students of color (Dunn & Moodie-Mills, 2012; Singh, 2013).

The risks of sexual exploitation among trans youth of color were also elevated. In one study, more than half of ethnic minority transgender youth had experienced forced sex, while almost 60% had traded sex for money or resources. These youth were consequently also at high risk of becoming HIV positive (Garofalo et al., 2006).

In light of the challenges inherent to intersecting identities alongside concomitant increased risks, the resilience of trans youth of color is indisputable. Citing Munoz (1999, p. 37), Saketopoulou (2011) states,

> I always marvel at the ways in which nonwhite children survive in a white supremacist U.S. culture that preys on them. I am equally in awe of the ways in which queer children navigate a homophobic public sphere that would rather they did not exist. The [psychic] survival of children who are both queer and racially identified [as nonwhite] is nothing short of staggering.

Effective Work With Trans Youth of Color

An important consideration when exploring LGBTQ or trans youth groups or programs for trans youth of color is the racial/ethnic demographics within these programs. Will a Latino trans man be the only trans man of color in the group? If so, how might this impact him? How might it affect his ability to relate to peers and obtain the support he needs and deserves? Will the racial/ethnic demographics of the group facilitate an experience of greater connection, or will they reinforce his sense of being different?

There is no single right or wrong answer. It is entirely possible that a Latino trans boy will feel a part of a group of white trans male peers. On the other hand, he may not. What is essential is that these dynamics be addressed directly with the young person so they can make an informed choice about participation and are prepared to navigate the racial/ethnic context of the group. Similar dynamics can be true when a young trans woman participates in an LGBT youth group where the other young women are all cisgender peers.

After a young person joins a group, it is important to periodically check in about their experiences within the setting, including questions about any microaggressions directed toward the young person. It is also helpful to be attentive to ways a trans youth of color may feel torn between aspects of their identity or the multiple communities of which they are a part. Within this context, an Asian American trans young woman may feel she needs to prove to peers and/or adults that she is trans enough or Asian enough or feel she must prove her allegiance to both communities.

When working with trans youth from a different cultural background or community than that of the mental health professional, the clinician must watch and listen closely for the varied ways culture shapes the values, beliefs, customs, and traditions of both the transgender young person and their family. These aspects of the young person's cultural context must be integrated into the therapeutic process and/or program activities.

Given the intersections of race and gender identity in the lives of trans youth of color, effective interventions must incorporate knowledge of and sensitivity to both aspects of their identities. Mental health professionals must bring a nuanced understanding of the ongoing impact of systemic racism as well as transphobia within the larger culture. When working with transgender youth of color and their families, the focus can never just be about transgender identity alone. These young people and their families do not have the luxury of a single oppression in their daily lives.

Effective clinical work must incorporate the multiple aspects of the trans young person's identity and intersecting oppressions. The clinician needs to initiate conversations that explore the varying ways trans youth of color experience stigma and oppression, not only within the broader world but also within the Queer community. Youth of color may justifiably be anxious about these conversations—particularly in the presence of white mental health professionals. These conversations can only be effective when white mental health providers actively assume responsibility for unpacking their own internalized racism and work to recognize, acknowledge, and take responsibility for the racial privilege they hold within the larger society. Moving out from here, the work must focus on cultivating increased coping skills so that trans youth of color can sustain a positive sense of self and effectively navigate the world around them.

A recent study exploring resilience strategies among trans youth of color illuminated several ways these young people navigate the intersections of discrimination and prejudice toward both racial and gender identities (Singh, 2013). The first strategy highlighted how the young people were able to draw on their intersecting racial and gender identities to define themselves rather than allowing themselves to be defined by others. The second strategy revolved around their awareness of "adultism," defined as "the system where adults hold power and privilege in youths' lives" (p. 697). It was within this context that the young people experienced the greatest degree of racism and trans-prejudice. This dynamic led to the development of the third strategy for resilience—the young people's determination to learn to advocate for themselves within educational settings. This often included becoming student leaders.

Connections within LGBTQ communities and finding a place to belong within these communities formed another key aspect of their resilience. The final strategy involved the use of social media as a vehicle for developing greater understanding of the intersections of their identities. Interactions on social media also enabled the youth to broaden their support network beyond their immediate geographical location. The last two strategies are relational in nature, suggesting that a key aspect of their resilience involves making connections with others like them and finding a community in which they feel they belong. Maintaining a strong sense of their intersecting identities and becoming advocates for themselves and their communities strengthened their resilience.

PART 2

Trans Youth and the World Around Them

CHAPTER 7

Helping Families

W HEN I OPENED MY EMAIL THAT MORNING, THE FIRST
line read, "Please let us know if you can help our daughter,
but mostly her parents." It was from the father of a 13-year-old daughter who had sent an email to her parents two days earlier coming
out as a transgender boy. The daughter's disclosure was a complete
surprise to both parents. They knew very little about transgender
issues, had never met another trans person, and were totally confused by their daughter's announcement. What little they had heard
about transgender people was negative and made them worried for
her safety if this was true. The father was reaching out for support on
behalf of himself and his wife. They wanted to know how they should
respond. Could they set up an appointment to talk with me that
week? The urgency in their email was both clear and understandable.

Phone calls and emails like this are typical in my clinical practice. The past chapter focused on the coming-out process for gender-nonconforming and transgender youth, including social and
medical transition. However, coming out as transgender is not something children or adolescents do alone. A young person's disclosure
always involves the entire family. When children and teens socially
transition, parents, siblings, grandparents, and other extended family
members necessarily must also come out. In the same way that trans
youth cannot transition unnoticed, coming out as the parent, sibling,
or extended family of a transgender child is a very public act. Consequently, work with trans and gender nonconforming children and
adolescents always necessitates work with their families.

Recent research documents the pivotal role family acceptance
plays in the well-being of LGBT adolescents as they move into adult-

hood. This chapter begins with a brief overview of that research and then explores the challenges of the coming-out process for parents when their children disclose that they are transgender. The chapter focuses on the initial stage of work with families, including the range of emotional responses parents may experience, guidelines for supporting families as they navigate these feelings, information families need to support their children, and tasks parents must engage in as part of the coming-out process for the entire family. The chapter concludes with suggestions for engaging families.

Families come in many different shapes, sizes, colors, and configurations. The role of being a parent is taken on by biological parents, foster and adoptive parents, grandparents, aunts and uncles, older siblings, straight parents, Queer parents, and others. Children can have one parent, two parents, three parents, four parents, or more parents. Some families look like each other, while others do not. My oldest daughter once posted a family selfie from a family celebration with the caption "This is what a straight, gay, trans, multiracial family looks like!" This infinitely diverse set of possibilities forms the backdrop for my discussion of working with families of transgender children and adolescents. While I primarily use the word "parent," my understanding includes any and all of the primary caregivers in a young person's life.

As acknowledged earlier, the first thing people want to know about a child is whether "it's" a boy or a girl. The minute our child enters our life, she or he is sexed/gendered. In the earlier discussion on gender expression, we noted all the ways a child's world is gendered—from colors and clothing and hairstyles to baby toys, dolls, or action figures to hobbies. I participated in our school band from third grade through high school graduation, and even instruments were gendered—girls played clarinet or flute; boys played trumpet and trombone.

This means that from the moment our child arrives, we see them as our son or our daughter—one or the other, never both or neither. Despite rapidly growing transgender visibility, few parents think about whether their unborn child's birth-assigned sex will match their gender identity as the child grows up. There are parents today who may wonder about their children's sexual orientation, but rarely their gender identity.

A recent interaction between my colleagues and their obstetrician reflects the exception. When my colleagues were anticipating their first child, they chose not to know the baby's sex prior to birth. During a prenatal visit shortly before the due date, the obstetrician laughingly said to the dad, "Well, pretty soon now you'll know whether you have a son or daughter." Being trans-savvy and eager to upset the doctor's binary assumption, my colleague responded, "Well, yes, we'll know their sex, but it may be a while before we really know their gender." The obstetrician stared blankly for a moment, then quickly said, "Yes, of course."

As our children become part of our lives, our mind automatically begins to imagine their future. It's as if a movie of our child's life begins to play inside our heads. What will he or she look like when they start preschool? When they enter kindergarten? What kind of teenager will they be? We may picture their high school graduation, first job, or their wedding. Imagining their future is almost hardwired into us. However, among the many possible images that may cross our mind, few of us imagine our child coming out as transgender. Despite the increasing visibility of transgender people, when the doctor says she's a girl, we assume she will always be our daughter, and if he's a boy, we assume he's our son for life.

As these infants become toddlers and then preschoolers, some parents do notice gender-diverse behavior. A few may even question their child's gender identity at this early age. However, their child's disclosure about being transgender is completely unexpected for other parents. Either way, gender-diverse expression and disclosure are often confusing for parents, as reflected in the email at the beginning of this chapter. Some adolescents come out first as lesbian, gay, or bisexual and later disclose they are really transgender. Regardless of how parents learn about their child's trans identity, they typically experience a wide range of emotional responses, both initially and over time.

As a starting point, most parents need information about the differences between the basic concepts of sex, gender identity, gender expression, and sexual orientation as reviewed in Chapter 1. They often need education about the range of norms surrounding gender expression and the ways expression differs from gender identity. Like other people, parents may conflate sex and gender identity and fail to grasp that these concepts represent distinct aspects of ourselves. It can be a sea change for many parents to begin seeing gender identity as distinct from biological sex. Parents may confuse sexual orientation and gender identity, thinking being trans is the same as being gay.

Only a handful of parents have transgender people within their own families or social circles, and thus most need education about transgender people and their lives. Often the only information families have is from the media, much of which is still stereotypical and negative. Virtually all parents need education about transgender children and youth, including the material covered in the first section about gender diversity and nonbinary youth, social transitions, and the steps involved in medical interventions.

Some families are immediately accepting of their child's transgender or gender-diverse identity, even though they may have many questions. Other parents initially respond with denial or rejection and struggle to reach a place of understanding and acceptance. Regardless of their initial response, helping families navigate the journey from their child's disclosure to full acceptance and support is a crucial aspect of what good mental health providers do (Malpas, 2011).

The Critical Role of Family Acceptance

Recent research documents the pivotal role of family acceptance for LGBTQ adolescents in terms of their risk and/or well-being as young adults (Ryan et al., 2009; Ryan et al., 2010). While acceptance and support from peers and other adults is important, these recent studies indicate that family acceptance is the critical mediating variable for LGBTQ young adults' mental, emotional, and physical well-being. When families fail to communicate acceptance, Queer youth face enormous risks for depression, anxiety, drug and/or alcohol abuse, unsafe sex, and suicide attempts. In light of this information, engaging parents and other caregivers becomes even more essential.

Envisioning family acceptance on a continuum, at one end there are families who are accepting of, and perhaps even celebrate, their children's transgender or gender-diverse identity. At the opposite end of the continuum are families who deny and/or reject their child's transgender identity or affirmed gender. Between these endpoints, families are found all along the continuum—less rejecting, tolerant, somewhat accepting, moderately accepting.

The Family Acceptance Project studied LGBT young adults, ages

21 to 24 years old, who came out to at least one parent during adolescence (http://familyproject.sfsu.edu). The youth who grew up in highly rejecting families consistently experienced lower self-esteem and increased mental health problems such as anxiety and depression, were more isolated, and felt more hopeless about their lives when they reached young adulthood (Ryan et al., 2009; Ryan et al., 2010).

In terms of life-threatening risks, Queer youth growing up in rejecting families were nearly six times as likely to report high levels of depression in young adulthood and more than eight times as likely to have attempted suicide compared to young adults who grew up in accepting families. They were more than three times likely to be using illegal drugs and more than three times as likely to be at high risk for HIV and other sexually transmitted diseases by the time they were 21 to 24 years old (Ryan et al., 2009; Ryan et al., 2010). These studies and others overwhelmingly document the significance of family acceptance in the ongoing well-being of Queer adolescents, including trans and gender-diverse youth (Eisenberg & Resnick, 2006; Needham & Austin, 2010).

This knowledge underscores our mandate to facilitate acceptance within families. Given the high number of suicide attempts in the wake of family rejection, the very lives of trans and gender-diverse children and adolescents depend on this work. Facilitating acceptance when families have staked out a position of rejection can seem daunting. Yet additional data from the Family Acceptance Project study offers incredibly good news. We don't necessarily need to move families from totally rejecting to fully accepting before seeing significant decreases in their young adult children's risk factors. Even moderate movement toward tolerance within a family makes a difference (Ryan et al., 2010). Each step along the continuum away from rejection and toward acceptance decreases LGBTQ young adult risk factors.

An equally important part of the Family Acceptance Project study included interviews with parents and youth. These conversations identified specific things parents did that communicated acceptance to their children as well as specific messages and practices that communicated rejection to their LGBTQ adolescents (Ryan et al., 2010).

Most of us have ideas about what parents of transgender young people might say or do that would communicate acceptance or rejection. However, having specific practices that are documented to increase or decrease risk factors opens new possibilities with these families. The research provides specific examples we can use with families to help parents assess the degree to which they are currently communicating acceptance or rejection. The quantitative data about risk factors illuminate how their current interactions with their transgender children may increase or decrease their child's well-being as young adults.

This information can shift the conversation with families from our opinion about what trans youth need from their families and open up a discussion of evidenced-based parental practices that increase positive outcomes for their trans children. The following chapter expands on these positive parental practices. It also explores strategies for engaging even rejecting families and building alliances that can contribute to both the immediate and long-term health of transgender youth. Helping parents understand what acceptance looks and sounds like to trans adolescents, and partnering with them to shift their interactions with their children, can make the critical difference for their children being not only healthy, but also literally alive as they enter adulthood.

SELF-ASSESSMENT QUESTIONS FOR PARENTS AND OTHER FAMILY MEMBERS

The questions below and on page 146 are adapted and expanded from research by the Family Acceptance Project (https://familyproject .sfsu.edu).

What can I do to communicate support to our trans child?

- When was the last time I initiated a conversation about my child's gender identity? Am I affirming, verbally and non-verbally, when my child discusses their gender identity?
- How willing am I to acknowledge and respect who they are in this moment - even if I don't fully understand or struggle with tensions between my faith and beliefs and embracing my child's life?
- Do I actively, regularly, and lovingly encourage my child's self-expression?
- Do I fully accept/respect the ways in which my child expresses their gender identity? How do I convey my acceptance/respect?

- Have I requested that all family members (including extended family) respect my child's gender identity and self-expression? Do I defend my child if their gender identity or expression is disrespected by family members?
- Have I explored/inquired about local opportunities for trans/LGBTQ positive and affirming social experiences for my child? Have I asked my child if there are local events, groups, activities that they would like to experience/join?
- Have I read/watched videos about transgender role models? Have I encouraged my child to read/watch videos about transgender role models? Have I discussed transgender role models with my child?
- Do I accept/respect my child's trans/LGBTQ friends/significant others? Do I take the time to get to know these friends/significant others? Do I invite these friends/significant others to our home?
- How do I express my love for my trans child? Am I confident my child knows and feels that I love them? In what ways am I attentive to my child's spoken and unspoken needs?
- Do I use my child's affirmed name and pronouns with them and others? Have I encouraged other family members to use my child's affirmed name or pronouns?
- Do I spend time with/do things with my trans child? Do I laugh with my child?
- Do I express my pride in my child? To them directly? To others in our life?
- Do I believe my child can have a meaningful life as a transgender adult? Do I believe they can find happiness and love?
- How do I help my child cultivate confidence in their unique gifts and abilities?
- Do I express interest in my child's life goals? How do I offer encouragement about ways they might achieve these goals without dictating their path? How do I express belief in my child's ability to achieve their life goals?

Are there ways my trans child might experience rejection from me?

- Do I intentionally or inadvertently dismiss or deny my child's transgender or non-binary identity with them? If so, how does my child respond?
- Do I avoid or refuse to have conversations with my child that focus on their gender identity or expression? If so, why do I do this? If so, how does my child respond?
- Have I pulled back emotionally from my trans child? Am I less verbally or emotionally affectionate with my child since their disclosure?
- Do I intentionally or inadvertently pressure my child to conform to certain cultural or societal feminine or masculine gender norms? Do I ever insist they dress, look, or act more (or less) feminine or masculine? If so, how does my child respond? If so, how do I respond? In what ways can I make amends with my child and strive for greater acceptance of varied gender expressions?
- Have I ever intentionally or inadvertently shamed my child for their appearance and/or self-expression? If so, how did my child respond? If so, how did I respond? Did I acknowledge I was wrong and recommit myself to embracing our diverse gender identities and expression?
- Have I ever intentionally or inadvertently harassed or abused my child because of their transgender identity? If so, how did my child respond? If so, how did I respond? Did I make amends with my child and seek to more fully understand their knowledge of themselves?
- Have I ever intentionally or inadvertently made fun of transgender people? If so and if my child was nearby, how did they respond? If so and if my child was not nearby, what (if anything) did I think and feel while and after making the joke? Do I think it is problematic to make jokes about transgender people?
- Have I ever excluded my child from family activities or events because of their gender identity or expression?
- Have I ever been embarrassed to bring my child to family activities or events because of their appearance,

mannerisms, or interests? Have I ever been afraid that other family members would disapprove of or disrespect my child's gender identity/expression? If yes, how did my child respond to these situations? If yes, how did I respond to these situations?

- Do I dislike my child's LGBTQ/transgender friends because of their gender identity/expression? Am I embarrassed by my child's LGBTQ/transgender friends? Have I ever discouraged my child from spending time with their LGBTQ/trans friends?
- Do I interfere with, or oppose, my child's ability to attend/join trans-affirming youth groups, events, or programs?
- Have I failed to act when my child has been teased or bullied for their self-expression? Have I minimized or ignored their reports of teasing? Have I overtly or subtly blamed my child when they are teased or bullied?
- Do I refuse to use my child's affirmed name or pronouns? Is my use of their affirmed name or pronouns inconsistent? Do I excuse others who fail to use my child's affirmed name or pronouns?
- Do I hold any negative feelings about my child's transgender identity? If so, what feelings do I have? How do I express these feelings? Do I express these feelings when my child is around? How does my child feel about the feelings I have regarding their transgender identity?

When Transgender Children and Youth Come Out

Parents may have a range of emotional responses following their child's self-disclosure. These initial emotional reactions must be explored and navigated before most parents can reach a place of authentic acceptance and support. The varying ways parents learn about their child's trans identity can shape their emotional responses and how these may challenge them and their family.

Sometimes Parents Know Early On

As in the vignette about Joey in Chapter 2, some children's gender-diverse (nonconforming) expression is evident as young as two or three years of age. Like Joey, some of these children announce their transgender identity at this age or shortly thereafter. For many of these parents, attempting to make sense of, and process, their child's gender identity begins while their child is young. A young child's gender diversity may be distressing to some parents, while other parents immerse themselves in learning more about childhood gender development. Parents may search for information on the Internet, look for books about gender-diverse children, or seek out a therapist knowledgeable about gender-diverse expression among young children.

At the same time, childhood gender diversity does not always prepare parents for later disclosure of their child's transgender identity.

> When Jonathan's (natal female) parents first met with me, they told me they had noticed his gender expression varying over the course of early childhood—alternately female, more often somewhat masculine. As progressive, feminist parents, they wanted to raise both children without rigid gender norms or expectations. They bought their son and daughter (Jonathan) both "girls'" and "boys'" books, toys, and games. Consequently, they said they had not been especially concerned when Jonathan's interest and presentation was more masculine. They occasionally wondered if "she" would grow up to be a lesbian and were fine if that turned out to be true.
>
> A year earlier, their "daughter" had come out as bisexual, and both parents were fully supportive. However, these progressive parents were still rocked by their 12-year-old's recent disclosure that "she" was a "boy" and stated that she had known she was a boy since first grade. Having a bisexual or lesbian-identified daughter was a "nonissue" for them, but being transgender was still something they knew little about, and what they had heard in the media worried them. While they never questioned their 12-year-old's ability to know their sexual orientation, they had real reservations about whether "she" could be certain about being a transgender boy.

When Parents Are Surprised

While Jonathan's parents noticed and wondered about his gender expression, a child's disclosure of a transgender identity is completely unexpected for some parents. It is often assumed that you can tell a child is transgender from their gender expression. Yet not all adolescents who come out as transgender exhibited gender-diverse interests and/or behavior during childhood. For some transgender youth, the gender dysphoria between their birth-assigned sex and their internal sense of themselves only fully emerges with the onset of puberty and the development of secondary sex characteristics. Parents in this situation may be surprised and feel unprepared for their child's disclosure.

These parents may experience a sense of shock in the days or weeks following their child's disclosure. As a result, they may shut down and experience few emotions. Alternately, they may be flooded with feelings and experience a sense of disorientation, as if their world and everything they knew to be true was turned upside-down overnight. Many parents may not know how to even begin processing this information about their child.

Most adults in the United States today know lesbian, gay, and bisexual people. They may be coworkers, neighbors, or even family members. Far fewer have someone in their life who identifies as transgender. It is unusual for parents with whom I work to have witnessed someone's gender transition other than in the media. Consequently, for many, a child's disclosure of transgender identity triggers tremendous confusion and numerous questions.

Parents want to know how this happened. How did my child become transgender? How can my daughter suddenly claim to be my son? How can this child I have always known as my son just announce he is really a girl and expect me to embrace him as my daughter? Is this for real? What should I do? In an effort to understand why their child became (or believes they are) transgender, some parents imagine chromosomal or hormonal irregularities are the problem and seek medical testing. However, there is no evidence to support the belief that transgender identity is the result of hormone imbalances (Olson, Schrager, Belzer, Simons, & Clark, 2014).

The parents' initial phone call or email may reflect distress and urgency, as indicated in the email that began this chapter: "Please let us know if you can help our daughter, but mostly her parents." In that email, the father continued:

> On Sunday our 14-year-old daughter told us she is a transgender boy. My wife and I are confused, angry, but mostly lost. We don't

know where to turn but need to get some help. We love our daughter very much and that will never change. We have no idea how to help her with this. Can you help us?

When parents experience this degree of distress, it is not unusual for me to spend 30 to 45 minutes talking with them on our first phone call prior to scheduling an intake.

The complete unexpectedness of their child's disclosure leads some parents to respond with denial. Coupled with their lack of relationships with transgender people and the negative portrayals in the media, these parents simply do not want to believe this could be true. They are flooded with confusion and distress. This isn't happening. She's/He's just confused. This will go away. It's just a phase.

This shock can lead to a sense of numbness that leaves parents feeling disconnected from themselves, their day-to-day lives, and their children. They may act as if nothing happened, refusing to acknowledge the word "transgender" was even spoken. Spouses may not discuss the child's disclosure with each other. There may be no conversation with close friends or family and no further conversation with their child after the initial disclosure. By not speaking about it, the parents can pretend it never happened. Denial can be a common response from extended family members as well.

Janet's mother and her husband lived across the country, and she visited them every summer with the kids for two weeks. Janet told her mother near the end of the year about her 15-year-old son coming out as a transgender girl. Her mother had little to say in response. While they talked twice a week, Janet told me a month later that her mother never mentioned this news again. After that session, Janet raised the topic again with her mother and asked whether her mom had any questions. She reported back that her mother didn't seem to clearly recall their earlier conversation.

Many parents, as well as other adults, experience a sense of disbelief when a child or adolescent discloses their transgender identity. They may tell the young person, "It's just a phase. You'll grow out of it. This may be how you feel right now, but you will change your mind as you grow up." In an earlier vignette, Jasmine's parents had great difficulty accepting their daughter's certainty that she was a woman. Despite her statement insisting that she was "an atypical woman, not an atypical man," from their perspective this was just a new obsession that would pass with time.

Some parents believe gender identity only becomes definite in adulthood. They do not believe it is possible for younger children, or even adolescents, to know they are transgender. When parents respond with disbelief or denial, it is critical to pay attention to the young person's mental and emotional state. Many transgender youth struggle with depression prior to coming out. Encountering denial from their parents can significantly raise the risk that their depression will deepen into hopelessness about the future. It can prompt adolescents to act out in self-destructive ways in an effort to break through their parents' denial and get them to pay attention to what they are telling them about their affirmed identity.

Is It My Fault?

Given historical, and sometimes still maintained, psychiatric theories regarding the etiology of transgender identity as well as the beliefs of some religious traditions, some parents question whether or not it is their "fault" that their children believe they are transgender. The parents worry that they did something wrong as parents. Perhaps they failed to adequately model what it means to be a man or woman and this led to their child's gender confusion or cross-gender identification. These worries are typically accompanied by feelings of guilt or shame. Parents also worry that other people will judge them when they learn their child is transgender. They worry that their own parents or siblings, their child's teachers, or their neighbors will think they failed as parents.

There is a particular way this concern can emerge for single parents and gay and lesbian parents. These parents are cognizant that they challenge normative notions that children need both a father and a mother in order to have appropriate gender role modeling. There is a good chance that someone has questioned or challenged them about this at some point in their journey. In my work with a gay couple who adopted a little girl, one man's parents repeatedly told him he should not go forward with the adoption, asking, "Aren't you worried your daughter won't have a female role model?" This was followed by the admonition that he was just "being selfish" in wanting to parent, because "it's not fair to raise a girl when you know she won't have a mother."

Fear and Anger

Almost all parents grapple with moments of worry, anxiety, and fear after their child's disclosure of being transgender. They are generally afraid for their child's physical safety as well as their emotional and social well-being. We live in a world where transgender people still experience considerable stigma and discrimination. Some trans people experience verbal harassment or physical violence. Other trans people encounter rejection from friends or coworkers. Given these realities, it is not surprising that parents worry. No parent wants to see their child harassed or bullied at school. No parent wants their child to lose a job simply because of who they are. No parent wants their child to be ostracized by classmates, coworkers, or friends. No parent wants their child to be the target of stigma, discrimination, or violence.

Compounding these fears is the fact that many parents (and youth) have no visible models of what a healthy, meaningful adult life can look like for a transgender person. The absence of interaction with transgender friends, neighbors, or coworkers, coupled with stereotypical media representations of transgender people as mentally unstable, unemployed, and targets of violence, means that some parents may not believe a healthy adult life is possible for their child. Religious beliefs condemning transgender people and the continuing diagnosis of gender dysphoria as a psychiatric illness can make it difficult to imagine a positive life ahead for their child. All of these dynamics contribute to the persistence of parental fear when their child comes out as transgender.

Loss and Grief

Many parents experience some sense of loss and grief as they imagine their child no longer being the son or daughter they have always known. At times, this grief can be profound. As discussed earlier, our relationship with our children is inherently gendered. We relate to them as boys/men or girls/women from our first moment with them. We are father and son, or father and daughter. We are mother and daughter, or mother and son. Consequently, it's not surprising that most parents experience loss as they imagine their child's gender transition.

These feelings of loss are sometimes compounded if their transgender child was the parents' "only boy" and now identifies as a girl, or if the "only girl" comes out as a transgender boy. In these situations, parents not only "lose" a son; they lose their only son/daughter. The vignette below illustrates the possible emotional complexities of this family configuration.

> Melissa, 13 years old, and her parents sought me out six months after she came out to them as a transgender girl. She was their only "son." Her father was an auto mechanic and her mom a hair stylist. They lived in a small town and drove several hours each way to see me.
>
> Both parents clearly loved Melissa and were supportive, though it was apparent within the first appointment that her mother was further along the continuum of acceptance than was her father. Melissa was ready to socially transition and impatient with having to come to family therapy before her parents allowed her to move forward. We began our first appointment with all of us together.
>
> As I gathered their family history, they all agreed that Melissa and her father had always been closer than Melissa and her mother were. But since Melissa had disclosed being transgender, Melissa and her mother had begun to spend more time together, while she and her father hung out less frequently. Her mom was teaching her how to put on makeup, and they had begun to look at hairstyles and different clothing styles. As the two of them told me about these new activities, it was clear they both enjoyed them. Melissa was eager to go shopping for new clothes, and her mother indicated that she was open to this.
>
> Melissa's father was quiet while they were talking with me. When I invited him into our conversation, he said that he was still struggling with all of this. He stated that he loved his child and wanted her to be happy, but he wasn't ready to call her Melissa and didn't think he could "handle" seeing her in a skirt. Melissa was upset and impatient with her father's response, and he seemed reluctant to say more.
>
> Later when I met alone with the parents, I came back to the father's reluctance and asked him to tell me more about his

thoughts and feelings since Melissa came out as transgender. I acknowledged that it was clear how much he loved her and I was interested in better understanding what else he might be feeling. As we talked, I learned that Melissa's birth name was Stephen, as was her father's and his father's. He too, had been his father's only son.

The fact that, as in many families, all three generations of "men" held the same first and last names was a source of connection and pride for Melissa's father. When Melissa transitioned, he would lose his son, his only son, his son who bore his name and his father's name, and since the father had no siblings, their family name would end with him. He would never have grandchildren that bore his last name. (Accurate or not, his assumption was if Melissa married she would take her husband's last name.)

Each of these pieces represented a huge loss to Melissa's father in that moment. It was his struggle with these losses that contributed to his reluctance to allow Melissa to socially transition. He loved and accepted Melissa, but he needed time and space to grieve.

Another dynamic at play in this vignette revolves around the father–son relationship being disrupted when Melissa came out. This is mirrored within other families—the parent who struggles most with feelings of loss is often the one whose gender matches the child's birth-assigned sex: father and son, or mother and daughter. There are unique ways this shared gender bond represents a key aspect of the parent's grief, as illustrated by the following vignette.

Just as fathers of trans girls mourn the loss of their sons, mother of trans boys mourn the loss of their daughters. Bart's mother cried throughout several of our early sessions. Her feelings of sadness and loss surfaced again when Bart socially transitioned at school and began going by his affirmed name and male pronouns, and again when Bart cut his hair and began shopping for guys' clothes with his father and older brother instead of his mother. The mom told me their relationship as mother and "daughter" had always been very close. Her "daughter" confided in her about everything. When she was young, they sometimes wore the same outfits. Her "daughter" was their second child, the first being Bart's older brother.

A few months after Bart socially transitioned, his mother arrived at one of our appointments angry and crying. "You won't believe what 'she' did this weekend!" she exclaimed. (Bart's mom was still often using female pronouns.) "My husband and I were out shopping with the younger kids. After we got back home, I noticed a large garbage bag by the back door. When I opened it, inside were all of Bart's pictures. She went through our entire home and took down every single photograph of her that was hanging up or sitting on a coffee table, and threw them in the garbage bag to go out with the trash!"

The mom was hurt and angry. "How can she do this to me? How can she expect me to forget she is my daughter? How could she be so insensitive to my feelings? These pictures are the only thing I have left of my daughter." To this mom, Bart's actions felt like he wanted to erase their relationship as mother and daughter, to deny that it had ever existed.

In some ways, this was what Bart wanted. For transgender adolescents, childhood pictures can be a reminder of the pain they felt when others couldn't see them for who they really were. Seeing them on the coffee table can trigger this grief; it can bring up painful feelings about missing out on their authentic childhood, of not getting to be the little boy or girl they knew they were inside, and all the things they missed out on as a result. Bart was horrified when he looked at the dress he had to wear for his kindergarten picture. He hated seeing the pictures of him and his mom in the matching dresses his mom had made.

From Bart's perspective, these were not his childhood photographs. He was not the three- or five- or eight-year-old in those family pictures. From his perspective, there were no pictures of Bart as a child. Seeing those pictures of a three-, five-, or eight-year-old little girl brought back years of feeling invisible. Bart had asked his mom to put his childhood pictures away the week before. He had tried to tell her how the pictures upset him. But his mother had refused. For her, the loss of her teenage daughter was hard enough; she couldn't face losing her little girl as well. The pictures represented all that was left of her.

Anger may be a significant aspect of grief for some parents. They want to know, "Why me? Why my child? Why our family?" They may be angry at having to make the adjustments required when a child comes out as transgender. They may be angry that their child's transition means they too have to come out; they have to tell their friends and family, neighbors and coworkers, that their son is becoming their daughter, or vice versa.

In working with families of gender-diverse and transgender children, it is critical to create a safe environment for parents to express these emotions without judgment. Without a safe, nonjudgmental space to acknowledge and express their feelings, these emotions can calcify and become barriers that make it difficult for parents to reach a place of full acceptance and support for their transgender child.

Even if their grief, fear, or anger sounds selfish in the moment, it is important to listen as fully as we would to any client's pain. We might think this moment shouldn't be about them—that it should be about their child's well-being. While there is truth to this, the parents' feelings in those moments are still very real. It is also important to remember that grief, loss, anger, and fear do not necessarily equal rejection. Sometimes parents need these initial emotional responses acknowledged and validated before they are able to reach back and recover the unconditional love they have for their child—transgender or not.

Parents may find it difficult to fully express their emotions when their children are present in a session. They may worry about upsetting their children. They may not want their child to hear how afraid they are, or their worries that "no one will ever love my child." These are valid concerns for both parents and children and typically reflect healthy boundaries between the parent–child subsystems. If we want to create a safe environment for parents to express these emotions, we need to meet with them apart from their children. As long as parents feel the need to censor or edit their emotional reactions and struggles, their ability to work through and resolve them is compromised.

Maintaining boundaries between the parent–child subsystems is also critical for the transgender child's emotional safety and well-being. Witnessing their parents' grief or anger can be unhelpful, or even unhealthy, for trans and gender-diverse youth. It can be difficult for a young transgender boy to hear his parent express strong feelings of loss without experiencing guilt about "causing problems" or upsetting his parent. When Bart's mother refused to take his childhood pictures down, his internal experience was that his mother did not accept him. Leaving the pictures of that little girl out meant, "You don't really believe I am a boy. You'll never accept me as your son." Interpretations like this can lead to hopelessness and despair for trans adolescents.

Consequently, creating safe space for parents is often critical to keeping the young person safe, as well as essential for parents as they explore, express, and navigate their own emotional journeys toward acceptance. When parents begin to express strong emotional reactions to their child's disclosure in a family session without seemingly recognizing the possible impact on their children, it is important to step in and establish this boundary. This can mean interrupting a parent and saying, "I'm going to step in for a minute and ask you to hold on to that thought. I think it might be important for us to talk about this further, and I'd like to do that when it's just the two [or three, if two parents] of us present."

Depending on the context in that moment, I may ask the young person to step out and immediately meet alone with the parents. If something feels unfinished with the child, I return to the conversation and find a way to bring it to a close for now. When the parents and I meet alone, I reopen the space for them to express their feelings. It is also important to educate parents about the potential difference between what they think they are saying and what their transgender child actually may hear—as in the vignette with Bart and his mom. When she insisted on leaving his childhood pictures up, she was initially unaware that what Bart experienced was a rejection of his authentic identity.

This means that much of our work involves translating between cisgender parents and transgender youth—translating Melissa's father's grief as a reflection of his love and not rejection, translating Bart's mother's desire to keep his childhood pictures up as a reflection of her deep connectedness to him, translating what a teen feels when parents continue to use their birth name or prior pronouns.

Parents do not always grasp the connection between using their child's affirmed name and whether their child feels accepted or rejected by them. Just as when Bart's pictures remained hanging, when parents use their child's birth name or former pronouns, transgender youth typically hear, "My parents do not see me for who I am. They do not accept me for who I am." Adolescent trans boys hear, "My parents still see me as their daughter." Young trans women hear, "They will never accept me as their daughter." Parents may believe they can differentiate between unconditionally loving their child and rejecting the child's trans identity (or what may be perceived as an transgender identity choice), but young people typically cannot differentiate between these two dynamics. While it takes most parents some time to consistently use a child's new name and pronouns, it is critical for them to understand what their child experiences when parents fail to use their child's affirmed name and pronouns.

At the same time as I emphasize the importance of using affirmed names and pronouns to make parental acceptance and support explicit, I work with trans children and adolescents to help them understand and be patient with their family's need for time to process the information and emotions surrounding the disclosure of the young person's trans identity. This may mean helping a teen understand why I may use their birth name initially when talking with their parents – "because this is the name your parents are using right now and I need to start where they are in order to help them make this transition with you. Just as it took you time to accept your identity and be ready to come out, it will take your parents some time to understand all of this and learn how to provide the support you need. They have known you as their son (or daughter) all of your life; even if they love you unconditionally, it often takes parents some time for them to transition to knowing you as their daughter (or son)."

Preparing for Disclosure

After the initial work of engaging and assessing trans children and adolescents and exploring the parents' thoughts and emotions surrounding their child's disclosure, work with families often shifts to preparing for the young person to come out to others and socially transition. This process is necessary when a young person has a clear transgender identity—meaning their affirmed gender differs from their birth-assigned sex—and is also often relevant when children and adolescents identify as gender-diverse or nonbinary.

In either context when children or adolescents begin to live fully in their affirmed gender and/or socially transition, disclosure is unavoidable. Some families share the news with extended family members immediately, well before any decisions have been made about potential future steps. Other families delay the disclosure. However, short of a complete relocation, there is simply no way to transition in private. Those around us inevitably witness the transformations in our children. This means that both young people and parents face repeated decisions about who to tell, how to tell them, exactly what or how much to tell them, and when to tell them. In working with families, it is critical to help families explore these decisions and weigh possible risks and benefits of disclosure.

Part of preparing to share the news of a child's transition with others includes helping parents explore with their young people the possible responses they may encounter from others and how they want to navigate these responses. Another aspect includes deciding exactly what, when, and where to share the news. Families need to marshal the emotional resources necessary for navigating the responses of those around them. It is possible that not everyone will be accepting or understanding. It can be helpful to think through how they might handle potential denial or rejection. How will parents feel if their own parents insist that their grandchild cannot be transgender? What if the grandparents are adamant that the child not be allowed to transition? What if they refuse to use the child's affirmed name and pronouns?

Parents face ongoing decisions about disclosing to coworkers, neighbors, and acquaintances. Even after their child transitions and is living in their affirmed identity, parents may encounter former colleagues or old friends with whom they have only occasional contact. In these situations, parents must quickly decide what to say when asked how their son or daughter is doing. If they only see that colleague briefly once a year, is bringing them up-to-date worth what might be an extended or difficult conversation?

Parents may need to educate their children's friends' parents about gender identity and expression. This means that parents are often on the front lines doing education and advocacy about transgender youth while they are still trying to navigate their own emotional responses. Juggling these two tasks is no small feat.

At the same time, both parents and young people need assurance that they have a right to be private about their personal identities and lives. They need to understand privacy as different from being secretive, deceptive, or inauthentic. Privacy can protect our families. We all have the right to decide what is public as opposed to what is meant only for those with whom we are most intimate. Parents and young people have the right to choose with whom and when they share information about their own or their child's gender identity. It is critical to support and empower families in making these decisions.

There are times when parents and children are on different pages about disclosure, as reflected in the following vignette.

> In one family session, Jenny, the family's teenage trans daughter, described an incident while shopping with her mother and brother. They ran into a woman who had been their neighbor when the children were little. They had not seen her in several years. She and the mother talked for several minutes, catching up on what had been happening in each other's lives. The woman turned and said hello to Jenny's brother, and then asked the mom, "Where's your other son?" The mom responded, "Oh, he's not here today." Jenny was upset in the family session and wanted to know why her mother hadn't introduced her.
>
> As we processed this incident, the mother said she thought about telling the woman of her "son's" transition, but they were in a hurry to get home and it seemed too complicated to get into as they waited to check out with their groceries. The daughter's interpretation of her mother's silence was that her mother was embarrassed of her.

As parents and families move beyond initial disclosures, they need the information presented in the earlier chapters about social and medial transitions. Parents need support in mapping out the steps involved in their child's social transition, such as obtaining a legal name change or deciding which gender to check on their child's college application. Parents need information about medical steps like puberty blockers or affirmed-gender hormone therapy. Over time, they will need information about surgeries as their child becomes a young adult. Both parents and youth need accurate information about the possible physical, mental, and emotional risks and benefits of these interventions.

What About School?

When a child is ready to socially transition, parents need to meet with the school to disclose their child's gender identity. Some school districts are well informed and immediately supportive. With one family whose young "son's" feminine gender expression was evident early on, the principal initiated a conversation with the parents to let them know they fully supported their child and would do whatever was necessary to ensure "his" experience in their elementary school was a positive one. This included supporting a gender transition if that emerged as the right path for this family.

Other school districts are not as informed or supportive, and parents may find they need to educate their child's teachers and school administrators. The school in the following vignette demonstrates an appalling need for education about transgender adolescents and their families.

> Constance was a single mother who worked as an administrative assistant for a local phone company. About five months after her 17-year-old transgender daughter, Brianna, began attending school as a young woman, Constance received a visit from child protective services while at her job. The principal of her daughter's high school had filed a report with them because she believed the mother's decision to allow Brianna to begin hormone therapy constituted neglect.
>
> Constance called me in a panic. She was terrified child protective services might remove her daughter while they "investigated" the case. The caseworker assigned to investigate was willing to speak with me. I was able to share Brianna's history of gender dysphoria, educate him about best practices with transgender youth, and assure him that Brianna was involved in ongoing counseling with me. I discussed our process around making the decision for Brianna to begin taking feminizing hormones and referred him to their pediatrician. We each wrote a letter to child protective services that affirmed the medical necessity and appropriateness of hormone therapy for transgender people, even adolescents. The case remained open for several months before Constance was fully cleared of these charges.

This vignette reflects the kind of advocacy families may need from their counselors, therapists, and medical providers. More information about how to work with schools and other youth-serving agencies and programs is presented in Chapter 9.

Meeting Other Families

Parents often need help to identify and develop appropriate support systems and networks. It is can be extremely beneficial to meet other parents with gender-diverse or transgender children. Parents whose children came out a while ago can be a great source of information and support for parents just beginning this journey. Some parents may have already navigated disclosure to extended family members. Others may have already met with their child's school and shared with teachers about their child's transgender identity. Other families may have tackled issues like bathrooms and locker rooms with the school or their children's summer camp. Their teenagers may already be taking hormone blockers, estrogen, or testosterone. As a result, they may have established relationships with trans-knowledgeable and -affirmative medical providers.

Several studies document the value of parent support groups for families with trans and gender-diverse children (Gold & MacNish, 2011; Pleak, 1999; Rosenberg, 2002). Talking with other families often helps parents let go of guilt or shame. Listening to the stories of other families can help parents name and move through their own fears about their child's safety and well-being. Parents who are beyond the initial waves of adjustment can be helpful for parents still struggling with grief and loss. Appendix B provides a listing of support groups and programs for families of trans youth.

Pacing the Work

When adolescents come out as transgender, they generally have been thinking about this for some time. It is not usually an announcement they make lightly. Most teens have been online researching the steps involved in transitioning for months before they share the news with their parents. When they finally come out, teens often experience a huge sense of relief, accompanied by an intense desire to finally be, and be seen in, their affirmed gender. As a result, adolescents often arrive for the first appointment ready to begin their transition yesterday.

On the other hand, their parents have usually just begun to process this information. Parents want answers to their questions. They may want to know how they can be sure their child really is transgender as opposed to simply exploring different gender identities and expressions.

Both information and emotional support are essential before parents can be ready to take active steps toward their child's gender transition. However, the distress associated with their gender dysphoria, coupled with normal adolescence impatience, frequently makes it difficult for trans youth to be patient with their parents' need for more time.

Given these dynamics, a significant amount of the initial work with families involves pacing the process between the parents and the adolescent. Providers must slow the rush to transition on the adolescent's part so there is time to explore the development of the young person's gender identity and expression. This means reassuring the youth that it is not too late for them to authentically be who they are in the world, that they won't miss out on everything, and that their parents won't take forever to catch up. At the same time, the parents must be gently nudged forward in order catch up to their child in terms of understanding about trans identity, emotional processing, and readiness to take potential next steps in this journey.

This balancing act is challenging. If an adolescent feels as if their transition is being unnecessarily delayed, they may experience this as a denial or invalidation of their affirmed gender. Holding them back for too long can communicate a lack of acceptance and support from you and their parents. This can create distrust of you. Throughout this process of pacing, it is essential to closely monitor the intensity of the adolescent's gender dysphoria. Delaying transition can lead to feelings of hopelessness and despair. The youth may imagine it will never be possible to be who they are in the world.

Once again, the clinician often serves as a translator—translating the parents' initial (or even ongoing) hesitation or reluctance regarding social and/or medical transition as an expression of love and caring—as a sign of their parents wanting the best for their child—rather than a sign that the parents do not believe them or reject their affirmed gender.

My style with families is to be flexible and fluid in terms of who is present from session to session, or even within a single session. I may begin a session with the entire family present and then meet separately with parents and the young person. This enables me to experience their interactions as a family, as well allow as the parents and young person to speak with me privately.

As discussed earlier, there are times when parents want and need to talk about their concerns and questions, or express emotional struggles without their child present. Children and adolescents as well often need a safe space, separate from their parents, to fully express their hopes, fears, frustrations, and challenges. This can include their impatience, frustration, or anger with their parents' timeline.

Our separate meetings lead back to family sessions where our individual conversations can be discussed together, particularly at stages in the work where decisions about next steps need to be made. Early on I make these decisions abut how to structure our sessions. Over time we may decide together who participates that day, and in what combinations, depending on their immediate needs.

This chapter focused primarily on the needs of parents during the initial stages of family work. The following chapter delves more deeply into complexities that can emerge as families move forward. In particular, the research about family acceptance will be explored as a resource for facilitating increased family acceptance. Interventions are described for work with rejecting families, navigating family disagreements about a child's identity or aspects of their transition, and engaging families from conservative faith traditions.

CHAPTER 8

Beyond Help to a Deeper Understanding

T HE PREVIOUS CHAPTER FOCUSED ON WHAT MENTAL
health professionals can do to provide for the basic needs of
families of transgender youth—engage them, provide education to
parents, support parents as they work through the range of emotional responses that often emerge in the wake of their child's disclosure, and connect families to peer supports. This chapter explains
the more complex work mental health professionals do with families,
with a particular focus on families who struggle with acceptance of
their child's trans identity. As indicated by earlier discussions of the
pivotal nature of family acceptance for trans youth, helping families
arrive at this place is essential.

The starting point is the premise that almost all parents love their
children and want what's best for them. Almost all parents want
their children to grow up to become happy, healthy adults. Mental
health professionals should start by assuming best intent, regardless
of what the family situation may look like initially. If the professional
is not operating with the assumption that everyone wants the same
thing—for the transgender child or adolescent to grow up knowing
they are loved and that their life has meaning—then this is not the
right person to be consulting.

In my experience of supervising and training providers, this is not
always the foundational assumption. Sometimes the starting point
is the things a transgender young person has told us about their parents—what their parents have said or done to them that felt or was
rejecting. Often our immediate response is to protect this young person. This is a totally natural response, given both our role and the
compassion that brings us to this work.

At the same time, this response tends to align us with the young person, positioning us on their side as their advocate—even their protector. Being positioned as an advocate is not in and of itself a bad thing; transgender youth need advocates. However, this positioning can mean the rejecting parents become the "bad guys" who have rejected and hurt their child. This can create a dynamic where we align with the young person against their parents. If this becomes our starting point for family work, it will be difficult to engage the parents and establish the alliance needed to facilitate greater acceptance.

The above dynamic has some roots within the initial wave of lesbian and gay community organizing. In the early days of the movement, many individuals were rejected when they came out about their sexual orientation. When these adults (and I was part of this generation) began developing support programs for lesbian and gay youth, parents and families were often viewed as the "enemy." Creating safe spaces for lesbian and gay youth meant spaces where families were not present. Adult leaders assumed rejection from parents, or at the least viewed these straight parents as unable to adequately understand their lesbian and gay children. Consequently, most programs for lesbian and gay youth focused on providing peer support with other lesbian and gay youth as well as connections to positive lesbian and gay adult role models. This philosophy remained in place within many agencies until fairly recently.

However, as discussed in the previous chapter, recent studies about risk and resilience among LGBT youth point to family acceptance as the critical mediating variable. The data emerging out of the Family Acceptance Project made the risks of family rejection unequivocally clear. Youth growing up in rejecting families were nearly six times as likely to report high levels of depression in young adulthood and more than eight times as likely to have attempted suicide compared to young adults who grew up in accepting families. Youth who grew up in rejecting families were more than three times as likely to be using illegal drugs and more than three times as likely to be at high risk for HIV and other sexually transmitted diseases as young adults (Ryan et al., 2009; Ryan et al., 2010).

Thus, one primary goal of therapy will be to provide specific recommendations about what parents can say or do to communicate acceptance as well as to educate parents about what they say or do that communicates rejection.

Assessing Family Support

Beyond understanding the distinctions between basic concepts about sex, gender identity, gender expression, and sexual orientation, the information most frequently needed by families is what we have learned from the Family Acceptance Project about risk factors and positive outcomes for transgender adolescents. (https://familyproject.sfsu.edu)

The need for parents to communicate acceptance is essential for their children to become healthy, happy, productive young adults. Therapists must discuss the specific parental behaviors that facilitate acceptance or rejection and help parents pay attention to the messages or behaviors they are communicating to their children.

Parental Messages or Actions That Communicate Rejection

This section has been adapted and expanded from research by the Family Acceptance Project (https://familyproject.sfsu.edu).

The verbal messages or actions listed below disrespect the transgender young person's sense of self. These actions communicate the message that there is something bad or wrong about the young person. They signal that who they are is not OK. Messages like this are internalized by the young person, often leading to depression and feelings of rejection and contributing to high risk factors among transgender youth. These message and actions are particularly damaging when they come from parents but are also problematic when they come from other important adults, such as grandparents, aunts, or uncles.

Accepting parents set boundaries that respect is required from everyone in the household or family. Not only do accepting parents themselves not engage in disrespectful comments or behaviors, but they also ensure that other family members do not act in these ways toward the transgender young person. If other family members do not feel it is OK for the youth to be transgender or to dress a certain way, accepting parents make it clear that while these adults can believe whatever they want personally, their words and actions must be respectful.

Verbal messages and behaviors that have been identified as communicating rejection to transgender youth included the following:

HARASSMENT OR ABUSE RELATED TO THE CHILD'S
TRANSGENDER IDENTITY.

As indicated in Chapter 6, nearly three quarters of trans youth experience verbal abuse from their families. More than one quarter report having been slapped, beaten, or hit very hard, and 13% to 20% report having been punched, kicked, or pushed very hard (Grossman & D'Augelli, 2007). Young trans women (typically perceived early on as gender-variant boys) are at highest risk for physical abuse within their homes (Koken et al., 2009).

MAKING FUN OF A CHILD'S AFFIRMED GENDER OR NONBINARY
IDENTITY; DEMEANING TRANSGENDER PEOPLE BY MAKING
JOKES ABOUT THEM OR PUTTING THEM DOWN.

When parents or other family members ridicule a trans young person or make fun of their gender identity or expression, it contributes to the trans young person feeling "less than." Similarly, when parents or other family members make demeaning remarks about transgender people in general, the trans youth internalizes these comments as a message about their own self-worth as well because they know they are part of this group.

TELLING A CHILD THAT WHO THEY ARE OR HOW THEY LOOK IS
SHAMEFUL.

Communicating any shaming messages diminishes the young person's sense of self and makes them feel less than human. Hearing the message that your parents or other important adults are ashamed of you signals that who you are is not good or worthwhile. Young people internalize this sense of shame, which puts them at high risk for self-harming behaviors.

PRESSURING A CHILD TO ACT MORE (OR LESS) FEMININE OR
MASCULINE.

This essentially constitutes pressuring a child to be other than who they are and creates a situation in which the young person feels compelled to develop and maintain a false self in order to obtain their family's acceptance and approval. Children internalize this requirement to be other than who they are and take in a message that says,

"If my parents only accept or love me when I am presenting a false self, this means my parents do not love or accept the real me."

EXCLUDING A CHILD FROM FAMILY ACTIVITIES OR EVENTS BECAUSE OF THEIR GENDER IDENTITY OR EXPRESSION.

This type of exclusion is punitive. It communicates that the young person is not wanted or welcome, reinforcing the message that who they are is not acceptable.

REJECTING A CHILD'S LGBTQ FRIENDS; NOT ALLOWING THE YOUNG PERSON TO SPEND TIME WITH THEIR FRIENDS; DENYING ACCESS TO TRANS-AFFIRMING YOUTH GROUPS, EVENTS, OR PROGRAMS.

Rejecting a child's friends when the child knows they are like their friends communicates rejection of the child as well. In addition, these actions isolate the young person, making them feel as if they are the only one like this. The isolation exacerbates the shame the young person has internalized.

BLAMING A CHILD WHEN SOMEONE TEASES OR BULLIES THEM FOR "NON-NORMATIVE" GENDER EXPRESSION OR NOT BEING A "REAL" GIRL OR BOY.

One adolescent I worked with was being bullied at school. When the young man disclosed this to his father, his father responded, "If you dressed like a real man, you wouldn't get pushed around." When parents blame their children for being bullied, it sends a message that the young person deserves the harassment because of who they are—in other words, who you are is not OK.

DISMISSING OR DENYING A CHILD'S TRANSGENDER OR NONBINARY IDENTITY.

One 13-year-old trans boy's father periodically told him, "You are not a boy; you were my daughter when you were born and you will always be my daughter." This kind of parental denial challenges the adolescent's reality as well as sending the message that the parent will never accept the young person's understanding of themselves.

NOT USING THE YOUNG PERSON'S AFFIRMED NAME OR
PRONOUNS, OR EXCUSING OTHERS WHO DON'T USE THE
CHILD'S AFFIRMED NAME OR PRONOUNS.

As challenging of an adjustment as this generally is for parents, refusing to use the young person's affirmed name and pronouns communicates disrespect for their identity. This is another way of dismissing
or denying the young person's sense of self. When Cheryl's parents
kept using her birth-assigned name, what she heard was, "We do not
see you as a girl. We do not believe you really are a girl." When parents continue to use the birth name and pronouns, the young person often begins to feel hopeless. They begin to assume other people
will never see them in their affirmed gender; they will never be able
to be their true self; others will never see them for who they really
are. This contributes to feelings of invisibility and, concomitantly,
isolation.

BEING UPSET (ANGRY, SAD, CRYING, DISAPPOINTED, AFRAID)
ABOUT A CHILD'S TRANS IDENTITY/AFFIRMED GENDER TOO
OFTEN WHEN THEY ARE PRESENT.

This is sometimes challenging for parents, depending on where they
are in their own emotional process. Julie, as 15-year-old trans woman,
told me, "My mom is always crying about my transition. I'll come in
the living room and find her looking at one of my childhood pictures
and crying. It makes me feel bad. I don't want to make my mom feel
sad all the time." When trans youth are exposed to intense parental
emotions like this, they tend to internalize the sense that they are
a/the problem, that they upset their parents and make their parents
feel bad, and that their parents are disappointed in them. All of these
messages contribute to low self-esteem and low self-worth—factors
that can contribute to increased risk for trans youth. It is critical to
create spaces where parents can process their emotional reactions
to their child's disclosure and/or transition apart from their child.
This can be in a session with you, with the parent's personal therapist
if they have one, or within a support group for parents of trans or
LGBTQ youth.

REFUSING TO DISCUSS A CHILD'S GENDER IDENTITY WITH THEM.

This is a more subtle message of rejection, but when youth come out as transgender and parents ignore the information and never bring the topic up again, this sends the message that being transgender (who they are) is something that is too bad, sinful, or wrong to talk about. It can also communicate the message that parents do not think this is important to discuss, which says to the young person, "You are not important enough for me to be interested in you, the things that are important to you, or who you are."

INSISTING THAT A CHILD KEEP THEIR AFFIRMED IDENTITY A SECRET.

Secrets tend to be things we are ashamed about. When parents insist that their child keep their affirmed gender (who they are) secret, it sends the message that there is something shameful about them.

TELLING A CHILD THAT WHO THEY ARE IS A SIN OR THAT GOD WILL PUNISH THEM FOR BEING TRANS.

Regardless of a parent's religious beliefs, this message clearly communicates to a young person that who they are is not acceptable.

Parental Messages or Actions That Communicate Support

This section has been adapted and expanded from research by the Family Acceptance Project (https://familyproject.sfsu.edu).

As opposed to sending messages that communicate rejection, there are many ways parents can communicate their love, acceptance, and support. This is true even when parents may still be struggling with their own beliefs or emotions. Verbal messages and behaviors that have been identified as communicating acceptance to transgender youth include the following:

INITIATING CONVERSATIONS ABOUT A CHILD'S GENDER IDENTITY/EXPRESSION; EXPRESSING INTEREST IN THEIR UNDERSTANDING OF THEMSELVES; KEEPING THE LINES OF COMMUNICATION OPEN, EVEN AFTER THE CHILD TRANSITIONS; NOT ASSUMING THERE'S NOTHING MORE TO TALK ABOUT NOW.

When parents or other adults initiate conversations about the child's gender identity or expression and express interest in hearing more about the young person's identity, this communicates the child's importance to the adults in their life. This kind of parent-initiated check-in is important even after trans youth have transitioned and seem to be doing well.

ESTABLISHING A "ZERO-TOLERANCE" POLICY FOR DISRESPECT, RIDICULE, TEASING, OR PRESSURE TO CONFORM TO NORMATIVE GENDER EXPECTATIONS WITHIN THE FAMILY; INSISTING ON RESPECT FOR A CHILD FROM EVERYONE IN THE FAMILY'S LIFE (THEY MAY NOT AGREE, BUT THEY MUST TREAT THE CHILD AS A HUMAN BEING WORTHY OF RESPECT AND DIGNITY).

It is essential to create a supportive home environment. Insisting that others respect the child, even if they do not agree that being trans is OK, is critical. When parents stand up for their child and do not allow others (including siblings or extended family members) to tease their child or advocate on their behalf if someone harasses them, they send a clear message of support. Demonstrating that a parent "has their child's back" is an assurance of love. The message the young person will hear is, "I can count on you to be there for me even if I'm trans."

VERBALIZING LOVE AND SUPPORT FOR A CHILD, INCLUDING THEIR GENDER IDENTITY/EXPRESSION.

It is essential for parents to verbally assure their child that they love them—even when they do not believe their child is transgender or when they feel the child's transgender identity is something they cannot accept. When parents struggle with the news that their child is trans, the parents may withdraw and become less communicative or affectionate. This sends a message that the parents are not comfortable or not OK with who the child is.

INTRODUCING A CHILD TO POSITIVE TRANSGENDER ROLE MODELS; TAKING A CHILD TO TRANS-IDENTIFIED OR TRANS-AFFIRMING YOUTH GROUPS AND ACTIVITIES.

Helping children find positive adult transgender role models and allowing them to participate in trans-affirming activities and support groups lets teens know that they are accepted and supported. Meeting positive adult role models reinforces a message that the child's future is hopeful and positive.

IF A CHILD HAS TRANS AND/OR LGBTQ FRIENDS, SUPPORTING THESE FRIENDSHIPS; IF A TEEN IS DATING SOMEONE, INVITING THAT PERSON INTO YOUR HOME;

When parents welcome their children's friends and dating partners into their homes, their children feel supported by their parents. Embracing their friends or partners also embraces them.

HOLD LOVE TO BE THE MOST IMPORTANT THING—MORE IMPORTANT THAN SOCIAL NORMS, FIRMLY HELD BELIEFS AND TRADITIONS, OR WHAT OTHER PEOPLE MIGHT THINK.

Holding love as the "most important thing" is an important aspect of communicating acceptance. When parents do this, they send the message that love for their child and their commitment to their child's well-being is more important than social or cultural norms, more important than firmly held beliefs, more important than what others may think. In conjunction with this, when parents "stretch" beyond their comfort zone to support their child's identity—even when it makes the parents uncomfortable—they communicate acceptance.

FOCUSING ON A CHILD'S HAPPINESS; SUPPORTING A CHILD—VERBALLY AND THROUGH THESE POSITIVE PARENTING PRACTICES—EVEN IF IT SOMETIMES MAKES YOU UNCOMFORTABLE.

These practices are challenging when parents are upset or uncomfortable with their child's trans identity or varying gender expression. At the same time, being a parent stretches all of us. Whether our children are transgender or not, there will be times when parenting means doing things that may not feel comfortable to us as parents. The style of parenting one child needs may not be our natural way of parenting, and yet, being present for this child and supporting them means we have to be willing sometimes to act in ways that are not the most comfortable for us. This is part of being a parent. When mental health professionals help parents to broaden this task beyond the specific needs of their transgender child and to see stretching beyond their comfort zone as inherent to being a parent, it can make it easier for them to communicate unconditional love and acceptance for their transgender child even when there may be ways that the parent is still not quite OK with their child's affirmed identity.

BELIEVING AND REGULARLY COMMUNICATING FAITH IN A CHILD'S ABILITY TO HAVE A HAPPY, HEALTHY, MEANINGFUL ADULT LIFE—A LIFE WITH THE POSSIBILITY OF FINDING LOVE, COMMITMENT, MEANINGFUL WORK, AND FAMILY.

Media images of transgender people are often negative. Consequently, many parents worry about their child's future and safety, especially early on. Yet, it is critical for parents to communicate faith in their child's ability to have a happy and fulfilling future as a trans adult— life with professional success, friends, and the possibility of finding love ad commitment and creating a family of their own. Enabling parents and other family members to navigate their own fears, questions, loss, or anger in order to be able to send a consistent message of love and support lies at the core of a mental health professional's work with families.

The following vignette illustrates some ways of the reasons why parents must make this effort:

> Sixteen-year-old Toshina and her parents came to see me about one year after she disclosed that she was a transgender woman. Since that point, her gender expression had become more feminine, though she had not yet fully transitioned at school. About to finish her sophomore year, Toshina was pushing her parents to let her start school in the fall as a girl. She also wanted to begin taking estrogen before the end of the year.
>
> Her parents, Jerome and Kim, had an uneasy truce with her trans identity. They were clear that they loved her and were not entirely rejecting of her being trans-identified, but they still used her male name and pronouns most of the time. They were OK with Toshina's clothes becoming a bit more feminine, but they drew the line at Toshina leaving the house dressed like her best female friends. They knew she used "Toshina" with her close

friends and that she had a boyfriend, but they were not ready for her to attend school as "Toshina."

Neither Kim nor Jerome told anyone in their extended family about Toshina's affirmed gender, including Kim's mother, with whom they were very close. Both parents had been raised in a Black Baptist church. While their personal religious beliefs had shifted since then, they worried about how relatives would respond if they allowed Toshina to transition.

About two months into our work, Toshina brought up a family wedding scheduled later that summer. Several of her cousins were bringing their girlfriends or boyfriends, and she wanted to invite her boyfriend, Marcus, too. She wanted to wear a dress like her girl cousins and wanted her relatives to know she was his girlfriend. The way Toshina's face lit up made clear how important this was to her. As Toshina and I discussed what this would mean for her, she talked about not wanting to pretend anymore; she wanted to be able to be real with her cousins. In part, she did want to show Marcus off just as her cousins would be showing off their girlfriends or boyfriends. However, she wanted her cousins and aunts and uncles to meet Marcus authentically—not assuming they were friends, but seeing Marcus as her boyfriend and seeing Toshina as she was, his girlfriend.

Kim and Jerome were hesitant. They weren't sure they were ready to be open about Toshina's affirmed gender with their parents and siblings. They thought they might be willing to tell other family members about Toshina coming out, but they worried that Toshina attending the wedding as a girl would be "too much" for some of their family members. The hard part was that their reluctance to allow her to be visible in her real self (as a young woman) made Toshina feel that her parents did not truly accept her for who she was or that they were embarrassed about her.

After my initial assessment process with Toshina and her parents, much of my work was with Jerome and Kim, given their reluctance about Toshina fully being out in the world. Toshina was clear about her identity and eager to transition. She was impatient and sometimes angry with her parents' hesitation, feeling as if one year was long enough for them to get used to her being their daughter.

In the course of conversations with the parents, we began to discuss the importance of family acceptance and support for Toshina. We discussed the risk factors if she did not feel accepted and supported, particularly by her parents. It was clear that Jerome and Kim loved their daughter very much. There was no question that they wanted her to grow up into a happy and healthy young adult. As we looked at the ways Kim and Jerome could communicate acceptance, we focused on three in particular:

- Hold love as the most important thing; make love more important than social norms or what other people might think.
- Focus on your child's happiness.
- Support your child even if it makes you uncomfortable.

The parents and I discussed the ways these practices are an important aspect of parenting, whether or not your child is transgender. We acknowledged, and even laughed about, the fact that children rarely grow up to be exactly the way we imagined they would—that each child, like each human being, is unique and sometimes requires different ways of parenting, including approaches that might not be natural or easy for us.

We discussed the importance of using Toshina's affirmed name and pronouns and how this reflected their acceptance of who she was—how using her affirmed name communicated that they saw her for who she really was, their daughter, Toshina. I suggested that they to try this at home more often, even if they were not ready to do so in public. Over time, Toshina reported that Jerome and Kim were calling her Toshina at home more often.

Kim initiated a conversation about Toshina's coming out with her mother, who was more supportive than Kim imagined she would be. At one point, the grandmother joined us for a family session because she wanted to understand Toshina better.

By late July, Jerome and Kim told Toshina she could invite Marcus to the wedding. They were still not entirely convinced this was the "right" thing to do, but they were willing to share Toshina's affirmed gender with the extended family.

The week after the wedding, Toshina was beaming when she came to see me. She talked nonstop for nearly 20 minutes about how amazing it was to be there as Toshina and have her cousins see her as Marcus's girlfriend. "I was able to be me," she said, "the real me, finally." It was clear that the wedding was a significant moment both for Toshina and her parents. Despite some lingering reservations, Kim and Jerome stretched beyond their personal comfort zone to make communicating their love and support to Toshina the most important thing in that moment.

Sharing findings about the high risks for young people growing up in rejecting families highlights just what is at stake and can enable parents to see the risks of maintaining behaviors that communicate rejection to their children. When parents know what parental practices increase greater positive young adult outcomes for their children, they are empowered to make choices that improve their child's quality of life. Rather than simply telling parents that they need to be accepting, therapists need to help parents see what acceptance and support look like in action.

Each positive parental behavior increases the young person's sense of acceptance, decreases young adult risk factors, and promotes greater positive outcomes for trans youth.

The vignette about Toshina and her parents illustrates how these findings can enable therapists to identify and work from common ground. Few parents want to see their children engaged in illegal drug use or alcohol abuse. Few parents want their children to experience debilitating depression or anxiety. Few parents want their children to feel so hopeless they attempt suicide. I have yet to meet a parent who wanted to bury a child. This sounds harsh, but it points to the fact that it is almost always possible to arrive at some piece of common ground in therapeutic work with families.

Almost all parents love their children and want the best for them. Even parents who deny that their child's gender identity could vary from the sex assigned at birth, even parents who are uncomfortable with their children coming out as trans, and even parents who believe being transgender is "wrong" generally still want their children to become happy, healthy, and alive young adults. In identifying this common ground of loving their children and wanting the best for them, therapists and parents can often reach beneath what might look like rejection and touch the hopes every parent holds for their children.

Begin Where the Family Is Right Now

Almost every social work or counseling textbook tells students, "Start where the client is." Yet, it is all too easy for therapists to jump ahead of the family, or individual family members, in an attempt to get them to where we believe they need to be—in full support of their transgender child. While this is the end goal, therapists need to remember that the starting point in therapeutic work is wherever this particular family is today. We have discussed the urgency and potential risk factors, especially for transgender adolescents. This means we do want to move the family toward acceptance, and as quickly as possible. At the same time, families will make this journey with us only if we start where they are right now.

Families typically get "stuck" at one of two points: accepting the child's transgender identity or reaching consensus about transition steps. Early on, families may struggle to believe that, or disagree about whether, their child actually is transgender. Further into the process, family members may have different opinions about whether or when the young person should socially transition or begin some aspect of a medical transition, such as hormone blockers or feminizing or masculinizing hormone therapy.

Starting where the family is means obtaining a full, detailed understanding of where the family, or individual family member, is stuck or in disagreement. In these moments, I ask myself: What barrier is currently keeping them from accepting their child? What stands in the way of their ability to fully support their child? What might enable greater acceptance from the family?

In my interactions with the parents (while I refer to parents in this section, the points equally apply to grandparents and other family members), I begin by asking them to tell me more about their concerns or objections. My goal is to understand in detail (rather than superficially) as much as possible about the parent's concerns. If they tell me, "I'm worried she won't have a good life," I don't let the conversation stop here. I draw them out further so I can really understand and appreciate what this specific parent worries about. I might have a hunch, but it is only a hunch until they tell me more. In the following example, the father's 15-year-old son, John, has recently come out as a transgender girl.

COUNSELOR: *Tell me what worries you about John's understanding of his gender identity. [I use "John" here because we are still in the initial sessions and the father is using "John"].*

FATHER: *I just don't think he can know at 15 whether he's transgender or not. He's too young. Teenagers are always exploring their identity. Today he thinks he's a girl. Tomorrow it will be something else.*

COUNSELOR: *It's true that exploring identity is often part of adolescence. Tell me more about how that connects to your reluctance to believe John's understanding of himself as a trans girl.*

FATHER: *I just don't think he should make a decision like this at his age. How does he know he'll still feel the same way in 10 years?*

COUNSELOR: *It worries you that he might change his mind later on?*

I might continue exploring the father's concerns with questions such as: "What if John did feel differently at 25 years old? What then? What do you imagine that might be like for John? For you? For other people in John's life? What do you worry might happen if John did change his mind later on? What would make you worry about this possibility?"

At this point, I do not attempt to dissuade the father from being concerned about John changing his mind. Even though I know most transgender people who come out in adolescence continue to identify as trans in adulthood, my goal in the moment is to fully hear the father's concerns or objections, to understand what this father in particular worries about, to understand clearly what worries the father in terms of who John is and how the father sees John's strengths or challenges.

Other directions to explore might include understanding the father and his history better. Are there aspects of the father's history that contribute to his concern for John? I might ask the father, "Have you known other people who felt one way as a teenager but felt differently as adults? Was there anything you felt strongly about or believed as a teenager that shifted in your adult life?" These questions allow me to learn more about the father's perspective and what experiences have shaped his view. A parent's concern for their child can be rooted in their own life narrative—or that of a close family member, such as a sibling. Getting this history out on the table can help us separate the father's earlier experiences from John's current disclosure of being transgender. It can sometimes help us clarify whether the father's worries are really about John or more reflective of the father's history and perhaps not true for John.

Listen and Validate

Coupled with reaching for a detailed understanding of the parent's concerns, it is essential for therapists to actively listen to the family's responses and validate their concerns. This is reflected in the previous example when the counselor acknowledges that identity exploration is often part of being a teenager. Rather than counter or debate whether this assumption is always true, I validate this as a fairly normative adolescent developmental task. The important piece right now is for the parents to believe the clinician truly hears and understands their feelings and concerns.

This process cannot be rushed. At this stage in the work with a stuck or rejecting family, you cannot challenge, object, debate, or argue with a family member very much. The goal is to build an alliance with the family (or family member), and this is only possible when they trust that you understand where they are in this moment. This means exploring how they view their parental role, how they understand what this particular child needs from them, what their hopes and dreams are for their child, and what things they worry about in terms of their child identifying as transgender or taking the next step in a gender transition.

If the parents are angry, stay present in their anger—for as long as it takes to get through it. If the parents are afraid, stay present in their fear—for as long as it takes to navigate and/or resolve it. As opposed to shying away from their feelings, lean into them and encourage them to express these feelings fully. We do this by drawing them out, by asking questions that demonstrate our interest in what is important to them and our willingness to listen and understand. We communicate our ability to appreciate their point of view. We acknowledge how the immediate situation would make them upset, fearful, and so forth. We acknowledge and validate the things the parent is angry or worried about.

In many ways, this parallels work with mandated clients. You cannot really begin the therapeutic process or engage treatment goals with most mandated clients until you fully engage the client's anger and resistance about having to be there. The starting point is the client's resentment around treatment not being their choice. You validate that being in treatment involuntarily would make many people angry. You acknowledge that their anger in this situation is understandable. You might even acknowledge that you, too, would feel angry about being required to attend treatment if you didn't want, or feel you needed, counseling.

The starting point to effectively engage involuntary clients is always listening to and validating their resistance, anger, and resentment. You cannot move beyond this initial work until the client experiences the sense that they have been heard, that you "get" why they are upset, and that you can appreciate that feeing upset is a reasonable response to their situation. It is the experience of being heard that creates a small opening for movement in a new direction. In the same way, when rejecting parents feel fully heard, you may discover a window of willingness to hear a different idea, or think outside the box, or explore the possibility of some middle ground between rejection and acceptance. The following vignette illustrates this process.

> Mr. Jamison was referred by another therapist. He and his wife were separated and lived in two different cities. Their only child (born female) was a freshman at an out-of-state college. About six months prior, the young person, now going by Stephen, had come out to his parents as a transgender man. Both parents were surprised by this and reported that their child's gender expression had always been fairly normative. They had never seen any indications of a more masculine gender identity before Stephen's announcement.
>
> The father had been talking with his therapist about Stephen's disclosure and had reached a place of relative acceptance, though he still had many questions. His wife, on the other hand, did not believe that Stephen was transgender. She thought this was just a phase and was very upset about Stephen's disclosure.
>
> The impetus for Mr. Jamison reaching out to me was that Stephen had recently told his parents that he wanted to begin taking testosterone. Mrs. Jamison was extremely upset about

this and thought a parent should do anything they could to prevent Stephen from beginning hormone therapy. Mr. Jamison was not particularly comfortable with Stephen starting hormones but also thought there wasn't much the parents could do to stop it, since Stephen was 19 years old. Mr. Jamison called and asked if I could do a family session with the three of them to help them work through their different ideas.

Our appointment began with Stephen announcing that it was not his choice to be there that day. He did not need therapy. It was his parents who needed it. He had only come as a courtesy to his parents because it seemed important to them.

As I gathered their family history and explored Stephen's recent disclosure, Mrs. Jamison became increasingly angry. While she did not believe Stephen really was a man, what she was most angry about was learning about Stephen's disclosure through Facebook. "She didn't even have the courtesy to tell me directly! I had to learn through her Facebook post to everyone. How could she not talk to me before she told all of her friends? It's just rude not to talk with me first." Mrs. Jamison was clearly enraged about this and kept returning to the point.

Stephen was clear that he did not want to talk about how he had come out to her. The only thing he wanted to talk about was the fact that he wanted to begin taking testosterone, and that he was going to begin whether his parents supported this or not—though he indicated he would rather have their support.

Mr. Jamison took a conciliatory role, trying to make peace between his wife and young adult child. At some point when it seemed Mrs. Jamison was not able to move beyond how Stephen disclosed, I suggested that Stephen step out for a while and allow me to meet with his parents alone.

After Stephen left, I began to more directly engage Mrs. Jamison around her anger. I encouraged her to tell me more about what in particular upset her about Stephen coming out on Facebook and not speaking to her beforehand. She responded, "How dare she treat me like this? She embarrassed me in front of my friends! How could she not talk to me about this first? I shouldn't be the last to find out something like this!"

I worked to listen, understand, and validate her anger. As we made space for her anger, we began to identify some of the emotions beneath her anger—feeling hurt, left out, unimportant, not needed anymore. I validated these feelings as well. I let her know I could appreciate her being upset and angry that Stephen hadn't spoken to her first, that I could see how this would make her feel left out of Stephen's life and, thus, unimportant. I acknowledged that I could see this was hurtful.

In terms of my own feelings, after about the first five minutes of this conversation, part of me became impatient with Mrs. Jamison's inability to move beyond the Facebook disclosure. From my point of view, this was done and over and there was nothing we could do to change how Stephen disclosed being transgender. Another part of me felt annoyed that this seemed to be all about her, with little acknowledgment of any feelings Stephen might have.

I knew this was a double-session assessment and that I would not be working with the family in an ongoing way. I was concerned about how urgently Stephen wanted to begin testosterone. I also had concerns about the degree of depression he seemed to be struggling with. I was concerned about enabling Mrs. Jamison to be prepared for this next step in Stephen's transition, even if she was not ready to accept it.

Mrs. Jamison was also enraged that there was an LGBT health center in the city where Stephen attended college. Stephen had told them he'd already had his first appointment there. He was going back next week to review his bloodwork, and if everything was good, he could start T that day. Mrs. Jamison was outraged about Stephen starting this quickly. "Isn't this unethical?" she asked. "How can any ethical medical doctor allow someone as young as 19 years to begin taking testosterone just like that? How can they even know whether she really is transgender that quickly?"

I initially attempted to explain the informed consent model, but I quickly realized this was positioning me as defending this approach in opposition to Mrs. Jamison's stance about it. I stepped back from explaining the model and refocused on acknowledging her feelings about it. I indicated that I could appreciate her concerns and understood her being upset that Stephen would be allowed to proceed with hormone therapy this quickly.

Despite the critical importance of these conversations, I was conscious of our limited time and began to shift our conversation away from her distress to talk about what Stephen needed from them now. I had to interrupt Mrs. Jamison and say that I could see she was still upset, yet I was also aware of how limited our time was and that I felt we needed to talk about next steps. My sense was that Mrs. Jamison would have happily continued to rage, but I also felt she had experienced enough acknowledgment to allow me to shift the focus.

As I interrupted here to shift the topic, I continued to acknowledge how important it was for her to have a place to express her anger. I encouraged her to follow up by talking with her own individual therapist about these feelings.

We were able to shift topics and discuss the likelihood that Stephen would begin testosterone shortly. We spent time addressing the effects and possible risks of hormone therapy. From there, I shifted to what Stephen needed from them most and introduced the Family Acceptance Project material about the importance of family acceptance. Over the next few minutes, we acknowledged that the parents were not entirely on board with Stephen beginning T. Still, it was essential that they communicate their unconditional love and support for him, especially given his depression. Mrs. Jamison struggled with this. She did not want Stephen to think she was OK with all this. We explored some ways she could acknowledge that she did still have many questions and concerns. She said she would continue to work with her therapist about these. She was able to then affirm that she loved Stephen unconditionally and that he would always have her support.

Throughout this session, it was essential for me to manage my own emotional reactions so that I could be patient and stay present with Mrs. Jamison's anger. It was critical for me to validate her objections and feelings about Stephen coming out on Facebook without talking with his mother beforehand. Without acknowledging and validating her rage, we would never have been able to address the importance of the parents' expressing their unconditional love to Stephen.

As addressed at the beginning of this chapter, sometimes our commitment to being an advocate for the transgender young person can interfere with building an alliance with their parents. It was important not to view Mrs. Jamison as the "bad guy" simply because she was stuck in her anger and rejection. If we want to facilitate a shift within the family, we cannot let our own emotional reactions—such as my impatience with her repeated return to the Facebook post—get in the way of building an effective alliance. When an alliance does not seem possible, at the very least we need to establish some connection with the parents. This is only possible as I come to deeply understand and appreciate the immediate situation through the eyes of the parents—not just through the eyes of the transgender young person.

There have been a few moments when I've needed to lean in quickly with parents and could not spend as much time building as strong of a connection as I normally would want to. These were situations when the risk seemed high—when the young person was acutely depressed and/or actively suicidal. In these situations, I needed the parents to set aside their objections more quickly and express their love for their child in order to keep their child alive. I still navigate this shift in conjunction with presenting the risks from the FAP. However, I convey a greater sense of urgency and lean into the risk factors alongside their role as parents rather than reaching for a well-formed alliance with them. As I lean in to press for change toward expressing greater support for their child, I might say something like this:

> I realize you still have a lot of feelings about James coming out as a transgender young woman. I know this is something you believe is wrong, and I respect the strength of your convictions.
>
> At the same time, I am aware—and I know you are as well—that James is extremely depressed. He acknowledged that he is thinking about suicide frequently and sometimes feels this is the only way out.
>
> I know how much you love your child and want the best for him. I know how seriously you take your responsibility as his parent.
>
> Given that, and what we know now about the risks for young people when they feel rejected by their families, I am wondering if there is any way we can hold your questions and concerns, your conviction that being transgender is wrong, in one hand and yet at the same time find a way to reassure James that you love

him unconditionally. [In some situations with religious families, I might be bold enough to say, "that you love him unconditionally just as God, his Creator, does.] I wonder if there is a way to reassure James that you love him as he is, whether he is transgender or not—even if your beliefs have not changed. I wonder if there is any way—without changing what you believe—to hold your love for James, and keeping him safe and alive, as the most important thing in this moment.

I know we have a lot more to talk about in terms of how to work all this out—the differences between what you believe and James believing he is a girl. And I realize I am asking you to do something that may be difficult for you to juggle. But in this moment, what I want to most ensure is that James will be here so we can do this work together, so we can find a way through this. And what he needs to know most right now is that you, as his parents, love him unconditionally—whether he is transgender or not. He needs to know his life has value to you.

I am aware that what I have said above is intense. I only lean into these words when the situation with a young person's life seems truly at a crisis point and I need the parents to engage in an accepting way regardless of their beliefs. You'll notice that I am clear I am not trying to change their beliefs. While people's beliefs can shift over time, pushing them to change what they think or feel rarely works in the moment. What I am seeking here is a short-term "fix," not a long-term solution. The work of finding a way for the family to navigate their differences will need to continue after the crisis has passed.

The Nature of the Family's Struggle

The clinical focus while exploring and validating the parents' struggles has been to reflect on what may be at the core of their conflict and what the family may need to move toward greater acceptance. By starting where the family is at that moment, therapists gain a more thorough understanding of the parents' perspective. They have a better sense of what their specific concerns or objections are, thus enabling them to more accurately assess where parents are stuck. This sets the stage to develop effective interventions that align with where the family is in the moment.

At this point, I return to my original questions in light of the information I've learned about the nuances of the family's struggles and/or conflicts. What barrier keeps them from accepting (or communicating their acceptance) their child? What stands in the way of fully supporting their child? What might enable greater acceptance from the family?

There are several barriers that can prevent acceptance within families of trans youth. Often these barriers fall into one of two categories. In the first scenario, the barrier involves a knowledge gap; there is some area in which the family needs more information, and it is this lack of understanding that inhibits greater acceptance. In the second scenario, the barrier typically lies within the emotional realm. There is some emotional conflict that blocks greater acceptance, or some buried emotion that needs to surface before it can be resolved. Again, the goal of the earlier focus on deeply exploring the parents' perception of the immediate situation was to gather enough information to assess the nature of the barrier at this stage in the process. Knowing what has them stuck enables you to develop an intervention in line with the family's needs.

PARENTS: WHILE READING THE FOLLOWING MATERIAL, THINK ABOUT YOUR OWN NEEDS AND RESPONSES TO YOUR CHILD.

When the Barrier Involves the Lack of Information or Knowledge

Some families get stuck because they need more information about transgender issues. As a therapist assesses where they are stuck, the knowledge gap becomes clear. For example, it may become apparent that the parents still struggle with the difference between concepts of sex, gender identity, gender expression, and sexual orientation.

> Janelle came in to our appointment upset and told me her mom had "done it again." "She went off again on this long thing about if I liked girls, why did I have to transition? Couldn't I just be a boy that liked girls like most boys do? What was the big difference? She just doesn't get it. I'm not a boy. I'm a girl—a girl who likes

other girls. When she goes off like this, I feel like she still doesn't accept me as a girl."

I raised this with Janelle's mother when she and I met during the second part of the appointment. This was not the first time the mom and I had discussed the differences between biological sex and gender identity, but what became clear in this conversation was that the mother was conflating gender identity, gender expression, and sexual orientation. Janelle's mother did not fully understand that gender identity and sexual orientation are two different aspects of who we are—that we all have both a gender identity and a sexual orientation.

The mom thought if Janelle liked girls, it would have been a lot easier to "just stay a boy." The mom didn't understand that when Janelle imagined being close with her girlfriend, she envisioned herself as a girl too. As we worked through these concepts, the mother gained a clearer understanding of the differences between her daughter's gender identity as a young woman and her sexual orientation as a woman attracted to other women.

Other times, it becomes clear that parents need more information about transgender children or adolescents in particular. They may have some knowledge about trans adults from the media but question how a young person could know they are transgender. Sometimes the parents appear stuck in fear, but what emerges is that the need for specific information about puberty blockers (or another aspect of transition) is more important than space to express their fear. In this scenario, the barrier is not so much an emotional one as it is the lack of information. Once the parents gain more knowledge about hormone blockers, their fear diminishes. This illustrates the importance of closely assessing whether the barrier is about needing information as opposed to being more emotional in nature. A struggle that initially seems like an emotional need may turn out to be more rooted in inadequate information about a particular aspect of gender transition.

One other area of education that is helpful for many parents involves grasping the differences between what the parents intend and believe they are saying and what their children actually hear. Functioning as a family translator in this sense and helping parents understand how their transgender child hears certain statements is critical. For example, many parents struggle in making the adjustment to consistently using their child's affirmed name and pronouns. From the parents' perspective, when they forget and use the child's birth-assigned name or pronouns, they generally believe they are doing the best they can. They want their children to understand how difficult this is for them. They want their children to be more patient with them. They don't understand why their children get so upset when they just "make a mistake."

The missing link in this situation is that the parents are generally unaware of what their child is actually hearing when they "mess up" and use the old name or pronouns. While the parents perceive this as a "mistake" (and they are usually sorry for making this mistake), the trans youth hears their parent saying to them, "You are not who you think you are. I do not believe you are who you understand yourself to be. Who you are is not OK or real." This is a critical piece of information for parents, because it directly contributes to whether their child feels accepted or rejected.

PARENTS: DO YOU RECOGNIZE YOURSELF IN ANY OF THESE STATEMENTS? IT'S OK IF YOU DO! THIS IS ALL A LEARNING PROCESS AND A JOURNEY.

Ask Permission First

When a clinical assessment of the barrier reflects insufficient knowledge, two strategies can enhance the usefulness of the information that is shared. First, it is helpful to ask for permission before sharing new information with parents and family. For example, you could say, "Would it be okay with you if I shared some of what we're learning about transgender teenagers?" or "Would it be all right if I shared some of how we understand the differences between sex, gender identity, and gender expression?"

Asking permission typically decreases defensiveness and thus facilitates greater openness to processing the new information. Obtaining permission tends to create greater buy-in from parents to continue the discussion with you. Asking permission also levels the power differential between the parents/client and you as the professional/expert a bit and reinforces the family's self-determination. It reinforces their competence in receiving and making decisions about new information as opposed to being told what they should believe or do by an outsider. With families who are entrenched in their rejection, these factors can be critical in attempting to create an opening for positive change. With families from more conservative religious contexts, there may be an inherent wariness that an outside mental health professional (whose education is secular and not faith or scripture based) will attempt to change the family's beliefs. Therapeutic effectiveness rests on finding a way to navigate this initial distrust and build an alliance anyway.

How the Problem Is Framed

Another aspect that can determine effectiveness with families within conservative religious traditions relates to how the "problem" is framed. Some of these parents communicate rejection toward their child because the concept of transgender identity conflicts with their religious beliefs. In this situation, parents are often stuck because they cannot envision an alternative perspective or path. They cannot imagine a way through the impasse between their faith and their child's "choices."

This can appear to simply be about rejection, but a closer examination may reveal that the underlying barrier is more about needing fresh ideas or information that might illuminate a possible path through this conflict between the parents' faith beliefs and their love for their child. It is possible that the parents are not unwilling to be (more) accepting. Instead, with the knowledge they currently possess, the difficulty is their inability to envision a path through this impasse.

When this is the case, it is helpful to discuss whether the parents would be open to hearing how others have found a path through this dilemma. Would they be willing to explore other perspectives within their faith tradition? Would they be open to talking with other parents who have resolved similar concerns or conflicts? Would they be willing to talk with a pastoral leader/minister/rabbi/imam who might have fresh ideas on navigating this conflict between their faith/beliefs and their love for their child?

It can be useful to identify resources representing a range of faith communities that do accept and support transgender people. There are evangelical Christians who accept transgender people, such as Tony and Peggy Campolo and Matthew Vines. There are leaders within each branch of Judaism who are accepting. PFLAG can also be helpful in locating parents from different faith communities.

I am careful to stress that this is not about attempting to change parents' beliefs. If my goal is to change their beliefs or I send a message to that effect, I am likely to lose them. I am simply asking if they would be willing to listen to others who have shared similar struggles with the hope that those experiences might help these parents envision their own path through this dilemma. In this scenario, the underlying obstacle is the lack of ideas and information and not the rejection in and of itself. In the long run, the exact beliefs they hold may be less important than the actions the parents take to communicate acceptance and support for their transgender child or adolescent.

Always Check in Afterward

After providing new information, therapists should check in with the parents or family about their understanding of what was shared. For example, you can say, "How does that sound to you? Does any of what I shared resonate for you? Does any of what I just discussed ring true in terms of your experience with your daughter? Does this sound like something you might be open to?"

Following up with these questions will clarify whether the family understood what you presented as well as elicit feedback about how they are processing this information. It may also bring to the surface additional questions they may have about the conversation. Parents, too, should always feel comfortable asking questions and sharing feelings.

Reaching for Underlying Feelings and Creating Space for Emotional Expression

Sometimes an emotional block precludes full acceptance from families. It is important for parents to identify the emotions underneath the outer layer of rejection and then create space for these feelings to be expressed. Yes, the father worries that John may not be able to know he's transgender at 15 years old. Yes, the father worries that John will change his mind over time.

As a father shares these concerns, a therapist's role is to reach for the feelings that shape the father's worries. What emotions is this father experiencing underneath his concerns? Is it fear, anxiety, worry, anger, loss? As the father discloses his concern that John might change his mind, part of our work is to imagine, or be curious about, what feelings might drive that concern.

PARENTS, CAN YOU THINK OF SOME THINGS YOU HAVE SAID OR THOUGHT AND LINK THESE TO UNDERLYING EMOTIONS YOU HAVE?

Tentative language is helpful in reaching for underlying feelings. For example, as a therapist, you might say, "I wonder if underneath your worry that John may change his mind, you might also be afraid of losing him?" Or, "I could be way off base, but is there a chance that in addition to worrying about John, you also might worry about being an effective parent in this situation?" The tentative wording allows a parent to agree or disagree. If they agree, you can ask them to tell you more about this. If they disagree, they often go on to explain what they see as more accurate, or you can ask about this.

PARENTS, THE SAME IS TRUE FOR YOU. ALLOW YOURSELF TO EXPLORE WHAT YOU MIGHT BE FEELING IN A TENTATIVE WAY. THIS MAY GIVE YOU MORE SPACE TO ARRIVE AT A DEEPER UNDERSTANDING OF YOUR FEELINGS.

Anger is often a surface emotion when families are rejecting. Yet, anger is rarely the entire story for parents. When parents are angry about their child's self-disclosure as transgender, appear rejecting of this identity, or oppose a social or medical transition step, the underlying emotions are often fear, hurt, or sadness. These are the feelings the clinician needs to bring to the surface and acknowledge in order to facilitate movement toward greater acceptance. It is these feelings that are the real barrier to acceptance, not the parents' anger.

Therapy must provide a safe space for parents to explore and express these emotions. Bringing their grief, loss, fear, worry, anger, or disappointment out into the open where it can be acknowledged, expressed, and validated is essential for healing. As long as these feelings are hidden or unexpressed, the family will remain mired in conflict or rejection of their child's trans identity.

The following vignette illustrates these strategies for facilitating greater acceptance—beginning where the family is, drawing out their concerns and validating them, reaching for underlying emotions, and creating a safe space to express these emotions.

As part of a project that offered family therapy to LGBTQ youth identified as at risk of becoming homeless due to parental rejection, I met with Juan, a 17-year-old young man who had run away several times. He was a sharp-dressing teen who paid great attention to his appearance. His gender presentation was highly feminine. He sometimes identified as gay, sometimes as trans, but more often as a gender-fluid femme man.

In our first appointment, Juan told me how much his mother hated him for being "femme." They fought almost every time he left the apartment. He said he had run away before because of the mean things his mother would say to him when she was angry. He was clear that she rejected him because of his femme gender expression. Juan's primary affect in our early sessions was anger toward his mother's rejection of him, but there were moments when the hurt underneath his rage was apparent.

The first time I met Juan's mother, I asked to meet with her alone. I did not think Juan was emotionally able to engage with her in a constructive way yet, and given his description of their interactions, I did not want to subject him to additional experiences of her anger and rejection.

The mother's anger was apparent from the onset of our appointment. As I asked some initial questions about how she saw what was happening between her and her son, she launched into a tirade about his appearance. "It's not right for a young man to dress like that. It's just not right. All that makeup. Those girly clothes. It's not right."

She told me how much she disapproved of the friends he hung out with and the way they acted just like him. She hadn't raised her son to be like this. Yes, she was a single mom, but she had taught him what a man should be like. No real man prances around like a girl. Maybe she should have his uncle beat some sense into him.

At about that point, I knew that some of my colleagues would be ready to write the mom off as hopeless. She seemed as rejecting of her son as Juan had told me, and there was very little room to get a word in edgewise. Each time I attempted to shift the conversation or offer an alternate perspective, her rage resurfaced and took over the discussion. She did not want to hear anything else—and perhaps (I suspected) especially not from a white middle-class professional man who was likely judging her as a working-class single Puerto Rican mom who clearly had not raised her son to be a real man.

In my experience, anger is rarely our first emotion. Anger is an emotion that almost always layers on top of either fear or pain. Anger can protect us from the profound discomfort of feeling afraid and powerless; it can create a cushion against the pain of being hurt by someone or something in our life. Juan's anger toward his mother clearly functioned in part to protect him from the pain of her rejection of him. I wondered what might lie underneath his mother's rage.

I also deeply believe what I wrote earlier about most parents loving their children and wanting the best for them. In part, this is rooted in knowing from experience that there is absolutely nothing my children could do that would ever erase my love for them. When I reach beneath the anger of most parents, this profound unconditional love is almost always there, even if deeply buried or scarred in the moment. The understanding that anger is rarely our first emotion and my belief that deep love is at the root of most parents' psyche means I rarely accept what looks like parental rejection at face value. Instead, I maintain a passionate conviction that there is always more to the story.

As I met several more times with Juan's mother, I was able to engage her in telling me what he had been like as a young child, what he liked and didn't like, what made him laugh, what about him made her laugh, and what had made her proud of him. We explored her hopes and dreams for Juan. We talked about how she had tried to raise him and the kind of person she wanted him to be when he grew up. She told me that she and her sister had lived together for much of Juan's childhood, that her sister loved Juan as if he were her own son, and how they had raised him together, sharing child care and doctor's visits and parent-teacher conferences. She told me how much Juan loved his aunt. She was the one who had taught him to play baseball and bought him his first bike.

Her sister had been diagnosed with breast cancer two years before and was gone within the year. She and Juan were both devastated. As I brought us back around to what was happening between her and Juan now, I acknowledged that the depth of her love for her son was palpable. She nodded and began to tear up.

As we continued to talk, she began to tell me how afraid she was for her son. How terrified she was every time he left the apartment looking like "that"—"you know, like a girl." She had heard boys like Juan being called "faggots" or "maricón," getting beaten up, sometimes left for dead. When Juan's boyfriend picked him up, she worried they wouldn't make it to the nearest subway station 10 blocks away without someone harassing them. It was this fear that fueled her anger. Underneath all the anger, Juan's mother wasn't rejecting; she was terrified of losing him. This would have been difficult enough to navigate on its own, but so close on the heels of losing her sister, the fear was unbearable for her.

Within the next few weeks, I was able to bring Juan and his mother in together. With coaching, Juan was able to tell his mother how much her anger hurt him, how it made him feel as if she didn't love him anymore, and how this was even more painful alongside his grief about losing his aunt the year before. His mother was able to share her fears, how much she worried for his safety, how alone she had felt since her sister died. She told Juan she couldn't bear to think of losing him as well, and so she yelled at him for going out "like that." Together we were able to reframe the mom's rage. It didn't mean she rejected who he was. In fact, it meant the opposite. The intensity of her anger reflected the depth of her love for him, how important he was to her, and how much she wanted him to remain in her life.

Working with Juan and his mom confirmed my belief that as clinicians, we can never write a parent off. We can never blithely accept what may look and sound very much like rejection on the surface. There is almost always more to this story. It's our profound responsibility to reach for what may lie underneath the rage and disapproval. Our understanding now about the critical role family acceptance plays in the health and well-being of these young people demands that we reach for what might yet be love, buried deep beneath the parent's seeming rejection.

As illustrated above, when parents or other family members are deeply embedded in anger or rejection, one strategy is to try to step back from their anger for a moment and then invite memories of when the child was younger.

A therapist might say, "I wonder if you would be willing to step back from what you are feeling [or from what we have been discussing] for a moment? If you would be willing to shift gears and share some of how you felt when he/she was young. What were your feelings when he/she came into your life? What hopes or dreams did you have for them?"

These kinds of conversations often make it possible to link hopes and dreams to the importance of acceptance and support. These hopes and dreams can be realized, but only with love, acceptance, and support.

FOR PARENTS, WHEN YOU THINK BACK TO YOUR FEELINGS OR HOPES AND DREAMS FOR YOUR CHILD FROM EARLY ON ALONGSIDE WHERE YOU ARE TODAY, WHAT FEELINGS COME UP?

Even a small movement away from rejection and toward acceptance can decrease the young adult's risk factors (Ryan, et al., 2010). Given this, when family members have shared some of the positive dreams they held for their child, I may ask if there are one or two rejecting behaviors they might be willing to stop doing and one or two accepting behaviors they would be willing to begin doing. Many times the agreement I strive for is to have them try out these shifts for one to two weeks until we meet again. I frame the agreement in this short-term context. This is not about changing how they interact with the child permanently. It is about not doing or saying one or two things that convey rejection and trying out one or two accepting behaviors or messages for this brief time period so that we can come back and discuss it further.

It can be helpful to draw on a harm reduction framework. I ask the parents if they are willing to refrain from one rejecting behavior and begin practicing one accepting behavior, not because they have changed their minds and now believe being transgender is OK, but simply because of what we know now about the long-term impact of parental actions on children. I stress that my goal is not to change their beliefs but to increase the chances that their child will grow up to be healthy and alive.

Getting parents to stop even one rejecting message or action and begin even one new accepting practice can facilitate a greater sense of acceptance for the trans young person. It communicates that their parent is willing to try—that their parent loves them enough to try something different simply because it may make a difference for the young person. It demonstrates commitment to the youth on the parent's part.

Another intervention strategy involves exploring the value of love within families and what it looks like to live out this value within their family. I explore whether families can love each other without necessarily agreeing about everything with each other. I explore whether it is possible for families to express unconditional love and acceptance, without that necessarily meaning condoning every individual choice or behavior. I believe the answer to both questions is yes, though living this out within families can certainly be challenging. If love is a primary value for a particular family, this exploration can be worthwhile. Knowing what the research says about the pivotal importance of unconditional love for transgender adolescents supporting a family as they grapple with how to live out their love for each other, despite possible differences, can be invaluable.

Potential Pitfalls or Biases With Families From Conservative Faith Traditions

- Progressive or nonreligious therapists not understanding conservative religious beliefs
- Belittling conservative religious beliefs or minimizing their significance to families
- Prejudgment of these families
- Perceiving parents as not loving their child enough; viewing parents as placing a higher premium on their beliefs than on their child's well-being
- Pushing families to choose between their religious beliefs and their child rather than looking for ways to expand options/paths

Question: Can families from conservative faith traditions believe that being transgender is wrong or sinful and still accept their transgender child?

Reflection: This is a challenging question for many mental health providers as well as transgender individuals. There are some who would say this is not possible—that when parents believe it is wrong or sinful for their child to identify as transgender, this inherently equals parental rejection. In my experience in working with families, I am no longer sure this is always the case.

There is no question that there are many transgender youth growing up in families who understand trans identity to be "against God's will," and some of these parents do reject their children as a result of this belief. In some situations, this rejection is complete enough to result in the trans youth being kicked out of their family's home. However, I also believe that we, as mental health professionals, need to resist viewing acceptance and rejection as an either/or proposition. This is the same kind of polarized thinking that families from conservative faith traditions are often accused of.

Instead, as we can see from the Family Acceptance Project research, family acceptance and rejection can be viewed on a continuum, not just as polar opposites (Ryan, et al., 2009; Ryan, et al., 2010). This means that there can be degrees of acceptance and rejection within individual families. It means that acceptance and rejection are not necessarily mutually exclusive.

On a purely pragmatic level, if we operate with the assumption that acceptance and rejection are mutually exclusive and conclude that parents cannot view being transgender as sinful and accept their child, we preclude any possibility of engaging these parents and facilitating change or increased acceptance. And this is true whether or not we verbally express this opinion. Even if we are silent about our assumption, it is likely that our nonverbal communication will inevitably convey this judgment to the parents.

As fine as this line might be, I have worked with some parents from conservative religious communities who did find a way to hold their beliefs in one hand and yet also be clear about their unconditional love for their child. The mother of a 17-year-old nonbinary youth with whom I worked often read fundamentalist Christian literature while in my reception area. Yet, as I talked with this mother, it was evident that she had found a way to navigate her church's beliefs alongside her love for her child.

The mother remained unsure that it was OK to be transgender; the mother still believed that sex and gender identity were the same in "God's eyes." At the same time, she stated she loved her child unconditionally. When we met, the mother was able to acknowledge her own religious beliefs and her struggle with how all this fit together, yet simultaneously tell her child that she loved them unconditionally.

I did some coaching with the young person about being able to see that acceptance did not always have to equal agreement—that their mother could love them unconditionally, yet not always agree with them—in the same way that they might love a partner sometime down the road and not necessarily agree with that person about everything.

Some of you might be thinking you are not so sure this is possible. That you're not convinced the mother really unconditionally accepted her child if she still thought being transgender was a sin. You might think the young person would not feel loved if the mother still held those religious beliefs. I concede that this is a fine line. Nonetheless, I believe it is sometimes possible to help families walk this line and hold these two seemingly opposed positions in tandem without either canceling the other out. And if this is the closest I can get to acceptance in the moment and it means that there's a better chance that another transgender young person stays alive, I'll take it.

We need more research about families within conservative faith traditions who are accepting of their LGBT youth. We need to better understand how these families reach a place of acceptance even if their beliefs do not change. We need to understand what enables them to make this leap. Knowing how some families successfully navigate this dilemma might enable us to better understand how we can facilitate this movement into unconditional love and acceptance for other families—even when their religious beliefs may not change.

A Note for Clinicians: Beyond Gender Identity

A young person's gender identity is not always the whole story in working with their families. Many times the work may move well beyond the child's gender identity to engage other family dynamics that are less than optimal or unresolved.

In the course of working with one transgender adolescent, the nature of his struggles led to extensive family work around unresolved aspects of the parents' divorce, the father's largely unacknowledged addiction, and the impact of a grandmother's alcoholism.

In work with another family a generational pattern emerged of not discussing major events in the life of the family. It was sparked by my discovery several months into our work (ostensibly focused on a 13-year-old trans girl) that the mother had recently been diagnosed with her third round of breast cancer. Not only had no one told me about the mother's reoccurrence, neither parent had talked to their children about this – as in never mentioned it to the two young people.

As we processed this issue the father shared that his father had been tragically killed in an accident when he was only five years old. His mother never told him anything about the accident, and in fact never mentioned his father again. She just moved on as if there had never been a father in his life.

Both of these scenarios reflect the fact that while work with families of trans youth may begin with a young person's coming out as trans, it may go anywhere from that disclosure. It is important to be prepared for this likelihood and have an awareness of the level of your clinical skills in work with families. It may be that some families need to be referred to a more senior family therapist if more complex family challenges and patterns emerge as they did in these two families.

CHAPTER 9

All About School

I BEGAN SEEING MARCO (NATAL FEMALE) WHEN HE WAS IN fifth grade. His mother brought him to see me because a few months earlier he had told a school guidance counselor he was transgender and wanted to attend school as a boy. The guidance counselor then called his mother. While surprised by this news, Marco's mother indicated that she was supportive whatever his gender identity or expression.

We met from November through the following June. Over the course of my exploring Marco's sense of himself, meeting with his mother, and the two of them together, Marco remained clear about being a boy. At the end of fifth grade, Marco was emphatic about beginning middle school (sixth grade) as a boy. His mother and I agreed this was the right step. She met with his new school in August, and in September her son started middle school as Marco.

As he and I met each week, I checked in about how it was going at school. Were his teachers using "Marco" and male pronouns? How were his peers responding (some of whom had known him in elementary school)? Was he encountering any difficulties? Was anyone teasing him or asking personal questions? About two months into the school year, I asked these questions again. "How's it going being in sixth grade as Marco?" Marco's response was, "Well you know, now I can just do my work."

This opened up a conversation about how hard it had felt the year before, how distracted he had felt when his teacher and classmates saw him as a girl, how much he had hated going to school and hated hearing the girl's name everyone used for him. Socially transitioning and attending school as Marco removed these distractions and distress. Consequently, he was able to simply focus on what he was learning in classes. As the year went on, Marco's peer interactions and grades improved significantly compared to the previous year.

Marco was one of my first adolescent transgender clients. His response about simply being able to focus on his work caught my attention. It highlighted how much mental and emotional energy trans and gender-diverse youth expend not being seen in their affirmed gender—how distracting this can be, how much it keeps them from being present, and the extent to which this can interfere with academic enjoyment, performance, and success. Marco's growth and progress that next year illuminated the wide-ranging positive impact for a transgender young person allowed to fully be who they are in the world.

This chapter addresses transgender children and adolescents within educational settings. It begins by exploring ways to inform schools about a young person's social transition, including key issues, possible requests, and necessary decisions when meeting with school personnel. It outlines strategies to ensure that the school maintains a safe and positive learning environment as the young person attends school in their affirmed gender. This is followed by current research about harassment and bullying within schools and its impact on transgender and gender-diverse youth.

The second half of this chapter describes best practices to create and maintain supportive, inclusive environments for transgender and gender-diverse youth (and consequently for all students) within school settings. It reviews the May 2016 U.S. Education Department's Office for Civil Rights and U.S. Department of Justice's Civil Rights Division's Dear Colleague Letter ("DCL") affirming that all U.S. schools are prohibited from discrimination on the basis of gender identity or expression under Title IX of the Education Amendments of 1972 (20 U.S.C. §§ 1681–1688) and explicitly charged with protecting transgender students.

While many of these policies and practices are relevant to other youth organizations, the final section addresses additional considerations that may emerge in settings such as day and/or overnight camps and community youth programs (scout groups, sports teams, and arts, music, and performance activities). In addition to providing support for transgender and gender-diverse youth and their families, the chapter emphasizes the important role mental health providers can play in educating schools and advocating the full inclusion of trans and gender-diverse young people. The chapter ends with a series of best practice guidelines for schools, agencies, and other organizations.

Coming Out at School

It can be helpful to begin a child's social transition at school on the first day back from a break in classes. When possible, many families choose to have their child or adolescent socially transition with the start of the school year in September. This creates a fresh start with new teachers, who meet the young person in their affirmed gender and begin using their affirmed name and pronouns at the onset of the academic year. This can facilitate the consistent use of the youth's affirmed name and pronouns more smoothly as opposed to the teacher needing to shift to a new name midway through the year.

However, decisions about when a young person or family is ready to transition at school do not always fit this timetable. Some families begin social transition after the December/January break or upon returning from spring break. While teachers and classmates knew the young person in their birth-assigned gender and name for part of the school year, beginning after a break in classes creates a clear first day when the new affirmed gender is announced and recognized.

Other families simply agree on a start date with the school without connecting it to a school break (typically on Monday at the start of a new week). For preschool and elementary school youth, it may be less critical to begin a school transition in conjunction with the return from a break. Younger peers typically make the shift to a child's new name and affirmed gender more easily, without extensive explanations or discussion.

There are situations when the young person can begin going by their affirmed gender when they start a new school. This might be at the beginning of middle or high school. Some families relocate or find other ways for their child to have a complete new beginning in their affirmed gender, with neither teachers nor classmates having known the child prior to their social transition. At times, this choice is made because the parents and young person do not perceive the current school environment as supportive of transgender youth. Other times, the young person does not want to navigate, or feel capable of navigating, the disclosure and adjustment period that occurs when trans youth socially transition in a school where they were previously known in their birth-assigned sex/gender.

Meeting With the School

Social transitions at school begin with a meeting between the parents and the school. If the young person is older, they may also participate in this meeting. In the lower grades, where the child has a single teacher and classroom, the conversation often begins with parents informing the teacher that the child will be socially transitioning. The conversation typically moves from there to a meeting with a school guidance counselor or principal.

With middle and high school youth, if the parents have an existing relationship with someone at the school, such as a guidance counselor or assistant principal, it can be helpful to begin the conversation with that staff member. They are often able to outline next steps in terms of other staff who need to be included in planning and decision-making.

The initial focus of these meetings is disclosure about the child's gender identity and the intent to have the young person begin attending school in their affirmed gender using a new name and pronouns. During these meetings, the parents discuss how they would like their child's transition to be announced at school and in classes and discuss what type of accommodations may be necessary.

When the school has previously worked with transgender or gender-fluid students, the staff generally have basic knowledge about gender identity and expression and may have already developed policies for navigating the transition. If this is the first time a school has had a transgender students, the parents will need to be prepared to educate the staff—or point them to existing resources. They should also be prepared to advocate specific policies or accommodations. In these situations, mental health providers can play a key role in advocating the needs and rights of the young person.

It can be helpful for the parents to take some basic literature to this meeting or make it available to school staff beforehand. Possible resources include:

- Books about gender identity/expression among young people (such as this one)
- Resources geared toward transgender students in schools
    o Lambda Legal (http://www.lambdalegal.org/know-your-rights/youth/tgnc-friendly-schools)
    o The National Center for Transgender Equality (http://www.transequality.org/know-your-rights/schools)
- U.S. Department of Education Office for Civil Rights documents, May 2016
    o OCR "Dear Colleague" Letter on Transgender Students (http://www2.ed.gov/about/offices/list/ocr/letters/colleague-201605-title-ix-transgender.pdf)
    o OCR Examples of Policies and Emerging Practices for Supporting Transgender Students (http://www2.ed.gov/about/offices/list/oese/oshs/emergingpractices.pdf)

In the past, schools sometimes required a letter about the child's transgender or gender-fluid identity from their medical doctor or mental health provider that indicated that the child was diagnosed with gender dysphoria. However, the May 2016 DOE/DOJ letter explicitly states that transgender students do not need to produce a medical diagnosis or birth certificate; instead, a parent's or guardian's assertion that a student's gender identity differs from previous records or representations is sufficient for the school to be required to recognize that student's affirmed gender.

What to Discuss With School Personnel

The first request is typically for the school and all personnel to begin using the child's affirmed name and pronouns, even if there has been no legal name change yet. The school will generally not change the official school records without documentation of a court-ordered name change. However, parents still have the right to insist that the school find a way to ensure all class rosters reflect the child's affirmed name.

Families need to ensure that all teachers are informed about the child's gender transition and affirmed name and pronouns. This may be something parents want to do directly prior to the first day of the transition. Other times, the school will inform the teachers. It is important to ensure that school administration expects teachers to use the affirmed name and pronouns and communicates that this is essential for the student's well-being.

Some schools with dress codes have adopted gender-neutral uniforms. When this is not the case, parents need to be clear that their child will attend school in the uniform that matches their affirmed gender.

Two areas that have been contentious at times with schools have been the use of gendered bathrooms and locker rooms. Trans-affirmative school policies allow transgender and gender-diverse students to use the restroom and locker room that matches their gender presentation or affirmed gender. Some schools may still initially refuse to allow this or insist that the young person use a single-stall bathroom and a separate locker room space.

However, the May 2016 DOE/DOJ directive affirms that transgender students must be allowed to use the bathroom that corresponds with their gender identity—and that to do otherwise is discrimination against trans students. In addition to this directive, many recent court decisions have ruled that the federal Title IX law banning discrimination on the basis of sex also prohibits discrimination on the basis of gender identity and expression.

Many transgender children and teens will want to use the restroom that matches their affirmed gender. Mental health providers can work with parents to assess which decision is best in terms of their child's well-being and safety. This might include thinking about the particular school context and examining how safe a transgender boy will be in the boys' bathroom or locker room (or a trans girl in the girls' facilities). Children and adolescents are typically alone in bathrooms and locker rooms without adult supervision. This can create a risk for transgender and gender-diverse youth of being harassed or bullied by peers when adults are not present to intervene.

It is also generally possible for trans and gender-diverse youth to use an alternate restroom, such as one in the school nurse's office. This alternative space may be chosen because of safety concerns, as indicated above. Other times, trans youth choose this option because they do not feel ready to navigate gender-segregated settings with their cisgender peers. The decision to use gender-segregated facilities should always rest with the young person. They should never be "pressured" into using a gendered facility before they want to do so.

However, there may be situations where parents believe they need to overrule the child's choice about using gender-segregated facilities based on the concerns just discussed. When this occurs, it is essential to thoroughly discuss the reasons behind the parents' decision, make space for the young person's feelings to be expressed and acknowledged, and ensure that the young person understands that this decision does not reflect a lack of support or a denial of their affirmed gender.

Decisions about using gender-segregated or alternate facilities may evolve over time. A 14-year-old transgender girl may not feel comfortable using the girls' room at the onset of her social transition at school. But she may feel completely ready to do so six months later as she becomes more comfortable navigating school as a girl and peers more fully know and accept her in her affirmed gender. Regardless of the ultimate decision, these factors need to be considered prior to the child's social transition at school.

Historically, many schools balked at allowing transgender youth to participate in musical groups and sports that were gender-specific. John was actively involved with several school choirs prior to transition. When he began ninth grade as a boy, John asked to join the male a cappella choir. The music director was initially reluctant. After several conversations with the parents, John was allowed to join. However, the director required John to audition even though the a cappella choir was not an auditioned choir and none of the other singers were asked to audition.

Similarly, athletic coaches have resisted allowing transgender girls to play on girls' sports teams or transgender boys to play on boys' teams. With the May 2016 DOJ/DOE directive prohibiting discrimination against trans students, all schools must now allow transgender students to join the teams that match their affirmed gender.

It is essential that families and mental health providers know what rights transgender students are legally entitled to receive. Some states have enacted laws that prohibit discrimination against transgender people within their jurisdiction. However, currently there still are no federal laws prohibiting this discrimination. While the May 2016 directive issued by the Departments of Justice and Education serves this function for transgender students, it is likely that students and families will encounter school districts refusing to enforce the directive. Within days of its issuance, several lawsuits were filed challenging its requirements. It is also likely that some families will not be aware of the recent directive and the protections it affords them.

This means that mental health practitioners need to educate both youth and their families about the rights they are entitled to within their schools, informing them that the Departments of Justice and Education now require schools to allow transgender students to use the restrooms and locker rooms that match their affirmed gender and to participate in school groups, sports, and other gendered activities that match their affirmed gender. If the school requires students to wear a uniform, transgender students are legally entitled to wear the uniform that matches their affirmed gender. All schools are also now mandated to support trans students by using their affirmed name and pronouns.

Given that the directive may be contested for some time yet and some school districts may refuse to enforce the directive, organizations such as Lambda Legal and the Transgender Law Center can be helpful. These agencies will be tracking school districts that refuse to comply.

If you or someone you work with has experienced gender-based bullying, harassment, or discrimination at school, you (or they) have the right to file a complaint with the U.S. Department of Education's Office for Civil Rights (OCR). The National Center for Transgender Equality provides guidelines for filing a complaint at the following link on their website: http://www.transequality.org/know-your-rights/schools.

Student Privacy

Transgender students of any age have the right to privacy about their transgender history and identity. When a child first transitions, almost everyone at the school will know they are transgender. However, as the young person moves into successive grades or changes schools, new teachers will not necessarily know the child's history. Some transgender youth, especially middle or high school students, may want to "be stealth" at school (a term used within the trans community to indicate trans people who are not out or open about their trans identity or history).

Many trans adolescents simply want to attend school as a "regular" girl or guy. While they might choose to come out to certain individuals, they may not want all of their teachers or peers to know their transgender history. The young people fear—often rightfully so, unfortunately—that once others learn they are trans, it will change the way their peers or teachers see them.

Given this, it is important for parents and young people to talk about—possibly with a mental health professional—where, how, and to whom they want their trans history or identity disclosed. Parents have the right to ask the school which staff will be told their child is transgender. Transgender children and adolescents also have the right to know who has this information. Both youth and their parents have the right to have this information kept confidential and disclosed only to school personnel with a need to know (perhaps a school nurse who might be involved in the child's needing emergency medical attention).

Reinforcing this right to privacy is the fact that the young person's transgender identity requires a psychiatric diagnosis of gender dysphoria. Consequently, the information is protected medical information. It should not be disclosed without the family's awareness and permission. The only exception is a medical emergency where the information is needed.

If certain school personnel need to be aware of the young person's gender identity, this must be shared with their parents. Both young people and parents have the right to know who these individuals are, as well as when, where, and how the information will be disclosed. For adolescents in particular, it can be profoundly uncomfortable to unexpectedly learn that a teacher or school staff member knows about your transgender identity or, worse yet, to be publicly outed by one of these adults, even if unintentionally. In some contexts being outed like this may put them at risk of harassment or violence.

With younger children, families must think through how other parents in their child's grade will be informed. Sharing this news can allow other parents to talk with their children about their classmate's transition. Parents need to decide whether they want the school to disclose this information or whether they disclose the information themselves. I have worked with schools that wanted to share the information that a child was gender transitioning—typically because they believed this would help the process go more smoothly. I have also worked with schools that did not publicly disclose this information but instead addressed it on a case-by-case basis if other parents asked questions. When schools do disclose, this typically happens just prior to or on the first day the child attends school in their affirmed gender.

The Rights of Transgender Students (National Center for Transgender Equality

- You have the right not to be bullied or harassed because you are transgender or gender-nonconforming. If school administrators become aware of bullying or harassment, they must take action to end it.

- You have the right to equal educational opportunities regardless of your gender identity or expression or your race, nationality, or disability. This includes not being punished or excluded from school activities or events because you are transgender or gender-nonconforming.

- You have the right to present yourself in a way that is consistent with your gender identity, so long as you follow rules for how to dress that apply to all students.

- You have the right to use restrooms and other facilities that are consistent with your gender identity and can't be forced to use separate restrooms.

- You have the right to privacy concerning your transgender status and gender transition. Any such information kept in school records must be kept private and not shared without your permission.

- You have the right to join or start a Gay–Straight Alliance or pride club and to have your group treated like other student groups.

How Safe Are Schools for Trans and Gender-Diverse Youth?

GLSEN's (the Gay, Lesbian and Straight Education Network's) 2013 National School Climate Survey indicates that transgender, gender-queer, and other non-cisgender students faced the most hostile school environments. Additionally, gender-nonconforming cisgender students experienced more harassment at school than did gender-conforming cisgender students (Kosciw, Greytak, Palmer, & Boesen, 2014). Over half (56%) of the students reported that they often or frequently heard negative remarks about someone's gender expression, such as about someone not acting "masculine" or "feminine" enough, with remarks about someone not acting "masculine enough" occurring more frequently. One third reported hearing derogatory comments about transgender people (such as "tranny" or "he/she") often or frequently.

While these remarks were often made when teachers were not present, when school staff were present, only 10% of students indicated that they intervened most or all of the time. In addition, over half (55.5%) of the students had heard teachers or other school personnel also make negative remarks about a student's gender expression (Kosciw et al., 2014). The pervasiveness of these remarks signals that transgender, gender-nonconforming, and gender-queer youth are viewed as "less than" and are not welcome in that school setting. This directly impacts a trans youth's sense of self and safety. One young person said, "This past week has been nothing but 'Is that a boy or a girl?' said loudly behind me or people calling me 'mangirl.' It's making school feel much more unsafe and I hate walking through the halls" (Kosciw et al., 2014, p. 22).

The frequency of these remarks by staff and students furthers a climate of hostility within the school. More than half of the students (55.2%) surveyed reported that they had been verbally harassed at school because of their gender expression, with one in five having been harassed often or frequently. Almost one quarter (22.7%) had been physically harassed (e.g., shoved or pushed) because of their gender expression (Kosciw et al., 2014).

Numerous studies have shown that transgender students experience increased marginalization and discrimination as well as higher rates of harassment and bullying than do their lesbian, gay, and bisexual classmates (Greytak et al., 2009; McGuire, Anderson, Toomey, & Russell, 2010; McGuire & Conover-Williams, 2010). Transgender students also reported the lowest feelings of safety at school (Greytak et al., 2009). This lack of perceived (and often real) safety contributes to increased absences and decreased academic performance among transgender students (Greytak et al, 2009). Transgender students also demonstrate fewer hopes and goals for their future than their cisgender peers.

These experiences of harassment and bullying can significantly impact the health and well-being of transgender, gender-nonconforming, and gender-queer children and adolescents. Studies have found that increased abuse is linked to poorer physical and mental health, is associated with greater risk of HIV and other sexually transmitted infections, and can lead to decreased psychosocial adjustment (Espelage & Swearer, 2008; Russell, Ryan, Toomey, Diaz, & Sanchez, 2011; Toomey, Ryan, Diaz, Card, & Russell, 2010). This overall marginalization, isolation, harassment, and bullying correlates with increased suicidal ideation and attempts, with 45% of trans youth in one study reporting thoughts about suicide and 26% having attempted suicide (Grossman & D'Augelli, 2007).

Safety Plans

Given the increased risk of harassment and bullying, making a safety plan prior to the child's attending school in their affirmed gender is essential. The plan needs to identify a safe adult at school to whom the young person can reach out at any time if they are ridiculed, harassed, or bullied by other students. This is often a guidance counselor or a school nurse that the youth can easily access.

In discussing a safety plan, it is important to "walk a line" between the need to establish the plan and creating fear or anxiety about the possibility of harassment. The majority of youth I have worked with have positive social transitions with their peers at school and do not experience harassment. At the same time, the young person needs to know whom to seek out if something does occur. Even if the transition at school goes well, it is important to periodically inquire whether the youth has experienced any harassment or bullying or an uncomfortable question or remark from a classmate or staff member.

Studies of youth overall (non-trans-specific) indicate that harassment and bullying occur most often in middle school, with sixth grad-ers reporting the highest incidence (U.S. Department of Justice, 2014). This can include verbal harassment, such as being made fun of, called names, or insulted. It can be physical bullying, such as being pushed, shoved, tripped, or spit on. Sometimes the bullying involves students being forced to do things they don't want to do. Being excluded or shut out of friendship circles is also a form of harassment and bullying that can create tremendous isolation for a trans youth. The incidence of bullying tends to decrease as young people move into Grades 10 through 12 (U.S. Department of Justice, 2014).

It is important to recognize that young people may be reluctant to speak out when they are being harassed or bullied. One study indi-cated that 17% of third- through fifth-graders had been bullied but did not report this to anyone. The number of young people not reporting they are being bullied increases steadily as grade level increases; 43% of 9th- through 12th-graders failed to tell anyone what was happen-ing to them in school (Luxenberg, Limber, & Olweus, 2014).

Jimmy (natal female) began attending a private school as a boy as he started ninth grade. Things went smoothly that year. Jimmy did well academically, and his peers seemed very supportive. During the winter of 10th grade, Jimmy's grades began to drop. There were several instances when he cut classes or left school early. His parents felt he was not taking school seriously, and we met for several family sessions to address what was happening. His next report card had several failing grades, and the school placed Jimmy on academic probation. A set of improvement goals were outlined, and when Jimmy failed to meet these goals, the school asked him to withdraw.

Throughout this time, Jimmy appeared fairly unconcerned about his grades, which of course further infuriated his parents. Though I asked several times whether something was happening at school that was bothering him and directly asked if anyone was making fun of him or bullying him, Jimmy said no. He completed 10th grade through an online program, and his parents placed him in a new school the following fall.

It was only after being at the new school for two months (and doing well) that Jimmy disclosed that several 12th-grade boys had been calling him names and pushing him around during the

previous school year. Rather than telling anyone what was happening, Jimmy "set out" to get expelled. While this was clearly a
"creative" and "successful" strategy, disclosing the bullying could
have enabled Jimmy to process the abuse, prevented his expulsion from school, and decreased the conflict with his parents.

There are numerous reasons why a young person might not disclose harassment or bullying by classmates. There are negative messages about "tattling" or being a "snitch" among most youth. Many
young people are also afraid that if they tell someone, the bullying
will only get worse. For trans guys in particular (like cisgender boys),
stereotypical expectations for men to be "tough" and not admit any
vulnerability can often make it more difficult to acknowledge incidents of bullying.

Depending on the school response to incidents of harassment or
bullying, youth may not trust that school personnel will intervene
even if they do report what is happening to them. This may be especially true for transgender students. The GLSEN 2013 school climate report indicated that in addition to frequently hearing negative
remarks about gender expression (not acting "masculine" or "feminine" enough) or negative remarks specifically about transgender
people (e.g., "tranny" or "he/she"), 55.5% of LGBT students reported
hearing negative remarks about gender expression from teachers or
other school staff. Furthermore, 61.6% of the students who did report
an incident said that school staff did nothing in response (Kosciw et
al., 2014).

Given the reluctance many gender-diverse youth have about disclosing experiences of harassment and bullying, it is essential that
parents, mental health providers, school counselors, and others recognize signs that may point to possible abuse. Signs that a student
may be experiencing harassment or bullying include:

- Lost or destroyed clothing, books, electronics, or jewelry
- Frequent headaches or stomach aches; feeling sick or
  faking illness to stay home from school
- Changes in eating habits (suddenly skipping meals,
  binge eating, coming home from school hungry because
  they did not eat lunch), difficulty sleeping, or frequent
  nightmares

- Declining grades, loss of interest in schoolwork, sudden loss of friends or avoidance of social situations
- Feelings of helplessness or decreased self-esteem
- Unexplainable injuries
- Self-destructive behaviors, such as running away from home, harming themselves, talking about suicide, or suicide attempts (U.S. Department of Health and Human Services, 2016c)

Given the frequency of harassment as well as the reluctance many transgender and gender-diverse youth have about disclosing incidents of bullying, it is critical to develop a safety plan, proactively discuss reasons why young people might not report experiences of harassment or bullying, and work with the young person to identify a "safe" adult with whom they can disclose what is happening at school (or in other youth program/activity settings) should the need arise.

Creating a Supportive, Inclusive Environment

For teachers, school administrators, and parents the overarching aim must be to create, communicate, and maintain a safe, inclusive, and affirming learning environment for all students. To accomplish this, goals must be framed in terms of the school culture as a whole, and not simply focus on protecting transgender students alone. The best practices that follow do not simply make schools safe and affirming for trans and gender-diverse youth; these policies and practices make schools safe for all students—lesbian, gay, and bisexual youth; youth whose gender expression varies from what is considered normative for their birth-assigned sex; gender-expansive or gender-creative youth; youth whose gender identity and/or expression goes beyond the binary; and cisgender, gender-conforming, straight youth.

The policies and practices outlined here send a message that all students are safe and free to bring their "whole" selves to school, that every student can safely explore the many varied aspects of their identity, and that harassment and bullying are never acceptable by or toward any student. These policies and practices are essential regardless of whether the school is currently aware of transgender students in attendance.

The development of safe, inclusive educational settings is grounded in a fundamental belief in the inherent dignity of all human beings (including young people) and, concomitantly, that each person/student deserves to be treated with respect and kindness. This value stance guides the development of policies and practices that ensure that each individual in the school gives, and receives, respect and kindness. These policies must describe what respect and kindness look like in action—what behaviors or actions demonstrate these foundational values.

However, developing policies themselves is insufficient. To shape the academic environment, the school's core values of respect and kindness, along with policies that ensure that these values are lived out in each arena of the school, must be communicated and continually reinforced by all school personnel.

The first step in creating a safe, affirming, and inclusive learning environment begins with adopting a policy that prohibits any kind of harassment or discrimination. This must be a written policy that is communicated to all school personnel, parents, and students. The underlying rationale for ensuring the absence of harassment or discrimination—that students cannot learn when they feel unsafe—must be clear. School personnel need to know that while they can hold any "personal" beliefs they choose, they cannot discriminate against, ridicule, or harass any student (or colleague, supervisor, or parent). Students as well need to understand that their personal beliefs or attitudes cannot be expressed in ways that harass or discriminate against their classmates.

These policies have sometimes been called "zero tolerance for discrimination" policies. However, there are many concerns about the language and effectiveness of zero-tolerance policies. In many settings, these policies serve as punitive approaches that administer consequences to students perceived to violate the guidelines. The consequences often include suspension or expulsion, which removes students from the school environment but does not necessarily contribute to changed behavior. Numerous studies indicate that zero-tolerance policies are largely ineffective and disproportionately applied to youth of color (American Psychological Association, 2008; National Association for the Advancement of Colored People, 2005; Wald & Losen, 2003; Witt, 2007).

While consequences can be appropriate in some situations, the first line of action in reducing instances of harassment, bullying, or discrimination needs to be an educational one that focuses on what we want students to do—practice kindness, respect, openness to diversity and difference, acceptance—rather than focusing on what we want them to stop doing. Schools need to educate students about the ways harassment, ridicule, and bullying harm others as well as the perpetrator themselves. This necessitates ongoing education and discussion about the school's values and how they facilitate a positive environment for all students. When students' actions do not demonstrate values of respect and kindness, simply punishing them does not typically effect change. Instead, school personnel must be willing to meet with these students and explore what might lie beneath this behavior as well as support them in building more positive social skills.

Creating a safe, inclusive environment must include educating students about the many ways human beings differ from one another. It must include discussion of our diversity as a strength, and thus something to be valued and celebrated. Students need to learn constructive ways to disagree with peers who hold divergent beliefs and opinions. They need to learn positive skills for resolving conflicts. Students need information and training on how to be an "ally" rather than a "bystander"—on how to speak up when someone is being teased or bullied. Overall, a proactive, preventive approach, marked by education, skills training, and positive reinforcement, is increasingly being recognized as more effective than punitive measures in creating safe, inclusive school environments (American Psychological Association, 2008; Boccanfuso & Kuhfeld, 2011; Smith, 2013). **Advocates for Youth** has an excellent curriculum titled Taking a Stand Against Bullying for teaching youth how to step forward when they see someone being bullied (http://advocatesforyouth .org/3rscurric/documents/4-Lesson-4-3Rs-TakingaStandAgainst-Bullying.pdf).

Given that many gender-diverse youth report hearing negative remarks about "non-normative" gender expression or about transgender people being harassed by peers in the presence of school personnel who fail to intervene, schools need clear policies that direct all personnel to address harassment and bullying when it occurs and then bring the incident to a supervisor's attention. Some adults ignore instances of bullying because they perceive "teasing" to be "part of growing up" and fail to understand its negative impact on young people, both in the present and potentially long term (Espelage & Swearer, 2008; Russell et al., 2011; Toomey et al., 2010). These negative repercussions need to be addressed with staff. Other times, school personnel fail to intervene because they feel they do not know "how" to do this effectively. As a result, these policies must be accompanied by regular training for staff regardless of their position or role—for teachers, counselors, facilities workers, food services staff, and others.

The University of Delaware has an excellent set of recommendations for teachers and parents on how to address and intervene in cases of bullying (http://www.education.udel.edu/wp-content/uploads/2013/01/Bullying.pdf).

Developing Guidelines That Support Transgender and Gender-Diverse Students

All school districts need to develop guidelines that promote not only safety, but also the positive development and education of gender-diverse youth. While the starting point is creating an inclusive educational environment, this must be followed by specific policies that address the unique needs of gender-diverse students. This section outlines specific policies that protect and affirm these young people.

Areas School Guidelines Should Address

Policies and forms that reflect gender-inclusive language

Use of affirmed name and pronouns

Names on official school records

Use of bathrooms

Use of locker rooms

Typically gender-segregated activities, such as
sports teams, choirs, theater roles, etc.

Physical education classes

Dress codes

Confidentiality

Staff education

All school policies—not just those specific to gender-diverse students—need to reflect gender-inclusive language. Typically, students are referred to—verbally and in writing—as boys and girls or as young men and women. These categories must be broadened to include youth whose gender identity may not be reflected within the male/female binary construct. This can include eliminating the use of male/female language ("boys"/"girls") where possible, or by adding language such as "transgender" or "gender-diverse."

Shifting this language signals to staff, parents, and students that the school is aware that not all students fit within the binary gender construct. It communicates the school's understanding that some students may identify as gender-diverse. This is essential for several reasons. First, simply acknowledging the existence of gender-diverse youth is a sign of respect, validation, and inclusion. Second, these changes facilitate increased awareness of the presence of gender-diverse youth among both staff and parents. Third, including gender-diverse youth within school policies affirms trans youth and signals that the administration views them as important members within the school community. The latter not only positively impacts gender-diverse youth but sends a clear message of inclusion and affirmation to the entire student body.

Most official forms, such as applications or intake forms, require that we "check" the male or female box to indicate our sex/gender. Schools need to review these documents and ensure that gender-diverse students are able to identify themselves in ways that are consistent with their gender identity rather than being forced to choose a box that does not describe them.

Options for Revising Gender Language on Forms

1.   Sex assigned at birth _____
2.   Gender identity _____
3.   Male _____
4.   Female _____
5.   Transgender _____
6.   Other _____

Schools must develop policies that support the use of affirmed names and pronouns for all gender-diverse students. As indicated before, using the young person's affirmed name is a sign of basic respect. It also validates the student's affirmed gender identity. When school personnel insist on using a student's birth-assigned name despite requests for their affirmed name and pronouns, it sends the message that "we do not see you for who you are" and "we do not believe you are who you know yourself to be." As discussed previously, microaggressions like these invalidate the experiential self-awareness and reality of gender-diverse youth, demeaning them and communicating that they are lesser human beings. The fact that these incidents are small interactions does not diminish their cumulative effect and demeaning impact and power.

Policies about the student's affirmed name and pronouns must be addressed both in terms of how the youth is addressed informally by teachers, coaches, counselors, and peers and within official school records. While official school records may need to use a student's birth-assigned name until it has been legally changed, it is essential to develop policies that also allow the inclusion of the student's affirmed name. This policy becomes particularly relevant with substitute teachers, who rely on the "official" roster for students' names.

Josie socially transitioned between eighth and ninth grade, beginning high school in her affirmed gender. Several middle schools funneled into her high school, meaning that most students met Josie as a young woman; they did not know her before she transitioned. The family filed the name change petition in July, but the approval process was delayed. As a result, the legal name on the school records remained her birth name.

When the parents met with the high school in August, the principal and guidance counselor were very supportive. Despite the official records, her teachers were informed about her transition, and they consistently used "Josie" and female pronouns. However, the first time one of the regular teachers called out sick, the substitute teacher read the name on the official roster—her legal birth name, thus outing Josie as a transgender student to her classmates.

This illustrates the importance of developing guidelines that allow the use of a student's affirmed name, even when the legal name has not yet been changed. Without incorporating the youth's affirmed name within the official records, the student's trans identity may be inadvertently disclosed, potentially subjecting them to ridicule or harassment from peers as well as to experiencing the more internal negative consequences associated with microaggressions, such as fear, shame, and dysphoria.

Beyond developing gender-affirmative guidelines, schools must ensure that all staff receive adequate education and training. This should include information about gender development, gender identity, and gender expression; the particular needs of gender-diverse students; specific steps staff can take to be strong allies for trans youth; knowledge of local resources (such as trans or LGBTQ youth programs/groups); and information about signs that may indicate a student is at risk of drug and/or alcohol use, high-risk sexual behavior, self-harm, or suicide.

Providing education for parents also facilitates the development of safe, inclusive educational environments. The school's gender policies need to be shared with parents along with other standard informative material, or these policies can be included in the school handbook sent home with each student. Some school districts organize educational presentations about gender diversity, gender identity, and gender expression for parents, which may include relevant videos, presentations by medical and mental health providers knowledgeable about gender development and gender identity in youth, a panel of community members, or table displays run by affirmative local youth programs or agencies. Schools can develop a resource guide for families that includes books, websites, and local support groups and organizations.

Given the centrality of peer relationships, developing a safe, inclusive educational environment necessitates student education about gender identity and expression. This material can be incorporated into larger conversations about gender diversity or discussions about current events as well as explored in more focused ways, such as classroom reading and assignments, school assemblies, and student fairs. Curriculum development needs to include positive material about transgender and nonbinary youth and adults.

In addition to "verbal" or written materials and activities, safety and support can also be communicated visually in the selection of images within classrooms and hallways. One middle school I visited had "Safe Space" signs at the entrance to every classroom. One place these stickers and posters are available is through GLSEN. Hard copy stickers and posters can be purchased for a nominal fee; digital downloads are free. http://shop.glsen.org/products/glsen-safe-space-kit?variant=11303798214

Work with students needs to challenge myths and stereotypes about transgender people and offer factual information that will facilitate understanding. Students need education about the various forms harassment and bullying may take (verbal, physical, online, etc.) as well as the harmful effects of these behaviors for both the recipient and the perpetrator. All students must know the process for reporting harassment, bullying, or abuse, including abuse centered around gender identity and expression. Students need to know safe places to go when experiencing harassment and safe school personnel to talk with if this happens to them or a peer. Concomitantly, the school needs to develop clear procedures to immediately address incidents of harassment or abuse that are reported by students or school personnel.

Supporting the development of Gay–Straight Alliances (GSAs) or pride clubs within middle and high schools is an important way schools can facilitate a safe, affirming environment for transgender and nonbinary youth. GSAs create opportunities for trans youth to meet each other, thus decreasing isolation and increasing their sense of support. The activities these student clubs plan facilitate a more positive sense of self, leading to pride in who they are. The teacher advisor can provide critical support for trans youth within the GSA. Given their visibility in this role, they may also become an identified resource for students who might not feel safe or ready to attend the club.

Given the name, Gay–Straight Alliances allow students who are questioning sexual orientation and/or gender identity and expression to attend without identifying as LGBTQ. They create safe spaces for LGBTQ students who are not ready to out themselves. The engagement of both LGBTQ and cisgender and straight peers facilitates the development of LGBTQ allies among the student body. It increases the number of non-LGBTQ youth willing and trained in how to stand up when they see another student being harassed or bullied. The participation of non-LGBTQ students increases the number of students who are knowledgeable and affirming of their LGBTQ classmates. It leads to non-LGBTQ students initiating classroom conversations, speaking up about issues of discrimination, and taking responsibility to create a safer, more welcoming climate at the school. Several studies indicate that the very presence of a GSA in a school increases the sense of safety for gender-diverse youth (Russell, Muraco, Subramaniam, & Laub, 2009; Toomey, Ryan, Diaz, Russell, 2011).

Students have the right to start a GSA in their school when none exists. The Equal Access Act, passed in 1984, requires all federally funded secondary schools to provide equal access to extracurricular clubs. All school-affiliated student organizations, including a Gay–Straight Alliance or pride alliance, must be treated equally in comparison to other student clubs. If a school permits student groups, it cannot ban certain types of groups or single them out for unequal treatment.

Other Youth Program Settings

Many of the issues transgender and nonbinary youth encounter within their schools may also emerge within the context of other youth-serving programs and activities. Community programs and youth-serving agencies may resist using the young person's affirmed name and pronouns. Programs like scouting, community sports teams, and day/overnight camps may be gender-segregated, and their policies about accepting transgender children/youth vary. For example, the Girl Scouts organization has publicly affirmed that transgender girls are welcome. Their position states, "If the child is recognized by the family and school/community as a girl and lives culturally as a girl, then Girl Scouts is an organization that can serve her in a setting that is both emotionally and physically safe" (Girl Scouts, 2016). While the

Boy Scouts organization lifted its ban on gay members in 2013 and its ban on gay adult leaders in 2015, these shifts did not address inclusion of transgender members or leaders (ACLU, 2015).

Co-ed programs, whether day programs or overnight camps, may or may not allow transgender youth to use the restrooms that match their affirmed gender. Sleep-away camps may not allow transgender campers to bunk with peers of their affirmed gender. These are all challenges that parents and trans youth may encounter as the young person begins to move through the world in their affirmed gender.

Resources

Focused on creating safe and affirming schools for all students, regardless of sexual orientation, gender identity, or gender expression, **GLSEN** offers extensive resources for K-12 classroom discussions and activities, professional development materials for teachers and administrators, and programming support for GSA's and other student clubs. http://www.glsen.org

Advocates for Youth has two excellent resources for developing safe programs for LGBTQ youth:

1. "Tips and Strategies for Assessing Youth Programs and Agencies." http://www.advocatesforyouth.org/component/content/article/972-tips-and-strategies-for-assessing-youth-programs-and-agencies
2. "Creating Safe Space for GLBTQ Youth: A Toolkit." This article includes lesson plans for building respect and tolerance among youth and strategies for creating safe space within an organization. http://www.advocatesforyouth.org/publications/608?task=view

The Importance of Education and Advocacy

Many mental health providers view their primary role as a clinical one. However, when working with transgender or gender-diverse children and adolescents, it is essential to be prepared to function as both an educator and advocate and not solely as a clinician. Many schools and other youth programs need accurate information about transgender youth. While many parents take on this challenge, some program directors may not view parents as objective or reliable sources of information. They may view the parents as focused on their child's inclusion and not on what the director or board of directors may see as in the best interest of the program. Camp or program directors may feel they need to prioritize possible risks for the program over the needs or desires of an individual camper. Having a professional, who is often perceived as both an expert and more objective, speak to these concerns can play a significant role in shifting opinions about the full inclusion of gender-diverse children and teens, as illustrated in the following vignette.

> Johnson (natal female) and his parents first came to see me in the spring of his sophomore year in high school. He had recently come out to his parents through an email as a transgender young man. Working together over the course of the summer, the family and I came to a consensus that he would begin 11th grade in his affirmed male gender. Johnson's passion was theater, especially musical theater. He performed in every school production and had been involved with a local theater company for several years. There was some hesitation in both contexts about Johnson assuming male roles after he transitioned at school, but this was resolved fairly easily.
>
> In the spring of that academic year, the community theater company began making plans for their summer theater day camp for elementary-age children. Johnson had served as a volunteer junior counselor in this program for the past two years and thoroughly enjoyed the work. In May, his parents received a call asking them to come in and meet with the director. They were informed that Johnson would not be able to return as a junior counselor because a parent of a camper had heard he was transgender and was adamant about not wanting her children around Johnson. She threatened to pull her children out of the program if Johnson was there and indicated that there were other parents who would do the same.
>
> Both the parents and Johnson were understandably upset. This was the first significant negative response he had encountered about his gender transition. After processing their feelings about the director's decision, the parents and Johnson asked if I would talk with the director. Over the next several

weeks, the director and I spoke by phone on three occasions, each about 45 minutes long. At the onset, the director said there was no way he and the board of directors could risk having parents pull their children out of the program. The summer camp was the primary source of financial support for the fall and spring community productions. If too many families pulled out, the theater company could easily go under. They believed they could not take this risk for one adolescent when it might lead to the closing of the program for all young people. They wanted Johnson and his parents to understand that this was not about Johnson. The board and director wanted to support him in his transition. They did not want Johnson to feel upset about their decision but rather understand that it was solely financial and not about him.

I repeatedly acknowledged their fears about the possible financial loss if they allowed Johnson to return as a counselor and validated the difficulty of the board's decision. I focused on listening to and even drawing out their concerns. I acknowledged their understanding that this was a financial decision that they believed was best for the well-being and longevity of the overall program and its work with all youth in the community—transgender and cisgender. I worked to ensure that the director felt heard by me. It was critical that he felt I understood and appreciated their concerns, as well as their support for Johnson.

In the midst of these conversations, there certainly was a part of me that found it challenging to be patient and understanding about the board's refusal to accept Johnson back. There was a part of me that felt angry about their decision and the way it impacted my client. There was a part of me that identified with the rejection Johnson encountered in this situation. This part of me resisted—even resented—validating the board and director's concerns.

These internal responses could have made it easy for me to align with Johnson and his parents in a way that could have interfered with my ability to engage the camp director. As a family therapist, I knew it was essential to build an alliance with everyone in this community system. Without this, I would not be able to help the director and board shift their position.

As a clinician, I also knew that when a client is upset about something, it is not possible to shift their beliefs or focus on taking actions before listening to and acknowledging the feelings they are experiencing. When a client is angry about being mandated to treatment, clinicians must begin by staying with that anger—drawing it out, encouraging the client to fully express it, validating the reality and even the legitimacy of the client's anger. Even when the clinician believes the client is responsible for the actions that led to their being mandated, challenging the client's right to feel angry or dismissing it as irrelevant only increases the client's anger and resistance. When that occurs, the engagement process is sabotaged and the possibility of growth or progress is diminished or even eradicated.

These clinical tools—building an alliance with each member in a system and validating each member's feelings in the moment—are also critical advocacy tools. As mental health professionals, our clinical skills of sitting with our own countertransferential responses, rather than acting them out with clients, are essential to effective advocacy for transgender youth and their families. I could not afford to act out on my anger about the board's decision. There are some moments when I can channel or draw upon my anger about an unjust decision, but this must be a conscious and intentional therapeutic choice. I cannot be an effective clinician or advocate when I allow my emotions to determine my responses. Learning to transform clinical knowledge and skills into effective advocacy tools is invaluable in this work.

> When I sensed that the director truly felt heard about the challenges of their decision, I was able to lean into our newly established alliance and also indicate that the decision would likely lead to Johnson feeling rejected. I gently but firmly suggested that being told he could not return to camp because of his gender transition would send a message that who he was as a transgender youth was not acceptable.
>
> We went back and forth about these challenges several times. In the course of our initial phone call, I provided basic education about gender identity among adolescents and the needs of transgender youth. I addressed the importance of acceptance and support from the adults in their lives. As the call ended, I offered to forward fact sheets about gender identity and expres-

sion and transgender youth for him to share with the board of directors.

On our second call, the director reported back from his conversation with several board officers. He said they were still anxious about the potential financial risks if they allowed Johnson to return. I engaged him about the theater program they oversaw, asking him to tell me more about it. I asked him what was unique about their program, what its mission was, what they believed was the value of theater for children and teens. The director eagerly talked about the ways acting facilitates self-expression among youth. He expressed the board's belief that acting can help young people explore who they are within a safe context, that being involved with the theater allowed the young to try on varying ways of being in the world without needing to commit to any single way if it did not fit them. In discussing the program's mission, the director shared their commitment to creating an environment where young people could feel safe to express their thoughts and feelings and build self-confidence about their identity in the world.

Engaging the director about the program's mission opened the door for an intervention that held the potential for change within this system. I leaned into their commitment to create a safe space for all youth and linked this to their decision about Johnson. Again, gently but firmly, I suggested if Johnson was not allowed to return to camp, it would send a message that contradicted their mission, not just to Johnson, but to all the campers. The current decision would communicate that youth were not, in fact, able to bring their whole selves to the theater program— that instead there were some aspects of identity not welcomed within the group. Reaching back and acknowledging the board's concerns, I suggested that this message seemed to contradict their mission.

I could sense the director absorbing the impact of the board's decision to ban Johnson's participation that summer and how this negated the theater's commitment to creating a safe space for self-exploration and expression among the children and teens who participated. He acknowledged the tensions within this dilemma, yet indicated he was not sure how to navigate this with his board.

I shared that there was a gender identity/expression non-discrimination bill in that county. I stated that I hoped he and the board would allow Johnson to return to camp because it would be consistent with the message they wanted to convey to the young people. At the same time, it was also possible for the board to simply tell parents it was against the law to reject Johnson because he was transgender. He agreed to think about this and talk further with his board.

When we spoke the third time, the director told me our discussion about their mission had moved him. He and the board leaders had discussed this and decided that the right thing was to allow Johnson to return. I validated their courage in making this decision and said I believed it was the right thing to do and could even strengthen the values of their program.

We spent the remainder of that conversation strategizing about how to deal with parents who might oppose the decision to support Johnson's return as a counselor. One option was to inform all the parents about Johnson's transition and his return. Another option was to allow Johnson to return and respond to any parental objections individually as they arose. The director and board chose the latter approach. Camp staff, including Johnson, were told to direct questions or concerns from parents to the camp director or his assistant rather than responding to them on their own. This ensured consistent messaging about the board's decision being reflective of the camp's mission. In the end, the summer camp went smoothly with only one parent asking questions about Johnson's transition.

This vignette highlights the critical role mental health practitioners can play in advocating for gender-diverse young people and their families. This was a situation where my outside knowledge could have a greater impact than parental advocacy alone. In addition to needing information, the director needed to be able to process his fears about potential financial losses, explore how to address the issue further with the board of directors, and then strategize how to respond to potential parental objections. These conversations would have been difficult to work through with the parents, and he and the board did not have enough knowledge about trans youth and gender identity to explore alternative decisions without outside consultation.

The vignette also illustrates the openness and patience often required in advocacy efforts. The same skills that enable us to sit with an individual client's emotions and struggles without injecting our personal feelings or reactions can be called upon in building alliances with those who appear rejecting or unwilling to support transgender youth.

If I had reacted too strongly to the director's initial statements that they could "not afford" to allow Johnson to return, this could have prematurely terminated our conversation. If I had pushed my own "agenda" about full inclusion of trans youth too soon or too forcefully, the director might have felt his concerns were not taken seriously. If I had dictated what he should do rather than inviting and validating the challenges he faced, our discussion would likely have had a less positive outcome.

In addition to advocating for an individual young person, it is critical for parents and providers to address larger local, state, and federal policies and laws that impact transgender youth. This could include your local school board; neighborhood and community groups, agencies, or organizations; your local municipal government; state policies and legislation; and national concerns affecting transgender and gender-diverse young people and their families.

Mental health providers cannot work with trans youth and their families in a way that provides clinical services in a vacuum. Counseling and other therapeutic services must always be grounded in the social and legal context in which these youth and their families live. If clinicians attempt to ignore or distance themselves from the larger issues of societal stigma and discrimination that trans youth encounter daily, their therapeutic efforts will become irrelevant.

Organizational Best Practices for Schools

- Create a visibly welcoming environment. Use "Safe Space" posters and stickers. Have trans-relevant and trans-affirming information available in your reception area or lounge— brochures, fliers, or magazines.
- Update policies and forms to reflect gender-inclusive language.
- Ensure that written policies about kindness and respect are communicated to everyone, including personnel, parents, and students/young people.

- Be clear that staff can hold any personal belief but must adhere to the organization's policies about respect, kindness, and nondiscrimination in all interactions with young people.
- Provide staff training about gender development, gender identity, and gender expression. Educate staff about issues unique to trans youth, relevant and affirming community resources, and at-risk warning signs.

WITH TRANS YOUTH:

- Acknowledge, respect, and support a young person's gender identity and expression.
- Ask what name and pronouns the young person would like you to use. Then refer to trans and gender-diverse youth by their preferred name and pronouns. If you don't know what pronouns to use, ask politely and respectfully.
- Admit when you don't know something or make a mistake. Don't be afraid to apologize. Then move on. Don't linger on your apology.
- Allow all youth to express their gender identity through their choice of clothing, hairstyle, and accessories.
- Do not attempt to change a youth's gender identity or punish a youth for their gender expression. Do not label varying gender expression as "inappropriate sexual behavior."
- Treat information about a youth's gender identity as confidential to ensure their privacy.
- Don't make assumptions about a transgender young person's sexual orientation.
- Don't assume what path a transgender youth is on regarding hormones or surgery.
- Listen to the voices of transgender youth. Treat them as the experts on their lives.
- Don't expect one transgender youth to be the resident trans expert. As with any group, there is a lot of diversity within the trans community.
- Become comfortable with fluidity. Don't insist on binary identifications. Don't define someone else. Everyone has the right to choose the identities they feel best suit them.

- Trust that a young person's decision to present themselves as gender-different from their birth-assigned gender is not made lightly or without due consideration.
- Do not sensationalize or sexualize trans bodies. It is generally inappropriate to ask a transgender person how they have sex or what their genitals look like. (This includes asking what surgeries a trans person has had or intends to have.)
- Ensure access to trans-knowledgeable and trans-affirming medical and mental health providers.
- Ensure safe, respectful educational settings.
- Connect trans and gender-diverse youth to supportive community resources, programs, and services—or bring these resources to them.

FOSTERING A CLIMATE OF RESPECT:

- Educate young people about differences, including gender diversity and gender identity.
- Challenge put-downs and dispel myths and stereotypes. Stand up for gender diversity.
- Be an ally and advocate for trans and gender-diverse youth. Encourage ally building among youth.
- Educate young people about the ways harassment and bullying are harmful.
- Confront harassment and bullying when they occur. This will make all youth feel safer.
- Develop a clear system for reporting harassment or abuse.
- Promptly respond to all gender-based harassment and abuse.

PARENT EDUCATION:

- If appropriate in your setting, provide education for parents, including written communication about your organization's gender policy.
- Provide educational presentations for parents and opportunities for discussion about gender diversity and transgender identity.

INPATIENT OR RESIDENTIAL SETTINGS:

- Make placement decisions based on an individualized assessment.
- Best practice generally houses transgender youth according to their affirmed gender identity, not their birth-assigned sex. Mixed-gender housing can be appropriate for trans youth.
- Transgender youth should rarely be placed with peers of their birth-assigned sex, and then only for safety concerns. If this is unavoidable, ensure that all staff respect and acknowledge the young person's affirmed gender identity (e.g., by using the name and pronouns they request).
- Do not place transgender or gender-diverse youth in sex-offender programs or facilities; trans youth are not predators.
- Ensure that transgender youth have safe access to bathrooms—ideally a bathroom that matches their affirmed gender identity. If necessary, this can be a single-stall bathroom or a staff bathroom.
- Provide privacy and safety in shower facilities through a single-user facility, allowing showering at a different time from cisgender peers, or installing privacy barriers.
- Conduct necessary strip searches in a respectful and dignified manner. They should always be done in private and out of sight of peers or nonessential staff. Allow transgender youth to choose the gender of the staff person who conducts the search. Provide training in respectful and affirming treatment for trans and gender-diverse young people for all staff members.

CHAPTER 10

Beyond Coming Out

Living a Life

Much of the existing literature about trans youth focuses on the early stages of assessment and diagnosis, or how to support a young person in coming out and socially transitioning. There is very little that explores the types of challenges and clinical concerns that emerge after the initial wave of coming out as transgender and the youth is now living in their affirmed gender. This chapter addresses this gap by exploring the wide range of issues that can emerge with transgender adolescents beyond the initial stages of coming out and transitioning. Parents need to understand the complexity of these issues to remain centrally involved and supportive to their child. Therapists must understand them to provide the most effective clinical care.

Am I a "Real" Man or a "Real" Woman?

Many transgender adolescents struggle with the question of whether or not their affirmed gender identity is "real" in the sense of being true or valid. Younger transgender children may struggle with this question, but it's more frequently seen among adolescents. When present, this nagging question about being real represents both an internal and external struggle.

On a personal level, the issue involves the extent to which the transgender young person experiences themselves internally as a real man or a real woman. The question carries at least a piece of self-doubt. Insecurity about their affirmed identity emerges from internalized societal messages that posit gender identity as synonymous with biological sex, or more specifically genitalia. These messages are conveyed in overt and subtle ways, and it is virtually impossible for trans youth not to internalize them to some extent. Overt messages include arguments that people cannot know, or be sure of, their transgender identity as children or adolescents; viewing all adolescent trans identity as identity exploration or confusion; and negative stereotypes and rhetoric about trans people in the news or media. The underlying message is that a penis or vagina is what makes a man or a woman real.

More subtle messages include the frequency with which transgender youth (and adults) are often asked, "Have you had the surgery yet?" This question always refers to genital surgery and carries an implicit message that you are not a valid man or woman until your genitalia match those of a cisgender man or woman. Subtle messages are also conveyed when peers or adults refuse to use, or inconsistently use, the transgender young person's affirmed name or pronouns. This failure suggests that the other person continues to see the young person in their birth-assigned sex and not their affirmed gender—reinforcing the belief that gender is synonymous with body parts or sex.

It takes more effort for some individuals to shift to using a child's affirmed name and pronouns than it does for others because they have known them by their birth-assigned name and gender. Yet it is essential to understand the message conveyed to the trans adolescent when the birth-assigned name and pronouns continue to be used (even though this is often not the message the speaker intends to send). When adults use their birth-assigned name and pronouns, the trans adolescent hears, "You do not believe that my affirmed gender identity—my transgender identity—is real. You do not believe I am who I know myself to be. You do not believe I am really a man or a woman (in the sense that matches my affirmed gender)."

These messages, intended or not, challenge the trans adolescent's sense of self as well as their sense of reality. When an adult repeatedly tells them, "You are not who you think you are. You do not know who you are," the young person takes in the message, "You are not grounded in reality. You are crazy." With each of these messages, the transgender young person's sense of self takes a hit.

People who grow up as targets of discrimination and oppression typically internalize aspects of the stigmatized messages about their identity. It is impossible to be surrounded by negative messages about who you are without absorbing at least some of it. Transgender children and adolescents demonstrate tremendous self-awareness and confidence in their ability to define themselves despite ongoing continuous messages that counter their reality. Yet, that self-assurance can also be chipped away by repeated messages that deny the validity of their identity and even their existence.

How Do You Perceive Me?

Related to these identity challenges for trans young people are frequent questions about how others—family, friends, strangers—perceive them, and whether the perceptions of others will change once they learn about their transgender history and identity. When a young person's trans identity is not visible, there is often fear that once others discover their trans history, they will no longer be seen the same way or be seen as a real or regular guy or girl. These questions persist because they are often validated, as illustrated in the following vignette.

> Each year, I guest teach a session on transgender awareness for a colleague in an undergraduate social work course. A few years ago, the department chair sat in on the class. This year after class, my colleague told me that every time the department chair speaks about me, she uses female pronouns. The information stings. This woman has only met me post-transition, only met me with facial hair and male pattern baldness, only seen me in a suit and tie, only knows me as Elijah Nealy. What reason would she have for using female pronouns? There is a clear level of disrespect in the way she refuses to accept me for who I am in the world today. Her use of female pronouns also diminishes my identity. It says, "You are not Elijah Nealy. I don't believe you are who you say you are. You are not a man. You are really still a woman." The simple fact that the department chair knows I am a transgender man alters her perception of me as a man.

In the face of these internal and social struggles, mental health providers must empower trans youth to develop and maintain a solid sense of self despite being misgendered and invalidated. Clinical interventions need to focus around two dynamics. The first is providing a safe space to express and work through the emotions these interactions can generate—fear, insecurity, self-doubt, anxiety, anger, invisibility, hopelessness. This space can be created in individual work with trans youth, but it can be particularly powerful when this safe space is created within a group of trans adolescents and they are able to witness each other's feelings.

The second involves helping trans youth develop a set of tools for navigating these interactions and the concomitant emotions. One strategy might involve drawing on cognitive therapy interventions for challenging internal self-doubt as well as external messages that challenge their affirmed gender identity. Forming relationships with other transgender youth can significantly diminish their feeling that they are the only one struggling with these situations and emotions. This speaks again to the healing and empowering dynamic of group work with trans adolescents.

Body Image

Clinical work with transgender adolescents needs to explore and address issues of body image. This may specifically focus on having a penis or not having a penis, on having breasts or not having breasts.

But body image struggles often go beyond the young person's feeling about their genitalia. Imagine confronting the reality each morning that your reflection in the mirror does not reflect who you are. Imagine being unable to see yourself in the mirror or being unable to see yourself reflected in the world around you. Imagine being told you are a girl, but when you look at other girls you know that is not who you are.

This is not just about body image in the sense of being uncomfortable about some aspect of your body, such as weight, the shape of your nose, or having too many freckles. It is about not being able to see yourself other than in your own mind. Even more, it is the fact that the person you do see when you look in the mirror, the person people around you see when they look at you, is not who you are.

This aspect of body image and gender dysphoria can bring a transgender young person's grasp on reality into question. It can cause them to question the reality of their sense of self. Not being able to see yourself in the mirror can also engender a sense of invisibility or even unrealness. If I cannot see myself and if others cannot see me, am I real? Can I trust my perceptions? Can I trust my sense of reality? Is my internal gender identity and sense of self real?

This facet of body image and gender dysphoria can contribute to significant emotional distress and pain. It can generate a wide range of emotions that may vary over time and across different situations and contexts—anxiety, fear, worry, insecurity, anger, invisibility, grief, sadness, pain, depression, and hopelessness. Again, clinical interventions need to focus on making time, space, and safety for trans youth to explore and express these emotions. Their feelings need to be acknowledged and validated.

Trans youth also need tools for managing these emotional dynamics, especially in moments when their feelings are intense. Cognitive behavioral therapy (CBT) interventions can be helpful, as can mindfulness techniques. Learning to sit with and tolerate these feelings, developing strategies for letting these feelings pass, identifying safe and understanding people to talk to when gender dysphoria erupts, and drawing on affirmations that assert and support their ability to live through their dysphoria can all be empowering for trans youth.

Another aspect of body image work involves learning to accept and live with what can change and what will not change. How much will hormone therapy alter their physical body? What can they realistically expect from top surgery? What remaining physical characteristics will they have to learn to live with? The struggles precipitated by these questions can be complex, as illustrated by the following vignette.

Barclay, a trans male high school senior, constantly struggled with his 5-foot-2-inch height. He had not begun taking testosterone until 17 years of age, toward the end of puberty. As a result, hormone therapy had not contributed to increased height.

Barclay hated this fact. Being shorter than all of his male peers made him feel insecure. It made him question whether he was really a guy and worry that his peers did not perceive him as a "real" man. When he talked about how short he was, Barclay often put himself down. Being short made him feel like a loser. It made him think that girls would never be attracted to him and would never want to date him.

In part, Barclay's struggles mirror those of body image struggles many teens grapple with. Transgender youth are not the only young people with ambivalent or negative feelings about their bodies or some parts of their bodies. In this sense, the challenge of my work with Barclay parallels that with any client struggling with body image: How can this individual reach a place of self-acceptance around their body or body parts? What tools do they need to more effectively navigate periodic moments of nonacceptance?

The work began with creating a safe enough space for Barclay to name and express the profound anger and grief he experienced about being "too short" and unable to change his height. This included grief and anger that he had not transitioned when he was younger when the outcome might have been different, as well as grief and rage that he had not been assigned male at birth. We explored the stages of grief and how these reflected the range of his emotions.

We also utilized CBT techniques to examine the validity of Barclay's belief that girls would never be attracted to him. How did he know this? We examined the evidence for this belief. We debated whether there might be any alternative interpretations of the situation.

Were there any girls in the world who dated shorter men? (Yes)

Were there any girls in the world who dated men shorter than they were? (Yes)

Were there short men who did have girlfriends or wives? (Yes)

Was it possible that girls might be attracted to him at some point even if he was not dating anyone right now? (Yes)

Over time, Barclay demonstrated increased acceptance of his height and developed tools to manage those moments when his insecurity was triggered, typically in social situations. Barclay was able to utilize the above questioning to challenge his assumptions in those moments and, thus, shift his internal emotional reaction. This enabled Barclay to remain more present with peers in those moments and thereby increase his opportunities for connecting with others—and maybe even finding a girlfriend (which he did over time).

Grief and Loss About Missing Out

Many transgender adolescents experience feelings of grief and loss about experiences they missed earlier in their lives when they were perceived in their birth-assigned sex rather than their affirmed gender. These experiences can include not being able to be a little boy or girl, not getting to play with affirmed-gender playmates or engaging in the games and activities other young boys or girls did, or not being able to freely have crushes on classmates the way cisgender peers did during middle school.

Another aspect of loss involves the lack of physical images from childhood—pictures or videos—that reflect their affirmed gender.

> Dahlia, a 15-year-old trans girl, participated in a girls' theater group that also focused on building positive self-esteem among young women. One week, the group discussed the importance of loving themselves even when they made mistakes or did not do as well as they hoped they would. The leader encouraged them to treat themselves the same way they would a young child if that child was hurting—to be kind, nurturing, and encouraging. As a reminder, the leader suggested each girl tape up a preschool picture of themselves where they could see it each day.
>
> As Dahlia described this to me, she exploded, "I don't have any pictures like that! So how am I supposed to learn to love myself? I hate that stupid little kid! He's not me!" When she paused for a moment, she began to cry. "I just wish I could see what I really looked like when I was five."

In addition to this more personal loss, trans youth may experience aspects of loss around their affirmed gender not being seen by family and childhood friends. For example, a young trans man may have been a "tomboy" as a child, dressed like a boy, and engaged in boys' games but not have gotten to visibly be a boy at that age. While his grief may partially be about his internal understanding of himself, it is more about how others perceived him at that time—that they did not see him as a little boy.

When youth transition in late adolescence or as young adults, they may experience loss and anger about missing out on their teenage years in their affirmed gender identity. These feelings can surface around missing out on normative developmental tasks and events. This could involve not being able to participate authentically, such as not being able to go to junior prom in their affirmed gender. Other times the loss may be the inability to engage certain activities at all, such as being stuck playing girls' softball when they belonged with the boys' baseball team.

Social anxiety resulting from gender dysphoria as well as feelings of not fitting in may have contributed to loss of connections with peers of their affirmed gender—such as never getting to giggle and laugh with other girls at sleepovers or join the "bro parties" on Friday nights. The development of birth-assigned secondary sex characteristics likely compounded their feelings of disconnection. Transitioning in late adolescence means young people are not authentically having crushes on peers or beginning to date and explore relationships in the same way their cisgender peers do.

Confusion

With the exception of transgender youth who socially transition in early childhood, many trans young people spend at least some time being confused or unclear about their gender identity. The confusion may emerge out of the dissonance between their internal sense of self and the perceptions of those around them, or it may be their own internal confusion—sensing something is wrong or off or not quite right in terms of their identity, yet not being able to clearly name what the problem is.

Many trans youth who become clear that their affirmed gender does not align with their birth-assigned sex are unable to disclose this immediately, often out of fear that others, especially family members, will not believe them or will reject them—or will even kick them out of their family and home. Some young people have a sense of their affirmed gender identity but are afraid to clearly name it, even to themselves. This fear can delay disclosure for weeks, months, or years.

Maintaining a false self during this period contributes to feeling inauthentic as well as disconnected from oneself and others. There is a cost attached to living with chronic fear, anxiety, and worry. It may negatively impact mental and emotional well-being, academic performance, self-esteem, and relationships with others. While coming out and being able to transition generally alleviates much of this tension, some of these emotions and their after-effects may persist long after youth begin living in their affirmed gender.

Shame

Despite increasing visibility and acceptance, we still live in a world replete with negative stereotypes and beliefs about transgender people. As discussed in the first section of this book, many people continue to believe biological sex equals gender identity. Others insist on viewing gender dysphoria as a psychiatric illness that needs to be treated until the individual can accept their birth-assigned sex.

Transgender young people grow up hearing these messages and invariably internalize some of them, resulting in negative and shameful feelings toward themselves. It is essential to explore these dynamics when working with trans adolescents. Adolescents do not always offer up or easily acknowledge internalized feelings of shame. A certain kind of creativity is necessary for engaging youth in these conversations.

In both group and individual settings, clients and I have brainstormed and listed on poster paper all the messages they have ever heard about transgender people. We have made collages with pictures that represent these messages and then discussed how the messages made, or make, them feel. We have named which messages they have rejected and which they worry may be true or make them feel shame or hopeless about their future.

It can be helpful to begin by asking what messages they have heard from others—in the media, online, in books, etc.—as opposed to directly asking whether they feel shame or what negative messages they believe. Adolescents are more likely to respond to the latter questions after numerous messages and stereotypes have been identified. In moving toward the impact of these messages, it can be helpful to begin by asking youth how they imagine that hearing these messages might affect transgender youth or people. Again, this keeps the focus off themselves and the need to immediately self-disclose. It allows them to name how others might feel in the face of these messages and how the stereotypes might impact other trans people's actions and choices. Having discussed with them their ideas about the impact of cultural messages on other trans youth, you might wonder out loud if they have ever felt affected by any of these messages.

Having completed some of the above activities, we have created other collages and art that reflect the strengths transgender youth bring to the world—images of feeling pride in themselves and of how they envision the world they want to create.

Feeling Isolated

Many transgender youth grow up feeling they are both different and alone. This is beginning to change with the increasing visibility of transgender people in U.S. culture, including trans children and adolescents. Yet, there is almost always some period of time when feeling isolated predominates—perhaps the period before they became clear that their discomfort is about gender identity, or the time during which they are too afraid to come out as transgender. Youth in more rural or isolated geographic areas may literally be isolated. There may be no nearby groups or centers for trans youth to meet one another. There may be an absence of medical or mental health providers with knowledge about trans youth.

Transgender young people growing up in conservative religious environments can experience profound isolation. These children are often less connected to the media, social media, and peers or families outside their faith community. This isolation, coupled with negative messages about LGBT people, may lead them to believe that not only are they the only one like this, but also that who they are is wrong, bad, sinful, and shameful.

Isolation diminishes the mental health and emotional well-being of transgender adolescents. It often causes them to pull inward and away from other people and the world around them. It can lead to loss of interest in activities they previously enjoyed. Isolation increases the risk that these youth will engage in risky or self-harming, self-destructive behaviors. Alternately, isolation can lead trans youth to stop caring and act out in ways that may be self-destructive and/or destructive of people and things around them.

When youth come out about being transgender, it is essential to facilitate connections with other trans young people—preferably in person at an LGBTQ Center or a Queer or trans youth group, but at the least through online forums, such as those available at the Gender Spectrum lounge. https://www.genderspectrum.org/stay-connected/ Meeting youth who are like them, finding trans youth who are proud of who they are, and discovering that other young people have faced many of the same struggles reduces their sense of isolation. Positive connections with other trans youth facilitate the development of a healthier self-esteem and a more hopeful outlook for their future.

Connecting trans youth to adult transgender mentors can also be useful. These adults serve as hopeful role models of being a transgender adult—doing things like attending college, obtaining a job, dating, finding a spouse, being a parent—things that many trans youth, and especially those who are isolated, fear are not possible for transgender people in light of pervasive negative societal messages.

Periods of Hopelessness and Despair

Many of the feelings just discussed—fear, shame, isolation—can trigger a sense of hopelessness and despair about the future. Trans youth may believe they will never get to be their true self—that being fully who they are in the world will never be possible. They may believe that their future opportunities are severely limited as a transgender person. They may worry that if they do come out and transition, life will be too overwhelming and difficult—that they will not succeed, that they will never be able to find a job or someone who will date them, let alone love and marry them. They may believe others will always ostracize them. They may envision a lifetime of ridicule, rejection, harassment, and even violence. They may not be able to imagine ever feeling good or proud about who they are.

While feelings of hopelessness generally decrease when trans youth come out and make connections with other trans youth, the feelings can sometimes persist. Even socially transitioning or beginning hormone therapy does not always eradicate the despair (e.g., Barclay's despair about ever finding a girlfriend). Alternately, it may abate only to be triggered by an event or interaction at a later date (e.g., having a boyfriend or girlfriend break up with them or being kicked out of their house for being transgender).

At other times, persistent grief can morph into despair. Examples include young trans women of color chronically being unable to obtain employment, or the loss of family acceptance as the cost of being one's authentic self. As mentioned in earlier discussions, struggles around body image can precipitate persistent grief and despair.

Young trans guys may grapple with intense anger and grief that they will never have a penis, never have a penis that works like a cisgender guy's, never have the penis they should have been born with, never have the penis that makes sex simple.

Mental health providers must closely and regularly screen for these emotional dynamics—even when a young person does not appear depressed or hopeless. When these negative beliefs about their future and concomitant emotions emerge, it is critical to reach for these beliefs and feelings in working with trans youth. Mental health practitioners need to create multiple safe spaces for transgender youth to identify, explore, express, process, and challenge these internal struggles.

It is also important to note that trans youth typically do not find it easy to take the risk to initiate these conversations with their therapist. Talking about these things is intensely personal and can be embarrassing. Most adolescents doubt adults will understand their feelings. Given this, how likely is it that a transgender teen would expect their therapist to "get" what it feels like to not have a "dick?" Or what it feels like to have one and not want it? Especially if their therapist is a man? Or is cisgender?

It is essential that mental health providers begin to grasp the nuances and depths of this grief and despair. Not every transgender youth is trapped in these feelings, and certainly most are not caught there all the time. Yet, despair can all too easily be triggered by the daily onslaught of microaggressions and big aggressions like harassment, discrimination, and violence. We cannot afford to be complacent about screening for these emotions. They are intimately connected to the fact that the rate of attempted suicide within the transgender community is 40% compared to 4.6% in the general population (James et al., 2016). Reaching for these feelings, helping trans youth to begin to name and express them, and finding tools to challenge and/or manage them are essential.

At the same time, it is essential to actively facilitate hope. Sometimes we spend time in sessions, or I have the youth do homework between appointments, to do an online search to find healthy, positive, successful transgender adults. Inviting transgender college students, young adults, parents, and others to speak at trans youth groups can be empowering for trans adolescents. We have watched video clips and Ted Talks by transgender people who are proud of their identity and are pursuing their passions. We have read articles and books by or about transgender youth and adults. All of these interventions challenge the hopelessness and despair that can result from internalized stereotypes, experiences of bullying or abuse, and feelings of fear, isolation, and rejection.

Lack of Parental Acceptance and Support

While many families I have worked with are immediately, or relatively quickly, accepting and supportive of their transgender children, there are parents whose immediate response is denial, disbelief, or rejection. These parents may not believe transgender identity exists. They may insist that their children are confused and need help to accept their birth-assigned sex (which they equate with gender). They may believe trans identity is a mental illness or sinful. They may send their children for reparative therapy.

Rejecting parents may cut off contact with the young person's friends if the parents perceive the friends to be bad influences. They may block Internet access because they do not want their teenager reading or watching stories of transgender people or talking with trans people online. Some parents become hostile and angry when a child discloses their trans identity. They may withdraw and stop talking with their child as a way of expressing their displeasure or disapproval. They may become so angry that they insist the young person leave the house, either immediately after the disclosure or at a later point. It is possible they may be verbally or physically abusive toward their child. This possibility emphasizes the need for safety planning with trans youth before they come out to family members.

Families that are not overtly hostile or rejecting may still not offer the support needed by their transgender child. They may deny a young person's desire to socially transition; they may refuse access to hormone blockers for a prepubertal child or young adolescent. They may not allow an older teen to begin feminizing or masculinizing hormone therapy.

When trans youth are living in these contexts, they may struggle with ongoing feelings of sadness and rejection, invisibility (their parents cannot see what they need) or insignificance (their needs are not important enough to respect), isolation, or despair about the future. When these rejecting family responses and consequent feelings persist, transgender youth may become at very high risk of self-harm and/or suicidality (Ryan et al., 2010).

For mental health professionals, finding ways to engage and retain these youth in your practice and/or programs is critical. Reaching out to their families and attempting to build an alliance or relationship with at least one or some members can go a long way toward diminishing the effects of familial rejection. Creating a safe space and empowering transgender youth to create their own families, comprising both peers and supportive adults in their lives, can be invaluable. While it has not been the norm in many cisgender white communities, in the face of family rejection, Queer people have been creating families of choice for decades. Some Queer youth of color create these life-sustaining families within the ballroom scene/community (Arnold & Bailey, 2009).

Resistance to Meeting Trans Teenagers or Adults

Having discussed the importance of connecting trans youth to other transgender teenagers or supportive cisgender peers, you may discover that some transgender adolescents are resistant to attending, or adamantly refuse to attend, transgender or even LGBTQ-identified activities, groups, and events. Mental health providers sometimes perceive this reluctance as a reflection of internalized shame and self-hatred. It can be viewed as denial of their trans identity or of being like other trans youth. It is sometimes attributed to social anxiety resulting from earlier periods of isolation or anxiety when the youth was forced to maintain a false self while navigating social situations in their birth-assigned sex.

While these assessments may be valid, they are not the only possible explanations for this resistance to trans community connections. It is critical to understand that not all transgender adolescents (or adults) use the language "transgender" to describe themselves; not all transgender adolescents (or adults) even identify as transgender. From their perspective, they may simply identify as a (young) man or a (young) woman without the "trans" adjective added onto their experience and identity. These youth often see themselves as having been a boy or a girl (their affirmed gender identity) from birth. They believe their physical bodies somehow developed differently from their true internal identity and perceive their birth-assigned sex as inaccurate.

These young people may not use language like "transitioning" because this is not how they experience what is happening. From their perspective, the social and medical transition is simply a process of righting what has been wrong from birth—both their bodies and others' perceptions of their sex or gender identity. They are not changing who they are; they are not transitioning to live as a different gender; they are simply finally being recognized as their true sex or gender in the world.

While it can be challenging to assess whether a youth's resistance to meeting trans peers is linked to internalized shame or social anxiety as opposed to not perceiving themselves as transgender, it is important not to jump to the conclusion that reluctance reflects the former. It is essential to first draw the young person out and carefully listen to their perceptions and understanding of their identity and life experiences. While the mental health profession perceives those whose gender identity does not match their genitalia at birth as transgender, it is important to always ask what language each client uses to describe themselves. You cannot assume the adjective "transgender" always fits. The language itself—"transgender"—suggests you are different. It suggests your identity as a man or woman needs to be qualified. Cisgender people do not need or use an adjective to qualify their sex or gender identity; they are men or women. For many young people (and adults), being a *transgender* woman or *transgender* man is not the same as simply being a woman or man.

Given this framework, these young people may legitimately not be interested in meeting transgender teens because they do not identify with them. They do not want to meet peers who identify as transgender because they do not relate to their experiences or understanding of themselves. Instead, these youth simply want to a "regular" guy or girl among their peers. They do not want to be seen as trans and they do not want to be out about their (trans) history because this is not how they perceive their identity and experience.

Mental Health Connections and Interventions

Cisgender mental health providers—gay and straight—may worry that they cannot fully grasp the nuances of the experiences of transgender youth. In some ways this is true. And it can be important to acknowledge that you cannot fully understand what it feels like to be in their shoes—and yet you are committed to listening and understanding as best you can.

At the same time, underneath the specific nuances and details of a transgender young person's life experiences lie the same human emotions we all encounter. Transgender youth are not alone in having moments of deep, deep grief. Transgender youth are not alone in the rage that can erupt from ongoing experiences of invisibility, marginalization, and oppression. They are not alone in facing profound experiences of loss or having "missed out."

While it is essential for you to listen and learn as much as you can about the details and the nuances of their day-to-day life experiences, the interventions you draw upon will come from the same toolkit you use with many of your clients. As has already been illustrated, CBT can be pulled from your toolkit to challenge dysfunctional or unhealthy beliefs that lead to anxiety or depression.

Austin and Craig (2015) stress the need for the adaptation of evidenced-based interventions for work within trans communities. Highlighting the effectiveness of cognitive behavioral interventions in treatment for depression, anxiety, and suicidality, they explore ways CBT can be adapted within a trans-affirmative context. Austin and Craig (2015) argue that negative messages about transgender people, coupled with experiences of victimization and discrimination, contribute to the phenomenon of minority stress (Meyer, 2003; Marshal et al., 2011) among some transgender individuals.

The interaction of these dynamics contributes to the development of negative thought patterns in trans and gender-diverse individuals about themselves and their future. Examples include: "There is something wrong with me." "Who I am is sinful." "I will never be successful." "No one will ever marry me; I am a freak." "My family hates me; why bother trying anymore?" "The [horrible] way this feels [or I feel] will never change."

From a cognitive behavioral perspective, when trans adolescents and adults internalize these negative societal beliefs, the messages generate feelings such as fear, anxiety, depression, and despair. As these emotional states persist, they lead to self-destructive choices and behaviors among transgender youth and adults, such as substance abuse, eating disorders, self-harming behaviors, and suicidality.

Austin and Craig (2015) go on to develop the following model for CBT interventions with transgender individuals (I have framed their model in terms of work with trans youth):

1. Create a safe, trans-affirmative environment where trans youth can name their experiences.

2. Help trans young people see the connections between their experiences and minority stress, as this helps trans youth move away from seeing themselves as the problem; instead, they begin to recognize that the "problem" lies with heteronormative cisgender beliefs and practices that marginalize and oppress transgender people.

3. Out of this shift, trans youth can begin to see themselves in a more positive light. This enables youth to challenge internalized negative beliefs and instead recognize their strengths: "I am not a failure. I am not only doing the best I can to navigate the oppression directed toward transgender people; I am doing an amazing job navigating an inherently destructive system. I am here; I have survived; I am stronger than the oppressive forces that would silence me."

4. Having developed a set of affirming and empowering beliefs about themselves and their future, trans youth are enabled to choose more empowering actions, such as seeking out increased community connections and becoming an advocate for themselves and their community.

This model of trans-affirmative cognitive behavioral interventions breaks the hold of negative internalized beliefs and concomitant anxiety, depression, and hopelessness. When replaced with positive, affirming beliefs, trans youth are empowered to make healthier, more constructive choices for themselves and their lives. The critical link that bridges the movement away from internalized beliefs to a more empowering framework is the understanding emerging from the minority stress model, which holds that the cause of their distress does not lie not within them but instead lies within oppressive dominant trans-prejudicial societal beliefs and their impact on transgender people.

Other evidenced-based practice models also offer possibilities for trans-affirmative interventions. Mindfulness-based work can be extremely helpful in empowering trans youth to manage their emotional reactions in the face of ridicule or rejection. These practices can decrease the stressors that typically accompany being different and on the margins.

Psychodynamic approaches may help some trans youth unpack and resolve early experiences of abuse, invisibility, and rejection that have become a stumbling block to their well-being and growth in the present.

Narrative therapy can empower transgender young people to find strengths within narratives that originally only seemed to speak of pain and rejection. These interventions can lead to the creation of new possibilities and new possible endings to their life narratives.

Living a Life

The remainder of this chapter comprises four vignettes exploring dimensions of life for transgender and gender-diverse adolescents beyond early transition. In some ways they reflect the normative developmental themes and tasks most teenagers and young adults encounter. Yet, there are unique dynamics and considerations for trans youth.

Each vignette is followed by reflection questions for both families and mental health professionals. Professionals can use these to help them think about the potential clinical concerns emerging in a young person's life or family. Parents and other family members can use them to illuminate and reflect on their own journey through the experience of having a trans child in their lives.

You may work through this section on your own and take time at the end of each vignette to think about or journal your ideas in response to the questions. Or you may want to review this section with a friend, family member, or colleague as a way to spark increased discussion around supporting transgender adolescents. The vignettes are followed by a deeper exploration of key themes and challenges.

Vignette One: Shifting Peer Relationships

Daniel was best friends with two girls prior to his transition. The three of them had known each other since elementary school and were inseparable all through middle school—sleepovers, trips with each other's families, hanging out after school. When Daniel socially transitioned in ninth grade, both girls were his number-one supporters and took an active role in easing his adjustment at school.

Daniel began masculinizing hormones during the fall of his sophomore year. Over the ensuing months as Daniel began to develop facial hair and build muscles by working out, he was more and more consistently viewed as a guy at school and less as "that kid" who transitioned. As these shifts occurred in how Daniel looked physically and was perceived by peers, the friendship between the two best girlfriends and Daniel also began to shift and in some ways became less close and intimate. The two girls no longer changed in front of him when they spent time at each other's homes. They began to leave Daniel out of some of their "girl talk." Their sleepovers became less frequent. As Daniel discussed this with me, I sensed he was feeling very sad about these shifts in his friendships with the two girls and missed the closeness they had shared prior to his transition.

REFLECTION QUESTIONS FOR PARENTS AND MENTAL HEALTH PROFESSIONALS:

1. How would you explore or open up conversation with Daniel about his emotions in this moment? What would you want to ask him or know about his feelings and their possible meaning for him?
2. Do Daniel's feelings in this vignette raise any concerns for you about the certainty of his male gender identity or his transition continuing to move forward?
3. How would you explore whether Daniel is feeling loss, regret, or both? What reactions do you have to transgender individuals who might experience feelings of regret?

Deeper Exploration

Friendships prior to transition with peers of the same and opposite gender often change after a transgender teen is read consistently in their affirmed gender. These shifts may be embraced as welcome changes, or they may spark feelings of loss and sadness as they did for Daniel.

The ways the two girls began to "pull back" from Daniel and leave him out of their "girl talk" represented a mixed experience. On the one hand, it was a clear affirmation that they saw him for who he was in his affirmed gender—a guy—and they began to interact with him the same way they interacted with other guys. He was no longer "one of them" in a way that affirmed his emerging manhood. On the other hand, no longer seeing him as one of their "best girlfriends" resulted in a loss of intimacy and sharing among the three of them.

In discussing this vignette, it is critical to differentiate between loss, regret, and ambivalence. Too often, people view a transgender person's expression of grief or loss about some aspect of their transition as an expression of ambivalence or regret about their decision to transition. When it is inaccurately perceived as ambivalence or regret, the provider may insist on further gender identity exploration. This misunderstanding of what the trans adolescent is experiencing can lead to a break in the therapeutic alliance. In some instances, these misperceptions have led providers to delay support for essential medical steps, such as beginning hormone treatment or pursuing surgeries. This history, and its continued occurrence, contributes to the anger and distrust many trans youth (and adults) feel toward mental health providers.

As Daniel and I discussed his feelings about the changing connections with his girlfriends, it became clear that he was experiencing grief and loss and not ambivalence or regret. As clinicians, we generally recognize that almost all significant life changes, even those we welcome, may be accompanied by moments of loss. Yet we sometimes fail to recognize this in work with transgender clients.

Having been your typical "pride-of-place" New Yorker for decades, I often thought that I would never be happy living anywhere else. However, in the summer of 2015, my family relocated to West Hartford, Connecticut, so I could begin my first tenure-track faculty position—something I had long anticipated and hoped for. I was incredibly excited about my new beginning professionally. It had been a long time coming. My family and I love West Hartford, and my new university colleagues and students are wonderful. I am more than happy to no longer have an hour subway commute to work shoved up against the bodies of a hundred strangers. I love sitting out in the silence of our yard at night. Yet there are things I miss about living in New York City. Missing these things and sometimes even feeling sad about them is not the same as regretting my decision to relocate.

The mental health system has been too quick to read a trans person's grief and loss as regret rather than helping the young person explore and express these feelings. What Daniel needed in that moment was a safe space to express his sadness, to talk about how it felt to be "left out again" even as he became more and more accepted as the young man he had longed to be, to freely explore his happiness about this affirmation of him as a guy alongside his sadness about no longer being "best friends." He needed acknowledgment that both emotions could simultaneously be true. He needed validation of both his joy and his grief.

As we made space for these emotions, we were able to move out from this specific situation and acknowledge that many life changes carry both joy and sadness. We were able to acknowledge that what Daniel was feeling was not just about being trans and thus different. Instead, these seemingly opposing emotions were reflective of our universal human experience. This takes the clinical work a step further. Being transgender can mean feeling different from others in a way that is isolating. It is essential to begin by validating the unique aspects of identifying as a young trans man or woman. Yet, it can be important to also stay attuned to commonalities that may exist with the experiences of other human beings, as this can offer an opportunity to bridge the trans adolescent's sense of isolation.

While some trans young women may have had many girlfriends prior to social transition, others may find themselves building female friendships for the first time. Similarly, some trans male teens were primarily friends with boys throughout their childhood. Others, like Daniel, may have been closer with female childhood peers. For both trans men and women, living in their affirmed gender means navigating different interactions and relationships with peers of the same and different genders—in a way that often varies from their experiences prior to their transition.

Beyond the possible shifting nature of prior close friendships, the ways other girls or guys respond to a transgender adolescent at school, parties, and other social settings necessarily shifts because their experience of the teen's gender has shifted. For some youth, this process is a positive experience of feeling more included than was true prior to transition, as illustrated by the following vignette.

> Cynthia, a 17-year-old trans woman, socially transitioned at the start of her senior year in high school. She had been a very socially awkward teenage "boy" whose gender expression was decidedly feminine. As a result, she never fit in or connected with boys, but also was rarely befriended by girls. She had spent both middle and high school on the periphery socially, with few

peer friendships of either gender. Within a few months of coming out and socially transitioning, Cynthia found herself much more accepted at school. Her peers began to invite her to parties, and by midspring, boys were calling her to go out with them. Being able to let go of maintaining a false self and relaxing into her affirmed gender enabled Cynthia to form positive peer relationships after she transitioned.

For some transgender youth, the struggle with social shifts and adjustments necessitated by their transition can be alleviated with information and social skills practice.

Jeremy, a 17-year-old trans man, had little experience spending time with male peers or being in male-only settings and conversations. He felt awkward around other guys once he transitioned. He had done mostly OK talking with girls before, but he felt he did not know how to start a conversation with guys. He worried they would not accept him. He found their talk about girls, girls' bodies, and sex very uncomfortable.

In our work, I encouraged Jeremy to talk with supportive adult men in his life about their experiences of being a teenage boy. I encouraged him to ask questions and, in this way, access the male socialization he had missed out on when younger. In regard to his discomfort with conversations about girls and sex, we explored different models of masculinity as a tool for helping Jeremy identify the kind of man he wanted to be, what values he wanted to hold as a man, and how he wanted to talk about girls, women, and sex as opposed to assuming that the presenting framework was the only one possible for young men.

There are transgender youth for whom symptoms of social anxiety are distinct and separate from their diagnosis of gender dysphoria. Cynthia's experience illustrates the way earlier manifestations of social anxiety may be reflective of gender dysphoria. Jeremy's struggles relate more to his lack of male socialization when younger.

As the young person's dysphoria is alleviated with their social transition and they are able to more fully be themselves in the world, earlier symptoms of social anxiety may dissipate. When social anxiety symptoms do not diminish, it can be reflective of deeply internalized negative beliefs, as described in the section on adapting CBT interventions. Alternately, the young person may meet the criteria for a diagnosis of social anxiety that is separate and distinct from the diagnosis of gender dysphoria.

Vignette Two: Shifting Intersections of Identity and Stigma

Robert, a young African American trans man, socially transitioned at the beginning of high school (9th grade) at a new school where he had received a full scholarship. That year was challenging for him as he struggled to fit in despite significant racial, class, and gender identity differences from most of his peers. He was disappointed he did not make the marching band. Despite these challenges, Robert managed to end the academic year with a B- average and several new friends.

While Robert had smoked weed a few times before, during 10th grade he began to get high with friends several times a week. His parents became increasingly worried about his pot use. Their concern was frequently expressed by yelling at Robert, and grounding him or taking away his cell phone when they found out he had been smoking.

In a session with me, both parents said they were worried Robert wasn't taking the full impact of his gender transition seriously enough. By this, they meant the impact of his now being a black young man in an urban area. As one parent said, "He's at a predominantly white affluent prep school, smoking weed with his friends in the park after school. If the police approach them, the consequences for Robert will be far greater than what happens to any of those white kids." While they were concerned about how weed might interfere with his learning, both parents were very frightened about Robert's immediate safety as well as the potential long-term consequences if Robert was arrested.

REFLECTION QUESTIONS FOR PARENTS:

1. In what ways can you relate to Robert's parents in this vignette?
2. Are there ways you can relate to Robert's challenges? What were your experiences around fitting in and feeling "part of" as a child or adolescent?

3. What would you need in order to manage your fear for Robert's safety and his future opportunities without losing sight of the pressures he is facing in the moment?

4. How might your emotions and responses vary based on your own racial/ethinic identity?

REFLECTION QUESTIONS FOR MENTAL HEALTH PROFESSIONALS:

1. How would you respond to the parents' worries in this session? In what ways would you more deeply engage their fears and address their current relationship with their son? What role would your own racial identity play into or shape this discussion with his parents?

2. What are your clinical hunches about the challenges or struggles Robert might be experiencing? How would you begin to raise or explore these dynamics with Robert? How would you decide whether to work with him individually versus with the family as a whole?

Deeper Exploration

For trans youth of color, the intersection of identities means multiple shifts in how others perceive them as well as multiple, and often shifting, aspects of stigma and marginalization. Robert attended elementary and middle school as a young African American girl. He began high school as a young black man. This was a significant shift in his identity—not just internally, but also in terms of how the world saw him. Young African American girls are not generally perceived to be threatening. Young black men, even at 14 years old, are seen as dangerous. While Robert had encountered racism before transitioning, the nuances and potential impact were different now. Indeed, his chances of being stopped and frisked by the police increased with his transition.

His parents worried that Robert did not fully grasp the implications of being seen as a young black man. They felt he assumed that because he attended an affluent, predominantly white prep school and smoked weed with his white friends at the park, he possessed the same privileges (or pass) that they held. The parents were legitimately terrified that if the police approached the young people, Robert's legal consequences—both immediate and long term—would be greater.

The work with Robert's parents began by listening to and validating their fears. It was important to not rush them through or past their anger but to instead make space for them to name and express it fully. Underneath the anger, their fears emerged, and at that point in time they had few places they could openly discuss their fears.

As I met with Robert, it was clear that he was much more cognizant of his shifting experiences of racism than he was willing to disclose to his parents. We spent much time discussing how it felt for him to be navigating the city as a young black man rather than a black girl—the different ways white people now responded to him while shopping or riding the subway. While racism had always been a part of his life experience, the experience shifted with his being recognized as a young man in the world.

At school, Robert navigated multiple levels of stigma. His previous schools had been more racially diverse. Now Robert was one of only a few African American students.

He faced the additional challenge of class stigma as well. His parents were lower middle class; only one parent worked full time, and the work was in the nonprofit world with a relatively low salary. Robert talked with me in sessions about his peers spending winter break in California, Florida, or Hawaii and spring break with their families in Europe; taking a last-minute four-day weekend trip to Iceland to see the Northern Lights; and visiting their summer homes in the Hamptons.

Over time, Robert expressed his anger and resentment about his family not doing similar things. "Why do we have to be poor? Why can't my parents get a different job? A job that makes money?" He often acted out this rage by not coming directly home after school or staying out past curfew on the weekends. And he smoked more weed, despite being repeatedly grounded. Though it was not apparent at first, it became clear over time that in some ways being grounded was a "respite" from navigating the uneven race and class tensions he felt with his peers.

Navigating multiple layers of stigma in terms of race, class, and transgender identity meant multiple challenges to "fitting in" at his new school. In part, smoking weed and becoming a pothead was Robert's initial way to establish an identity within his new high school. Always having weed made him popular. Peers who wanted to get high sought him out. He was invited to parties at their families' opulent apartments because he brought weed. He was a part of things as a pothead, despite his race, class, and gender identity differences. Becoming part of his affluent white peer group also mitigated his experience of increased racial stigma as a young black man. In his mind, he accessed privilege by association.

Robert's vignette illustrates the impact of intersecting identities for trans youth of color as discussed in Chapter 6. As a young black transgender man from a lower-middle-class family attending an affluent, predominantly white and cisgender prep school, Robert did not have the luxury of simply navigating his trans identity that first year he transitioned. In many ways, his identity as a transgender young man played the least significant role in his adjustment. In that context, his race and class identities were more salient.

Vignette Three: Dating and Relationships

Sandra transitioned socially during sixth grade and began hormone blockers shortly thereafter. During 10th grade, she began taking feminizing hormones. She had had crushes on boys before this, but now there were more school dances and parties at classmates' homes. Her interest in relationships and intimacy began to emerge more strongly.

One day, Sandra asked what to do about dating, as a trans woman. "Do I have to come out as trans? If so, when should I come out? If I do it right at the start, then it's their choice whether to date me or not. Maybe that would be better than getting my heart broken when they find out later on. Or, do you think it would be better to let them get to know me first? You know, so they get to know me as a person first and not just transgender? But then, what if we're at a party and he wants to make out like everybody else is doing? What if he finds out then that I'm transgender—like if he slips his hand between my thighs?"

REFLECTION QUESTIONS FOR PARENTS:

1. How comfortable would you feel having a conversation with Sandra about these concerns?
2. Could you focus on actively listening and help Sandra fully explore her thoughts and feelings, rather than giving advice or making suggestions too soon?
3. If you have a belief about the "right" choice or decision Sandra should make in terms of disclosing her identity or history, can you resist imposing your opinion?

4. How can you stay present with Sandra and manage your own fear and worry about her safety or being rejected and hurt by others?

REFLECTION QUESTIONS FOR MENTAL HEALTH PROFESSIONALS:

1. How would you help Sandra explore these decisions?
2. Do you have a belief about the "right" choice or decision Sandra should make in terms of disclosing her identity or history?
3. What feelings does this bring up for you?

Deeper Exploration

Dating and relationships are challenging for most adolescents, but for transgender youth there are unique ways in which this process is complex, as indicated in the vignette about Sandra.

Some teens (and their parents) struggle with questions about whether anyone will ever want to date or marry them. Beyond this, dating in and of itself is anxiety producing. "Does she like me or not?" "What if I like someone a lot and they don't like me?" "What if I'm really attracted to him and he doesn't like me that way?" Even for adults, dating puts our self-esteem on the line.

This process has added complications for transgender teenagers, particularly around issues of self-disclosure. For youth still attending the same school where they transitioned, this is not always an issue. But even in those settings, teenagers often meet friends of friends from other schools who may not know their transgender history. In your clinical work with transgender teenagers, they may want you to tell them how to date as a transgender young man or woman. This is something that many cisgender therapists might not have thought about—or at least they may not have grasped the complexities that can emerge for a transgender teenager.

It is challenging for young people to determine when to come out about their transgender history. Should they come out right at the very beginning so that it's known from the start that they're transgender? Disclosing at the onset means the potential dating partner makes their choice about whether they want to date with full information about their history. From a transgender teenager's perspective, being rejected at the beginning might be less painful than being rejected after they've had more time to really begin to like, or even love, that person.

Yet, on the other hand, the potential dating partner might decide not to date the individual simply because they're a transgender young man or woman. If the trans teen doesn't tell them right away and they date for a while instead, the other person might get to know them and like them enough that it wouldn't matter to them that they are transgender.

Another reason to delay disclosure is that you might not know how much you like somebody right away. You might think you like them when you first hook up, but after hanging out more, you could discover you don't like them enough for the relationship to go anywhere. In this case, waiting to disclose means you might not have to disclose. You could choose to disclose only if a dating relationship becomes more serious.

There is no single right or wrong answer to these questions, and certainly not one that fits every situation. Almost every transgender teenager, young adult, or adult has stories about disclosing to others and being ridiculed or rejected. Other times, the disclosure is simply awkward and the other person becomes extremely uncomfortable and doesn't know what to say or how to respond. One 18-year-old came out to someone at the beginning of their freshman year in college, and the other person's discomfort led them to laugh for the next 15 minutes. The 18-year-old shared that he just wanted to disappear in that moment.

Having to come out and disclose their transgender history makes most trans teenagers and young adults feel profoundly different. When Jack discussed a party he had attended the previous weekend, he told me, "Everyone else was off in a corner making out. Why can't I do that without having to think about being trans? I just want to be a normal guy coming onto a girl. But I can't. If we start making out and she feels my crotch, then what? I'm not even talking about having sex. I just want to be a normal teenage guy making out with a girl."

Having to navigate these situations can not only trigger anxiety, but it can also bring up anger about how unfair it is to have to disclose. The young person may feel resentful about being different—or as Jack said, not just being a normal guy. In many ways, this is an aspect of gender dysphoria. Sometimes cisgender therapists think gender dysphoria is only about how a young person feels about their body. In fact, the DSM frames gender dysphoria in terms of discomfort or distress about one's body or body parts. In reality, however, gender dysphoria is about much more than body parts and how a body is configured. Gender dysphoria is also about feeling different. It can include feeling anger about not being born a boy or a girl.

As parents and clinicians, it's important for us to explore our own thoughts and feelings surrounding a young person's decisions about whether to disclose their transgender history in a dating situation. Many times trans women are accused of deceiving a male partner when they do not disclose their transgender history at the onset. Transgender women have been assaulted, and even murdered, simply because their cisgender heterosexual male partner was outraged that he had fallen for someone he later "discovered was really a man" (given his perspective that trans women are not real women).Many of these men avoid conviction because lawyers, judges, and juries agree that they have been unfairly deceived and that they cannot be held responsible for their rage upon discovering the trans woman's history.

Some of us may have internalized these beliefs and feel that a dating partner deserves to have this information from the very beginning. Reflecting this belief to a young transgender woman will likely shut down the conversation and convey that you do not believe she really is a woman. Other counselors might push young trans men or women to disclose their history right away out of wanting to protect the client—not wanting them to be hurt if the partner rejects them sometime later. As is true in other clinical scenarios, attempting to shield our clients from being hurt is not generally helpful.

Instead, the work needs to be around helping a transgender young person explore the pros and cons of these decisions, or how that individual young person perceives these pros or cons. This is a conversation you might have many times, perhaps each time the young person has a crush on someone new. It's important to help your transgender client explore the risks of disclosing at the onset versus the risks of waiting to disclose. It's important to help them explore their feelings about these decisions. It's important to make space for the anxiety, frustration, or anger they may have about dating and disclosure. It's also important to help them develop skills for managing these situations as they occur. It can often be helpful to brainstorm their worst-case scenarios and role-play different ways to respond.

Vignette Four: Navigating Sexuality and Intimacy

Demaris is a 17-year-old Latina trans woman who transitioned during ninth grade. Her friends have become increasingly sexually active with their partners. A few months ago, Demaris began dating a girl she "really likes; I mean I really like her." Over the past few weeks, Demaris and her girlfriend have begun spending more time together. She says they've "made out" and slept together once, "but we didn't really have sex."

As you try to explore this with her, she becomes increasingly agitated. "You just don't get it! What am I supposed to do in bed with a girl? How can I even let her see my body? I want her to touch me, but not like this. How do I tell her I don't want her to touch me there? I don't even know what to call it! I don't even like saying the word 'penis.' It reminds me how wrong my body is. I mean like I can't even touch myself there—even when I'm alone and horny."

REFLECTION QUESTIONS FOR PARENTS AND MENTAL HEALTH PROFESSIONALS:

1. What emotions or concerns come up for you as Demaris is expressing her feelings? How comfortable would this conversation be for you?
2. For parents, how might your cultural and familial norms and beliefs, as well as your own sexual history impact this conversation?
3. In Demaris' words, do you "get" it?
4. For therapists, what intersecting clinical themes might be occurring in this moment?
5. How would you respond to Demaris in this moment? What language or words would you use to discuss her concerns/struggles/feelings?

Deeper Exploration

Exploring intimacy and sexuality are normal developmental tasks for adolescents and young adults. This might include becoming sexually intimate, but even if not, most adolescents are thinking about and exploring their beliefs and values about sexuality as well as imagining what it would be like to be sexually active in the future. Just as in the previous vignette, these developmental tasks have added complexities for transgender young people.

For many transgender youth, there are several concerns. The first is often, "Is another girl [or guy] going to be happy having sex with me with these body parts?" The second may be more personal: "How can I have a satisfying sexual life with someone else when I still have body parts that match the sex I was assigned at birth?" A third area of concern may involve the young person's discomfort with masturbation depending on the degree of their dysphoria about their body. Trans youth may not only worry about whether another will want to have sex with them; they may struggle themselves with how to be sexual in their current bodies.

The mechanics of sex can be complicated enough for a young person who hasn't been sexually intimate before, but for trans youth the stakes are even higher. What does a young trans woman do in bed with a penis? What does a young trans man do about not having one? What about their breasts? Or the absence of breasts? The young person's own personal (internal) gender dysphoria can be challenging enough, but how do they jump over this in order to have sex with another person? Good sex? Relaxed sex? Sex they enjoy?

It is critical to make space for trans youth to explore these concerns, or even to reach for them if the young person has not raised them. It's difficult for most teens to talk about sex with adults—even with their therapist or counselor. So it's essential to be sensitive to the degree that these may be particularly vulnerable conversations for trans youth to engage in. For trans youth, these may not only be awkward and embarrassing conversations, but they may also generate shame. Conversations about sex may intensify their dysphoria in the moment and following a session in the sense of having to name and openly discuss their bodies and body parts when they might rather ignore or dissociate from these aspects of self. Transgender youth may also have difficulty believing that a cisgender therapist in particular will "get it"—that is, will understand what navigating their bodies and sex is like for them as opposed to cisgender youth. Again, becoming sexually intimate is new, unfamiliar, and anxiety inducing for many—maybe even most—teens, but gender dysphoria creates added layers for trans youth.

Even the choice of words may be a challenge. Not all trans women are comfortable using the word "penis." The word itself may generate too much dysphoria. Other trans women may be fine using this term to describe their body part. Many trans men are not comfortable using the word "vagina." Others do not experience dysphoria about this term. Others still might use the word "man-gina," or call their clitoris their "dick." Given these varying levels of comfort, it's critical for clinicians to explore how trans men and women, as well as gender-queer youth, feel about their current body parts and the vocabulary each young person uses to discuss their body.

It's essential to be comfortable discussing sex in detail, to be open and explore creative ways trans youth may experience sex and sexuality, and to embrace an understanding of sex significantly broader than vaginal intercourse.

To become effective in exploring these areas with all youth, cisgender and sometimes transgender, clinicians often need to augment their knowledge and understanding of trans sexuality. Ways to do this can include reading transgender novels that include sexual relationships, reading erotica written by transgender men and women or gender-queer individuals, attending open workshops at transgender conferences, and listening to trans people's stories. The goal is to develop a greater understanding of how transgender people creatively navigate gender dysphoria and sex. By doing so, providers can help adolescents and young adults "think outside the heteronormative box" when intimate with themselves and partners.

In addition to the dynamics of being sexual with others, some trans youth struggle with pleasuring themselves.

> Sam had socially transitioned almost three years before and had been on testosterone for one year now. He and Aneisha had been dating nine months and were sexually active. He expressed on many occasions how happy it made him to know she was attracted to him and how wonderful he felt making love to her.
>
> It was six months before Sam acknowledged that he never let Aneisha touch or pleasure him. Sam said it made him think about his body not being what he wanted it to be and he didn't want to think about this. As a result, Sam had never climaxed when they had sex. Despite the fact that Aneisha had indicated that she was not only comfortable with but attracted to Sam's body, he could

not relax and be present with her in this way. Just imagining being touched by her increased Sam's dysphoria to the point that it became intolerable for him.

As we explored this further, Sam hesitantly acknowledged that he was not even comfortable touching himself intimately. He was too uncomfortable with his current body parts to even masturbate, let alone let someone else touch him. While Sam wanted to (in fact, as he put it, "I'm horny all the time") and occasionally tried to masturbate, the mental and emotional impact of his dysphoria made it difficult for him to climax alone or with others.

Many transgender youth are asked intrusive and inappropriate questions about their bodies and sexuality. Inappropriate questions generally reflect the curiosity of the adult and not the interest or needs of the young person. At the same time, it is important to recognize the challenges inherent in initiating these conversations, especially for adolescents, and normalize the discomfort around conversations about bodies and sexuality.

Collazo, Austin, and Craig (2013) offer helpful questions to facilitate conversation when youth indicate an interest in discussing sexuality and intimacy:

- What words do use to refer to your genitals?
- What terms do you use to describe the sexual activities between you and your partner(s)?
- What are your feelings about the parts of your body that are often associated with sexuality?
- Do your feelings about these parts of your body interfere with your ability to engage in sexual activity?
- Do these parts of your body cause shame or embarrassment during sexual activity?
- How do your gender and biological sex impact the kinds of sexual activities in which you engage (or won't engage) on your own or with others?

Given that most existing literature focuses on the initial stages of disclosure and social transition, this chapter has sought to explore concerns that may emerge beyond those stages. Families and mental health professionals typically have little understanding of the unique challenges transgender youth face. With few opportunities for advanced education about transgender adolescents, most mental health professionals lack the knowledge necessary to provide effective clinical interventions that address the issues trans youth encounter once they are living full time in their affirmed gender.

CHAPTER 11

Preparing for College and Work

Young Adult Developmental Tasks

TURNING 18 TYPICALLY MARKS THE ENTRY INTO ADULT-
hood. It's the time when many young people move out into
the world on their own more fully. Whether they are moving into
the world of work full time or headed to college, young adulthood
is the time when youth are expected to transition out of the safety
of parents, home, and the high school structure and move toward
increased independence with the ability to support themselves. They
are expected to move into adult roles and responsibilities and establish a commitment to a work identity. This can involve learning a
trade, finding work, and/or pursuing higher education.

While many young people have held jobs during adolescence by
choice or necessity, even for them, there is something different about
turning 18. It signals a new stage in all our lives—that moment when
the world around us declares us "legal" in many states. With this, the
expectations of those around us begin to change, and our own expectations of ourselves change in response.

When I worked at a residential treatment program for 12- to
24-year-olds, a colleague had a plaque in her office that read, "Young
adults, leave home now while you still know everything." Some
young adults enter the world this way, confident of their ability to
make it, maybe even cocky at times. Other young adults are more
anxious and fearful of being independent.

The expectation to become independent can make it difficult for
new adults to share their fears with their family. The world and their

peers tell them they shouldn't need their family anymore; they're an adult now; they should be able to handle what comes up on their own now. And they, too, want to prove they can do things on their own. They're supposed to be launching—moving away from their families, developing their own social circles, and beginning their own separate adult lives. Their self-esteem depends on meeting these ambitious and often ambiguous expectations.

Erik Erikson (1950) identified the core developmental task of young adulthood as Intimacy vs. Isolation. This speaks to the importance of exploring and developing relationships during this time period. While adolescence is a time of identity exploration, young adulthood is when we begin to settle into a core identity that comfortably reflects our understanding of ourselves. With this maturing sense of self we become able to develop adult relationships with those around us. It's a stage in our lives when we are challenged to share ourselves more intimately with others. Beyond developing adult friendships and collegial relationships, this is a time when we explore more longer-term commitments with individuals outside our family. This includes the potential of choosing a life partner. Ideally, we choose and learn to maintain intimate relationships that reflect a sense of commitment, safety, and care.

From Erikson's (1950) perspective, failure to successfully navigate these developmental tasks of young adulthood becomes evident when young adults avoid intimacy and are fearful of commitment and relationships. When these patterns emerge, the young person is at risk of isolation, loneliness, and, over time, depression.

Some college students and working young adults make friends quickly. They get involved in socializing with coworkers or join student activities and campus groups quickly. They are excited about being on their own—being able to make their own choices about when, or whether, to come in at night, with no one around to nag them to do their chores. Meeting new people, sometimes from around the globe—new friends whose life experiences are often radically different from their own—is stimulating for these youth. They revel in the newness of creating a life for themselves and finding a sense of belonging in a place and space that is totally their own, untouched by the people and places that have shaped so much of their lives until now.

Other young adults find it more difficult to build new friendships and feel isolated during that first semester, or even first year, away from home. They may find it too overwhelming to form relationships with coworkers outside the structure of the workplace. Their social anxiety and struggles may cause them to turn inward and become depressed, or to reach for drugs or alcohol to facilitate socializing. Many of these young people want to be able to talk with family about feeling lonely, but like every other young adult, they also want their parents to think they're doing great on their own.

The Impact of Being Trans on Normal Developmental Challenges

Transgender young adults encounter all of the aforementioned young adult developmental challenges and tasks—with the added assignment of navigating these as a transgender young adult. "Should I be out on campus? Should I be stealth? Is there such a thing as part out and part stealth? What if I can't make friends? What if nobody wants to date me? What if I'm stealth and we're all out drinking and I end up making out with someone and they discover I'm trans then? Will I be safe? Will being outed ruin everything? Will I lose all my friends?" All of the questions from the vignettes about dating, sexuality, and intimacy come into play when trans youth head off to college.

Many college students don't tell their parents much about their day-to-day lives. Some parents complain they can't get their kids to call them even once a month. There are particular ways that this is compounded for transgender youth. Because their parents are cisgender, trans young people are not always sure their parents will "get" or understand the challenges they are facing, as the following vignette illustrates.

> Dayton spent his summers in high school working as a junior counselor at a sleep-away camp. He socially transitioned during his freshman year in college and reached out that spring to let the camp directors know about his new affirmed name and pronouns. Many camps have not encountered trans campers or counselors, and consequently have not yet developed trans-affirmative and inclusive policies. In Dayton's situation, the director told him they could not put him in the cabin with the other male junior counselors and school age campers. They felt it wouldn't be appropriate for him to sleep or shower there. Instead, they

would put him in a cabin with older male camp personnel. The directors also didn't want him to use the men's room in the main bathrooms in the center of camp. They would designate a separate bathroom for him to use.

Dayton was very upset by the director's conversation and decisions, and rightfully so. The conversation was permeated with microaggressions. The message from the camp directors was, "You are not a man like other men; therefore, you cannot room, shower, or shave with other boys and men." Their conversation clearly told Dayton, "You are not really a man, because if we really saw you as a man, this conversation would never happen."

Dayton attempted to talk with his father about the conversation with the camp director. His father, who was totally supportive of Dayton's transition, responded that he could see how this might be hard, but that Dayton needed to try and see this from the camp director's point of view. They had other campers to consider. "And besides, you can't expect everyone to get this overnight. You've got to be patient with people and give them time." Dayton's father totally missed the microaggressions. As upset as Dayton was about the camp director's decision, he was even more devastated by his father's inability to understand what it had felt like to him and to grasp the underlying message that Dayton was not really a man.

The fact that most young adults want their parents to think they're doing great sometimes means trans college students do not discuss microaggressions they may be dealing with or fears they struggle with. They might not tell their families about the verbal harassment they have encountered on campus. One first-year trans woman called her parents weekly and told them how great everything was going at college. She never told them how, at one of the country's most progressive colleges, she had to walk through the entire first year being misgendered on a daily basis.

Transgender college students can be at risk of isolation. This can be especially true on smaller campuses where there are no transgender (or even LGBTQ) student groups or in rural areas where they are few trans-affirmative off-campus resources. When trans young adults have decided to be stealth on campus or at work, they may also struggle with feeling isolated. These decisions will be discussed in more detail later in this chapter.

Preparing for College

Given some of the above dynamics, transgender high school students may have much anxiety about how to navigate being trans on campus. Many of their parents may also be anxious. Beyond the usual parental anxieties of a child being away from home for the first time, most parents experience additional concerns specific to their child's trans identity, such as whether they will be accepted and whether they will be safe.

Colleges are increasingly developing programs and resources specifically for transgender students. Some have active trans student groups. Some have gender-neutral or even trans housing options. It is important for young people and parents to research the colleges the young person is interested in and explore how Queer- or trans-affirmative the school is. Much of this research can be done online. Is there a Queer student center? What trans or LGBTQ student activity groups exist? Are there Queer or gender-neutral dorms? What are the policies about trans students in dorms of their affirmed gender? If trans women can room in the women's dorms, who has to know about her trans history? Does her roommate need to know?

For Reflection

Do you think her roommates should know? Do you think her female roommates have a right to know? If so, why? What is important to you about her roommates knowing?

Other important trans-related questions include whether or not the campus health center prescribes or monitors hormone therapy, or if they have nearby medical providers who are willing to do this. Are there trans-identified or trans-affirmative and knowledgeable counselors at the college counseling center?

Even when a student intends to be stealth on campus, most trans youth and their families choose to come out with an admissions counselor in order to be able to freely ask about trans resources on campus. Prospective students should feel free to ask for a campus tour that includes the LGBTQ student center. They should also ask to meet with current trans students and talk about their experiences on campus and in classes. Given the increasing number of gender-fluid and trans students, most admissions offices are prepared for these questions and concerns. If they are not, this tells a prospective student something about the gaps in their ability to ensure transgender students are respected and embraced at this university. Additional questions trans students may want to ask as they consider different colleges are included in the following text box.

How Trans-Friendly Is This Campus?

(Adapted from Trans Youth Equality Foundation)

- Percentage of out LGBTQ students?
- Percentage of out transgender students?
- Percentage of out LGBTQ faculty?
- Percentage of out LGBTQ administrators?
- Existence of LGBTQ studies or courses?
- Is the first-year orientation program inclusive of LGBTQ issues?
- Are nondiscrimination policies inclusive of LGBTQ people?
- Do nondiscrimination policies include gender identity and expression?
- How are records changed for transgender students to reflect their correct pronouns and name?
- Is there an LGBTQ or Pride student center at this school?
- What kind of activities exist for meeting other transgender/LGBTQ students?

- Is there access to inclusive, knowledge-able counseling services for transgender students?
- Are there any trans-identified counselors? Support groups for trans students?
- Are the health center staff and physicians trained in transgender sensitivity and healthcare?
- Are wellness programs or sex education pro-grams inclusive of transgender people?
- Are there any records of LGBTQ students being harassed? What are the policies for how the college handles complaints about harassment?
- What are the housing policies for transgen-der students? Can trans students room with other students of their affirmed gender? If so, who must be notified about the student's trans history?
- Are there gender-queer or gender-neutral housing options?
- Are there gender-neutral bathrooms on campus?
- What state legislative protections exist in this location for transgender people?
- What social and community opportuni-ties exist in surrounding towns for LGBTQ people?

Additional resources for trans youth in the college application process are included at the end of this chapter.

Navigating College

Some transgender individuals transition and go on to live their lives in their affirmed gender, choosing not to disclose their transgender history. This practice is called stealth. Some transgender young people want to be stealth when they attend college. Some may have been stealth in high school, and college is just an extension of this norm (this would generally be true if the youth changed schools after transitioning).

However, for many transgender adolescents, college marks the first moment when they have the opportunity to meet new friends without everyone knowing they are transgender. These youth usually transitioned in middle or high school. If they remained in the same school district, their history of transitioning was always known by most of their peers. Even if their transition went well and they had many friends and were embraced as just another high school student, in their minds, at least, they were likely always the transgender girl or transgender boy.

Beginning college without disclosing your transgender history can be a healing, liberating, and empowering experience for many trans youth. For trans youth who can pass as their affirmed gender, it is often the first moment of moving through the world as a young man or young woman without the adjective "transgender" attached. It can be the first moment of feeling what it might have been like to be assigned your affirmed gender at birth, to have no one questioning your gender identity, to have no worries about whether the reason that girl dropped you was because you are transgender or wondering if this is why you weren't hired for that job at the mall.

However, there are some challenges to being stealth in college, as the following vignette illustrates.

> Derek spent his first two years living in the male dorms on campus. During this time, he became good friends with three other (cisgender) guys. They hung out all the time—worked out together, partied together, hung out with their girlfriends together. Because Derek was stealth, they did not know about his trans history.
>
> The spring of their sophomore year, the guys decided they all wanted to get an apartment off campus the next year. When Derek brought this up with me, he was torn between wanting to

get the apartment with the guys because of how good it felt to be one of them and being terrified that the other guys would find out he was trans if they all lived together. On campus, Derek had his own room, but in the apartment the guys would be sharing rooms. Derek didn't want to make a big deal about needing his own room, but he worried about guys walking around in their boxers or briefs or heading back to their rooms naked after a shower.

What he worried about most was that he would stand out as the weird guy who was too self-conscious to let the other guys see his body, and especially his body below the waist—in other words, whether his dick was different. Standing out like this meant the other guys would get curious. They'd want to know why Derek was so uptight. He worried they might take it upon themselves to "loosen him up" and discover that his genitals didn't match his gender identity.

When he imagined what might happen next, it was not violence he worried about. What troubled him was that these guys he had become friends with would no longer see him as one of them. From that moment on, they would see him differently; he would be the "trans guy," not just a "guy."

In contrast, some transgender youth begin college knowing they want to be out; they want to be openly involved in Queer or trans groups on campus. Some trans youth become advocates and leaders on campus. One transgender man I worked with challenged the policies of a national male fraternity, successfully getting them to recognize and accept trans men as members. One transgender woman challenged the admissions policies at a women's college. A stealth trans male student was elected president of the student body in his senior year without anyone knowing about his transgender history. The day after his election, he came out as a trans man in the campus newspaper and challenged everyone's assumptions.

Each of these young adults found their voices and their power on campus. They demonstrated tremendous courage in their willingness to be out as advocates. Their involvement and activism strengthened their self-esteem and self-confidence. Yet, it is crucial to remember that this openness and visibility can have a price attached to it for transgender people. Just as the young adults at the helm of the current Black Lives Matter movement are lightning rods for our society's prejudice and racism, out trans youth on campus must navigate frequent microaggressions and sometimes outright harassment and discrimination. This remains true even at the most progressive and trans-affirmative colleges.

Sophia took a gap year between high school and college and began her social transition the spring before starting college. She was tall and lanky, and when she headed to college that August, she still had some physical characteristics that might suggest male gender to others.

She had been accepted into a very liberal and progressive college. She began school with all of her identity documents saying "Sophia." This was the name on the roster in all of her classes. This is how she introduced herself to new classmates and roommates. Yet Sophia was misgendered the entire fall semester. Even when she met someone new and introduced herself as "Sophia," the other students often used male pronouns to refer to her. This experience was not something she had expected in a school with a reputation for being trans-affirming. We spent several sessions when she was back in New York City shoring up her resilience for navigating these microaggressions.

Sophia also encountered anxiety about going into the small town adjacent to the college campus. She found herself feeling afraid of being "read" as trans in town, and with this, fear of potential harassment or violence. Again, this was not something she had anticipated. Sophia had felt relatively safe in the urban environment of New York City (a dynamic reflective of her racial privilege as a white trans woman, as this would not likely be the experience of most trans women of color in NYC—or anywhere).

The following vignette continues to explore the nuances of decisions about being out or stealth on campus.

Jason came to see me during late fall of his junior year at college. He had socially transitioned and begun testosterone the previous summer. He had also changed schools during the summer so he could begin his junior year fresh—where there would not be anyone who knew him prior to his transition. As he told me in his first appointment, Jason wanted people to see him as a regular guy and felt they wouldn't if they knew his history. The only person on campus who knew about his trans history was his girlfriend, with whom he roomed. He was incredibly happy about this move. It felt as if he had been waiting all his life to just be a guy.

Jason came to see me because he wanted to discuss stressors between him and his girlfriend. He felt as if she was too possessive sometimes and wanted him to spend all his time with her. He wanted to be able to hang out with his guy friends more often. She was also on his case because she felt he didn't open up much emotionally. She told him she never knew what he was feeling. Jason said, "I just find it hard to talk about my feelings."

As the fall semester progressed, Jason talked about the friendships he was making at his internship on campus. He was really connecting with some of the other guys. He mentioned once that he sometimes wished he didn't have to keep his trans status secret, but he was convinced that his peers wouldn't see him the same way if he came out to them about being trans.

During the spring semester, Jason's friendships with the guys in his internship became stronger. They spent a lot of time together studying, running, working out, and watching movies. One night when they got pizza together, the other guys were bragging about their sports accomplishments in high school. They were all laughing and having a good time together. In contrast, Jason talked to me about feeling left out, and asked, "What am I supposed to say to them? All my trophies are from girls' swimming and diving." Over the next month, Jason seemed increasingly stressed about juggling the tension of being "stealth" and began to pull back from his friends.

REFLECTION QUESTIONS FOR PARENTS AND PROFESSIONALS:

1. How would you help Jason explore his decisions about being stealth versus coming out? What are the possible risks or benefits of either choice?
2. Is Jason's fear that others will see him differently if they knew he is trans "valid?" How would you help Jason explore/navigate/live with this fear?

3. What decision do you think is best in terms of Jason's mental and emotional well-being? Do you think being out is healthier than being stealth? What if his choice is different from yours?

Older LGBT-staged identity development models generally posit being "out" as essential to emotional health and well-being (Cass, 1979, 1990; Coleman, 1982; Troiden, 1988, 1989). Being "out" is equated with being proud of one's gender identity and sexual preferences. To be closeted (or stealth) is viewed as being ashamed of one's identity. Historically, these models have contributed to negative notions about being stealth.

However, it is essential that mental health professionals not impose their beliefs about being out as opposed to being stealth. The decision to be out or stealth is not clear-cut for many transgender individuals. There are nuances to these decisions that many cisgender families and therapists fail to grasp. Many trans people, children and adolescents included, simply want to be (seen as) their affirmed gender, as both Derek and Jason did; they simply want to be a young woman or a young man. They do not always want to be seen as a transgender boy or a transgender girl—because this typically suggests that they are something other than "just a girl" or a "real" boy. For transgender youth, the price of being out often means that others see them as different and concomitantly as less than real.

In contrast to the assumptions within earlier LGBT identity development models, Devor's (1997) discussion of the final stages of trans male identity development (Integration and Pride) concluded that most trans men were well integrated into society as men with their trans histories largely invisible. They did come out to those who needed to know about their history. Most of these men neither conscientiously hid nor disclosed their transgender backgrounds. Instead, disclosure was differential and strategic. They came out as trans when it was important or necessary in some way. When this information about their history was not relevant, it remained private.

Jason and I spent four to five weeks exploring his concerns about coming out to his buddies. We weighed the value of being seen as a regular guy, and we weighed the cost of his having to hold a part of himself out of these relationships. As we discussed the latter, Jason was clear that part of the cost for him was feeling isolated. I validated his fear that his friends might see him differently, acknowledging that yes, this could happen, and that it does happen often. I indicated that there was no right or wrong answer; this was something every trans person has to struggle with and sort out for themselves.

We discussed the option of his becoming more involved in the LGBTQ student group; perhaps this would open the door to some relationships where Jason could feel more comfortable being out. I pushed gently once or twice as to whether Jason could be 100% sure his friends would see him differently if he disclosed. I asked him to think about the different guys in his major that he felt close to and whether there was any guy in particular he wished he could come out to, or a guy he thought might still see him as a guy after disclosure.

Jason identified one friend he thought might be OK knowing about his history. We began to imagine what it might be like for Jason to come out to him. Two weeks later, Jason came in and shared that he had come out to this friend and that their conversation had been positive. We acknowledged what a difficult choice this was and the risk it involved for Jason. In the following weeks, Jason reported feeling relief about having someone else on campus who knew his life story and with whom he did not need to "edit" his thoughts and conversation to make sure they did not suspect his trans history.

It is critical for providers to listen and explore what is important to each particular trans young person as they navigate decisions about being out or stealth. It is also important for practitioners to create this space for them to explore their own thoughts and feelings without weighing in with their own opinion. The goal is to empower the young person's ability to sort through these decisions for themselves, knowing there is no right or wrong answer and that every choice has risks. What is important is for them to have support as they decide who they want to be in a given context—without pressure to assent to what the provider assumes is "best" for them.

Some trans young adults find ways to manage the stressors of remaining stealth. One resource can be developing connections with trans friends online. This offers the opportunity to talk more about day-to-day microaggressions and stressors with peers who understand without the risks of being outed on campus or at work.

Employment

Transgender youth may experience numerous stressors as they move into the work world. Some of these stressors involve whether or not the young person has been able to legally change their name and gender marker on their identification documents. It can be extremely stressful for a young person to apply for employment when their identity documents do not match their affirmed gender presentation. It can also be difficult to put themselves "out there" in early transition when they may still be viewed as their birth-assigned sex.

In these situations, trans youth may have many questions about applying and interviewing. "Should I tell them I'm transgender during the interview process? Or should I just wait and see whether they offer me the job?" Many trans youth have fears about discrimination in hiring. They may worry that they will not be hired simply because of their trans identity or their nonconforming gender expression.

These fears are often legitimate. As presented in the Introduction, a recent national study indicated unemployment rates for transgender people were three times higher than those of the general population, with trans people of color unemployed two – three times more often. Sixteen percent (16%) of respondents who had ever been employed reported losing at least one job because of their gender identity or expression. Twenty-seven percent of those who held or applied for a job the prior year reported being fired, denied a promotion, or not hired for a job they applied for because of their gender identity or expression (James et al., 2016).

Transgender women, and women of color in particular, are at highest risk of employment discrimination. One way that discrimination plays out is that many employers will not hire someone who presents as a woman but also has physical characteristics that may be read as male. This is especially true of jobs that require interaction with the public, but it is often true even for behind-the-scenes positions. These dynamics add to the anxiety trans young adults feel as they head into an employment interview—a situation that is inherently anxiety-producing for almost all of us.

Trans young adults who are employed and have not yet come out about being transgender worry about being fired if they do come out as trans. This anxiety often persists even when their job seems fairly secure. One young adult trans woman I worked with had many pieces of evidence that her employers valued her contribution. Her supervisor and boss had clearly articulated her value to their organization. She had been promoted twice in two years, and her annual reviews were extremely positive. Yet, none of this diminished her anxiety about being fired if she came out as trans. She was terrified of the possibility of losing her job and delayed coming out for almost a year.

Another young adult trans woman who had not yet come out worked in a predominantly male work environment. While it generally seemed fairly progressive, there were occasional inappropriate jokes by coworkers along race and gender lines. This woman, too, worried about her coworkers' response as well as the possibility of being terminated.

What compounds the fear and anxiety about losing employment is that terminations are not generally framed as being about gender identity or expression. Being let go from a job may be presented as necessary downsizing; the rationale may be the need to reorganize departments and positions. It is generally difficult to prove that termination was discriminatory.

While there is recourse in some areas when trans people are unjustly terminated on the basis of gender identity or expression, this does not solve everything. They do not automatically get their job back. Even if they file a lawsuit against their former employer, they are still unemployed in that moment. They still have rent and bills to pay. They still have to get out there and look for a new job. And now, they also have legal fees.

Within the context of the workplace environment, some transgender young adults are challenged by persistent experiences of feeling awkward and uncomfortable. Sometime this may be because of ways that coworkers interact with them, such as by ridiculing them. Other times, it is experiences of being outed by others, as the following vignette illustrates.

George was a barista at a local coffee shop. He had been presenting as male, and had generally been perceived as male, for several months when he obtained this job. He was incredibly excited to get it because he needed it to help pay for his college costs.

He had to come out to his supervisor when he was hired because he had not been able to get all of his documentation changed over yet, including his legal name change. He went by his male name with coworkers, and none of them questioned his male gender identity. However, the roster printed out each morning listing the employees that were coming in to work that day always had George's birth-assigned name on it because it was still his legal name. His boss said he couldn't figure out a way to get it to print George's affirmed name.

So, periodically, George would have to deal with a coworker looking over the roster and asking, "Who's this? I don't know anybody named Gloria. We don't have a Gloria working here." And then George would have to out himself as trans in response.

Failure to Launch

I have worked with numerous transgender young adults who "failed to launch" in the sense that they stayed home with their families and did not take any actions toward establishing an adult life for themselves. Many of these young adults were not working. Some had attended college and returned home. Others had not gone to college or obtained employment.

The way many of these young people were "stuck" developmentally often reflected unresolved gender dysphoria. They were typically just coming out as trans sometime after high school. They were between 18 and 24 years old. For the most part, they had spent all of their adolescence living in a false self. As a result, they had not accomplished many basic adolescent developmental tasks, and consequently were unable to begin assuming young adult tasks.

Some had come out earlier as transgender, but their own internalized trans-prejudice kept them from beginning to transition. They often felt they did not have the right to transition. They had been told it was wrong to feel the way they did, that it would be "selfish" to transition, that wanting to be a different gender meant they were mentally ill, and that no one would ever love them, be friends with them, or hire them if they transitioned.

Others were living with and dependent on unsupportive families. As we worked together, it became clear that they were simply
unable to move into their adult lives in their birth-assigned sex.
They could not conceive of going to college or getting a job as they
were in that moment—still inhabiting their birth-assigned sex. They
were trapped—unable to afford a medical transition on their own,
unable to imagine college or employment as they were, and dependent on families who were unwilling to support these steps. It was
this dilemma that held them back developmentally. As we worked
through these challenges—and this typically involved considerable
work with their families—most of these young people were able to
transition and move forward with their adult lives.

This chapter has briefly discussed some of the tasks and challenges
facing transgender young adults as they move from adolescence into
their adult lives. As noted, trans young adults must navigate all the
usual young adult developmental tasks. However, these are sometimes complicated by the added dimension of being trans.

Resources for Preparing for College

**College reviews for ranking LGBT and sometimes T rankings
specifically:**
- https://www.campusprideindex.org/
- http://www.princetonreview.com/search-results?q=lgbt
- www.thetaskforce.org/downloads/reports/reports/
  CampusClimate.pdf

Human Rights Campaign resources:
- **"Explore: Campus and Young Adult"** – http://www.
  hrc.org/explore/topic/campus-young-adult
- **"GenEQ: Guide to Entering the Workforce"** – http://
  www.hrc.org/resources/geneq-guide-to-entering-the-
  workforce?_ga=1.199576935.810963094.1424645452

Campus Pride is a "national nonprofit . . . organization for student
leaders and campus groups working to create a safer college environment for LGBT students. The organization is a volunteer-driven
network 'for' and 'by' student leaders. The primary objective of Cam-

pus Pride is to develop necessary resources, programs and services to support LGBTQ and ally students on college campuses across the United States." https://www.campuspride.org/

TONI Project (Transgender On-Campus Nondiscrimination Information) "is a first-of-its-kind space for students to share college and university policies important to transgender people. Use this site to learn about campus housing policies, health plans, and curricula, or add and edit information about the school you currently attend." http://www.transstudents.org

"The Top Ten Trans-Friendly Colleges and Universities" (*The Advocate*) – http://www.advocate.com/politics/transgender/2012/08/15/top-10-trans-friendly-colleges-and-universities

"College Campuses Are More Trans-Inclusive Than Ever, but Still Have a Long Way to Go" (by Joseph Erbentraut, *Huffington Post*) – http://www.huffingtonpost.com/2015/05/18/trans-friendly-colleges _n_7287702.html

Lambda Legal resources:
- **"Transgender Students in College"** – http://www.lambdalegal.org/know-your-rights/college/transgender/transgenderaud1
- **"FAQ About Transgender Students at Colleges and Universities"** – http://www.lambdalegal.org/know-your-rights/transgender/in-college-faq

PART 3

Supporting Trans Youth

CHAPTER 12

The Mental Health Professional

T HIS CHAPTER BEGINS WITH A DISCUSSION OF OUR ROLE AS mental health professionals in working with transgender youth and their families and the training needed to effectively fulfill this role. The tasks outlined in the WPATH Standards of Care for mental health professionals are presented, as are challenges that can emerge as a result of the "gatekeeper role."

Mental health professionals are not immune to cultural messages about gender as binary or the belief that sex and gender identity are synonymous. Given this, examining our own ideas and beliefs about gender is an essential starting point. This chapter explores how these internalized attitudes and beliefs may interfere with effective clinical practice with trans youth. Possible provider "missteps" that create barriers in the therapeutic relationship with transgender clients are discussed. The final section explores our intersecting social locations and how these potentially impact our work, as well as the challenges of navigating our emotional responses to this work with transgender youth and their families.

The Importance of Training and Consultation

Few graduate schools or professional educational programs in social work, psychology, mental health counseling, or family therapy include curriculum on working with transgender clients. As a result, despite the increasing visibility of transgender children and adolescents, few mental health providers are prepared to work effectively with these young people and their families.

The WPATH Standards of Care (2012) recommend the following

minimum credentials for mental health professionals working with transgender or gender-diverse children and youth (p. 13):

1. A master's degree or its equivalent in a clinical behavioral science field.
2. Competence in using the Diagnostic Statistical Manual of Mental Disorders and/or the International Classification of Diseases for diagnostic purposes.
3. Ability to recognize and diagnose coexisting mental health concerns and to distinguish these from gender dysphoria.
4. Training in childhood and adolescent developmental psychopathology and competence in diagnosing and treating the ordinary problems of children and adolescents.
5. Documented supervised training and competence in psychotherapy or counseling.
6. Knowledge of gender-nonconforming identities and expressions and the assessment and treatment of gender dysphoria.
7. Continuing education in the assessment and treatment of gender dysphoria and work with transgender and gender-nonconforming clients. Knowledge about current community, advocacy, and public policy issues relevant to trans clients and their families.

As recommended earlier, mental health providers working with transgender children and adolescents should have training and experience in working with children and teenagers in general. It is also important for them to assess their level of competence with family therapy. A basic level of knowledge and skills can be sufficient for the initial work with families when their child is exploring gender identity or expression or beginning to transition. Basic knowledge of family work may also be sufficient if the child's gender identity is the primary issue. However, if more complex family concerns or history emerges, it may be important to refer the family to a provider specifically trained in family therapy.

It is essential to seek out training and supervision before you begin working with transgender youth and their families. Reading this book is a great start. While I have tried to make it as comprehensive as possible, it really provides the basic foundation upon which you must continue learning about transgender youth and gain increased skills for working with them and their families. Attending face-to-face trainings is important as well, because they offer the opportunity to ask questions in the moment as well as interact with colleagues.

Today there are numerous training opportunities around the United States. A great way to get started in your training is to become a member of WPATH. WPATH recently developed a certification program for mental health providers that offers the in-depth training needed to become a gender specialist. WPATH has a biennial international symposium where gender experts from around the world gather to share new research, therapeutic interventions, and best practices in health and mental health care for transgender people. WPATH is establishing a U.S. chapter (USPATH) that will hold its first symposium in February 2017. The directory of medical and mental health providers on its website offers an opportunity to begin to network with other professionals working with transgender youth in your local area or state.

Other professional trainings around the United States are offered in conjunction with several annual conferences. These include Gender Spectrum's original conference on the West Coast, Gender Spectrum East, the Philadelphia Trans Health Conference, and the Gender Odyssey Conference. There are numerous smaller conferences and events for transgender people hosted by local or statewide transgender organizations. Many of these have begun to include professional training opportunities as well.

Local agencies and institutions may provide trainings and seminars, as do many professional organizations and associations. If you have difficulty finding training in your geographic area, ask your professional association, your local university, or a larger social service agency to invite a trainer to provide a training in your area. If you participate in an annual conference focused on different training opportunities, ask the organizers to invite someone in to do a pre-conference training institute.

When you begin working with transgender children and youth, it is critical to access supervision from someone experienced with this population. If you have worked with transgender adolescents before but not younger trans or gender-diverse children, this is another important area for seeking consultation. In addition to providing clinical supervision, this individual can be helpful in beginning to

develop a referral base of other mental health and medical providers who work with transgender young people. You will need to find
medical providers who are able to prescribe and monitor hormone
blockers and feminizing and masculinizing hormone therapy.

In thinking about your level of competence for specific referrals, it
can be helpful to revisit the assessment chapter to determine when it
might be best to refer a transgender youth to a colleague with greater
expertise in this area. As noted there, therapists with a foundational
level of knowledge are often able to work effectively with youth
exploring gender identity and expression. However, when youth
begin to clearly assert a transgender identity and desire to transition,
it is important for them to work with a gender specialist.

If the young person has significant mental health concerns, is at
risk of suicide or self-harm, is actively using drugs or alcohol in a way
that negatively impacts their life, or is using sex for validation of their
gender identity, it is also essential for them to work with a gender
specialist. If there is no one with this expertise in your geographic
area, WPATH may be able to help you locate an experienced clinician
from whom you can seek consultation.

The Role of Mental Health Providers

- Assessment and diagnosis of the young person's gender dysphoria

- Supportive counseling and family counseling

- Assessment and treatment of any other mental health concerns

- Assessment of eligibility and readiness
  to access hormone therapy or surgical
  interventions

- Provision of referrals for medical
  interventions

- Education and advocacy within the
  community

- Provision of information and referrals for
  peer support for youth and family

The WPATH Standards of Care (2012) outline several primary tasks for mental health providers when working with gender-diverse and transgender children and adolescents (p. 14). The first task involves assessment and diagnosis of the child's or adolescent's gender dysphoria. As discussed in Chapter 3, this includes completing a general psychosocial evaluation as well as gathering a detailed history of the young person's gender expression and identification. Depending on the age of the child, this information is generally gathered from both the young person and their parents. The goal in this first step is to assess the nature, extent, history, and intensity of the young person's gender dysphoria.

The second task is to provide supportive counseling for the young person as well as family counseling. These interventions focus on exploring gender identity and expression; providing education about biological sex, gender identity, and gender expression; and alleviating distress associated with gender dysphoria. Related to this process is the need to assess and treat any other mental health concerns that might be present.

As the young person and their family consider a medical transition, the mental health professional is responsible for assessing the adolescent's eligibility and readiness to access hormone therapy or surgical interventions. If the teenager meets the eligibility requirements and their family is ready, the mental health professional should ensure that the family has the information needed to make an informed decision about proceeding with that aspect of the child's medical transition. It is the mental health professional's responsibility to refer the client and their family to knowledgeable and competent medical doctors who can oversee the medical transition.

When working with transgender children and adolescents, the mental health professional should take an active role in educating and advocating for the young person within their community in settings such as schools, faith communities, camps, and other community programs and activities. This role is particularly important given the high risk of harassment and bullying for gender-diverse and trans youth.

Finally, it is critical that mental health professionals provide information and avenues for transgender children youth and their families to access peer support regarding their gender dysphoria and, if relevant, gender transition.

Is Psychotherapy Required?

The WPATH Standards of Care (SOC) (2012) differentiate between the process of assessment and diagnosis and the provision of psychotherapy (p. 28). Mental health providers familiar with earlier versions of the Standards of Care may be aware that psychotherapy was previously required before a transgender individual could begin hormone therapy or access surgical interventions. This is no longer true. Participating in psychotherapy is helpful for many transgender individuals, but it is no longer a requirement before clients can medically transition. Discontinuing this requirement reflects the evolving understanding that gender dysphoria is not pathological and does not require psychotherapeutic intervention (though it can be helpful for many youth).

That said, the vast majority of transgender and gender-diverse young people I work with do see me for psychotherapy for at least a period of time beyond the assessment phase. The overall goal for therapeutic interventions with trans and gender-diverse children and adolescents is to enhance their mental, emotional, and social well-being as they navigate what it means to be a trans youth in the world—at home, at school, and in the community. Within this overarching goal, clinical work can be helpful in at least three areas.

One is processing the internal and external experiences of gender identity and dysphoria that have occurred prior to the youth's seeking assessment and/or coming out as transgender or gender-diverse. This may include the young person's feelings of confusion, fear, not fitting in, or isolation. It may necessitate working through the emotional aftermath of early experiences of familial or social marginalization, bullying, or discrimination.

The second area addresses much of what has been discussed within this book—exploring and clarifying one's gender identity and expression, making decisions about how to live authentically in the world, where appropriate moving through the process of gender transition, and enhancing acceptance from those within the young person's support network.

The third area is exploration of post-disclosure and post-transition challenges, such as building increased coping skills for moving through the world as a gender-diverse, nonbinary youth or young person now living in their affirmed gender. This can include learning to respond to intrusive questions from others, navigating experiences of ridicule or bullying, or making decisions about when, where, and with whom to share one's transgender history.

As transgender children grow up, new developmental issues emerge—both typical childhood and adolescent developmental tasks and others that may be related to the young person's trans history or identity. Post-transition clinical issues that may emerge for transgender children and youth involve the possibility of reemerging dysphoria or body image work, dating and intimacy, exploring the varying ways their social interactions shift as they live in their affirmed identity, and other issues addressed in the chapter on advanced clinical interventions with adolescents. At the same time, it is important to acknowledge that some transgender youth may be able to navigate these challenges without ongoing psychotherapy. The support of their family and friends may be sufficient.

As discussed within the two chapters on work with families, family therapy is often helpful and many times essential to the long-term well-being of the transgender young person. The three phases of work just described—before, during, and after transition—can apply equally to family work. As discussed, many parents can benefit from support in exploring and working through the range of emotions they experience when their child comes out as transgender. Parents too, need information and support while their children make a gender transition. For many parents, there are other emotions or challenges that develop over time—such as when their child attends sleep-away camp for the first time in their affirmed gender, begins dating, or enters high school or college. Each of these occasions may raise new questions and concerns for families.

While many transgender children and teens benefit from ongoing therapeutic work, it is important to remember that it is not required before a young person can medically transition. Furthermore, while all transgender youth need to navigate these challenges, not all trans youth require the support of a therapist to do so. Some may be able to address these tasks with the support of family or with support from a trans adolescent support group, as indicated by the following vignette.

Tyler was an 11-year-old boy who socially transitioned when he turned 10. His social transition at school went smoothly, and he was doing well emotionally, socially, and academically. Extended family members were all very supportive. There were no present-ing mental health concerns.

Tyler saw a therapist several times for assessment and diag-nosis of his gender dysphoria before transitioning. However, he did not like the therapist and did not want to continue seeing her. Tyler's mother contacted me because she wanted a thera-pist who could work with them moving forward, particularly as they approached potential decisions about the use of hormone blockers. Tyler was decidedly not interested in seeing a thera-pist and stated there was nothing he wanted or needed to talk about.

Tyler did not identify as transgender; he simply identified as a boy. As a result, he did not see a need, nor did he want, to talk about being transgender. While he had experienced significant dysphoria prior to socially transitioning, this had largely abated now that he was living as a boy with full support and acceptance from family and friends.

I met with Tyler's mother several times to gather a psychoso-cial and gender history. We discussed his social transition in terms of how they had planned it and how well he had been doing since then. She confirmed that Tyler seemed happy and that she had no concerns about his mental or emotional well-being.

With a bit of pressure from his mom, Tyler reluctantly agreed to come see me for at least one appointment. During that con-versation, Tyler was clear that he felt he did not need to be in therapy. I discussed situations in the future where talking with the therapist might be helpful but agreed that he seemed to be doing very well right now.

When his mother and I met later, we both believed it could be useful for Tyler to have an ongoing connection with a therapist so that if challenges arose in the future, he would have a place to process them. However, in the face of Tyler's resistance to ther-apy at the present time, we agreed that it was more important to respect Tyler's self-determination that he did not need to be in therapy. He was doing well and the SOC do not require psycho-therapy. Furthermore, insisting that Tyler attend therapy might discourage him from the process at a later time when it might be necessary. We terminated at that point, knowing that Tyler was welcome to return if therapy seemed helpful at a future time.

The Gatekeeper Role

While psychotherapy is not required prior to medical interventions, it is the mental health professional's responsibility to assess eligibility for these steps. This necessitates meeting with clients for some period of time in order to conduct the assessment. The SOC do not specify the number of sessions required for assessment and/or to determine eligibility and readiness. Mental health professionals vary in their approach to this process. Some providers establish a set number of appointments for all clients. Others vary the number of sessions based on the needs of individual clients.

The fact that it is the mental health professional and not the client who makes the decision about access to medical interventions creates the dynamic of providers as gatekeepers. Within the context of the SOC, the professional is the linchpin in determining whether trans youth or adults can move forward with their desired medical interventions. A licensed mental health professional must provide a letter to the medical doctor (see samples in Appendix C) stating that the client meets the criteria for gender dysphoria and is ready to begin hormone therapy or proceed with the identified surgical intervention.

Functioning in the role of the gatekeeper can challenge the therapeutic relationship. A recent study of transgender individuals indicated that the gatekeeper role became a barrier for them in two different ways. One occurred when clients experienced the clinician as overly controlling or noncollaborative in the gender assessment process. The other way the role became a barrier was when clients perceived the therapist to be treating it in a superficial or pro forma manner. An example of the latter was a provider saying, "We'll just do the eleven appointments you need, and then I'll give you the piece of paper" (Mizock & Lundquist, 2016, p. 152).

There are also inherent contradictions within the gatekeeper role that convey mixed and stigmatizing messages to clients. On the one hand, the SOC state that gender identities are diverse and that there is nothing pathological about gender dysphoria. At the same time, transgender individuals are required to seek mental health assessment and clearance before they can transition. Within the SOC, gender dysphoria is no longer considered a psychiatric illness. Yet it remains in the DSM, and trans people continue to need a psychiatric diagnosis in order to fully be who they are in the world.

If being transgender is truly not a psychiatric illness, then why is a mental health assessment required? If being transgender is not a mental illness, why can't transgender individuals make their own decisions about medical interventions without needing approval from a mental health provider? Plastic surgery does not require a mental health assessment; these are decisions cisgender individuals are allowed to make on their own despite the fact that the surgery alters their physical appearance and body. Requiring a mental health assessment and diagnosis reinforces the stigma associated with being transgender and undermines client self-determination and autonomy.

The required assessment and hoped-for clearance leads many transgender individuals to understandably feel that they must prove they are transgender in order to justify their medical transition. If they fail this test, the mental health professional has the power to withhold the required clearance letter that will allow them to proceed. While the DSM outlines specific criteria, mental health professionals may interpret the criteria differently. This leaves open the possibility that a particular transgender youth might not meet the clinician's understanding of gender dysphoria criteria and not be allowed to medically transition. These repercussions can lead to the development of resentment and anger on the part of the client, as illustrated by the following vignette.

> A number of years into my own transition, I made the decision to pursue lower surgery. I was a well-respected clinical social worker whose practice focused almost exclusively on work with transgender children, adolescents, and adults and their families. I trained regularly in these areas and supervised other clinicians. I was happily married and parenting three young people.
>
> Despite these aspects of my life, the SOC required mental health letters from two different professionals diagnosing me with (at that time) gender identity disorder. This meant I had to seek out clinicians I did not know, pay for my appointments with them, and share my life history despite my lack of need for psychotherapy at that time. Despite my expertise in this area and the fact that I had been living as a man successfully for several years, I was dependent on the judgment of a mental health professional diagnosing me and determining whether I was ready for lower surgery, just as all transgender individuals are.

This creates a tremendous power imbalance and thus vulnerability, even for someone like me who holds power as an experienced mental health professional. It is also a definite recipe for resentment, given the sense of powerlessness that accompanies another individual having the power to determine whether you will be allowed to access something inherent and essential to who you are as a gendered human being. It is essential that we grasp the tensions and potential impact of these dynamics bound up in our role within the SOC as a gatekeeper.

Nonbinary trans youth can encounter particular challenges within this framework. Many are increasingly deconstructing the binary understanding of gender and view their identities along a continuum. They do not necessarily identify as men or women. They may not want to transition in the sense of living in the "opposite" gender. They may choose some medical interventions and not others. Mental health professionals with older understandings of gender identity disorder and narrow definitions of what it means be transgender can present barriers for nonbinary youth in obtaining the diagnosis and clearance needed to access medical interventions. The following vignette illustrates the type of scenario where older understandings of transgender identity could pose a barrier for these young people.

> Casey, an 18-year-old gender-diverse young person, identified as being "transgender on the masculine spectrum." Casey used gender-neutral pronouns and did not identify as a "transgender man" or use that language. They sought me out because they wanted a letter for chest reconstruction surgery
>
> Casey reported that since the onset of puberty, they had experienced gender dysphoria about their chest. Though they did not intend to fully transition and live as a man, they deeply desired a flat, male-appearing chest and believed this was an essential aspect of their gender identity on the masculine spectrum. Casey explained that a flat chest would more accurately represent who they understood themselves to be and allow them to be more comfortable moving through the world.
>
> While Casey experienced dissonance between their affirmed gender identity (transgender on the masculine spectrum) and the development of breasts during puberty, their self-presentation did not fully align with older understandings of transgender identity. Casey did not desire to be a man or to be perceived as one.

Casey did not necessarily believe they experienced the feelings and responses of most men.

The DSM only requires that the individual meet two of the six identified criteria. However, some mental health professionals might question the "legitimacy" of Casey's transgender identity knowing that Casey did not intend to live full time as a man. These challenges contribute to Casey and others feeling a need to prove their affirmed gender identities and justify chosen medical interventions.

The SOC also tasks mental health professionals with diagnosis, assessment, and treatment of any other mental health concerns. This can lead trans youth to feel they cannot be honest about certain struggles, such as depression, anxiety, or self-harming behaviors, out of fear that these factors might negatively influence the clinician's assessment about their eligibility to proceed with their transition. They fear the provider might deny the requested medical intervention—or delay clearance—believing that the other mental health concerns require further treatment before the youth can proceed.

Each of these dynamics has the potential to disrupt authentic engagement, both at the onset and within the course of the therapeutic relationship and process. While individual clinicians have not created this environment, the gatekeeper role and concomitant need to prove one's transgender identity can precipitate resentment toward the mental health professional and their regulatory role.

It is critical that mental health professionals not become defensive when clients express resentment or anger about these dynamics. Instead, open discussion of the contradictory and stigmatizing protocol is essential. Mental health providers need to authentically acknowledge the ways the gatekeeper role can hinder the development of rapport and trust. As in other contexts where clients are mandated to treatment, open acknowledgment and discussion of the power differential can help to defuse its potential negative impact. With this dynamic out in the open, clinicians and transgender clients are often able to be creative in how they navigate the tensions.

It is critical to be transparent about your assessment and diagnostic process, including the criteria you use to make a decision about whether or not to write the required letter. This is especially true with older youth and young adults who are not interested in pursuing therapy and simply request a gender assessment and letter. Mental health providers should acknowledge their inability to promise the letter prior to meeting to conduct the assessment. Clarity about expectations, such as the number of sessions you require, contributes to engagement and trust. However, there are times when these power dynamics cannot be resolved, leading some transgender clients to terminate the therapeutic relationship.

Exploring Our Assumptions and Subtle Bias

Effective clinical practice always starts with looking at and knowing ourselves. While the evidenced-based interventions we draw on may be rooted in science, ethical and is also relational. Knowing who we are—our family history; our cultural background; our attitudes, beliefs, and values; our varying social locations—plays a part in making us who we are, and thus who we bring into our relationship with clients.

During the first semester in my MSW practice class, I use an exercise with students that focuses on naming different aspects of who we are as well as identifying the history and experiences that shaped us. We explore our attitudes, beliefs, and values and how these might impact our work with clients—especially when we are unaware of them. One of the exercises is titled "What pushes my buttons?" A series of snippets about a client situation are provided, and students are asked to rate the degree to which they had a positive or negative reaction toward the client based on the information provided. Once they have rated their reaction, they identify the underlying beliefs that led to their reaction.

Our negative or judgmental reactions typically stem from internalized beliefs. We may have openly been taught these beliefs by the adults around us growing up, or we may have absorbed them from the larger culture. The beliefs can include every aspect of who we are and who we were told we should be. They include what we were taught about others and how they should act or behave. They include what we believe is the "right" way to do things.

Having grown up within a heteronormative, binary gender culture, all mental health professionals are at risk of internalized biases (or beliefs) that may interfere with their clinical relationship with transgender children and adolescents. Bias can be overt, or it can be present in the form of subtle lingering questions within our mind. Consequently, it is critical for us as providers to strive for increasing

self-awareness and regularly assess whether and how our social locations, lived experiences, or internalized beliefs may be affecting our
work with trans youth or their families.

Straight cisgender therapists—and sometimes lesbian, gay, or
bisexual therapists—who grew up within gender-normative environments may find that working with transgender children and youth
challenges their internalized assumptions about human beings, gender, and the world in which we live. Cisgender privilege means that
our own gender identity is often something we did not need to think
about. If you were assigned female at birth, you simply identify today
as a woman; if you were assigned male at birth, you identify today
as a man. It may be a new concept to understand biological sex and
gender identity as distinct aspects of ourselves that may not always
align perfectly. Before we can educate families about biological sex,
gender identity, and gender expression, we need to grapple with our
own understandings and assumptions about these different aspects
of who we are as human beings.

Is My Bias in the Way?

- Can a child or adolescent know they are a gender other than that assigned at birth? At what age can someone know this for certain?

- Don't all transgender youth have mental health issues and need therapy?

- Does a transgender identity reflect inadequate, incomplete, or aberrant gender development?

- Can an adolescent truly be transgender if their gender expression was normative in childhood?

- Do we really need to challenge the binary gender construct?

- Can families from conservative faith traditions believe being transgender is sinful or not real and still accept their transgender child?

QUESTION: Do I really believe a three-year-old child assigned female at birth can know he is a boy? Do I believe a nine-year-old child assigned male at birth can know she is a girl? Do I believe a teenager can know they are transgender?

REFLECTION: Internalized assumptions that young children, pre-teens, or even teenagers cannot be certain about a transgender identity can challenge our ability to validate a young person's affirmed gender. Lingering doubts that young children can be sure of their gender identity create a dynamic where transgender children must prove their affirmed gender to us—a dynamic that undermines their own sense of agency. This can also lead to unnecessary delays in their social transition or medical interventions, potentially creating increased dysphoria and associated risk factors.

   This is not to say that exploring a young person's understanding of their gender and how they came to this understanding is inappropriate; exploration is important. But we need to ensure that our questions encouraging exploration do not cross a line into questions that damage the young person's sense of self.

QUESTION: Don't all transgender youth have mental health issues and need therapy?

REFLECTION: Earlier beliefs about transgender people as mentally ill, as well as the ongoing categorization of gender dysphoria within the DSM, can alter our assessment of the mental and emotional well-being of trans youth. Internalized stigma contributes to an overemphasis on risk factors that can cloud our recognition of young people's inherent strengths and resilience.

   It takes a tremendous sense of self for any child or adolescent to assert that their gender identity does not match the sex they were assigned at birth. The strength it requires for a young person to be sure enough to proclaim, "I am a girl," when from the day they were born everyone has said, "You are a boy," cannot be underestimated. This kind of self-assurance challenges assumptions that transgender children and teens are more likely to be depressed or anxious or experience other types of mental illness than are their cisgender peers. The types of questions emerging from these assumptions can lead trans youth to believe they are mentally ill simply because they are transgender. Unexamined assumptions about increased mental health problems among trans young people can also contribute to an inflated assessment of symptoms and the degree to which they impair a young person's day-to-day functioning.

QUESTION: Is there any part of me that still believes being transgender reflects inadequate, incomplete, or aberrant gender development?

REFLECTION: This is another area where lingering unexamined internalized beliefs can contribute to seeing psychological problems in transgender children and teens where none exist—or to unnecessarily extend exploration about how sure the child is of their gender identity. Many mental health providers were taught that the emergence of transgender identity reflected poor gender role modeling from parents. Having teachers and professional mentors espouse these beliefs early in our professional education can embed them in such a way that they continue to be acted out in subtle or unconscious ways that stigmatize trans youth.

QUESTION: Can an adolescent truly be transgender if their gender expression was normative in childhood? Doesn't the absence of gender-variant expression mean the young person is not really transgender?

REFLECTION: Both providers and parents often struggle with the internalized narrative that transgender identity always emerges in childhood and is evident through "gender-variant" interests and behavior. Many mental health professionals still question whether an adolescent whose parents report they were a "girly-girl" as a child could truly be a (transgender) boy. Again, these subtle questions can lead providers to unnecessarily prolong the assessment phase and delay the young person's ability to even socially transition.

QUESTION: Do we really need to challenge the binary gender construct? Isn't this just another adolescent/young adult phase that will pass?

REFLECTION: Those of us who grew up amid strong heteronormative gender roles and an understanding of gender identity and biological sex as always aligned may be challenged by the extent to which adolescents and young adults are already deconstructing the gender binary. We may question why this is necessary or resist the ways it feels awkward to us.

Providers in some trainings object to the inconvenience of being asked to use gender-neutral pronouns by trans youth. They indicate that they feel the young people are just "being difficult" and that this should not be supported within a treatment setting. Other providers think gender diversity among teens reflects their natural developmental individuation; it is a way to differentiate themselves from adults and not a real identity.

Again, these attitudes and beliefs belittle and undermine a young person's sense of self. They send a message that the young person is not capable of knowing who they are. They also signal that the young person's identity is less important than the adult provider's comfort.

Therapist "Missteps"

Many transgender individuals, including trans and gender-diverse adolescents, report negative experiences in therapy (Grossman & D'Augelli, 2007; Poteat, German, & Kerrigan, 2013; Xavier et al., 2013). Several factors contribute to this problem. As noted earlier, most mental health professionals have not received training around working with transgender children and adolescents. Coupled with this, the training some clinicians received may have conveyed older pathological understandings regarding the development of transgender identity. In addition, many mental health professionals reflect the heteronormative cisgender assumptions with which they grew up, and these beliefs and attitudes continue to shape much of the general public's understanding of transgender individuals.

A recent qualitative study of the experiences of transgender individuals receiving medical and mental health services conducted by Mizock and Lundquist (2016) revealed numerous "missteps" mental health professionals made with transgender clients. If this work is new to you, understanding what these therapists did that contributed to a disconnect in the therapeutic alliance may help you avoid these difficulties in your future work. If you already work with transgender children and adolescents, it may be helpful to reflect on whether any of these factors played a role in client situations when there was a breach in the therapeutic relationship.The discussion below describes each of these potential missteps by mental health professionals working with transgender individuals as reported by participants in Mizrock & Lundquist's (2016) study.

Assessing Potential Missteps (Mizock & Lundquist, 2016)

- Do my clients need to educate me about being transgender?
- Do I have a tendency to link any problems a trans client is struggling with back to their gender identity?
- To what extent have I deconstructed my narrow binary understandings of gender, gender identity, and gender expression?
- Do I ever feel uncomfortable discussing gender identity and expression with clients?
- Am I really aware of the wide range and diversity of transgender narratives?
- Is there any part of me that believes transgender identity needs to be "fixed?"
- Do I believe gender dysphoria is a mental illness and that all trans people should be in treatment?

EDUCATION BURDENING occurs when trans youth and/or their families need to assume responsibility for educating their therapist. Given the absence of professional education about working with the transgender community, it is not surprising that many transgender adolescents and adults are forced to educate their mental health provider about their needs. Even clinicians with basic knowledge about gender identity and expression and aspects of transitioning often miss the nuances of a transgender child's or adolescent's experiences.

When the responsibility for our education falls to our clients, the focus of the therapeutic relationship shifts from the client to the professional. Instead of being free to explore their current feelings and challenges, the trans adolescent must bring us up to speed on what it is like to be transgender or educate us about the effects of taking estrogen. This significantly limits what the young person is able to gain from their work with us.

GENDER INFLATION occurs when mental health professionals view all of a trans young person's difficulties as being connected to their transgender identity, regardless of whether or not this is the case. Years ago, a lesbian couple I knew sought out family therapy because of some struggles their daughter was having academically. When they stopped going after only three appointments, I asked what had happened. They told me that the therapist insisted on seeing all of their daughter's struggles in school as the result of her having lesbian parents.

This happens less frequently today in terms of lesbian and gay clients, but it still often occurs with transgender youth. When trans young people seek us out, it may be that some of the things they struggle with are connected to their experiences as a transgender youth. However, they may also face challenges that are totally unrelated to this one aspect of their identity.

GENDER NARROWING reflects the experiences of trans clients with clinicians who hold very narrow views of gender and gender identity and expression as well as limited narratives about transgender identity development and life experiences. This is another misstep that can occur even when mental health professionals have had some education about transgender individuals. The key piece here is "narrow" views about gender and only being aware of "limited" narratives about trans experience.

The mother who had difficulty believing her child really was a boy because he still liked the color pink held narrow views about gender. She was only familiar with trans narratives where trans men were normatively masculine. Some mental health professionals might also question this young person's male identity because his gender expression was not masculine enough. Historically, the psychiatric establishment held that "real" transgender people were all heterosexual;

a trans woman could not be a "real" transsexual if she was attracted to other women. Some clinicians continue to hold these views about transgender narratives.

GENDER AVOIDANCE reflects experiences when mental health providers are reluctant to engage in conversations about the young person's gender identity or expression. Some trans youth have told me that they attempted to discuss their gender identity numerous times with their previous therapist, but the clinician always changed the topic. Others have shared experiences of being told that what they felt was "a phase," or that "all teenagers explore gender." Some transgender teens report feeling as if a previous therapist was uncomfortable talking with them about sex. Sometimes the provider lacked basic information about work with transgender youth. Other times, the provider had some basic awareness but little understanding of the nuances of trans experiences.

GENDER GENERALIZING occurs when clinicians assume all transgender people and their narratives are the same rather than seeing the wide diversity among the trans community. Gender generalizing can occur when a provider has worked with only a few trans young people and makes the assumption that their experiences are reflective of all trans youth. Other times, these assumptions occur because providers do not attend to the role of intersectionality in the lives and experiences of trans young people. For example, if a provider has worked only with white trans women or middle-class trans women, they may assume that the narratives and experiences of other trans women are similar. In truth, the life experiences of transgender young people are incredibly diverse. This diversity is shaped by other aspects of their identities, such as their racial/ethnic identity, the context in which they grew up, and the socioeconomic realities of their lives.

GENDER REPAIRING, often called reparative therapy, reflects providers who believe that transgender identity needs to be "fixed" or corrected in some way. In the vignette about Joey in Chapter 2, the parents had been working for a year with a professional who viewed Joey's gender-diverse behavior as needing correction and redirection to more normative boys' interests and activities. Similarly, Leelah Alcorn's parents insisted she see a therapist who focused on changing or repairing her belief that she was a young woman. These understandings of trans identity are highly problematic in terms of increasing risk for self-harm among trans youth. Reparative therapy has been discredited by all major medical and mental health care associations as well as banned for use with minors in several states.

GENDER PATHOLOGIZING is similar to gender repairing in that it, too, represents older beliefs that gender dysphoria is a mental illness requiring treatment. However, gender pathologizing does not always lead to corrective therapy. It may be that providers simply understand gender dysphoria as a mental illness—perhaps reflective of inadequate gender role modeling when the youth was a child, dissociative coping mechanisms that led to an alternate gender identity, or the manifestation of aspects of borderline personality disorder.

The Intersections of Social Locations

> Location of self is the name of a process in which the therapist initiates a conversation with a family about similarities and differences in their key identities, such as race, ethnicity, gender, class, sexual orientation, and religion, and how they may potentially influence the therapy process. Implicit in this communication is the idea that these identities are meaningful and embedded in the work. (Watts-Jones, 2010, p. 405).

This section briefly explores some of the ways our varied social locations may impact our work with transgender children and youth and their families. One significant aspect of social location in working with transgender youth involves our relationship to gender identity and expression and whether we stand in the center or on the margins of heteronormativity.

Similarities and differences in social location between mental health professionals and their clients are neither good nor bad, in and of themselves. The crucial part is being aware of our locations and willing to critically reflect on how these might impact the therapeutic relationship. In my work with MSW students, I find that they sometimes assume that similarities between clients and workers are best and that differences create problems. For example, they may assume a female worker is better able to connect and relate with a female client. They tend to assume a Latino male worker is best suited to work with a Latino male client. Concomitantly, their assumption is that if their own racial/ethnic identity is not Latino, this client will be less able to relate to them.

Sometimes similarities in social locations between workers and clients can facilitate the beginnings of trust and rapport. Similarities can mean that the worker intuitively understands cultural nuances or contextual dynamics that a worker outside that social location might miss or fail to adequately appreciate. For example, when I am working with a young transgender man, there are ways that I "get" the repeated ways others question his masculinity. I see these dynamics where a cisgender therapist might miss them, simply because these are shared experiences between that young person and me.

However, these same similarities can also cause us to miss things. As a trans male therapist, it is easy for me to assume that I understand my trans male client's experience because we share this social location. Yet this is not always valid. As a white trans male therapist, I cannot assume I understand my Asian client's narrative simply because we are both trans men. If I make this assumption, I am likely to miss the nuances, and maybe the more obvious dynamics, of his life experiences of marginalization in terms of race and ethnicity.

Further, our shared similarity around gender identity might mean I am less attentive to the differences between us. Because their social location differs, a cisgender therapist might pay closer attention to the details of a transgender client's story—precisely because they realize they do not share the same life experiences.

As mentioned earlier in this book, those of us raised as heteronormative straight cisgender therapists did not generally need to think about our own gender identities. Given our location at the center of heteronormativity, it may sometimes be difficult to envision or comprehend the challenges trans youth experience in their daily lives on the margins of gender normativity. It is not impossible for us to do so, but we need to begin by examining our own privilege in these aspects of our identity and how that privilege limits us.

Those of us who experience privilege in many aspects of our social locations may struggle to appreciate the impact of the microaggressions, verbal harassment, discrimination, and violence many trans young people encounter. This can challenge our ability to emotionally connect with the way these experiences affect transgender youth—particularly trans youth with multiple stigmatized identities, such as youth of color or transgender youth living with disabilities.

Related to this dynamic is the way those of us who are white frequently fail to grasp the impact of the intersections of race and gender identity among trans youth of color and their families. All too often, those of us who are white do not initiate conversations about racial identity and experience within the context of clinical practice—with transgender youth or any clients. Because our place of privilege around race allows us to not think about race in our day-to-day lives, we miss the reality of its pervasive and chronic impact on the lives of trans youth and families of color. When this happens, we fail to appreciate the ways racial stigma intersects with, and amplifies, stigma around gender identity and expression.

Lesbian, gay, and bisexual mental health professionals sometimes have a window into the lives of trans youth because of their shared position on the margins of sexuality and gender. Yet these positions are not identical. As in other arenas of similarity, LGB clinicians need to be careful not to assume that their experience is the same or that they understand when they likely do not fully grasp the lived realities of transgender youth. A gay male counselor with feminine gender expression as a child might assume that the five-year-old gender-diverse natal male with whom he currently works will grow up to identify as a gay man—because their childhood gender expression is similar. The risk is that this assumption of sameness could mean that this clinician fails to fully explore his five-year-old client's gender identity.

Beyond self-awareness, it is incumbent on me to initiate conversations about social location with trans youth and their families. This is especially true where I hold aspects of privilege or power.

In my work with Juan and his mother (Chapter 8), I highlighted our need to reach beneath the surface to find the underlying emotions driving the mother's anger or rejection. I noted the intensity of the mother's anger, even in my meetings with her, and how this made it difficult to have a dialogue. Each time I attempted to shift the conversation or offer an alternate perspective, her rage resurfaced and took over our discussion. It felt as if she did not want to hear an alternative perspective on what might be occurring between her and her son.

I also noted my suspicion that she particularly might not want to listen to the opinions of a white middle-class professional man (me) who (in her eyes) was likely judging her as a working-class single Puerto Rican mom who clearly had not raised her son to be a real man (since he dressed like a "faggot"). Without question, the dominant white culture routinely judged her.

In this relationship, I held privilege and power as the therapist, as a man, as a white man, as the one with a graduate education, and as one who never had been a single mother raising a son of color in a white dominant society marked by systemic racism and violence toward dark-skinned men. Given these intersecting aspects of privilege, she had every right not to expect me to understand her life experience. Given my privilege and power in this relationship, it was my responsibility to acknowledge this reality with Juan's mother and to open the door to a discussion about how our differences in social locations might facilitate or hinder our work together. It was only as I entered this conversation that we were able to begin to build a modicum of authenticity and trust, without which change could not have emerged.

Managing Our Own Emotional Responses

Similarities in social location can also intensify our connection with clients. As a trans man, I need to stay conscious of the moments when I identify with transgender youth. This is a strength I bring to my work. Yet my ability to relate can morph into enmeshment. The fact that I, too, experienced family rejection can make it easy for me to slide into rescuing a trans young person whose family rejects them. The following vignette examines the potential impact of our own emotional responses and how we need to navigate these effectively.

> I had been working with Brian (17-year-old trans male) and his family for 10 months. He came out as transgender to his parents about 3 months before they came to see me for therapy. It was challenging to engage Brian given how acutely depressed he was. His depression was visible in every aspect of his speech and body language. There were often long silences when I asked a question. When he did respond, I had to lean in very close, and even then his voice was so soft I sometimes missed what he said.
>
> His parents struggled with his disclosure about being trans-

gender at first, especially his mother. I spent a lot of time helping them understand gender identity and expression, as well as how these differed from sexual orientation. Within their cultural context, sex and gender identity were one and the same. You were whatever sex you were born, and there was no possibility for changing this.

Over time both parents became more accepting and together we made the decision that Brian would socially transition at school that coming fall. His father met with the counselors and teachers to set everything up. Mom made an appointment and took Brian to see a doctor about beginning puberty blockers.

Throughout this time, Brian's depression remained a focus. He had frequent suicidal ideation and a history of cutting himself. Conducting a suicide assessment was part of every session. Brian and I would re-affirm his commitment not to harm himself weekly. Several times he seemed unsure about his ability to make this commitment and I brought his parents in to discuss whether it was possible to ensure he would not harm himself that weekend, or whether we should have him hospitalized.

Brian's depression diminished somewhat when he transitioned at school. He began coming out of his room for dinner, going for walks with his brother and parents, playing with the family dog again, and even meeting up with friends on occasion.

One week toward the end of our session, Brian seemed upset. When I asked about this, he shrugged it off.

I asked a second time whether there was something important he thought I should know. He wiggled his hand back and forth as if to say "maybe."

I said, "I'll take that as a yes" and waited for a few moments. When he remained silent, I asked if he was worried about telling me what was upsetting him.

He nodded yes.

I asked if he could tell me what he was worried about.

Brian said, "I'm worried you'll think someone is a terrible person."

I thought for a moment and then asked, "Is the person you're worried I'll think is terrible part of your family?"

He nodded yes again.

I shared there wasn't much someone could do that would

make me think they were a horrible person. I said people had told me about things they did that were hurtful to others, but that didn't make me think they were horrible people. I said that most of the time when we hurt someone else, it's because we were hurt in the past. And this meant we needed help, not that we were horrible.

Brian was quiet for a few minutes more.

Then he said, "We were watching TV this week in the living room—me, my mom, and my brother. Somehow the subject of abortion came up and we were discussing it."

He paused for a minute and curled himself even deeper into my couch, as if he wanted to disappear.

Then he whispered, "I asked my mom, if she had known I was transgender before she had me, would she have aborted me?" He stayed curled in a ball on the couch and continued, "And she said yes."

In that moment, I had an overwhelming desire to scoop Brian up and hold him close. I wanted to rock him in my arms. It took everything within me to simply sit quietly with him while he cried.

I also wanted to scream at his mother (who I genuinely liked), "What in the world were you thinking? How could you ever say something like that to your child? How can you not understand the impact of saying, 'Yes, I would have had an abortion if I knew you would be trans?'"

I couldn't do any of those things. Instead, I had to sit with my emotional responses so I could be present with Brian. I acknowledged how much his mother's answer hurt him. I told him this was not about him. There was nothing wrong with who he was. This was about his mother's pain and confusion. I said I needed to meet with his mother to help her work on her pain so she didn't keep hurting him.

An hour later as I walked to my car to go home, I was still entertaining a fantasy of rescuing Brian and taking him home to live with me. I'll be his parent. He doesn't deserve to live with this. He doesn't deserve to hear things like this. I'll take care of him.

Throughout the week, I moved in and out of my worry for Brian, my desire to protect and rescue him, and my anger toward his mother. I spent some time writing about my emotional responses, and I talked with a colleague about how the session affected me. I had to meet with Brian's mother the next week, and in order to do that effectively, I knew I had to have a better handle on my own feelings.

Being angry with his mother wouldn't work. I could not go into a conversation with her on the attack. I could not let my alliance with Brian or my desire to protect him alienate me from his mother. Yes, he needed an advocate. What that meant was that I needed to find my place of compassion for his mother. I needed to find the place I had told Brian about—the place where I knew that when we hurt others, it's because we were hurt before. I could only be the kind of advocate Brian needed if I was his mother's advocate as well. I had to believe she loved him despite how much the response in the living room didn't sound like love.

When the family arrived the following week, I asked to talk with Brian's mom and dad first. We had a moment or two of checking in about how the week had been and how they thought Brian and his older brother were doing.

I took a deep breath and said, "Last week when Brian and I met, he shared a situation that really upset him. He told me that the week before you [looking at his mom] and his brother and he were watching TV and the subject of abortion came up. Brian said he asked if you [still looking at mom] had known he would be transgender, would you have aborted him? He told me you said yes."

The mom responded quickly that she hadn't been serious. She told me she and Brian's older brother had a warped sense of humor; they said things like that but never meant them. Brian never got their humor.

She sounded a bit defensive. I worried she thought I was judging her.

I said I could see how this might be true, that maybe Brian hadn't understood it was a joke. (Inside, part of me was thinking, "How in the world could a parent joke about something like aborting a child?" However, I sat with my feelings.)

I said to the mom, "You know, there have been one or two other times when Brian has felt hurt by things you've said to him." I reminded her of a conversation we'd had when he told her he felt hurt when she said he would never be a boy. "I know you love Brian deeply [and I did know this, despite her comment to him]. I know you've been incredibly supportive of his transition. You were the one who called the doctor to get him on hormone blockers so he wouldn't get his period anymore. You're the one who takes him to his doctor's appointments. I can see by your actions that you love and support him and want him to be happy. But at the same time, it seems like there are these moments when anger leaks out. Saying yes, you would have aborted him, even if it was a joke, feels angry and hurtful to me. It makes me wonder if there is something underneath that anger that keeps leaking out."

The second I finished that last sentence, Brian's mother began sobbing about how hard this was for her. That she loved Brian very much. That he was her baby, her baby girl. That it felt like she was losing her baby girl.

Here was the pain underneath the anger. The grief and loss she felt as her baby girl, her only daughter, became her son, Brian. The loss she felt was huge. As we talked, it also became clear that she felt guilty about her grief.

This is a long vignette, but it illustrates the emotional complexity of our work with transgender youth and their families. It illustrates the challenge of managing our own emotional responses in order to stay engaged with each member of the family. Being Brian's advocate meant maintaining my relationship with his mother and holding the belief that she loved him despite the hurtfulness of what she said to him.

In the moment when Brian disclosed this conversation to me, I had to validate how painful it was for him to hear that response, how painful it would be to hear your own mother say she wished you hadn't been born. But I also had to be careful not to sabotage the possibility of healing by attacking his mother.

When I leaned into the conversation with Brian's mom, my attitude and tone of voice had to be matter-of-fact. There could not be a trace of judgment about her telling Brian she would have aborted him. When she first explained this as a joke, I rolled with that, acknowledging that it might be true that Brian had just missed the humor.

This is what it means to manage our own emotional responses in the work we do with transgender youth. This is what navigating our countertransference can look like at times.

As mental health professionals, we bring who we are as individuals—our social locations and life narrative, our education, training, and clinical experience—to the work of empowering and supporting trans youth and their families. This chapter highlighted the importance of education and clinical supervision. It reviewed our role within the context of the WPATH SOC, explored the potential challenges of the gatekeeper role, and examined internalized assumptions or missteps that can hinder our relational connections with trans youth and their families. The final section explored the potential impact of our social locations and illustrated the complexities of navigating our emotional responses in this work.

CHAPTER 13

Top 10 Life-Affirming Practices for Adults in the Lives of Trans Kids

1. ## Use their affirmed name and pronouns.

   Work at this, no matter how hard or awkward it may feel to you.

   Work at it, even if you're not sure it's the "right" thing to do.

   Because it is the right thing to do.

   This says to the young person: I see who you are and I accept you for who you are.

   Every human being needs and deserves this.

2. ## Don't lose sight of their resilience.

   Despite all the challenges trans youth face, be careful not to focus on the problems.

   Transgender youth are so much more than their struggles in life.

   One of my "failure to launch" youth had spent the five months after high school graduation in her room. Literally in her room. Not going out with friends. Not coming out to talk with her parents. Only coming out for food after everyone else had gone to bed at night. She had been accepted to college but refused to go.

   She had survived high school by maintaining her false self as a boy. We worked together the fall after high school graduation as she came out to her family and socially transitioned. The next fall, she went off to college. She's the young woman who spent her entire first year being misgendered. Did she retreat and hide out again? No. She became an activist instead.

Midway through college, she transferred into a women's college, stealth. A women's college that still did not admit trans women. Two weeks after she arrived on campus, she came out. She lived through all kinds of horrible remarks from other women students that year. But she did not back down. Despite being harassed, she made friends and found allies. By the end of that academic year, the college revised its admission policy and began openly accepting transgender women.

Trans youth need to see their own incredible resilience.

They need to have this resilience reflected back to them on a regular basis.

3. Appreciate the courage it takes to be who they are in this world.

Every day. Just doing day-to-day stuff.

Marissa, a 20-year-old trans woman, was harassed on the subway ride from her apartment in the Bronx down to my office every single time she came to see me. While we often spent the first 10 to 15 minutes processing these encounters, this never deterred her from returning to see me. Neither did these experiences ever sway her own sense of herself.

How many people do you know who are this dedicated to their own mental health and well-being? How many people do you know who are so strong in their own self-determined sense of themselves that they can withstand ongoing harassment from others on their daily subway commute?

4. Do not reduce what they are feeling to body parts.

Being a man or a woman, or both, or neither, is about much more than body parts.

This is true for transgender youth and for all human beings.

If you are a woman who had a double mastectomy because of breast cancer, would you stop being a woman?

The first time I told a therapist I thought I wanted to gender transition, their response was, "But do you want a penis? A penis? Is that what you want—a penis?" That was the last time I mentioned this there. It was also the last time I mentioned it to anyone for another five years. Do not reduce what trans youth are feeling to body parts.

In case I haven't been clear, this also means you do not ask intrusive questions about what surgeries young people have had or want—unless they indicate they want to discuss this with you.

5. Pay attention to the intersections and impact of trauma.

Being told you are not who you know yourself to be is trauma.

Being marginalized and discriminated against is trauma.

Look for the ways trauma is reflected in the lives of the trans youth around you.

A colleague asked me to see a young adult African American trans woman pro bono. Given some of her past experiences, my colleague felt it was critical that this young woman talk with a transgender therapist.

We spent the first appointment gathering the usual intake information.

When the young woman arrived for our second session, she looked me straight in the eyes and asked, "Can I be real with you?"

I said, "I would be honored if you would trust me enough to do that."

She spent the next 45 minutes raging in my midtown office suite that I shared with six other therapists. Her rage was the eruption of trauma—racial, gender, gender identity, gender expression, and spiritual trauma. Years of being told she was mentally ill. That her belief that she was a woman was a delusion. Psychosis. Years of being passed around from one mental health clinic to another. Years of being dismissed as difficult and too angry by one white-dominant LGBT organization after another.

When you are with trans youth of color, it is never enough to simply talk about gender identity and expression.

For youth of color, gender, gender identity, gender expression, sexual orientation, and any other aspect of their lives always happens in the context of, and at the intersection of, their racial/ethnic identity.

Those of you who are people of color know this. It's my readers who look like me—white—who need to hear this and deeply take it in.

We are the only ones who imagine we can talk about gender identity and expression without talking about race. We imagine this because we generally don't have to think about race in our day-to-day lives.

This no longer works.

We have to begin to think about the impact of race and racism in everything we say and do.

We need to ensure that trans youth of color know that Black Lives Matter.

Black Trans Lives Matter.

6.   Introduce them to trans adults who are thriving.

Trans youth are often surrounded by images of and messages about transgender people as mentally ill, sick, perverted, sinful, unemployed and unemployable, single forever, unable to be loved by anyone, and without the ability to form a family of their own.

Hopelessness settles in when our future seems impossible.

Being able to begin your medical transition can seem like decades away at 13 or 16 years old.

Being poor and not having a way to afford hormones or surgery can feel impossible.

Living in a home with a family that rejects who you are can make you feel crazy.

Thinking that you will have to live all your life with a body that does not fit, or with the world around you calling you a boy when you are a girl, or calling you a girl when you are a boy, can make life not seem worth living.

Give them opportunities to thrive right now.

It is not enough to promise "It gets better" later on. They might not make it till later on.

We have to create opportunities for life to be better right here and now. In our organizations, our agencies, our faith communities, our youth programs, our schools, our neighborhoods, our families.

7. Connect them to their peers.

Even today, many transgender youth feel isolated and alone. As if there is no one else like them. That they are the only one whose gender doesn't fit. This is especially true for trans youth growing up in rural areas or in conservative faith communities.

Connecting with their peers is essential for their growth and well-being. If there is no trans youth group where you live and work, find a way to start one. Find people who will commit to starting one with you.

Being with people like us diminishes the impact of internalized oppression.

Being with people like us strengthens our resilience.

Being with people like us empowers us to take risks and embrace our lives.

Being with people like us generates possibility and hope.

8. Be willing to step outside the box.

Transgender children and youth do not just need counselors or therapists or parents.

They need advocates.

This means that those of you trained in clinical therapy, which typically happens in an office, are going to need to get out of your office if you are really committed to working with trans youth.

You are going to need to educate their school and their teachers. You are going to need to attend meetings with child welfare workers and insist that they find a trans-affirmative placement. You are going to need to train the clinicians at your local adolescent inpatient psychiatry unit, because otherwise your trans clients will have no safe place to be hospitalized when their depression and suicidal hopelessness overwhelms them. You are going to need to step outside your comfort zone and work with the extended family when necessary.

One Friday night in early September, I took a commuter train an hour outside New York City to meet with the extended family of a seven-year-old trans girl I worked with who had just begun second grade as a girl.

Her parents lived in and were part of a tight-knit Roman Catholic immigrant community. Many from the grandparents' generation still spoke minimal English. Conflict within the extended family had exploded when the two parents revealed their decision to allow their daughter to attend school that year as a girl. The parents were frantic. They both worked and their siblings and parents had always shared childcare. Now the mother's sister refused to pick up her niece. The grandmother never wanted to see the child again.

Relatives were calling the parents and coming by their house and screaming at them that this was a sin, an abomination to God, and that they would be punished for doing this to their child. They were threatening to disown the parents and their two children.

So there I was, on the train, headed to the parents' home. When I arrived, there were 24 members of their extended family gathered in their living room—aunts, uncles, siblings, the grandmother and grandfather. I spent the next two hours facilitating the most amazing and most challenging family therapy session I have ever had the privilege of leading.

Was it comfortable or easy? No. But by the end of the night, the seven-year-old trans girl was on her grandfather's lap again and he was calling her by her affirmed name. Several sisters had come to understand the decision of the parents and were talking with family members who were still upset. One week later, the mom called me to let me know that the grandmother had done a 180-degree turn and was embracing her new granddaughter.

You have to be willing to step outside the box.

9. Never give up on a family—no matter how rejecting they appear to be today.

I've tried to write about all the ways we need to work with the families of transgender youth. Knowing what we know today about how pivotal family acceptance is for trans youth, we cannot afford to give up on a family.

Remember that what looks like rejection is rarely the whole story. Lean into the truth that almost all parents want their children to be happy and healthy as adults. When parents are angry, remind yourself that underneath anger, there is almost always fear or hurt. Reach for these feelings instead.

Can transgender youth survive without family acceptance? Yes, certainly many can and have. But the odds are against them. And the risks are high. Their road as a young adult is likely to be bumpy. I know. I lived this.

If you have transgender youth in your life whose families have rejected them, become a parent, aunt, uncle, or sibling to them. Claim them as part of your family. Introduce them to the reality and life-affirming power of kinship families and families of choice. Tell them about the people in your life who got you through that weren't blood family.

10. Say I love you often.

If you are a parent or another relative, say "I love you" every single day.

Say "I love all of you."

Say "I love you" even when you are still struggling to understand all this.

Say "I love you" even if you think being transgender is wrong or sinful.

Still say "I love you."

You may have to say, "I don't get this. I have always been taught this is wrong. Nonetheless, I love you. All of you. Always."

Every human being needs to know the people close to them love them.

For those of you who are professionals, it may feel as if saying "I love you" doesn't fit the context of your relationships with trans youth. Maybe so, but . . .

Find another way to say it then.

Find another way to express your connectedness.

Find another way to express their value and worth in the world.

Find another way to say they matter to you.

APPENDIX A: LEGAL ISSUES

Transgender children, youth, and their families are living today in the midst of a rapidly changing legal environment and one that is increasingly supportive of transgender youth. During May and June 2016, we witnessed sweeping changes in added protections for transgender children, youth, and adults.

In May 2016, the U.S. Education Department and the U.S. Department of Justice jointly issued a document affirming that the provisions of Title IX prohibiting discrimination on the basis of sex, also provides protection against discrimination on the basis of gender identity and expression. That same month, the U.S. Department of Health and Human Services (HHS) released their final rule on Section 1557 of the Patient Protection and Affordable Care Act and made it explicit that Section 1557 prohibits discrimination based on gender identity and sex stereotyping in any hospital or health program that receives federal funds, as well as most health insurance coverage. The following month, the U.S. Department of Defense announced that the ban on transgender people serving in the military would be lifted.

Federal protections for transgender children and youth

Hate Crimes

In October 2009, President Obama signed the FY2010 Defense Authorization Bill, which included the Matthew Shepard/James Byrd Jr. Hate Crimes Prevention Act. This historic legislation is the first federal law to recognize the existence of, and provide civil rights protections for, transgender people. It provides for the tracking of hate crimes based on sexual orientation, gender identity, gender, and disability, providing assistance to local authorities and gathering information about these crimes.

Discrimination

While a number of states have legislation that specifically protects transgender people, there is no single federal law that prohibits discrimination. Despite this, transgender people are protected on the basis of other federal laws, such as Title VII (workplace), Title IX (schools), and FHA (housing). Local and federal courts have increasingly ruled that gender identity and expression are included within these other statutes. This means despite the absence of a federal non-discrimination bill, transgender and gender-diverse individuals are currently protected from discrimination. In fact, these rulings have already overturned discriminatory policies and practices in many locations.

The wave of "bathroom bills" that moved through state legislatures during 2016 emerged, in part, as a response to these federal agencies' interpretations of existing federal laws (such as Title IX and VII). More recent lawsuits reflect states suing the federal government for its interpretation of the existing sex discrimination laws.

However, it is critical to continue advocating for federal non-discrimination legislation as the absence of a federal law means a lack of explicit protection. Historically, this gap allowed child welfare agencies to deny trans-related medical and mental health care to youth-in-care, state and local criminal justice systems to deny services and protections for transgender inmates, and health insurance companies to deny claims for trans-related healthcare.

At the same time, many mental health professionals and families fail to realize that despite the absence of a federal law prohibiting discrimination, transgender individuals are protected within existing "sex discrimination" protections and can file claims now with the appropriate federal agencies if they believe they have experienced discrimination. As stated earlier, the 2016 U.S. Department of Education and the U.S. Department of Justice letter affirm that the provisions of Title IX prohibit discrimination on the basis of sex and gender identity and expression. The HHS final rule on Section 1557 of the Patient

Protection and Affordable Care Act prohibits discrimination based on gender identity and sex stereotyping within healthcare and health insurance. Together these rulings affirm that transgender children, youth, and adults are currently protected against discrimination in any form. It is critical that all medical and mental health professionals, as well as school personnel and families be cognizant of these protections and educate trans youth and their families about their right within these federal statutes.

Some agencies, organizations, schools, healthcare practices, health insurance companies, employers, and others will disregard the inclusion of gender identity/expression within these protections and act in ways that are discriminatory toward trans people. The fact that transgender people are protected does not eliminate discrimination anymore than the long-standing protections in Title IX mean we no longer witness organizational discrimination against women.

However, recent directives and rulings make it clear that if trans young people experience discrimination, they are protected and have the right to legally seek redress. The following organizations help trans youth and their families find legal counsel when they have been discriminated against because of their gender identity or expression.

Lambda Legal Help Desk: Provides information and resources regarding discrimination related to sexual orientation, gender identity and expression, and HIV status. You can contact the Help Desk by calling 1-866-542-8336 or completing the online Help form at http://www.lambdalegal.org/help/online-form

The Transgender Legal Defense & Education Fund: can be contacted at 1-646-862-9396, or through their website, http://www.transgenderlegal.org/

National Center for Lesbian Rights (which also advocates for and provides services for transgender persons): Legal Help Line: 1.800.528.6257 or 415.392.6257.

ACLU LGBT Rights Project: Responds to complaints of LGBT or HIV discrimination. Reports can be filed on their website. https://action.aclu.org/secure/report-lgbthiv-discrimination

GLAD: Legal Advocates and Defenders for the LGBTQ Community: Primarily focuses within New England states, but can provide legal referrals outside this area. They can be reached through their website http://www.glad.org/

The following sections review legislation, guidelines, and resources for transgender children, adolescents, and adults within the context of specific environments. Given the rapidity of recent changes, it is likely legal protections for trans youth will continue to shift and evolve, expanding protection in some areas and jurisdictions and possibly reducing or revoking them in other locales. Please consult the following websites for the most up-to-date legal information for transgender youth and adults.

National Transgender Center for Equality:
http://www.transequality.org

Lambda Legal: http://www.lambdalegal.org

Schools

Historically discrimination against trans youth in schools has typically taken the form of refusing to use the young person's affirmed name and pronouns or refusing equal access to bathrooms or locker rooms according to their gender identity. Trans youth have been singled out for disparate treatment compared to their cisgender peers, e.g., every student gets to use the restroom according to gender identity except trans students. May 2016 represented a sea change in this arena when the U.S. Education Department's Office for Civil Rights and the U.S. Department of Justice's Civil Rights Division jointly issued a Dear Colleague Letter ("DCL") about transgender students' rights and schools' legal obligations under Title IX of the Education Amendments of 1972 (20 U.S.C. §§ 1681-1688).

This letter affirmed that Title IX prohibiting discrimination on the basis of sex also prohibits discrimination on the basis of gender identity and expression. The letter clarified the understanding that all U.S. schools are prohibited from discrimination on the basis of gender identity/expression and are explicitly charged with protecting transgender students.

The letter affirms that transgender students must be allowed to use the bathroom corresponding with their gender identity – and that to do otherwise constitutes discrimination against trans students. The letter explicitly states that transgender students do not need to produce a medical diagnosis or birth certificate; instead, a parent's or guardian's assertion that a student's gender identity differs from previous records or representations is sufficient for the school to be required to recognize that student's affirmed gender.

In addition to this letter, the Department of Education released a set of emerging best practices for implementing the directive prohibiting discrimination against transgender students (U.S. Department of Education, 2016). The booklet provides examples of policies and emerging practices that some schools are already using to support transgender students. Topics covered include policies for how the school is informed about the student's gender transition, confirmation of the student's gender identity, communication with parents, privacy of the student's gender identity, use of the student's affirmed name and pronouns, name and gender change on school records, access to sex-segregated activities and facilities, dress codes, staff training, and the role of school nurses and mental health personnel (social workers, psychologists, guidance counselors). The document includes links to these policies, along with other resources that may be helpful as educators develop policies and practices for their own schools.

Links for the two U.S. Department of Education's Office for Civil Rights documents released May 2016 are provided below.

OCR "Dear Colleague" Letter on Transgender Students:
http://www2.ed.gov/about/offices/list/ocr/letters/colleague-201605-title-ix-transgender.pdf

OCR Examples of Policies and Emerging Practices for Supporting Transgender Students:
http://www2.ed.gov/about/offices/list/oese/oshs/emerging practices.pdf
http://www.ed.gov/ocr

In light of these guidelines, if you or someone close to you has experienced gender-based bullying, harassment, or discrimination at school, you have the right to file a complaint with the U.S. Department of Education, Office for Civil Rights (OCR). The National Center for Transgender Equality provides guidelines for filing a complaint at the following link on their website. http://www.transequality.org/know-your-rights/schools

College

Legal Guide for Trans College Students
http://www.lambdalegal.org/sites/default/files/publications/downloads/2015_college-fs-v16_singlepages-2.pdf

Healthcare

In May 2016, the U.S. Department of Health and Human Services (HHS) released their final rule on Section 1557 of the Patient Protection and Affordable Care Act and made it explicitly clear that Section 1557 prohibits discrimination based on gender identity and sex stereotyping in any hospital or health program that receives federal funds. Section 1557 also extends nondiscrimination protections to individuals enrolled in a variety of health related coverage and includes both healthcare and health insurance. This rule became effective July 18, 2016.

Covered entities that must comply with this ruling include:

- Health insurance issuers, hospitals, health clinics, physicians' practices, community health centers, nursing homes, state Medicaid agencies, and other recipients of assistance, such as grants, property, federal Medicaid matching funds, Medicare Part D payments, and financial assistance under Title I of the ACA
- State-based and federally-facilitated Health Insurance Marketplaces
- All health programs and activities administered by HHS

The final rule states that one's gender identity "may be male, female, neither, or a combination of male and female." The document also specifies that protections for gender expression are included within its understanding and discussion of gender identity. Consequently, it is clear that both transgender people who gender transition and nonbinary trans individuals are included in these rights and protections.

Specific nondiscriminatory requirements of the HHS final rule include:

- Individuals cannot be denied healthcare or health coverage based on their sex, including their gender identity and sex stereotyping
- Categorical coverage exclusions or limitations for all health care services related to gender transition are discriminatory
- Individuals must be treated consistent with their gender identity, including in access to facilities. Furthermore, transgender individuals have the right to be referred to by the name and pronouns they use, regardless of what is on their insurance or identification documents. Refusing to refer to a person by the person's pronouns and name in use, or asking inappropriate questions about genitalia or surgical status in an effort to determine the person's "true" gender, is a form of harassment
- Individuals have a right to privacy. It is inappropriate for healthcare providers to invite hospital staff not involved in the patient's care to observe the patient's body for any reason other than legitimate training purposes. What this means is that under no circumstances should a person not directly involved in the patient's treatment be permitted to observe or participate in examination of the patient. In addition, information about a patient's transgender status or transition-related services that can identify a patient or can be used with other available information to identify a patient constitutes protected health information under HIPAA.
- Access to hormone therapy: If a transgender individual is admitted to a hospital and is currently taking hormones, that treatment should not stop unless there is a medical reason to do so.

As with the DOE/DOJ nondiscrimination directive to schools, there will be healthcare entities and insurers that will challenge this ruling. Nonetheless, the HHS final rule makes it clear that discrimination toward transgender people within healthcare is prohibited.

Lambda Legal, the Human Rights Campaign, Hogan Lovells, and the New York City Bar revised their guide to trans-affirming hospital policies to include the new May 2016 final HHS rule on Section 1557 of the Patient Protection and Affordable Care Act. These guidelines, *Creating Equal Access to Quality Health Care for Transgender Patients: Transgender-Affirming Hospital Policies* (5/2016), can be found on the Lambda Legal website below.

> http://www.lambdalegal.org/sites/default/files/creating_equal_
> access_to_quality_health_care_for_transgender_patients_-_
> final.pdf

The National Center for Transgender Equality (NCTE) has an excellent publication about health care rights and transgender people that includes guidelines for how to file a complaint about discrimination with the HHS Office for Civil Rights (OCR). Complaints can not only be filed by the individual who experienced the discrimination, but also by someone else, such as a friend, family member, or local community member. Instructions for filing complaints against specific types of healthcare facilities (such as hospitals, nursing homes, Veterans Health Administration) are also included. This publications can be accessed through NCTE's website, http://www.transequality .org/know-your-rights/healthcare

Health Insurance

As indicated above, the May 2016 HHS rule on Section 1557 of the Patient Protection and Affordable Care Act specifies that all health insurers receiving federal funds—most private insurers, state Medicaid, the Indian Health Service, and CHIP (Children's Health Insurance Program) programs—must provide transgender-related medical care in the same way they cover any other medical care. Insurers are no longer legally able to categorically deny a medical procedure simply because the member is transgender or because the procedure is related to a medical transition (Transgender Center for Equality, 2016).

Specific requirements state that covered entities (all health insurers receiving federal funds) cannot:

- Deny or limit coverage for a claim, or impose additional cost-sharing or other limitations or restrictions on coverage, for sex-specific health services provided to transgender individuals just because the individual seeking such services identifies as belonging to another gender.
- Categorically exclude coverage for all health services related to gender transition, or deny or limit coverage or impose additional cost-sharing or other limitations or restrictions on coverage for specific health services related to gender transition if those result in discrimination against a transgender individual.

While this provision became effective July 18, 2016, health insurance plans that implement changes annually have leeway to comply with this rule beginning on or after January 1, 2017.

The full text of the rule for Section 1557 of the Patient Protection and Affordable Care Act and relevant fact sheets can be found at http://www.hhs.gov/civil-rights/for-individuals/section-1557/

Selective Service

People who were assigned male at birth are required to register with the Selective Service within thirty days of their eighteenth birthday. This includes those who may have transitioned before or since then.

People who were assigned female at birth are not required to register with the Selective Service regardless of their current gender or transition status. However, when people who were assigned female at birth apply as men for federal financial aid, grants, and loans, they may be asked to document that they are exempt.

To request a Status Information Letter (SIL) that shows you are exempt, you can either download an SIL request form from the Selective Service website http://www.sss.gov/PDFs/SilForm_Instructions.pdf or call them at 1-888-655-1825.

The exemption letter is free of charge and does not specify the reason for exemption so it will not force trans men to out themselves in any other application process.

In June 2016, the U.S. Department of Defense announced that the ban on transgender people serving in the military would be lifted. The policy will be phased in during a one-year period. Effective immediately, service members may no longer be involuntarily separated, discharged or denied reenlistment solely on the basis of gender identity. Service members currently on duty will be able to serve openly. The link below offers more information:

http://www.defense.gov/News/News-Releases/News-Release-View/Article/821675/secretary-of-defense-ash-carter-announces-policy-for-transgender-service-members

In terms of trans-related healthcare for military personnel, the Department of Veterans Affairs (VA) recognizes the importance of treating gender dysphoria as a medical condition by covering hormone therapy, but denies coverage for trans-related surgical care. In May 2016 Lambda Legal and the Transgender Law Center, with co-counsel WilmerHale, petitioned with the US Department of Veterans Affairs (VA) to change the rule that categorically excludes transition-related surgery for transgender veterans. This petition can be read at the following link, http://www.lambdalegal.org/in-court/legal-docs/petition_va_20160509_surgery-for-transgender-veterans

Changing Legal Documents

Specific information about obtaining a legal name change, changing name and gender marker on a driver's license, and birth certificate policies for each state, as well as federal requirements for updating passports, social security, selective service, and immigration can be found on the **National Transgender Center for Equality ID Documents Center at,** http://www.transequality.org/documents

Legal Name Change

A court order from a judge in your local jurisdiction is generally required to legally change your name. Some states do allow for common law name changes: if you live with a new name for a certain period of time, it automatically becomes official without needing to process any documents. However, transgender people are generally advised to take advantage of more concrete legal procedures when available, because banks and other institutions generally decline to recognize a common law change.

It is important to be aware that a court ordered name change does not change the male/female gender marker on identity documents. Requirements for changing one's gender marker are outlined below. The National Transgender Center for Equality (NCTE) website provides information about the specific requirements and laws within each state. http://www.transequality.org/documents

The petition asking the court to issue the name change is completed by filing the required paperwork. In many settings these forms can be downloaded from the county courthouse website and filed with the county clerk in person or through the mail. If a trans youth is considered an adult in that jurisdiction they can petition the court themselves. When the name change is for a minor, the parents (or other legal guardian) must petition the court. A fee is generally involved, and some courts require that a lawyer represent you.

As a rule, the courts' primary concern is to ensure that the name change petitioner is not evading creditors or the criminal justice system. This means that the process of changing your name as a transgender individual should be pro forma. Yet some courts ask invasive questions about a person's gender transition and/or may require additional documentation as to why the name change is indicated or should be granted. It varies by state whether the judge can request confirmation of the DSM gender dysphoria diagnosis in the form of a letter from the transgender person's medical or mental health provider.

Having obtained a court-ordered name change, transgender young adults and parents of trans children and teens are able to have most legal documents reissued to reflect the new name. These documents include official school district records, college transcripts, driver's permits and licenses, passports, and social security cards and records. A number of LGBT community centers around the country have name change projects where pro bono lawyers assist transgender people (including youth and/or their parents) in completing and filing necessary court paperwork.

Name and Gender Marker

As indicated previously, a court ordered name change does not alter the male/female gender marker on identity documents. Requirements for changing one's gender marker are outlined below. The **National Transgender Center for Equality** (NCTE) website provides information about the specific requirements and laws within each state. **http://www.transequality.org/documents**

Passport

Passport documentation is handled on a federal level, and the requirements are available on this website (https://travel.state.gov/content/passports/en/passports.html). The court-ordered name change allows these documents to be reissued with the new name.

On June 9, 2010, the U.S. State Department stopped requiring proof of gender-confirming surgery (lower surgery) for issuing passports and consular birth certificates to transgender people and began asking instead for proof of "appropriate clinical treatment for gender transition to the new gender" to better reflect the individualized nature of treatment for gender transition. The letter documenting "appropriate clinical treatment for gender transition to the new gender," must be from a medical doctor (not a mental health provider). Sample text for this letter is available on the passport site (https://travel.state.gov/content/passports/en/passports.html) and at http://www.transequality.org/know-your-rights/passports

Social Security

Your Social Security card lists only your name and Social Security number – not your gender. However, the Social Security Administration (SSA) maintains information in its computer records on everyone who has a Social Security number, including name, date of birth, and gender. Social security documentation is handled on a federal level, and the requirements are available on their website (https://www.ssa.gov/).

The SSA modernized its long-standing policy on gender marker changes in 2013 and no longer requires gender confirming (lower) surgery. Under current policy, a transgender person can change their gender on their Social Security records by submitting either government-issued documentation reflecting a change or certification from a physician confirming that they have had appropriate clinical treatment for gender transition. Additional information is available at http://www.transequality.org/know-your-rights/social-security

Driver's Permits/Licenses or Other State ID

Driver's licenses and permits and state identification are handled on a state level, generally by the Department of Motor Vehicles. Presenting the court-ordered name change generally allows your name to be updated on these documents.

Each jurisdiction sets its own requirements for changing the gender marker (or in some states, refusing to change these markers). In many states a letter from a medical doctor or licensed mental health clinician (sometimes a PhD clinician is required) confirming gender identity will suffice (providers should check the directions on that state's website regarding the specific information required in this letter). Departments of Motor Vehicles in about half the states have removed surgical requirements completely for those applying to change their gender marker on their drivers licenses.

Some states have simplified gender marker changes by providing standardized forms instead of having legal or medical approvals submitted by letter. At the Washington, DC Department of Motor Vehicles, the applicant fills out the top half and the health or social service professional fills out the bottom. The use of forms helps applicants avoid the subjective determination of particular clerks who may not know the legal specifics or may have prejudices of their own.

School Records and Transcripts

See information above under "Schools" about the May 2016 DOE/DOJ directive to all U.S. schools prohibiting discrimination against transgender students. It explicitly states that transgender students do not need to produce a medical diagnosis or birth certificate; instead, a parent's or guardian's assertion that a student's gender identity differs from previous records or representations is sufficient for the school to be required to recognize that student's affirmed gender. Under Title IX, a school must treat students in a manner consistent with their gender identity even if their education records or identification documents indicate a different sex. In the past, Title IX investigations have been resolved with agreements committing school staff and contractors to use pronouns and names consistent with a transgender student's gender identity.

Lambda Legal offers a guide to updating and amending school records that outlines a student's rights under the federal Family Educational Rights and Privacy Act (FERPA) that protects the privacy of student educational records. Transgender students who wish to change their name and gender marker on their educational records can seek such an amendment under this federal law.

This law applies to K-12 and higher education students. When a student is under 18, their parent or legal guardian must make this request. Students also have the right to have earlier school records amended if their name and gender marker was changed after completing their education at that institution. Schools that refuse to amend a transgender student's records violate the student's right to privacy under FERPA.

Additional details, including a sample FERPA letter for addressing a local school and guidelines for filing a written complaint with the Family Policy Compliance Office of the U.S. Department of Education, can be found on the Lambda Legal website, http://www.lambdalegal.org/node/31111

Birth Certificates

Birth certificates are more difficult to change than other documents. The requirements to have a new birth certificate issued vary widely by state (some large cities issue birth certificates as well). Many of the state, local and territorial jurisdictions that administer birth certificates require a court order to change or amend them (the individual must petition a judge for an order stating that they are now male or female) and/or a letter from a surgeon certifying sex-reassignment surgery (SRS).

California, Vermont and Washington have removed surgical requirements completely for those applying to change a birth certificate. Tennessee is the only state that has a statute specifically forbidding the correction of gender designations on birth certificates for transgender people. Some other states prohibit it through either court decision or agency practice. The **National Transgender Center for Equality** (NCTE) website provides information about the specific requirements and laws within each state. **http://www .transequality.org/documents**

What to Do If the Youth and Families You Work with Experience Discrimination

Before a crisis situation occurs:

1. Know what local or state-wide protections exist for transgender youth in your area
2. Explore whether there is an LGBT legal association in your area or state or any LGBT-identified lawyers in your area who might be helpful if needed. Even if an individual lawyer is unable to take on a case, they may be able to write a letter affirming the transgender young person's legal rights in that setting.

The following vignette demonstrates the possible impact of a letter from an attorney in these situations illustrating how the letter alone may preempt the need for a court case.

Even though Jake had transitioned almost one year before and obtained his legal name change, his high school still refused to allow him to use the men's bathroom or locker room. His parents met with school officials several times but the school district refused to change its policy. Jake's family reached out to a local LGBT-affirmative attorney. The attorney drafted a letter documenting the numerous court rulings indicating that Title IX prohibits discrimination on the basis of gender as well as sex and thus protects transgender students from discrimination. The attorney's letter put the school district's legal counsel on notice that if they refused to allow the young man to use male facilities the school district would be open to a lawsuit they would not likely win. Within a few weeks of receipt of this letter, the district revised its policies to allow transgender youth to use the bathrooms and locker rooms matching their presenting or affirmed gender identities.

When there are no local resources:

1. Reach out to the legal departments at one of the LGBT legal organizations identified below and ask for their advice or assistance with your situation.
   Lambda Legal Help Desk: 1-866-542-8336
   The Transgender Legal Defense & Education Fund: 1-646-862-9396
   National Center for Lesbian Rights Legal Help Line: 1.800.528.6257 or 415.392.6257

ACLU LGBT Rights Project, https://action.aclu.org/
secure/report-lgbthiv-discrimination
**GLAD: Legal Advocates and Defenders for the
LGBTQ Community**, http://www.glad.org/

2. Form a coalition with other agencies and organizations in
your area to address the need for more trans- affirmative
policies in your situation and advocate legal protections for
transgender youth and adults. Build alliances with progressive trans-affirmative religious leaders and communities.

As indicated earlier, given the rapid evolution of policies and laws
regarding the rights of transgender individuals, the information
within this appendix may have changed. For the most up-to-date
legal information about key issues please visit the websites below:
National Transgender Center for Equality: http://www.transequality.org
Lambda Legal: http://www.lambdalegal.org

Fact sheets about numerous legal topics, including changing documents, employment, youth, healthcare, hospital rights, college students, etc. are available from Lambda Legal.
http://www.lambdalegal.org/know-your-rights/transgender

References

20 U.S.C. §§ 1681-1688; Dear Colleague Letter: Transgender Students
(May 13, 2016), www.ed.gov/ocr/letters/colleague-201605-title-ix-
transgender.pdf.

U.S. Department of Education, Office of Elementary and Secondary
Education, Office of Safe and Healthy Students, Examples of Policies
and Emerging Practices for Supporting Transgender Students (May
2016).

Section 1557: Protecting Individuals Against Sex Discrimination
http://www.hhs.gov/sites/default/files/1557-fs-sex-discrimination
-508.pdf

Section 1557: Coverage of Health Insurance in Marketplaces and
Other Health Plans

http://www.hhs.gov/sites/default/files/1557-fs-insurance-
discrimination-508.pdf

APPENDIX B: RESOURCES

I. General Information And Resources

National LGBTQ Rights and Advocacy Organizations

- **Human Rights Campaign** is the "largest civil rights organization working to achieve equality for lesbian, gay, bisexual, transgender and queer Americans." http://www.hrc.org/
- **National Center for Transgender Equality** is a "national social justice organization devoted to ending discrimination and violence against transgender people through education and advocacy on national issues of importance to transgender people." http://www.transequality.org/
- **National LGBTQ Task Force** is a social justice organization that "builds power, takes action and creates change to achieve freedom and justice for lesbian, gay, bisexual and transgender people and their families." The website provides reports, research, training, and information on advocacy opportunities, among other resources. http://www.thetaskforce.org/
- **PFLAG** is "a grassroots, chapter based organization" that provides "support for families, allies and people who are LGBTQ"; educates "about the unique issues and challenges facing people who are LGBTQ; and advocates in "communities to change attitudes and create policies and laws that achieve full equality for people who are LGBTQ." https://www.pflag.org/
- **Trans Advocacy Network** is "an alliance of transgender organizations that work at the state and local level, coming together to build a stronger trans movement by facilitating the sharing of resources, best practices, and organizing strategies." http://transadvocacynetwork.org/

- **The American Academy of Pediatrics (AAP)**, founded in 1930, is a professional membership organization of 64,000 primary care pediatricians, pediatric medical sub-specialists and pediatric surgical specialists dedicated to the health, safety, and well being of infants, children, adolescents and young adults. The AAP website offers a wide range of helpful materials about child health and wellbeing for parents. https://www.aap.org/

  Additional resources can be located on their companion website, www.healthychildren.org

  The AAP guidelines for gender-diverse and transgender children align with those recommended by the WPATH Standards of Care for the Health of Transsexual, Transgender, and Gender Nonconforming People. [See http://www.wpath.org/]

  The following two AAP documents are particularly helpful:

  - *Gender Identity Development in Children* — https://www.healthychildren.org/English/ages-stages/gradeschool/Pages/Gender-Identity-and-Gender-Confusion-In-Children.aspx
  - *Gender Non-Conforming and Transgender Children* — https://www.healthychildren.org/English/ages-stages/gradeschool/Pages/Gender-Non-Conforming-Transgender-Children.aspx

  When searching for web-based resources, parents and providers may come across a website for an organization formed in 2002 called the American College of Pediatricians (ACPeds). It is important not to confuse this smaller organization with **The American Academy of Pediatrics (AAP)** discussed above.

  Membership in the ACPeds is open to qualifying healthcare professionals who share the College's Mission, Vision and Values. The (ACPeds) vision states: "The American College of Pediatricians promotes a society where all children, from the moment of their conception, are valued unselfishly. We encourage mothers, fathers and families to advance the needs of their children above their own. We expect societal forces to support the two-parent, father-mother family unit and provide for children role models of ethical character and responsible behavior." www.acpeds.org

  The ACPeds 2016 position statements, *Gender Dysphoria in Children* and *Gender Ideology Harms Children,* <u>do not</u> reflect the consensus regarding best practices for the care of gender-diverse and transgender youth as outlined in the WPATH Standards of Care. In contrast, the "American College of Pediatricians urges health professionals, educators and legislators to reject all policies that condition children to accept a life of chemical and surgical impersonation of the opposite sex as normal and healthful."

This recommendation is further described by their statement that, "A person's belief that one is something one is not is, at best, a sign of confused thinking; at worst it is a delusion," and their position that, "Conditioning children to believe the absurdity that they or anyone could be "born into the wrong body," and that a lifetime of chemical and surgical impersonation of the opposite sex is normal and healthful is child abuse."

https://www.acpeds.org/gender-dysphoria-in-children-summary-points

https://www.acpeds.org/the-college-speaks/position-statements/gender-dysphoria-in-children

https://www.acpeds.org/the-college-speaks/position-statements/gender-ideology-harms-children

Crisis/Suicide Hotlines

- **Anti-Violence Project** (AVP) is a New York City-based organization that "empowers lesbian, gay, bisexual, transgender, queer, and HIV-affected communities and allies to end all forms of violence through organizing and education, and supports survivors through counseling and advocacy." In doing so, it runs a 24-hour hotline to support anyone in crisis at 212–714–1141. http://www.avp.org/
- **GLBT National Help Center** serves "gay, lesbian, bisexual, transgender and questioning people by providing free and confidential peer-support" through the GLBT National Hotline (1–888–843–4564), the GLBT National Youth Talkline (1–800–246–7743), Online Peer-Support Chat, and Trans Teens Online Talk Groups. http://www.glbthotline.org/
- **Trans Lifeline** is "dedicated to the well being of transgender people" and runs a suicide "hotline staffed by transgender people for transgender people." The phone numbers are 1–877–565–8860 (United States) and 1–877–330–6366 (Canada). http://www.translifeline.org/

- **The Trevor Project** provides "accredited, free and confidential phone, instant messaging and text messaging crisis intervention services" and "offers the largest safe social networking community for LGBTQ youth, best practice suicide prevention educational trainings, resources for youth and adults, and advocacy initiatives." Call 1–866–488–7386, text the word "Trevor" to 202–304–1200, or chat using the portal on the website. http://www.thetrevorproject.org

Legal Advocacy Organizations and Resources

- **American Civil Liberties Union** provides information and resources regarding federal, state, and local laws pertaining to transgender people. https://www.aclu.org/
    - *"Know Your Rights: Transgender People and the Law"* — https://www.aclu.org/know-your-rights/transgender-people-and-law
- **Lambda Legal** is "committed to achieving full recognition of the civil rights of lesbians, gay men, bisexuals, transgender people and those with HIV through impact litigation, education and public policy work." http://www.lambdalegal.org
    - *"Transgender Rights Tool Kit"* — http://www.lambda legal.org/publications/trans-toolkit
- **National Center for Lesbian Rights** is "committed to establishing legal protections that ensure transgender youth can live safely, and are supported and affirmed in our society." http://www.nclrights.org/
- **Sylvia Rivera Law Project** "works to guarantee that all people are free to self-determine their gender identity and expression, regardless of income or race, and without facing harassment, discrimination, or violence. SRLP is a collective organization founded on the understanding that gender self-determination is inextricably intertwined with racial, social and economic justice." http://srlp.org/about/
- **Transgender Law and Policy Institute** "brings experts and advocates together to work on law and policy initiatives designed to advance transgender equality." www.transgenderlaw.org
- **Transgender Law Center** "works to change law, policy, and attitudes so that all people can live safely, authentically, and

free from discrimination regardless of their gender identity or expression." http://transgenderlawcenter.org/

- **Transgender Legal Defense & Education Fund** "is committed to ending discrimination based upon gender identity and expression and to achieving equality for transgender people through public education, test-case litigation, direct legal services, and public policy efforts." http://www.transgenderlegal.org/

LGBTQ Media Resources

- **The Advocate** is a print and digital media resource that focuses on news and issues relevant to the LGBTQ community. http://www.advocate.com/
- **GLAAD** "rewrites the script for LGBT acceptance" and is a "dynamic media force" that "tackles tough issues to shape the narrative and provoke dialogue that leads to cultural change." https://www.glaad.org/
- **Trans News** "is designed to be an uplifting part of your day, where you can discover and share breaking news from around the web that celebrates the lives and achievements of transsexual, transgender and gender variant people. Trans News is an important reminder that despite the negative news we're so often bombarded with, there are a lot of really good, inspirational stories to be heard!" http://transnews.org/

General Information and Resources

- **"Injustice at Every Turn: A Report of the National Transgender Discrimination Survey"** (National Gay and Lesbian Task Force and National Center for Transgender Equality) — http://www.thetaskforce.org/injustice-every-turn-report-national-transgender-discrimination-survey/
- **"LGBTQI Terminology"** (by Eli R. Green and Eric N. Peterson at the LGBT Resource Center at UC Riverside) — http://www.ahwg.net/uploads/3/4/5/5/34557719/lgbtterminology.pdf
- **"LGBTQQIA Terminology"** (SF Youth Health Connect's Adolescent Health Working Group) — http://sfyouthhealthconnect.org/lgbtqqia-resources.html
- **"Our Trans Loved Ones: Questions and Answers for Par-**

ents, Families, and Friends of People Who Are Transgender and Gender Expansive" (PFLAG) — https://www.pflag.org/ourtranslovedones
- "Supporting and Caring for Our Gender-Expansive Youth" (Human Rights Campaign and Gender Spectrum) — www.hrc.org/youth-gender or www.genderspectrum.org/youth
- Trans Bodies, Trans Selves: A Resource for the Transgender Community (edited by Laura Erickson-Schroth, 2014, New York, NY: Oxford University Press) [BOOK]
- Transgender 101: A Simple Guide to a Complex Issue (by Nicholas M. Teich, 2012, New York, NY: Columbia University Press) [BOOK]
- "Frequently Asked Questions about Transgender People" (National Center for Transgender Equality) — http://www.transequality.org/issues/resources/frequently-asked-questions-about-transgender-people
- World Professional Association for Transgender Health (WPATH) is an "interdisciplinary professional and educational organization devoted to transgender health." http://www.wpath.org/

II. Information And Resources For Transgender Youth

General Information and Resources

- Advocates for Youth "partners with youth leaders, adult allies, and youth-serving organizations to advocate for policies and champion programs that recognize young people's rights to honest sexual health information; accessible, confidential, and affordable sexual health services; and the resources and opportunities necessary to create sexual health equity for all youth." http://www.advocatesforyouth.org/
- Gender Spectrum provides "consultation, training and events designed to help families, educators, professionals, and organizations understand and address the concepts of gender identity and expression." It features a wide variety of resources, including downloadable fact sheets, supportive videos, toolkits, etc.,

as well as supportive online forums where transgender youth can converse with one another. http://www.genderspectrum.org/

- **It Gets Better Project** works to "communicate to lesbian, gay, bisexual and transgender youth around the world that it gets better, and to create and inspire the changes needed to make it better for them." http://www.itgetsbetter.org/
- **Lambda Legal's resources regarding the transgender youth experience:**
  - *"FAQ for Transgender and Gender-Nonconforming Youth"* — http://www.lambdalegal.org/know-your-rights/transgender/trans-youth-faq
  - *"Immigration Protection for Undocumented Immigrant Youth"* — http://www.lambdalegal.org/publications/immigration-protection-for-undocumented-immigrant-youth
  - *"Info for Transgender Youth"* — http://www.lambdalegal.org/know-your-rights/lgbtq-teens-young-adults/info-for-transgender-youth
  - *"Resources for LGBTQ Youth"*—http://www.lambdalegal.org/publications/fs_resources-for-lgbtq-youth
- **Trans Youth Equality** "provides education, advocacy and support for transgender and gender non-conforming children and youth and their families" by sharing "information about the unique needs of this community, partnering with families, educators and service providers to help foster a healthy, caring, and safe environment for all transgender children." http://www.transyouthequality.org/
  - *"Coming Out"* — http://www.transyouthequality.org/coming-out
  - *"Disclosure"* — http://www.transyouthequality.org/disclosure

Artistic Expression Information and Resources

- **Artistic Expressions of Transgender Youth** (by Tony Ferraiolo, 2015; available on Amazon.com) [BOOK]
- **Dreams of Hope: Queer Youth Arts** is an example in Pittsburgh of the myriad ways in which "the power of the arts" can pro-

vide lesbian, gay, bisexual, trans, queer, and allied (LGBTQA) youth a welcoming environment to grow in confidence, express themselves, and develop as leaders. This organization's creative contributions educate audiences, build awareness, and increase acceptance." http://www.dreamsofhope.org/
- **Trans Life and Liberation Art Series** "creates collaborative portraits about and with living trans people on the frontlines of our liberation movement. It centers trans women and femmes of color, as well as incarcerated and disabled trans people of color. Participants work with a trans artist of their choice to create a portrait they love, and all artists and participants are paid." http://translifeandliberation.tumblr.com/

Reading Lists for Children

- **"Transgender Friendly Young Children's Books"** (Goodreads) — http://www.goodreads.com/list/show/20314.Transgender_Friendly_Young_Children_s_Books_
- **"Transgender Reading List for Children" (PFLAG)** — https://www.pflag.org/transkidsbooks
- **"6 Picture Books About Transgender Children" (by Allison McDonald;** Scholastic) — http://www.scholastic.com/parents/blogs/scholastic-parents-raise-reader/6-picture-books-about-transgender-children
- **"Reading for Children" (TransYouth Family Allies)** — http://www.imatyfa.org/resources/recommended-reading/for-children/
- **"Gender-Expansive and Transgender Children: Books for Students"** (Welcoming Schools) — http://www.welcomingschools.org/pages/looking-at-gender-identity-with-childrens-books/

Reading Lists for Teens

- **"Great Books for Trans Teens (and the People Who Love Them)" (A Room of One's Own)** — http://www.roomofonesown.com/trans-teens
- **"Booklist for Trans Teens"** (Goodreads) — http://www.goodreads.com/list/show/11446.Booklist_for_Trans_Teens

- **Leewind.org** focuses on literature with LGBTQ themes. It also features specific reading lists with transgender and gender-nonconforming themes. http://www.leewind.org/
- **"Books About Transgender Issues for Teens" (by Anne Rouyer;** New York Public Library) — https://www.nypl.org/blog/2015/06/16/transgender-books-teens
- **Trans Youth Equality Foundation reading list for teens** — http://www.transyouthequality.org/suggested-reading-for-youths-12-18/
- Testa, R., Coolhart, D., Peta, J., Lev. A., (2015). *The gender quest workbook: A guide for teens and young adults exploring gender identity.* Oakland, CA: New Harbinger Publications.

Camps for Trans Youth

- **Trans Student Educational Resources** (TSER) list of over 50 camps throughout the United States and Canada. http://www.transstudent.org/camps
- **The Naming Project Summer Camp** is located in Minnesota and "is for 14–18 year-olds or those who have completed 8th–12th grades who are of any sexual orientation or gender identity or expression who are interested in discussing and understanding sexuality and gender in terms of their own spiritual journey and are excited to spend time with other teen campers and staff while canoeing, swimming, hiking, singing, doing arts and crafts." https://www.thenamingproject.org/summer-camp/
- **Trans Youth Equality Foundation** offers summer and fall retreats in Maine for trans youth. http://www.transyouthequality.org/youth-retreats-camps/
- **Youth Project's Camp Coyote** "is a chance to get together with other trans-identified youth from across Nova Scotia to share experiences, spend time in a safe space, meet new people, and experience camp the way you want." http://www.youthproject.ns.ca/camp.php
- **Camp Aranu'tiq** provides summer camps in New England and California for trans and gender-diverse children, teens, and their families. http://www.camparanutiq.org

Healthcare

- **Gay and Lesbian Medical Association (GLMA)** works to "ensure equality in healthcare for lesbian, gay, bisexual and transgender (LGBT) individuals and healthcare providers." www.glma.org
- **Lambda Legal's resources regarding transgender healthcare:**
    - *"Creating Equal Access to Quality Health Care for Transgender Patients" (Lambda Legal, Human Rights Campaign, Hogan Lovells, and NYC Bar)* — http://www.lambdalegal.org/sites/default/files/publications/downloads/fs_20160525_transgender-affirming-hospital-policies.pdf
- **National LGBT Health Education Center** "provides educational programs, resources, and consultation to health care organizations with the goal of optimizing quality, cost-effective health care for lesbian, gay, bisexual, and transgender (LGBT) people." http://www.lgbthealtheducation.org/
- **University of California,** *San Francisco's Center of Excellence for Transgender Health* works to "improve the overall health and well-being of transgender individuals by developing and implementing programs in response to community-identified needs." http://www.transhealth.ucsf.edu/
- **World Professional Association for Transgender Health (WPATH)** promotes "evidence based care, education, research, advocacy, public policy, and respect in transgender health." On their site, you will find guidelines for ethical practices for professionals as well as international standards of care for individuals with gender identity disorders. There are many resources on this site. www.wpath.org

III. Resources And Information For Parents

General Information and Resources

- **The Gender and Family Project at The Ackerman Institute for the Family** empowers youth, families and communities through gender affirmative services, training, and research.

GFP promotes gender inclusivity as a form of social justice in all the systems involved in the life of the family. Multidisciplinary family-oriented services for gender expansive children and teens include: parent support groups and play groups for children in English and Spanish, sibling group, support group for adolescents, psychological evaluation, family therapy and parental coaching, training for schools and health professionals, liaising for medical and legal referrals, research on the needs of trans youth and families. GFP is a project of The Ackerman Institute for the Family, one of the premier institutions for family therapy and family therapy training in the United States. http://www.ackerman.org/gfp

- **Family Acceptance Project (FAP)** "is a research, intervention, education and policy initiative [based at San Francisco State University] that works to prevent health and mental health risks for lesbian, gay, bisexual and transgender (LGBT) children and youth, including suicide, homelessness and HIV – in the context of their families, cultures and faith communities." http://familyproject.sfsu.edu/
  - *"FAP Booklet for Parents of LGBTQ Youth" (download in English, Spanish, or Chinese; there is also a version for Mormon families)* — http://familyproject.sfsu.edu/family-education-booklet

- **Gender Spectrum** provides "consultation, training and events designed to help families, educators, professionals, and organizations understand and address the concepts of gender identity and expression." It features a wide variety of resources, including downloadable fact sheets, supportive videos, toolkits, etc., as well as supportive online forums where parents of transgender children can converse with one another. http://www.genderspectrum.org/

- **Mermaids** is a United Kingdom–based organization that "is passionate about supporting children, young people, and their families to achieve a happier life in the face of great adversity" and which works "to raise awareness about gender issues amongst professionals and the general public." It features a wide variety of resources, including downloadable fact sheets, supportive videos, toolkits, etc. http://www.mermaidsuk.org.uk/

- **"Our Daughters and Sons: Questions and Answers for Par-**

ents of Lesbian, Gay, Bisexual, and Transgender Youth and Adults" (PFLAG) — https://www.pflag.org/sites/default/files/ Our%20Daughters%20And%20Sons.pdf

- **Trans Youth Family Allies** is a nonprofit organization that "empowers children and families by partnering with educators, service providers and communities, to develop supportive environments in which gender may be expressed and respected." It features a wide variety of resources, including downloadable fact sheets, supportive videos, toolkits, etc. http://www.imatyfa.org/

Books for Parents With Transgender Children

- Angello, M., & Bowman, A. (2016). *Raising the transgender child: A complete guide for parents, families, and caregivers.* Berkeley, CA: Seal Press.
- Brill, S., & Pepper, R. (2008). *The transgender child: A handbook for families and professionals.* San Francisco, CA: Cleis Press, Inc
- Brill, S., & Kenney, L. (2016). *The transgender teen: A handbook for parents and professionals supporting transgender and non-binary teens.* Jersey City, NJ: Cleis Press.
- Duron, L. (2013). *Raising my rainbow: Adventures in raising a fabulous, gender creative son.* New York, NY: Random House, Inc.
- Ehrensaft, D. (2011). *Gender born, gender made: Raising healthy gender-nonconforming children.* New York, NY: The Experiment, LLC.
- Ehrensaft, D. (2016). *The gender creative child: Pathways for nurturing and supporting children who live outside gender boxes.* New York, NY: The Experiment, LLC.
- Kilodavis, C. (2009). *My princess boy.* New York, NY: Simon & Schuster Children's Publishing Division.
- Kriger, I. (2011). *Helping your transgender teen: A guide for parents.* New Haven, CT: Genderwise Press.
- Nealy, E. C. (2017). *Transgender children and youth: Cultivating pride and joy with families in transition.* New York, NY: W. W. Norton & Company, Inc.

IV. Resources And Information For Students And Educators

Resources for Students and Advocates in School Settings

- **American Civil Liberties Union resources for students and educators:**
  - *"Know Your Rights: LGBT High School Students – What to Do If You Face Harassment at School"* — https://www.aclu.org/know-your-rights/lgbt-high-school-students-what-do-if-you-face-harassment-school
- **Campus Pride** works "to develop necessary resources, programs and services to support LGBT and ally students on college campuses across the United States." https://www.campuspride.org/about/faqs/
- **Gay, Lesbian, & Straight Education Network (GLSEN)** "strives to assure that each member of every school community is valued and respected regardless of sexual orientation or gender identity/expression." http://www.glsen.org/
- **"LGBTQ Student Resources & Support: Creating More Welcoming Environments for LGBTQ Teens and College Students" (Accredited Schools Online)** — http://www.accreditedschoolsonline.org/resources/lgbtq-student-support/
- **Genders & Sexualities Alliance Network's** "overall strategy for fighting for educational justice is to work with grassroots, youth-led groups and GSAs, empowering them to educate their schools and communities, advocate for just policies that protect LGBTQ youth from harassment and violence, and organize in coalition with other youth groups across identity lines to address broader issues of oppression." https://gsanetwork.org
- **GLSEN Day of Silence** "is a student-led national event that brings attention to anti-LGBT name-calling, bullying and harassment in schools. Students from middle school to college take a vow of silence in an effort to encourage schools and classmates to address the problem of anti-LGBT behavior by illustrating the silencing effect of bullying and harassment on LGBT students and those perceived to be LGBT." http://www.dayofsilence.org/
- **Lambda Legal's resources for students and educators:**

- *"Bathrooms and Locker Rooms: Understanding Your Rights"* — http://www.lambdalegal.org/know-your-rights/youth/bathrooms-and-locker-rooms
- *"Bending the Mold: An Action Kit for Transgender Students"* — http://www.lambdalegal.org/publications/bending-the-mold
- *"How Schools Can Support Transgender Students"* — http://www.lambdalegal.org/know-your-rights/youth/tgnc-friendly-schools
- *"National Day of Silence: The Freedom to Speak (Or Not)"* — http://www.lambdalegal.org/publications/fs_2016_day-of-silence-faq
- *"Preventing Censorship of LGBT Information in Public School Libraries"* — http://www.lambdalegal.org/publications/fs_preventing-censorship-of-lgbt-information-in-pubilc-school-libraries
- *"A Transgender Advocate's Guide to Updating and Amending School Records"* — http://www.lambdalegal.org/publications/fs_2014_ferpa-faq
- **"Queer Youth Advice for Educators: How to Respect and Protect Your Lesbian, Gay, Bisexual, and Transgender Students" (WhatKidsCanDo.org)** — http://whatkidscando.org/publications/pdfs/QueerYouthAdvice.pdf
- **Schools in Transition: A Guide for Supporting Transgender Students in K–12 Schools (American Civil Liberties Union, Gender Spectrum, Human Rights Campaign, National Center for Lesbian Rights, National Education Association)** — http://www.nclrights.org/wp-content/uploads/2015/08/Schools-in-Transition-2015.pdf
- **Trans Student Educational Resources (TSER).** http://www.transstudent.org/
- **U.S. Departments of Education and Justice resources for students and educators:**
  - *Examples of Policies and Emerging Practices for Supporting Transgender Students* — www.ed.gov/oese/oshs/emergingpractices.pdf
  - *"Dear Colleague Letter on Transgender Students"* — http://www2.ed.gov/about/offices/list/ocr/letters/colleague-201605-title-ix-transgender.pdf

- **"Watch Kids Share Eloquent, Empathetic Reactions to Cait-lyn Jenner"** (**Time**) — http://time.com/3915842/caitlyn-jenner-transition-kids-react/
- **Welcoming Schools** is an initiative of the Human Rights Campaign that provides a "comprehensive approach to creating respectful and supportive elementary schools with resources and professional development to embrace family diversity, create LGBTQ-inclusive schools, prevent bias-based bullying and gender stereotyping, and support transgender and gender-expansive students." http://www.welcomingschools.org/

V. Resources For Allies Of, Advocates For, And Professionals Working With Transgender Youth

Camps — Resources for Staff and Parents

- **"Talking Transgender at Camp"** is a webinar that explores "the emerging area of transgender campers" and "how they can fit into traditional resident camps." http://www.acacamps.org/staff-professionals/events-professional-development/recorded-webinar/talking-transgender-camp
- **"TransgenderStaffatCamp"**isawebinarthatexplores"theemerg-ingareaoftransgenderstaffandhowtointegratethemintotypical camp settings." http://www.acacamps.org/staff-professionals/events-professional-development/recorded-webinar/transgender-staff-camp
- **"Transgender Youth—The Role Camps Might Play"** (**by Sarah Holder**) is a 2011 article on the American Camp Association's website discussing how camps can provide a safe and supportive environment for transgender youth and how camp leaders can cultivate such an environment. http://www.acacamps.org/resource-library/camping-magazine/transgender-youth-%E2%80%94-role-camps-might-play

Child Welfare and Juvenile Justice

- **A Place of Respect: A Guide for Group Care Facilities Serving Transgender and Gender Non-conforming Youth**

(**National Center for Lesbian Rights and Sylvia Rivera Law Project**) — http://www.nclrights.org/wp-content/uploads/2013/07/A_Place_Of_Respect.pdf

- **"Entitled to Treatment: Medical Care for Transgender Adolescents in the Juvenile Justice System" (Southern Poverty Law Center)** — https://www.splcenter.org/20160408/entitled-treatment-medical-care-transgender-adolescents-juvenile-justice-system

- **"Hidden Injustice: Lesbian, Gay, Bisexual, and Transgender Youth in Juvenile Courts, The Equity Project" (The Center for HIV Law and Policy)** — http://www.hivlawandpolicy.org/resources/hidden-injustice-lesbian-gay-bisexual-and-transgender-youth-juvenile-courts-equity-project

- **"Information Packet: Transgender Youth in Child Welfare Settings" (National Center for Child Welfare Excellence at the Silberman School of Social Work)** — http://nccwe.org/downloads/info-packs/Rider.Sikerwar.pdf

- **Lambda Legal's resources regarding the transgender youth experience in the child welfare and juvenile justice systems:**
  - *"Getting Down to Basics" (Lambda Legal and the Child Welfare League of America)*—http://www.lambdalegal.org/publications/getting-down-to-basics
  - *"Know Your Rights: LGBTQ Youth and Youth Living With HIV in Foster Care and Juvenile Justice Systems"* — http://www.lambdalegal.org/publications/xfs_know-your-rights-lgbtq-and-hiv-youth-in-foster-care
  - *"Your Right to HIV Treatment in Prison and Jail"* — http://www.lambdalegal.org/publications/fs_your-right-to-hiv-treatment-in-prison-and-jail

- **National Center for Child Welfare Excellence (NCCWE)** "takes a broad child welfare perspective, embracing an interest in policies and practices that promote the well-being, safety and permanency of all children and youth while devoting special attention to those facing significant challenges in their environments." http://www.nccwe.org/

- **Recommended Practices: To Promote the Safety and Well-Being of LGBTQ Youth and Youth at Risk of or Living With HIV in Child Welfare Settings (The Child Welfare League** of America) — http://www.lambdalegal.org/publications/ recommended-practices-youth

- **Safe and Respected: Policy, Best Practices, & Guidance for Serving Transgender & Gender-Nonconforming Children and Youth Involved in the Child Welfare, Detention, and Juvenile Justice Systems (New York City's Administration for Children's Services)** —http://www1.nyc.gov/assets/acs/ pdf/lgbtq/FINAL_06_23_2014_WEB.pdf
- **"The Unfair Criminalization of Gay and Transgender Youth: Research Brief" (Center for American Progress)** — https://www.americanprogress.org/issues/lgbt/ report/2012/06/29/11730/the-unfair-criminalization-of-gay- and-transgender-youth/

Conferences for Trans People, Their Families, and Provider Training

Many of the conferences listed below offer programming for transgender people and training for medical and mental health providers, families, transgender children, teens, and young adults. Check individual conference sites for specific details. There are an increasing number of smaller local conferences in addition to the larger ones listed here.

- **Trans Student Educational Resources** list of over 100 conferences, most of which are in the United States and Canada. http://www.transstudent.org/conferences
- **Asterisk Trans* Conference** is a college conference focused on building "community for trans* people and allies," addressing "trans* health and well-being," and providing "education and resources for trans* youth advocates." http:// asteriskconference.blogspot.com/
- **Gender Conference East** "provides a safe and supportive space dedicated to the needs of children and youth across the gender spectrum, as well as their families and the professionals working with them." http://www.genderconferenceeast.org/.
- **Gender Infinity Annual Conference** seeks to "create affirming spaces for families, learners, advocates, and providers to advance relationships, knowledge, and resources that empower gender diverse individuals. In our journey together we promote

justice, equity, and hope in the celebration of infinite gender possibilities." http://genderinfinity.org/2016conference/
- **Gender Odyssey Conference** offers programming that "is focused on the needs and interests of transgender and gender-nonconforming people across North America and around the world." http://www.genderodyssey.org/conference/
- **Gender Spectrum** "provides consultation and training to help professional groups and organizations understand youth's evolving conceptions of Gender identity and the impact this has on current and future practices in their field." https://www.genderspectrum.org/
- **GLMA's Annual Conference on LGBT Health** "educates practitioners, policy advocates, educators, administrators, researchers and students—from across the health professions—about the unique health needs of LGBT individuals and families." http://www.glma.org/index.cfm?fuseaction=Page.viewPage&pageId=1068&parentID=1063&nodeID=1
- **National Black Trans Advocacy Conference** is a "distinct educational and empowerment program event, home to nearly 300 plus trans and gender non-conforming individuals" and allies "focused on advancing black trans equality." https://www.blacktrans.org/conference/btac-welcome.html
- **Philadelphia Trans Health Conference** "offers a space for trans people and [their] allies, families, and providers to come together to re-envision what health means for trans people." http://www.trans-health.org/
- **Pride Works** is "an annual conference for lesbian, gay, bisexual, transgender, and queer/questioning (LGBTQ) youth, their allies, and the adults in their lives. The mission is to inform our communities about the realities of growing up gay, lesbian, bisexual or transgender, and to inspire them to respect and support LGBTQ people and to advocate for positive change." http://prideworks.com
- **True Colors Conference** works to "improve and enrich the lives of LGBTQIA+ youth in school, at home, within the social service system and in the community by creating a forum through which LGBTQIA+ youth and their allies may develop the skills and strategies necessary to educate themselves and

society about their needs and concerns, advocate for positive change at a variety of levels, from the personal to the political, and build leadership among adults responsible for the health and well-being of young people." http://www.ourtruecolors.org/Programs/Conference/index.html

Spirituality, Faith, and Religion

- **Advocates for Youth** lists faith-based organizations that affirm and support transgender people. http://www.advocatesforyouth.org/sercadv/1378?task=view
- **"Explore: Religion & Faith" (Human Rights Campaign)** — http://www.hrc.org/explore/topic/religion-faith
- **Center for LGBTQ and Gender Studies in Religion** is located at the Pacific School of Religion in Berkeley California. It works "to advance the well-being of lesbian, gay, bisexual, queer and transgender people and to transform faith communities and the wider society by taking a leading role in shaping a new public discourse on religion, gender identity and sexuality through education, research, community building and advocacy." http://clgs.org/
- **Crossing Paths: Where Transgender and Religion Meet (Unitarian Universalist Association's Office of Bisexual, Gay, Lesbian and Transgender Concerns)** — http://www.transfaithonline.org/fileadmin/TFexplore/UUA_crossingpaths.pdf
- **Institute for Welcoming Resources** is a program of the National LGBTQ Task Force that provides "the resources to facilitate a paradigm shift in multiple denominations whereby churches become welcoming and affirming of all congregants regardless of sexual orientation and gender identity." http://www.welcomingresources.org/
- **Keshet** "is a national organization that works for full LGBTQ equality and inclusion in Jewish life." http://www.keshet online.org/
- **The Naming Project** is a faith-based organization that works to "create places of safety for youth of all sexual orientations and gender identities where faith is shared and healthy life-giving community is modeled." https://www.thenamingproject.org/

- **Religious Institute** "is a multifaith organization dedicated to advocating for sexual health, education, and justice in faith communities and society." http://religiousinstitute.org/
- **"Stances of Faiths on LGBTQ Issues: Islam – Sunni and Shi'a" (Human Rights Campaign)** — http://www.hrc.org/resources/stances-of-faiths-on-lgbt-issues-islam
- **Transfaith** "affirms, empowers, and engages transgender and gender non-conforming people and their communities" and "cultivate diverse expressions of gender-affirming spiritual vitality." http://www.transfaithonline.org/
- **Transgender Muslim Support Network (Tumblr)** — http://trans-muslims.tumblr.com/

Book on Spirituality, Faith & Religion

- Beardsley, C., & O'Brien, M. (eds.) (2017). *This is my body: Hearing the theology of transgender Christians.* London: Darton, Longman, and Todd Ltd.
- Dzmura, N. (ed.) (2010). *Balancing on the Mechitza: Transgender in Jewish community.* Berkeley, CA: North Atlantic Books.
- Hertzer, L. (2016). *The Bible and the transgender experience: How scripture supports gender variance.* The Pilgrim Press.
- Hornsby, T., & Guest, D. (2016). *Transgender, intersex, and Biblical interpretation.* Atlanta: SBL Press.
- Kundtz, D. L., & Schlager, B. S. (2007). *Ministry among God's queer folk: LGBT pastoral care.* Cleveland, OH: Pilgrim Press.
- Ladin, J. (2012). *Through the door of life: A Jewish journey between genders.* Madison, WI: University of Wisconsin Press.
- Mollenkott, V. (2001). *Omnigender: A Trans-religious approach.* Cleveland, OH: Pilgrim Press.
- Mollenkott, V., & Sheridan, V. (2003). *Transgender journeys.* Cleveland, OH: Pilgrim Press.
- Sheridan, V. (2001). *Crossing over: Liberating the transgendered Christian.* Cleveland, OH: Pilgrim Press.
- Siraj al-Haqq Kugle, S. (2013). *Living out Islam: Voices of gay, lesbian, and transgender Muslims.* New York, NY: NYU Press.
- Tanis, J.E. (2003). *Trans-gendered: Theology, ministry, and communities of faith.* Cleveland, OH: Pilgrim Press.
- Tigert, L. M., & Tirabassi, M. C. (2004). *Transgendering faith: Identity, sexuality, and spirituality.* Cleveland, OH: Pilgrim Press.

- Zeveloff, N. (Ed.). (2014). *Transgender and Jewish*. New York, NY: Forward Association.

Professional Literature

- Angello, M., & Bowman, A. (2016). *Raising the transgender child: A complete guide for parents, families, and caregivers*. Berkeley, CA: Seal Press.
- Brill, S., & Kenney, L. (2016). *The transgender teen: A handbook for parents and professionals supporting transgender and non-binary teens*. Jersey City, NJ: Cleis Press.
- Brill, S., & Pepper, R. (2008). *The transgender child: A handbook for families and professionals*. San Francisco, CA: Cleis.
- Davis, C. (2008). Social work practice with transgender and gender nonconforming people. In G. Mallon (Ed.), *Social work practice with lesbian, gay, bisexual, and transgender people* (2nd ed., pp. 83–112). New York, NY: Routledge.
- Dresher, J., & Byne, W. (2013). *Treating transgender children and adolescents: An interdisciplinary discussion*. New York, NY: Routledge.
- Ehrensaft, D. (2011). *Gender born, gender made: Raising healthy gender-nonconforming children*. New York, NY: The Experiment, LLC.
- Ehrensaft, D. (2016). *The gender creative child: Pathways for nurturing and supporting children who live outside gender boxes*. New York, NY: The Experiment, LLC.
- Fish, L. S. & Harvey, R. G. (2005). *Nurturing queer youth: Family therapy transformed*. New York, NY: Norton.
- Krieger, I. (2011). *Helping your transgender teen: A guide for parents*. New Haven, CT: Genderwise Press.
- Lev, A. (2004). *Transgender emergence: Therapeutic guidelines for working with gender-variant people and their families*. New York, NY: Haworth Press.
- Mallon, G. (2008). *Social work practice with lesbian, gay, bisexual, and transgender people* (2nd ed.). New York, NY: Haworth Press.
- Mallon, G. P. (Ed.). (2009). *Social work practice with transgender and gender variant youth* (2nd ed.). New York, NY: Routledge.
- Mallon, G. P. (2010). *Lesbian, gay, bisexual, transgender and questioning youth issues: A youth worker's perspective* (2nd ed.). Washington, DC: Child Welfare League of America.

- Malpas, J. (2011). Between pink and blue: A multi-dimensional family approach to gender nonconforming children and their families. *Family Process, 50*(4), 453–470.
- Nealy, E. C. (2017). *Transgender children and youth: Cultivating pride and joy with families in transition.* New York, NY: W. W. Norton & Company, Inc.
- Pleak, R. (2011). *Gender variant children and transgender adolescents. Child & Adolescent Psychiatric Clinics, 20*(4).

General Reading

- **"The Year's 10 Best Transgender Nonfiction Books" (The Advocate)** — http://www.advocate.com/arts-entertainment/books/2014/11/05/years-10-best-transgender-non-fiction-books
- Boylan, J. F. (2003). *She's not there: A life in two genders.* New York, NY: Broadway Books.
- Brown, M. & Ramsey, C. (1996). *True selves: Understanding transsexualism - for families, friends, coworkers, and helping professionals.* San Francisco, CA: Jossey-Bass.
- Erickson-Schroth, L. (2014). *Trans bodies, trans selves: A resource for the transgender community.* Oxford and New York: Oxford University Press.
- Green, J. (2004). *Becoming a visible man.* Nashville, TN: Vanderbilt University Press.
- Herman, Joanne. (2009). *Transgender explained for those who are not.* Bloomington, IN: AuthorHouse.
- King, N. (2014). *Queer & trans artists of color: Stories of some of our lives.* CreateSpace Independent Publishing Platform.
- Malpas, J. (2016). The transgender journey: What role should therapists play? *The Psychotherapy Networker, April/May.*
- McBee, T. P. (2014). *Man alive: A true story of violence, forgiveness, and becoming a man.* San Francisco, CA: City Lights Publishers.
- Mock, J. (2014). *Redefining realness: My path to womanhood, identity, love, & so much more.* New York, NY: Atria Books.
- Coyote, I. & Spoon, R. (2014). *Gender failure.* Vancouver, BC: Arsenal Pulp Press.

Videos

(Available on YouTube unless otherwise noted)

- **"A Transgender Man's Path to Freedom"** — presented by Seeker Stories
- **"Becoming Me"** — presented by In the Life Media
- **"Beyond the Gender Binary"** — a TED Talk by Yee Won Chong
- **"Beyond the Gender Binary: Understanding Transgender Youth"** — a TED Talk by Dr. Margaret Nichols
- **"Doctors Speak Out for Trans Youth"** — Human Rights Campaign
- **"Equality Utah: A Mormon Mom's Story of Unconditional Love for Her Transgender Son"** — presented by Equality Utah
- **"Fifty Shades of Gay"** — a TED Talk by iO Tillett Wright
- **"Home"** — an original song by the theatriQ Youth Ensemble, presented by Dreams of Hope
- **"How I Help Transgender Teens Become Who They Want to Be"** — a TED Talk by Norman Spack
- **"I Am Transgender"** — a TED Talk by Rev. Allyson Robinson
- **"Just Call Me Kade"** — presented by Frameline
- **"Media Bias: Trans Youth"** — presented by In the Life Media
- **"My True Gender Identity"** — a TED Talk by Niklaus Fluetsch
- **"New Medical Treatments for Transgender Adolescents"** — a TED Talk by Norman Spack
- **"Out Youth: A Safe Place to Be Yourself"** — presented by Out Youth
- **"The Real Pain and Tragedy Faced by Transgender Youth"** — a TED Talk by Daniella Carter
- **"Trans Love in the Black Community: Living Color"** — presented by NBC News
- **"Trans Youth Advocate Jazz Jennings: 'I Am Saving Lives'"** — presented by MSNBC
- **"Trans Women of Color Collective: Shifting the Narrative"** — presented by Lourdes Hunter
- **"Transgender Women of Color Share Their Stories"** — presented by sampson247
- **"Transgender Youth Bust Myths!!"** — presented by My Genderation
- **"Transmen Documentary, Parts 1–4"** — presented by Tiffany Gibson

- "Unheard Voices of Transgender Youth" — presented by arts4justice
- "Voices of Transgender Adolescents in Healthcare" — presented by the University of Michigan Health System's Adolescent Health Initiative
- "Watch Kids Share Eloquent, Empathetic Reactions to Caitlyn Jenner" — presented by Time (http://time.com/3915842/caitlyn-jenner-transition-kids-react/)
- "Why I Must Come Out" — a TED Talk by Geena Rocero
- "Why Is Gender Identity So Important?" — a TED Talk by Rikki Arundel

APPENDIX C: SAMPLE MENTAL HEALTH LETTERS

THERE ARE CERTAIN SITUATIONS IN WHICH A TRANSGEN-der young person will need or benefit from a letter from a licensed mental health professional. *Carry Letters* can be useful for trans youth who present in their affirmed gender, but whose identity documents still reflect their birth-assigned sex as their gender marker. If youth are questioned by legal authorities, these letters from their medical doctor or licensed mental health professional are sometimes helpful in "explaining" the difference between the young person's gender presentation and the gender marker on their identity document, such as their driver's license. As the samples reflect, these letters do not generally need to be lengthy.

A letter from a medical provider or licensed mental health professional is often required when a transgender young person wants to change the gender marker on their driver's permit or license. While a sample letter is provided, specific requirements vary from state to state. Parents and/or professionals need to contact the Department of Motor Vehicles to find out the exact content and wording required within their state.

The recommended content of letters required for medical transition (hormone blockers, gender-affirming hormone therapy, and surgeries) can be found on pages 26-28 of the WPATH Standards of Care (2012). These letters need to set out detailed facts that support the diagnosis and recommendations. The Standards of Care indicate that hormone therapy and top surgery require one letter from a licensed mental health professional. Lower surgery requires two letters from licensed mental health professionals, one of whom must have an M.D or Ph.D. These letters must state that the client meets the DSM-V criteria for gender dysphoria.

With health insurance coverage increasingly covering transgender-related healthcare, including medical transition, it is important to cite the WPATH Standards of Care (2012) guideline specifying that hormone therapy (including hormone blockers) and both top and bottom surgeries are "appropriate and essential medical treatment" for gender dysphoria. This guideline is reinforced by noting that these treatments are considered medically necessary by all major United States medical and psychiatric organizations. I have provided sample text below and you will see this text in each of the sample letters addressing medical interventions:

> It is my diagnosis that [full name] fully meets the criteria for Gender Dysphoria (302.85, DSM V). The appropriate and essential medical treatment for Gender Dysphoria includes both hormonal treatments and gender-confirming surgeries. These treatments are considered medically necessary by all major United States medical and psychiatric organizations and are recommended by The World Professional Association for Transgender Health (WPATH) Standards of Care.

The sample letters provided in this appendix describe hypothetical composites and offer suggested text. They are not in any way guaranteed to achieve their goals. All medical providers and licensed mental health professionals providing letters like these need to ensure that the content meets federal and state requirements, as well as those specified by individual health insurance carriers.

Carry Letter

[Mental health professional's name, credentials]
[Office address]
[Telephone and email]
[Date]

To Whom It May Concern:

This letter serves to confirm that FULL LEGAL NAME (can place preferred name here) is a transgender person/man/woman (whichever applies) and is in treatment with me for Gender Dysphoria (DSM 302.85; ICD-10-CM, F64.1). XX's appearance and gender expression may vary from that expected from ID gender markers. (In other words, he/she/they may not look the way you might think a man or woman would/should.) This is not for the purpose of deception but is part of their treatment for gender dysphoria.

As a New York State clinical social worker, I have worked with many transgender and gender-nonconforming clients over the past 20 years—first as the director of adolescent and adult mental health services at the LGBT Community Center in New York City and then, for the past 12 years, in my private clinical practice. I am a social work professor at the University of Saint Joseph, West Hartford, CT. I provide training for medical and mental health professionals throughout the tri-state area on best practices for work with transgender and gender-nonconforming persons. I have been a member of the World Professional Association for Transgender Health (WPATH) for 12 years.

If you have any questions, please feel free to contact me.

Sincerely,

[Mental health professional's name, credentials]

Letter for DMV to Change Gender Marker

[Mental health professional's name, credentials]
[Office address]
[Telephone and email]
[Date]

Department of Motor Vehicles
[Mental health professional's state]

As a New York State clinical social worker, I have worked with many transgender and gender-nonconforming clients over the past 20 years—first as the director of adolescent and adult mental health services at the LGBT Community Center in NYC and then, for the past 12 years, in private clinical practice. I teach gender identity/expression and transgender care at Columbia University School of Social Work and offer postgraduate clinical training in work with transgender clients at the Institute for Contemporary Psychotherapy in New York City. I have been a member of the World Professional Association for Transgender Health (WPATH) for the past 12 years and participate in the Gender Working Group at Columbia Presbyterian Psychiatric Institute in New York City.

This letter serves to confirm that [client's full name] is in treatment with me for Gender Dysphoria (302.85). [Client's name] is a transgender man/woman and has been living full time as a man/woman for the past two years. He/She has legally changed his/her name and should be considered male/female in all legal jurisdictions. Please update all legal gender markers to read "male"/"female".

Thank you for your assistance with this matter. If you have any further questions, please feel free to contact me.

Sincerely,

[Mental health professional's name, credentials]

Letter for Hormone Blockers

(This sample is for a young trans man,
adapt as appropriate for young trans women)

[Mental health professional's name, credentials]
[Office address]
[Telephone and email]
[Date]

Dr. [doctor's name]
[Doctor's address]

RE: [Client's preferred first/last name] (legal name: [first/last]), DOB [client's date of birth]

Dear Dr. [doctor's name]:

I am writing on behalf of my client, [preferred name], a 13-year-old trans-masculine-identified individual (natal female) who has been seeing me for regular individual psychotherapy since [date]. I have also seen him several times in conjunction with his mother, [name]. [Client's name] resides with his mother and younger brother in [town, state] and is completing eighth grade in school. [Client's name]'s parents are separated, but both are involved in their children's lives.

As a NYS clinical social worker, I have worked with many transgender and gender-nonconforming clients, both adolescents and adults, over the past 20 years—first as the director of adolescent and adult mental health services at the LGBT Community Center in NYC and then, for the past 12 years, in private clinical practice. I teach on LGBT issues, including gender identity/expression at Columbia University School of Social Work, and offer postgraduate clinical training in work with transgender individuals at several psychotherapy institutes. I have been a member of WPATH for the past 12 years and am a member of an ongoing peer consultation group for work with trans and gender-variant children and adolescents.

[Client's name] and his mother report that he has experienced cross-gender identification since early childhood. From the ages of three to five years, [client's name] never liked dresses and preferred to wear boys' clothes. By the first grade, his mother reports, [client's name]'s best friends were always boys. [Client's name] reports that as a child, he always wished he was a boy but never knew it was possible to transition. [Client's name]'s gender dysphoria increased with the onset of puberty. There was a brief period during the fifth grade when [client's name] reports he tried to fit in better at school by dressing more like a girl, but he says it never "felt right." His mom reports conversations with her husband while [client's name] was young in which she discussed [client's name]'s consistent masculine gender presentation/ expression.

In [month year)], [client's name] came out to his parents about being transgender and began socially transitioning within his family and at school. He cut his hair, bought more masculine clothes, and began binding his chest. His mother met with his school guidance counselor, and the school began using his preferred name, [client's name], and male pronouns. His transition at school at school this year has gone very well. [Client's name] reports positive relationships with peers. He knows several other transgender youth at his school. [Client's name] is a bright young man with a great sense of humor and makes friends easily (though he was rather shy as a young child).

[Client's name]'s mother brought him to see me this past March because she felt he needed someone to talk to about his trans identity and his experiences transitioning as an adolescent male. The family has begun coming out about [client's name]'s transition with close friends and family. Both parents are supportive of [client's name] and his transition.

In meeting with [client's name] and his mother over the

past three months, it is my diagnosis that [client's name] meets the DSM-5 criteria for Gender Dysphoria (302.85). He reports significant gender dysphoria in relation to living as a transgender male in a body that does not match his internal gender identity. He experiences particularly acute gender dysphoria (self-hatred, depression, anxiety) in relation to his monthly menses. [Client's name] strongly wants to proceed with hormone blockers at this time. There are no current psychiatric concerns that would preclude moving forward.

I believe hormone blockers now would alleviate some of [client's name]'s gender dysphoria, thus lessening risks for depression and anxiety. His parents fully support this decision. As outlined in the WPATH Standards of Care for gender dysphoria, hormone blockers are medically necessary for transgender youth. I believe beginning hormone blockers will enhance [client's name]'s mental and emotional well-being, both in terms of his comfort within his body and in his ability to move more comfortably in the world. It is my recommendation that [client's name] be allowed to proceed at this time. Please feel free to contact me if you have any further questions.

Sincerely,

[Mental health professional's name]

Letter for Feminizing/Masculizing Hormone Therapy

(This sample is for a young trans woman,
adapt as appropriate for young trans man)

[Begin letter; format as appropriate]
[Mental health professional's name, credentials]
[Office address]
[Telephone and email]
[Date]

Dr. [doctor's name]
[Doctor's address]

RE: [Client's preferred first/last name] (legal name: [first/last]), DOB [client's date of birth]

Dear Dr. [doctor's name]:

I am writing on behalf of my client, [client's name], a 16-year-old trans-feminine-identified individual (natal male) who wants to begin feminizing hormone therapy. [Client's name] first saw me on [date]. I have seen her on a weekly basis since then for continued gender assessment and supportive psychotherapy. I also regularly meet with [client's name]'s father, [name], and with both of them together. While the father has experienced some of the emotions many parents of transgender youth struggle with, he clearly supports [client's name] in moving forward with her gender transition.

[Client's name]'s father is a single parent. Her biological mother was ill and unable to care for her. At that time, they lived in Montana and were part of a very supportive community.

In [year], when [client's name] was eight years old, her father relocated them to the New York City area in [year]. Initially, [client's name] attended a private school, but that proved to be a negative experience. [Client's name] and her father then moved to [town], where she attended school for one year. After this, they moved to their current home in [town], where [client's name] has been attending high school.

[Client's name]'s gender presentation has always been more feminine. Her father reports that when she was three years old, she would wrap a bath towel around her head and pretend it was long, flowing hair. Her favorite clothing at seven years old was a princess dress.

[Client's name] reports "always feeling like a girl." She presents with profound gender dysphoria that causes significant distress and interferes with her ability to engage productively in other areas of her life. She has extreme difficulty navigating men's restrooms and feels tremendous dis-ease about her male body, especially when showering or looking at herself in the mirror. She reports feeling very angry when peers call her "bro" or "dude."

In [month year], [client's name] came out as transgender to her father and a few friends. Since then, she has come out widely at school with teachers and classmates. She has begun to use "[client's name]" consistently as well as to dress and do her hair more femininely. Her goal is to begin school this coming fall fully presenting as a young woman. This includes obtaining a legal name change and beginning feminizing hormone treatment.

One area of concern is the ongoing conflict between the father and [client's name]—often centered around [client's name]'s failure to follow through on chores, not completing homework and sometimes refusing to attend school, and frequent angry outbursts toward her father.

We have discussed these areas in my work with [client's name] and her father. These struggles seem partly related to [client's name]'s gender dysphoria as well as to the stressors accompanying moving repeatedly, the loss of their family/ community supports in Montana, and the challenges for [client's name] of establishing new peer relationships in several different schools. When we first began meeting together, we attempted to focus on the family conflicts and [client's name]'s failing school performance before moving forward with hormone therapy. While there has been some improvement in these areas, both remain critical areas of concern.

It is my assessment at this time that withholding feminizing hormone treatment has become psychologically harmful for [client's name] and is leading to more severe gender dysphoria. While we will continue to focus on these other areas in therapy, my hope is that beginning hormone treatment may diminish her gender dysphoria and thus lead to enhanced self-esteem, fewer emotional outbursts and less anger, and improved ability to focus on school work.

As a NYS clinical social worker, I have worked with many transgender and gender-nonconforming clients, both adolescents and adults, over the past 20 years—first as the director of adolescent and adult mental health services at the LGBT Community Center in New York City and then, for the past 12 years, in private clinical practice in Manhattan and Westchester County, New York. I teach on LGBT issues, including gender identity/expression at Columbia University School of Social Work, and offer postgraduate clinical training in work with transgender clients at several psychotherapy institutes. I have been a member of WPATH for the past 12 years.

In meeting with [client's name] over the past several months, it is my diagnosis that she meets the DSM-5 criteria for Gender Dysphoria (302.85). [Client's name] believes that beginning feminizing hormone therapy is the next step in her transition. There are no current psychiatric concerns that would preclude beginning estrogen. She does not report current depression except occasionally in relation to her struggles in living as a transgender female in a body that does not match her internal gender identity.

As outlined in the WPATH Standards of Care for gender dysphoria, hormone therapy is medically necessary for transgender youth and can begin in adolescence. I believe this step will enhance [client's name]'s life in terms of both her emotional comfort within herself and her ability to move more comfortably in the world as a young woman. Her father supports initiating feminizing hormone therapy. It is my recommendation that [client's name] be allowed to begin treatment with estrogen at this time. Please feel free to contact me if you have any further questions.

Sincerely,

[Mental health professional's name, credentials]

Letter for Gender-Confirming Surgeries

(This sample is for a young trans woman, adapt as appropriate for young trans man. In the final paragraph, you would generally state the specific surgery, e.g., vaginoplasty, chest reconstruction, phalloplasty.)

[Mental health professional's name, credentials]
[Office address]
[Telephone and email]
[Date]

Dr. [doctor's name]
[Doctor's address]

RE: [Client's preferred first/last name] (legal name: [first/last]), DOB [client's date of birth]

Dear Dr. [doctor's name]:

As a New York State clinical social worker, I have worked with many transgender and gender-nonconforming clients over the past 20 years—first as the director of adolescent and adult mental health services at the LGBT Community Center in NYC and then, for the past 12 years, in private clinical practice. I teach gender identity/expression and transgender care at Columbia University School of Social Work and offer postgraduate clinical training in work with transgender clients at several institutes. I have been a member of the World Professional Association for Transgender Health (WPATH) for the past 12 years.

From [date] to [date], I met weekly with [client's name] for gender evaluation and assessment as well as supportive psychotherapy. She was referred to me by a clinical colleague after disclosing to that colleague that she wanted to begin to gender transition.

[Client's name] is a nearly 21-year-old transgender woman (natal male) who according to her report "always felt female." This gender dysphoria intensified during adolescence. [Client's name] was born and raised in Manhattan with her parents, [names], and one sibling. I have met with [client's name]'s family on several occasions, and they are very supportive of her gender transition.

During the year we worked together in New York City, [client's name] came out as transgender with her friends, socially transitioned, and developed a supportive intimate personal relationship. She attended a weekly transgender women's support group and participated in a weekend transgender conference that spring. She began hormone therapy in June [year].

In the fall of [year], [client's name] began her undergraduate studies at College X as an out transgender woman. She has done well both academically and socially. She returned this fall as a sophomore and is looking to transfer schools for the next year. She is a math major who also has extensive musical interests. [Client's name] and I continue to meet for psychotherapy when she is home for weekends in New York City and during college breaks, including numerous times this past summer.

It is my diagnosis that [client's name] fully meets the criteria for Gender Dysphoria (302.85, DSM-5). The appropriate and essential medical treatment for Gender Dysphoria includes both hormonal treatments and gender-confirming surgeries. These treatments are considered medically necessary by all major United States medical and psychiatric organizations and are recommended by the World Professional Association for Transgender Health (WPATH).

Given [client's name]'s current level of gender dysphoria (mental and emotional distress), it is my belief that the gender-confirming surgeries [specify exact surgery] scheduled with Dr. [name] are medically necessary and essential for [client's name]'s mental and emotional well-being. Given her diagnosis, the surgery should be completed as soon as possible. If you have any questions, please feel free to contact me at the above phone or email. Thank you very much.

Sincerely,

[Mental health professional's name, credentials]

REFERENCES

Almeida, J., Johnson, R., Corliss, H., Molnar, B., & Azrael, D. (2009). Emotional distress among LGBT youth: The influence of perceived discrimination based on sexual orientation. *Journal of Youth and Adolescence, 38*(7), 1001–1014.

American Civil Liberties Union. (2015). *Don't clap just yet for the Boy Scouts*. Retrieved February 5, 2016, from https://www.aclu.org/blog/speak-freely/dont-clap-just-yet-boy-scouts

American Psychiatric Association. (2000). *Diagnostic and statistical manual of mental disorders* (4th text rev. ed.). Arlington, VA: American Psychiatric Association.

American Psychiatric Association. (2013). *Diagnostic and statistical manual of mental disorders* (5th ed.). Arlington, VA: American Psychiatric Association.

American Psychological Association. (2008). Are zero tolerance policies effective in the schools? An evidentiary review and recommendations. *American Psychologist, 63*(9), 852–862.

Arnold, E., & Bailey, M. (2009). Constructing home and family: How the ballroom community supports African American GLBTQ youth in the face of HIV/AIDS. *Journal of Gay and Lesbian Social Services, 21*(2–3), 171–188. doi: 10.1080/10538720902772006

Austin, A., & Craig, S. (2015). Transgender affirmative cognitive behavioral therapy: Clinical considerations and applications. *Professional Psychology: Research and Practice, 46*(1), 21–29.

Bernal, A. T., & Coolhart, D. (2012). Treatment and ethical considerations with transgender children and youth in family therapy. *Journal of Family Psychotherapy, 23*(4), 287–303. doi: 10.1080/08975353.2012.735594

Best, C., Minshew, N., & Strauss, M. (2010). Gender discrimination of eyes and mouths by individuals with autism. *Autism Research,* 3, 88–93.

Boccanfuso, C., & Kuhfeld, M. (2011). *Multiple responses, promising results: Evidence-based, nonpunitive alternatives to zero tolerance.* Washington, DC: Child Trends. Retrieved February 12, 2016, from http://www.childtrends.org/wp-content/uploads/2011/03/Child_Trends-2011_03_01_RB_AltToZeroTolerance.pdf

Bockting, W. O., Knudson, G., & Goldberg, J. M. (2006). Counseling and mental health care for transgender adults and loved ones. *International Journal of Transgenderism, 9,* 35–82. doi: 10.1300/J485v09n03_03

Bockting, W. O., Miner, M. H., Swinburne Romine, R. E., Hamilton, A., & Coleman, E. (2013). Stigma, mental health, and resilience in an online sample of the US transgender population. *American Journal of Public Health, 103*(5), 943–951. doi: 10.2105/AJPH.2013.301241

Bouris, A., Guilamo-Ramos,Butler, J. (2004). Undoing Gender. New York, NY: Routledge. V., Pickard, A., Shiu, C., Loosier, P. S., Dittus, P., & Waldmiller, J. M. (2010). A systematic review of parental influence on health and well-being of lesbian, gay, and bisexual youth: Time for a new public health research and practice agenda. *Journal of Primary Prevention, 31,* 273–309.

Bowling, C. (2016, June 10). Georgia judge refuses to change transgender man's name. *The Atlanta Journal-Constitution.* Retrieved June 25, 2016, from http://www.ajc.com/news/local/georgia-judge-refuses-change-transgender-man-name/bkVOOaAZEGNjOQ1g26TB6I/

Brill, S., & Pepper, R. (2008). *The transgender child: A handbook for families and professionals.* San Francisco, CA: Cleis.

Budge, S., Adelson, J., & Howard, K. (2013). Anxiety and depression in transgender individuals: The roles of transition status, loss, social support, and coping. *Journal of Clinical Consulting Psychologist, 81*(3), 545–557.

Butler, J. (2004). *Undoing Gender.* New York, NY: Routledge.

Cass, V. (1979). Homosexual identity formation: A theoretical model. *Journal of Homosexuality, 4,* 219–235.

Cass, V. (1990). The implications of homosexual identity formation for the Kinsey model and scale of sexual preference. In S. S. Reinisch (Ed.), *Homosexuality/heterosexuality: Concepts of sexual orientation* (pp. 239–266). New York, NY: Oxford University Press.

Cohen-Kettenis, P. (2001). Gender identity disorder in DSM? *Journal of the American Academy of Child and Adolescent Psychiatry, 40*(4), 391–391. doi: 10.1097/00004583-200104000-00006

Cohen-Kettenis, P. T., Delemarre–van de Waal, H. A., & Gooren, L. J. (2008). The treatment of adolescent transsexuals: Changing insights. *Journal of Sexual Medicine, 5*(8), 1892–1897. doi: 10.1111/j.1743-6109.2008.00870.x

Cohen-Kettenis, P. T., & Kuiper, A. J. (1984). Transseksualiteit en psychotherapie. *Tijdschrift voor   Psychotherapie, 3*, 153–166.

Coleman, E. (1982). Developmental stages of the coming out process. In J. W. W. Paul (Ed.), *Homosexuality: Social, psychological, and biological issues* (pp. 149–158). Beverly Hills, CA: SAGE.

Collazo, A., Austin, A., & Craig, S. (2013). Facilitating transition among transgender clients: Components of effective clinical practice. *Clinical Social Work Journal, 41*(3), 228–237. doi: 10.1007/s10615-013-0436-3

Connor, J. J., & Rueter, M. A. (2006). Parent–child relationships as systems of support or risk for adolescent suicidality. *Journal of Family Psychology, 20*, 143–155. doi:10.1037/0893-3200.20.1.143

Coolhart, D., Baker, A., Farmer, S., Malaney, M., & Shipman, D. (2013). Therapy with transsexual youth and their families: A clinical tool for assessing readiness for gender transition. *Journal of Marital and Family Therapy, 39*(2), 223–243.

Davenport, C. W. (1986). A follow-up study of 10 feminine boys. *Archives of Sexual Behavior, 15*, 511–517.

Deruelle, C., Rondan, C., Gepner, B., & Tardif, C. (2010). Spatial frequency and face processing in children with autism and Asperger's syndrome. *Journal of Autism and Developmental Disorders, 34*, 199–210.

Devor, H. (1997). *FTM: Female-to-male transsexuals in society.* Bloomington, IN: Indiana University Press.

de Vries, A. L. C., Noens, I. L. J., Cohen-Kettenis, P. T., van Berckelaer-Onnes, I. A., & Doreleijers, T. A. (2010). Autism spectrum disorders in gender dysphoric children and adolescents. *Journal of Autism and Developmental Disorders, 40*, 930–936.

de Vries, A., Steensma, T., Doreleijers, T., & Cohen-Kettenis, P. (2010). Puberty suppression in adolescents with gender identity disorder: A prospective follow-up study. *Journal of Sexual Medicine, 8*(8), 2276–2283.

Diamond, G., Shilo, G., Jurgensen, E., D'Augelli, A., Samarova, V., & White, K. (2011). How depressed and suicidal sexual minority adolescents understand the causes of their distress. *Journal of Gay and Lesbian Mental Health*, 15(2), 130–151. doi: 10.1080/19359705.2010.532668

Drummond, K. D., Bradley, S. J., Peterson-Badali, M., & Zucker, K. J. (2008). A follow-up study of girls with gender identity disorder. *Developmental Psychology, 44*(1), 34–45.

Dunn, M., & Moodie-Mills, A. (2012, April 13). *The state of gay and transgender communities of color.* Center for American Progress. Retrieved from http://www.americanprogress.org/issues/lgbt/news/2012/04/13/11493/the-state-of-gay-and-transgender-communities-of-color-in-2012/

Durso, L. E., & Gates, G. J. (2012). *Serving our youth: Findings from a national survey of service providers working with lesbian, gay, bisexual, and transgender youth who are homeless or at risk of becoming homeless.* Los Angeles, CA: Williams Institute with True Colors Fund and Palette Fund.

Egan, S. K., & Perry, D. G. (2001). Gender identity: A multidimensional analysis with implications for psychosocial adjustment. *Developmental Psychology, 37*(4), 451-463. doi: 10.1037//0012-I649.37.4.45I

Ehrensaft, D. (2011). Boys will be girls, girls will be boys: Children affect parents as parents affect children in gender nonconformity. *Psychoanalytic Psychology, 28*(4), 528–548. doi: 10.1037/a0023828

Ehrensaft, D. (2012). From gender identity disorder to gender identity creativity: True gender self child therapy. *Journal of Homosexuality, 59*(3), 337–356. doi: 10.1080/00918369.2012.653303

Ehrensaft, D. (2014). Listening and learning from gender-nonconforming children. *Psychoanalytic Study of the Child, 68,* 28–56. Retrieved from http://www.ncbi.nlm.nih.gov/pubmed/26173325

Ehrensaft, D. (2016). *The gender creative child: Pathways for nurturing and supporting children who live outside gender boxes.* New York, NY: The Experiment, LLC.

Eisenberg, M.E., & Resnick, M.D. (2006). Suicidality among gay, lesbian and bisexual adolescents: The role of protective factors. *Journal of Adolescent Health, 39,* 662–668.

Erikson, E. H. (1950). *Childhood and Society.* New York, NY: W. W. Norton & Company, Inc.

Espelage, D., & Swearer, S. (2008). Addressing research gaps in the intersection between homophobia and bullying. *School Psychology Review, 37*(2), 155–159.

Garofalo, R., Deleon, J., Osmer, E., Doll, M., & Harper, G. W. (2006). Overlooked, misunderstood, and at risk: Exploring the lives and HIV risk of ethnic minority male-to-female transgender youth. *Journal of Adolescent Health, 38*(3), 230–236.

Girl Scouts. (2016). Social issues: Frequently asked questions [Web page]. Retrieved January 19, 2016, from http://www.girlscouts.org/en/faq/faq/social-issues.html

Gold, M., & MacNish, M. (2011). *Adjustment and resiliency following disclosure of transgender identity in families of adolescents and young adults: Themes and clinical implications.* Washington, DC: American Family Therapy Academy.

Goldberg, J. M., & Ashbee, O. (2006). Fit or fatphobic: Trans people, weight and health [Web article]. Vancouver, BC, Canada: Vancouver Coastal Health. Retrieved June 28, 2016, from http://www.rainbowhealthontario.ca/wp-content/uploads/woocommerce_uploads/2014/08/Weight%20and%20health.pdf

Gorton, R., Buth, J., & Spade, D. (2005). *Medical therapy and health maintenance for transgender men: A guide for health care providers.* San Francisco, CA: Lyon-Martin Women's Health Services.

Grant, J. M., Mottet, L. A., Tanis, J., Harrison, J., Herman, J. L., & Keisling, M. (2011). Injustice at every turn: A report of the national transgender discrimination survey. Washington: National Center for Transgender Equality and National Gay and Lesbian Task Force.

Green, R. (1987). *The "sissy boy syndrome" and the development of homosexuality.* New Haven, CT: Yale University Press.

Green, R., & Fuller, M. (1973). Group therapy with feminine boys and their parents. *International Journal of Group Psychotherapy, 23*(1), 54–68.

Greenson, R. R. (1964). On homosexuality and gender identity. *The International Journal of Psychoanalysis, 45,* 217-219.

Greytak, E., Kosciw, J., & Diaz, E. (2009). Harsh realities: The experiences of transgender youth in our nation's schools: A report from the Gay, Lesbian, and Straight Education Network (GLSEN) [Web article]. Retrieved February 6, 2016, from http://www.glsen.org/sites/default/files/Harsh%20Realities.pdf

Grossman, A. H., & D'Augelli, A. R. (2007). Transgender youth and life-threatening behaviors. *Suicide and Life-Threatening Behaviors, 37*(5), 527–537.

Grossman, A. H., D'Augelli, A. R., Howell, T. J., & Hubbard, S. (2006). Parents' reactions to transgender youth's gender-nonconforming expression and identity. *Journal of Gay and Lesbian Social Services, 18*(1), 3–16. doi:10.1300/J041v18n01_02

Grossman, A. H., D'Augelli, A. R., & Salter, N. P. (2006). Male-to-female transgender youth: Gender expression milestones, gender atypicality, victimization, and parents' responses. *Journal of GLBT Family Studies, 2*(1), 71–92.

Grov, C., & Bimbi, D. S. (2006). Race, ethnicity, gender, and generational factors associated with the coming out process among gay, lesbian, and bisexual individuals. *Journal of Sex Research, 43*(2), 115–121.

Hembree, W. C., Cohen-Kettenis, P., Delemarre-van de Waal, H. A., Gooren, L. J., Meyer, W. J., III, Spack, N. P., . . . Montori, V. M. (2009). Endocrine treatment of transsexual persons: An Endocrine Society clinical practice guideline. *Journal of Clinical Endocrinology and Metabolism, 94*(9), 3132–3154. doi: 10.1210/jc.2009–0345

Hill, D., Menvielle, E., Sica, K., & Johnson, A. (2010). An affirmative intervention for families with gender variant children: Parental ratings of child mental health and gender. *Journal of Sex and Marital Therapy, 36*(1), 6–23.

Ignatavicius, S. (2013). Stress in female-identified transgender youth: A review of the literature on effects and interventions. *Journal of LGBT Youth, 10*(4), 267–286. doi: 10.1080/19361653.2013.825196

Intersex Society of North America. (n.d.). Myth #10: Intersex is extremely rare [Web page]. Retrieved September 15, 2015, from http://www.isna.org/faq/ten_myths/rare

James, S., Herman, L., Rankin, S., Keisling, M., Mottet, L., & Anafi, M. (2016). The Report of the 2015 U.S. Transgender Survey. Wash, DC: National Center for Transgender Equality

Janssen, A., Huang, H., Duncan, C. (2016) Gender variance among youth with autism spectrum disorders: a retrospective chart review, *Transgender Health* 1:1, 63–68, DOI: 10.1089/ trgh.2015.0007.

Kelleher, C. (2009). Minority stress and health: Implications for lesbian, gay, bisexual, transgender, and questioning (LGBTQ) young people. *Counselling Psychology Quarterly, 22*(4), 373–379. doi: 10.1080/09515070903334995

Kerr, D. C. R., Preuss, L. J., & King, C. A. (2006). Suicidal adoles-

cents' social support from family and peers: Gender-specific associations with psychopathology. *Journal of Abnormal Child Psychology,*1-12.

Klein, D., Goldenring, J., & Adelman, W. (2014, January 1). HEEADSSS 3.0: The psychosocial interview for adolescents updated for a new century fueled by media. *Contemporary Pediatrics.* Retrieved June 5, 2016, from http://contemporarypediatrics.modernmedicine.com/contemporary-pediatrics/content/tags/adolescent-medicine/heeadsss-30-psychosocial-interview-adolesce

Knudson, G., De Cuypere, G., & Bockting, W. (2010). Response of the world professional association for transgender health to the proposed DSM 5 criteria for gender incongruence. *International Journal of Transgenderism, 12*(2), 119-123. doi: 10.1080/15532739.2010.509214

Koken, J. A., Bimbi, D. S., & Parsons, J. T. (2009). Experiences of familial acceptance-rejection among transwomen of color. *Journal of Family Psychology, 23*(6), 853-860.

Kosciw, J. G., Greytak, E. A., Palmer, N. A., & Boesen, M. J. (2014). *The 2013 National School Climate Survey: The experiences of lesbian, gay, bisexual and transgender youth in our nation's schools.* New York, NY: GLSEN.

Kuklin, S. (2014). *Beyond magenta: Transgender teens speak out.* Somerville, MA: Candlewick Press.

Kuvalanka, K., Weiner, J., & Mahan, D.(2014). Child, family, and community transformations: Findings from interviews with mothers of transgender girls. *Journal of GLBT Family Therapy, 10*(4), 354–379.

Lament, C. (2014). Transgender children: Conundrums and controversies—An introduction to the section. *Psychoanalytic Study of the Child, 68,* 13–27. Retrieved July 2, 2016, from http://www.psotc.com/transgender.pdf

Lev, A. I. (2004). *Transgender emergence: Therapeutic guidelines for working with gender-variant people and their families.* New York, NY: Haworth.

Lev, A. L. (2013). Gender dysphoria: Two steps forward, one step back. *Clinical Social Work Journal, 41*(3), 288–296. doi: 10.1007/s10615-013-0447-0

Liu, R., & Mustanski, B. (2012). Suicidal ideation and self-harm in lesbian, gay, bisexual, and transgender youth. *American Journal of Preventive Medicine, 42*(3), 221–228.

Lowder, J. B. (2014). Listen to Leelah Alcorn's *final words. Slate.com.*

Retrieved November 10, 2015, from http://www.slate.com/blogs/
outward/2014/12/31/leelah_alcorn_transgender_teen_from_
ohio_should_be_honored_in_death.html

Luxenberg, H., Limber, S. P., & Olweus, D. (2014). *Bullying in U.S. Schools: 2013 status report.* Center City, MN: Hazelden Foundation.

Mallon, G. P. (n.d.) Facilitating a discussion of transgender issues: A primer. New York, NY: National Resource Center for Permanency and Family Connections. Retrieved on September 25, 2015 from http://www.hunter.cuny.edu/socwork/nrcfcpp/info_services/download/Facilitating%20Discussion%20of%20Transgender%20Issues%2002%2022%202011.pdf

Malpas, J. (2011). Between pink and blue: A multi-dimensional family approach to gender nonconforming children and their families. *Family Process, 50*(4), 453-470.

Malpas, J. (2016). The transgender journey: What role should therapists play? *The Psychotherapy Networker, April/May.*

Marshal, M. P., Dietz, L. J., Friedman, M. S., Stall, R., Smith, H. A., McGinley, J. . . . Brent, D. A. (2011). Suicidality and depression disparities between sexual minority and heterosexual youth: A meta-analytic review. *Journal of Adolescent Health, 49,* 115–123.

McGuire, J., Anderson, C., Toomey, R., & Russell, S. (2010). School climate for transgender youth: A mixed method investigation of student experiences and school responses. *Journal of Youth and Adolescence, 39,* 1175–1188.

McGuire, J., & Conover-Williams, M. (2010). Creating spaces to support transgender youth. *Prevention Researcher, 17*(4), 17–20.

Mele, C. (2016, June 13). Oregon court allows a person to choose neither sex. *New York Times.* Retrieved from http://www.nytimes.com/2016/06/14/us/oregon-nonbinary-transgender-sex-gender.html?_r=0

Menvielle, E. (2012). A comprehensive program for children with gender variant behaviors and gender identity disorders. *Journal of Homosexuality, 59*(3), 357–368. doi: 10.1080/00918369.2012.653305

Meyer, I. (2003). Prejudice, social stress, and mental health in lesbian, gay, and bisexual populations: Conceptual issues and research evidence. *Psychological Bulletin, 129,* 674–697.

Meyer, I. (2007). Prejudice and discrimination as social stressors. In I. H. Meyer & M. E. Northridge (Eds.), *The health of sexual minorities:*

Public health perspectives on lesbian, gay, bisexual, and transgender populations (pp. 242–267). New York, NY: Springer.

Mizock, L., & Lundquist, C. (2016). Missteps in psychotherapy with transgender clients: Promoting gender sensitivity in counseling and psychological practice. *Psychology of Sexual Orientation and Gender Diversity, 3*(2), 148-155.

Mul, D., & Hughes, I. A. (2008). The use of GnRH agonists in precocious puberty. *European Journal of Endocrinology, 159*(Suppl. 1), 53–58. doi: 10.1530/EJE-08-0814

Mustanski, B., Andrews, R., Herrick, A., Stall, R., & Schnarrs, P. (2014). A syndemic of psychosocial health disparities and associations with risk for attempting suicide among young sexual minority men. *American Journal of Public Health, 104*(2), 287–294.

Mustanski, B., Newcomb, M., & Garofalo, R. (2011). Mental health of lesbian, gay, and bisexual youths: A developmental resiliency perspective. *Journal of Gay and Lesbian Social Services, 23*, 204–225.

Nadal, K. L. (2013). *That's so gay! Microaggressions in the lesbian, gay, bisexual, and transgender community.* Washington, DC: American Psychological Association.

Nadal, K. L., Skolnik, A., & Wong, Y. (2012). Interpersonal and systemic microaggressions toward transgender people: Implications for counseling. *Journal of LGBT Issues in Counseling, 6*, 55–82.

National Association for the Advancement of Colored People. (2005). *Interrupting the school to prison pipeline.* Washington, DC: Author.

National Center for Transgender Equality. (2016). Healthcare rights and transgender people. Retrieved October 31, 2016 from http://www.transequality.org/sites/default/files/docs/kyr/KYR-Healthcare-May-2016.pdf

National Coalition of Anti-Violence Programs (NCAVP). (2015). *Lesbian, gay, bisexual, transgender, queer, and HIV-affected hate violence in 2014.* New York, NY: Ahmed and Jindasurat.

Needham, B. L., & Austin, E. L. (2010). Sexual orientation, parental support, and health during the transition to young adulthood. *Journal of Youth and Adolescence, 39*, 1189–1198.

Nemoto, T., Bödeker, B., & Iwamoto, M. (2011). Social support, exposure to violence and transphobia, and correlates of depression among male-to-female transgender women with a history of sex work. *American Journal of Public Health, 101,* 1980–1988.

Nuttbrock, L., Hwahng, S., Bockting, W., Rosenblum, A., Mason, M., Macri, M., & Becker, J. (2010). Psychiatric impact of gender-related abuse across the life course of male-to-female transgender persons. *Journal of Sex Research, 47*(1), 12–23.

Olson, J., Schrager, S., Belzer, M., Simons, L., & Clark, L. (2014). Baseline physiologic and psychosocial characteristics of transgender youth seeking care for gender dysphoria. *Journal of Adolescent Health, 57*(4), 374–380.

Olson, K., Durwood, L., DeMeules, M., & McLaughlin, K. (2016). Mental health of transgender children who are supported in their identities. *Pediatrics, 137*(3). doi: 10.1542/peds.2015-3223

Pauly, I. B. (1965). Male psychosexual inversion: Transexualism: A review of 100 cases. *Archives of General Psychiatry, 13,* 172-181.

Pleak, R. (1999). Ethical issues in diagnosing and treating gender-dysphoric children and adolescents. In M. Rottnek (Ed.), *Sissies and tomboys: Gender noncomformity and homosexual childhood* (pp. 34–51). New York, NY: New York University Press.

Pollock, L. & Eyre, S. (2012). Growth into manhood: Identity development among female-to-male transgender youth. *Culture, Health, and Sexuality: An International Journal for Research, Intervention and Care, 14*(2), 209–222.

Poteat, T., German, D., & Kerrigan, D. (2013). Managing uncertainty: A grounded theory of stigma in transgender healthcare encounters. *Social Science and Medicine, 84,* 22–29.

Pyne, J. (2014a). Gender independent kids: A paradigm shift in approaches to gender non-conforming children. *Canadian Journal of Human Sexuality, 23*(1), 1–8. doi: 10.3138/cjhs.23.1.CO1

Pyne, J. (2014b). Health and wellbeing among gender independent children: A critical review of the literature. In E. M. A. P. Sansfacon (Ed.), *Supporting transgender and gender creative youth: Schools, families, and communities in action.* New York, NY: Peter Lang.

Rekers, G. A. (1972). *Pathological sex-role development in boys: Behavioral treatment and assessment.* Los Angeles, CA: University of California.

Resilience. (n.d.). In *Merriam-Webster's online dictionary* (11th ed.). Retrieved May 15, 2016, from http://www.merriam-webster.com/dictionary/resilience

Rosenberg, M. (2002). Children with gender identity issues and their parents in individual and group treatment. *Journal of the American Academy of Child and Adolescent Psychiatry, 41*(5), 619–621. doi: 10.1097/00004583–200205000–00020

Russell, S., Ryan, C., Toomey, R., Diaz, R., & Sanchez, J. (2011). Lesbian, gay, bisexual, and transgender adolescent school victimization: Implications for young adult health and adjustment. *Journal of School Health, 81*(5), 223–230.

Russell, S., Muraco, A., Subramaniam, A., & Laub, C. (2009). Youth empowerment and high school gay–straight alliances. *Journal of Youth and Adolescence, 38*, 891–903.

Ryan, C., Huebner, D., Diaz, R. M., & Sanchez, J. (2009). Family rejection as a predictor of negative health outcomes in white and Latino lesbian, gay, and bisexual young adults. *Pediatrics, 123*, 346–52.

Ryan, C., Russell, S., Huebner, D., Diaz, R., & Sanchez, J. (2010). Family acceptance in adolescence and the health of LGBT young adults. *Journal of Child and Adolescent Psychiatric Nursing, 23*(4), 205–213.

Saketopoulou, A. (2011). Minding the gap: Intersections between gender, race, and class in work with gender variant children. *Psychoanalytic Dialogues, 21*, 192- 209.

Sausa, L. A. (2005). Translating research into practice: Trans youth recommendations for improving school systems. *Journal of Gay and Lesbian Issues in Education, 3*(1), 15–28.

Schwartzapfel, B. (2013, March 14). Born this way? *American Prospect.* Retrieved from http://prospect.org/article/born-way

Shelton, J. (2015). Transgender youth homelessness: Understanding programmatic barriers through the lens of cisgenderism. *Children and Youth Services Review, 59*, 10–18.

Sherer, I., Baum, J., Ehrensaft, D., & Rosenthal, S. M. (2015). Affirming gender: Caring for gender- atypical children and adolescents. *Contemporary Pediatrics, 32*(1), 16-19.

Simons, L., Schrager, S., Clark, L., Belzer, M., & Olson, J. (2103). Parental support and mental health among transgender adolescents. *Journal of Adolescent Health, 53*(6), 791–793.

Singh, A. (2013). Transgender youth of color and resilience: Negotiating oppression and finding support. *Sex Roles, 68*, 690–702.

Singh, A. A., & McKleroy, V. S. (2011). "Just getting out of bed is a revolutionary act": The resilience of transgender people of color who have survived traumatic life events. *Traumatology, 17,* 34–44.

Smith, S. (2013, December 6). Zero-tolerance policies in schools are often destructive: Fueling a school to prison pipeline. *Alternet.* Retrieved February 12, 2016, from http://www.alternet.org/education/zero-tolerance-policies-schools-are-often-destructive-fueling-school-prison-pipeline

Spack, N. P., Edwards-Leeper, L., Feldman, H. A., Leibowitz, S., Mandel, F., Diamond, D. A., & Vance, S. R. (2012). Children and adolescents with gender identity disorder referred to a pediatric medical center. *Pediatrics, 129*(3), 418–425. doi: 10.1542/peds.2011-090

Strang, J. F., Kenworthy, L., Dominska, A., Sokoloff, J., Kenealy, L. E., Berl, M. . . . Wallace, G. L. (2014). Increased gender variance in autism spectrum disorders and attention deficit hyperactivity disorder. *Archives of Sexual Behavior, 43,* 1525–1533.

Sue, D. W. (2010a). *Microaggressions and marginality: Manifestation, dynamics, and impact.* Hoboken, NJ: John Wiley & Sons.

Sue, D. W. (2010b). *Microaggressions in everyday life: Race, gender, and sexual orientation.* Hoboken, NJ: John Wiley & Sons.

Toomey, R., McGuire, J., Russell, S. (2012). Heteronormativity, school climates, and perceived safety for gender nonconforming peers. *Journal of Adolescence,35,* 187-196.

Toomey, R., Ryan, C., Diaz, R., Russell, S. (2011). High school Gay-Straight Alliances (GSAs) and young adult well-being: An examination of GSA presence, participation,and perceived effectiveness. *Applied Developmental Science, 15,* 175-185.

Toomey, R., Ryan, C., Diaz, R., Card, N., & Russell, S. (2010). Gender-nonconforming lesbian, gay, bisexual, and transgender youth: School victimization and young adult psychosocial adjustment. *Developmental Psychology, 46*(6), 1580–1589.

Tosh, J. (2011). "Zuck off!" A commentary on the protest against Ken Zucker and his "treatment" of childhood gender identity disorder. *Psychology of Women Section Review, 13*(1), 10–1.

Trans Youth Equality Foundation (n.d.). *College 101: College and school concerns.* Retrieved on March 31, 2016 from https://static1.squarespace.com/static/530651b5e4b0b4d1ce2d7a88/t/55a40491e4b072c329fe56b1/1436812433259/College+and+School+Resources.pdf

Travers, R., Guta, A., Flicker, S., Larkin, J., Lo, C., McCardell, S., &

van der Meulen, E. (2010). Service provider views on issues and needs for lesbian, gay, bisexual, and transgender youth. *The Canadian Journal of Human Sexuality, 19*(4), 191-198.

Troiden, R. (1989). The formation of homosexual identities. *Journal of Homosexuality, 17,* 43–73.

Troiden, R. (1988). *Gay and lesbian identity: A sociological analysis.* Dix Hills, NY: General Hall.

U.S. Conference of Mayors. (1996). *HIV prevention programs targeting gay/bisexual men of color* (HIV Education Case Studies). Washington, DC: Author.

U.S. Department of Education, Office of Elementary and Secondary Education, Office of Safe and Healthy Students. (2016, May). *Examples of policies and emerging practices for supporting transgender students.*

U.S. Department of Health and Human Services. (2016a). Patient Protection and Affordable Care Act: Section 1557: Coverage of health insurance in marketplaces and other health plans [Web page]. Retrieved from http://www.hhs.gov/sites/default/files/1557-fs-insurance-discrimination-508.pdf

U.S. Department of Health and Human Services. (2016b). Patient Protection and Affordable Care Act: Section 1557: Protecting individuals against sex discrimination [Web page]. Retrieved from http://www.hhs.gov/sites/default/files/1557-fs-sex-discrimination-508.pdf

U.S. Department of Health and Human Services. (2016c). Warning signs [Web article]. Retrieved January 29, 2016, from http://www.stopbullying.gov/at-risk/warning-signs/#bullied

U.S. Department of Health and Human Services, Administration for Children & Families, Family & Youth Services Bureau. (2014). *Street outreach program: Data collection project executive summary.* Retrieved on March 21, 2016, from http://www.acf.hhs.gov/sites/default/files/fysb/fysb_sop_summary_final.pdf

U.S. Department of Justice, Office of Justice Programs, Bureau of Justice Statistics. (2014). National crime victimization survey: School crime supplement, 2013.

U.S. Department of Justice, Civil Rights Division, & U.S. Department of Education, Office for Civil Rights. (2016, May 13). Dear colleague letter on transgender students [Official letter]. Retrieved from www.ed.gov/ocr/letters/colleague-201605-title-ix-transgender.pdf

Van Schalkwyk, G., Klingensmith, K., & Volkman, F. (2015). Gender identity and autism spectrum disorders. *Yale Journal of Biological Medicine*, 88, 81–83.

Wade, S. (1991, Winter). Cultural expectations and experiences: Three views. *Open Hands*, pp. 9–10.

Wald, J., & Losen, D. (2003). Defining and re-directing a school to prison pipeline. Cambridge, MA: Harvard Civil Rights Project.

Wallace, R., & Russell, H. (2013). Attachment and shame in gender-nonconforming children and their families: Toward a theoretical framework for evaluating clinical interventions. *International Journal of Transgenderism*, 14(3), 113–126.

Wallien, M. C.-K., P. (2008). Psychoasexual outcome of gender-dysphoric children. *Journal of the American Academy of Child and Adolescent Psychiatry*, 47(12), 1413–1423.

Watts-Jones, D. T. (2010). Location of self: Opening the door to dialogue on intersectionality in the therapy process. *Family Process*, 49, 405–420.

Wingerson, L. (2009, May 19). Gender identity disorder: Has accepted practice caused harm? *Psychiatric Times*. Retrieved from http://www.psychiatrictimes.com/articles/gender-identity-disorder-has-accepted-practice-caused-harm

Witt, H. (2007, September 5). School discipline tougher on African Americans. *Chicago Tribune*. Retrieved from http://www.chicagotribune.com/chi-070924discipline-story.html

Woodford, M., Paceley, M., Kulick, A., & Hong, J. (2015). The LGBTQ social climate matters: Policies, protests, and placards and psychological well-being among LGBTQ emerging adults. *Journal of Gay and Lesbian Social Services*, 27(1), 116–141. doi: 10.1080/10538720.2015.990334

World Health Organization. (1992). *International statistical classification of diseases and related health problems* (10th revision). Geneva, Switzerland: Author.

World Professional Association for Transgender Health (WPATH). (2012). *Standards of care for the health of transsexual, transgender, and gender nonconforming people*. Retrieved from http://www.wpath.org/site_page.cfm?pk_association_webpage_menu=1351&pk_association_webpage=3926

World Professional Association for Transgender Health (WPATH) Board of Directors. (2010). *De- psychopathologisation statement released May 26, 2010* Retrieved from http:// wpath.org/announcements_detail.cfm?pk_ announcement=17

Xavier, J., Bradford, J. Hendricks, M., Safford, L., McKee, R., Martin, E., & Honnold, J. (2013). Transgender health care access across Virginia: A qualitative study. *International Journal of Transgenderism,* 14, 3–17. Retrieved from http://www.tandfonline.com/doi/pdf/10.1080/15532739.2013.689513

Zucker, K. J. (1985). Cross-gender identified children. In B. W. Steiner (Ed.), *Gender dysphoria: Development, research, management* (pp. 75–174). New York, NY: Plenum Press.

Zucker, K. (2005). Gender identity disorder in children and adolescents. *Annual Review of Clinical Psychology, 1,* 467–492.

Zucker, K., & Bradley, S. (1995). *Gender identity disorder and psychosexual problems in children and adolescents.* New York, NY: Guilford Press.

Zucker, K. J., Wood, H., Singh, D., & Bradley, S. J. (2012). A developmental, biopsychosocial model for the treatment of children with gender identity disorder. *Journal of Homosexuality, 59*(3), 369–397. doi: 10.1080/00918369.2012.653309

Zuger, B. (1978). Effeminate behavior in boys from childhood: Ten additional years of follow-up. *Comprehensive Psychiatry, 19,* 363–369.

Zuger, B. (1984). Early effeminate behavior in boys: Outcome and significance for homoesexuality. *Journal of Nervous and Mental Disease, 172*(2), 90–97.

ACKNOWLEDGMENTS

I T IS MY FIRM BELIEF THAT OUR LIVES ARE INHERENTLY relational. Nothing we accomplish, that's worth accomplishing, happens in a vacuum. While I might be able to "screw up" my life on my own, anything positive I accomplish not only rests on my own abilities and gifts but also is grounded in the support of those I am blessed to acknowledge as partners in this journey.

My spouse, Alexandra, witnessed the evolution of this book from start to finish. She has steadfastly been her generous, thoughtful, optimistic self, willing to listen to my ruminations, cheer me on when the end seemed far off, and provide the space I needed to be immersed in this endeavor.

Several colleagues and friends provided support in critical moments: Monica McGoldrick illuminated a path forward at a time when I was so far behind and overwhelmed that giving up seemed like a logical solution; Robin Gorsline stepped in toward the end and carried my share of responsibilities in an endeavor that we cochair; and the unwavering Anne Stockwell kept me focused on what I could "pack into the stream of life" rather than my own limited ends.

While I am fully responsible for the content, I want to thank my colleagues John B. Steever, M.D., and M. Dru Levasseur, Esq., for their willingness to review the medical transition chapter and legal appendix, respectively.

Two of my students, Jason Cassese and Shari O'Reilly, scoured the Internet to find and annotate relevant listings for the resource appendix.

My intelligent, creative new colleagues at USJ have embraced me, checked in with me, and kept me focused on the importance of this work.

My editor at W. W. Norton & Company, Deborah Malmud, envisioned the possible value of my contribution from the onset and held fast to that belief throughout the challenges of writing my first professional book. The creativity she brought to help me shape my ideas and insights was invaluable. My appreciation also goes out to the other staff members at Norton who helped move this book to fruition.

I am immensely grateful for the transgender youth and their families with whom I have been privileged to work. Sharing this journey toward increased authenticity and wholeness has been an incredible blessing in my own life. Their vulnerability has taught me to be more courageous; their commitment to connection has impelled me to more fully hold love as the most important thing.

And now faith, hope, and love abide, these three;
and the greatest of these is love.
                    [I Corinthians 13:13, NRSV]

INDEX

abuse, 247
  parental, related to child's transgender identity, 168
  safety assessment and asking about, 34, 42
  trans youth and, 124
  see also bullying; emotional abuse; harassment; physical abuse; verbal abuse
ACA. *see* Affordable Care Act (ACA)
academic environment, supportive and inclusive, creating, 215–18, *see also* school(s)
acceptance
  agreement and, 199
  communicating to trans child, questions for family members, 144–45
  educating students about, 217
  hopes and dreams and, 196
  transgender adolescents and, 126
  for young person coming out, 59
  see also family acceptance; love
acculturation process, immigrant families, rejection of transgender youth, and, 131
ACLU. *see* American Civil Liberties Union (ACLU)
acquaintances, parents and disclosure to, 159
Adam's apple, tracheal shave for reduction of, 111
adolescence
  emergence of trans identity in adolescence, 117–22
  parents seeking information about gender identity in, 33

  see also transgender adolescents; trans youth of color
adolescents
  DSM criteria for gender dysphoria in, 29–31
  gender transition and, xxi
adultism, trans youth of color and, 135
adults
  DSM criteria for gender dysphoria in, 29–31`
  young, developmental tasks of, 269–71
  see also life-affirming practices for adults in lives of trans kids
advocacy
  parents and, 159
  transforming clinical knowledge and skills into, 227
  WPATH Standards of Care and, 291
  youth program settings and, 224–30
  see also advocates; education
advocates
  mental health providers and role of, 224–30
  see also advocacy
affirmative counselors or therapists, referrals to, 43
affirmed gender identity, 13
  assessment, medical intervention framework, and, 87
  choosing a new name and, 70
  coming out at school and, 203
  confusion and, 242–43
  living in, social transition, and, 74–78
  making fun of, within family, 168
  mental health of transgender children supported for living in, 76

campus health centers and, 273

cisgender people and health insurance coverage for, 114

HHS final rule nondiscriminatory requirements and, 333

hormone/puberty blockers, 88–92

providing parents with information about, 160

psychiatric diagnosis and access to, 24

sample letter for, 374–77

trans adolescents and, additional thoughts, 97–99

transgender men and testosterone, 88, 92–94

for transgender women, 88, 94–97

trans women from lower socioeconomic brackets and access issues with, 95–96

see also feminizing hormone therapy; hormone blockers; masculinizing hormone therapy

hospital policies, trans-affirming, 334

hotlines, providing information about, 34

housing

federal protection and, 328

homeless LGBT youth and discrimination in, 124

hurt

anger and, 325

as real barrier to family acceptance, 192

hyperfemininity, transgender adolescents and, 119

hypermasculinity, transgender adolescents and, 119

hysterectomy

hormone therapy dosage reduction after, 97

lower surgeries and, 109, 110

identity and stigma, shifting intersections of

deeper exploration of, 258–60

reflection questions for mental health professionals, 258

reflection questions for parents, 257–58

vignette, 257

immigrant families, rejection of transgender youth and, 131

inclusive school environment, creating, 215–18

Indian Health Services, transgender-related medical care and, 115, 332

information sources, families and need for, 47

inpatient settings, best practices for, 233

intake process

asking question about gender/gender identity/expression during, 35–36

asking questions about sexual orientation during, 37–38

Integration and Pride stage, in "transgender emergence" model, 58

Internet, transition-related care information on, evaluating, 113

intersectionality

gender generalizing and, 308

trans youth of color and, 129

intersex conditions

complexity of biological sex and, 5

surgery and, 4–5

intersex condition specifier, DSM-5 on gender dysphoria in adolescents and adults and, 30

intimacy, avoidance of, 270

Intimacy *vs.* Isolation (Erikson), as core developmental task of young adulthood, 270

involuntary clients, listening to and validating feelings of, 181

irreversible medical interventions, 88

isolation, 212, 244–45, 294

family rejection and, 247

transgendered college students and, 272–73

transgender youth and, 119

validation and bridging trans adolescent's sense of, 255

Jannsen, A., 42

jobs

loss of, xxiii

transgender youth and, 282–84

see also employment; workplace environment

Judaism, accepting leaders within each branch of, 191

juvenile justice resources, 357–59